Track & Field
COACHING
ESSENTIALS

USA
TRACK & FIELDᔆᴹ

Will Freeman
Editor

Human Kinetics

Library of Congress Cataloging-in-Publication Data

Track & Field coaching essentials / USA Track & Field ; Will Freeman, editor.
    pages cm
Includes bibliographical references and index.
1. Track and field--Coaching--United States. I. Freeman, Will. II. USA Track & Field.
GV1060.675.C6U72 2014
796.42--dc23

                              2014023040

ISBN: 978-1-4504-8932-4 (print)

The web addresses cited in this text were current as of *September 2014,* unless otherwise noted.

Developmental Editor: Cynthia McEntire; **Associate Managing Editor:** Nicole Moore; **Copyeditor:** Patsy Fortney; **Indexer:** Dan Connolly; **Permissions Manager:** Martha Gullo; **Senior Graphic Designer:** Keri Evans; **Cover Designer:** Keith Blomberg; **Photographs (interior):** © USA Track & Field, unless otherwise noted; **Photo Production Manager:** Jason Allen; **Art Manager:** Kelly Hendren; **Associate Art Manager:** Alan L. Wilborn; **Illustrations:** © Human Kinetics, unless otherwise noted; **Printer:** Sheridan Books

Human Kinetics books are available at special discounts for bulk purchase. Special editions or book excerpts can also be created to specification. For details, contact the Special Sales Manager at Human Kinetics.

Printed in the United States of America   10 9 8 7

The paper in this book is certified under a sustainable forestry program.

Human Kinetics
P.O. Box 5076
Champaign, IL 61825-5076
Website: www.HumanKinetics.com

In the United States, email info@hkusa.com or call 800-747-4457.
In Canada, email info@hkcanada.com.
In the United Kingdom/Europe, email hk@hkeurope.com.

For information about Human Kinetics' coverage in other areas of the world,
please visit our website: **www.HumanKinetics.com**

Contents

CONTENTS

CONTENTS

Preface

Vern Gambetta

Coaching is the cornerstone of any sustainable sport development system. A sound coaching education program is the foundation for coaching excellence. It is only fitting that this new and revised coaching manual is being published on the 30th anniversary of the start of the USATF coaching education program. This work is a compendium, a resource on all the events in track and field as well as sport psychology, physiology, and biomechanics. It is intended to be a text for Level 1 coaches, but in my estimation, it goes well beyond that. Because of its breadth and depth, it will also serve as a reference for coaches at all levels on the foundations of technique, training, and supporting sciences. Its strength lies in the fact that it was written by coaches for coaches, which makes it a definitive work.

A brief overview of the history of USATF coaching education is appropriate to put this work in context. Basically, the program started with a discussion I had with Berny Wagner when he was executive director of the Track and Field Association of the United States. When he became national coach/coordinator of The Athletics Congress (TAC, forerunner to USATF), we continued our discussions on the need for coaching education. Berny took it upon himself to connect Gary Winckler and me with Joe Vigil and Al Baeta at the TAC convention in Reno in 1981. We became a subcommittee of the men's and women's track and field committees to explore the possibility of beginning a coaching education program. The committee chairs—John Randolph on the men's side and Harmon Brown on the women's side—went out of their way to support the program. Over the next year, we researched other programs around the world and explored the unique needs of coaches in the United States. From this we put together the structure of the program, which was composed of three levels.

We presented the program structure at the 1982 TAC convention in Philadelphia, and it was approved. I was appointed director of the coaching education committee, which included Joe Vigil and Gary Winckler. During the year of 1983, we selected our first group of instructors and outlined the curriculum. We convened at California State University at Long Beach in December 1983 to train the instructors and review, revise, and finalize the curriculum. Each aspect of the Level 1 curriculum was presented, critiqued, and revised on site. Somehow we accomplished this monumental task, and the first Level 1 schools were held in January 1984. Two years later, in December 1986, the first Level 2 school was held at the U.S. Olympic Training Center at Colorado Springs. In the past 30 years, more than 30,000 coaches have been certified at Level I.

No one was paid. The whole program started with $3,000 in seed money from the men's and women's development committees. From that $3,000 has grown arguably one of the most successful programs ever undertaken by USATF. It proves that drive, determination, and dedication with heavy doses of idealism can result in success.

This coaching manual is another landmark in the program. It represents a major revision and upgrade of the Level 1 program. The future of the program is exciting, and this manual will be a major factor in ensuring consistency of instruction and a common terminology for coaches.

The journey to better coaching begins in part 1 with the fundamentals of coaching our exciting and versatile sport. How do coaches reach athletes and get them to connect with the program and the sport? How do coaches maintain integrity and encourage athletes to win the right way? Coaches Rick McGuire and

PREFACE

Will Freeman address these topics and more in part I.

Part II presents the scientific realities of track and field coaching, including the psychology of athletes, the biomechanics and physiology of bodies in motion, and the best training practices. Coaches Freeman, Robert Chapman, and Vern Gambetta explore these topics, presenting very technical information in a very accessible way.

Part III covers the running events and relays, including sprints, relays, endurance running, racewalking, and hurdles. Joe Rogers, Joe Vigil, and Andrew Allden discuss all aspects of the track side of track and field.

Part IV is all about the jumping events: pole vault, long jump, triple jump, and high jump. Jeremy Fischer's expertise in these areas is key for coaches looking to help their athletes jump farther and higher.

Finally, in part V, Lawrence Judge covers every aspect of the throws: shot put, discus, hammer, and javelin. He describes the key differences and similarities in the training of athletes in the various throwing events and how to develop individualized programs to address each thrower's strengths and weaknesses.

Note: Track and field events are measured in meters, which are roughly equivalent to yards. Where the text mentions distances in meters (such as setting cones at 30 meters for a drill), you can replace the number of meters with yards.

The Level 1 coaching program certainly has made a difference in the quality and depth of coaching in the United States. This work, assembled so brilliantly by Will Freeman with assistance from Terry Crawford, will be a real difference maker to our sport.

Acknowledgments

This book is a collaboration of a talented group of coaches. Joe Vigil, Vern Gambetta, Joe Rogers, Larry Judge, Jeremy Fischer, Robert Chapman, Rick McGuire, and Andrew Allden were involved in refining and adding to the previous USATF Level 1 materials to create this text. All master teachers and coaches, the members of this talented group have been invested in coaching education for many years. Also, it is important to thank Ian Whatley, Iain Hunter, and Dave Mills, who contributed to the endurance running and racewalking chapter.

W. F.

Special thanks to Terry Crawford, director of coaching for USATF, and to all the staff at Human Kinetics. They have been a great help in making this project come to fruition.

Several master teacher–coaches were involved in getting the USATF coaching education program off the ground—Vern Gambetta, Joe Vigil, Al Baeta, Dan Pfaff, Bob Myers, Gary Winckler, Rick McGuire, Ralph Vernacchia, George Dunn, Gary Wilson, Phil Lundin, and Kevin McGill. Their insights have inspired and motivated coaches to be better teachers.

PART I

Fundamentals of Coaching Track and Field

Positive Coaching

Rick McGuire, PhD

Consider carefully the role of the track and field coach. Most educational resources for coaches focus on the track and field part of the role with very little on the coaching aspect. However, coaches don't coach the sprints; they coach the sprinter. Coaches don't coach the high jump; they coach the high jumper. Coaches don't coach track and field; they coach track and field athletes. The defining challenge of the coach, therefore, is to build the person in the athlete. There is an art and science to coaching the person. Everything that coaches do should therefore focus on helping each ath-lete become a better, prouder, happier, more effective, and more fulfilled person.

Based on the direction of the leadership of the high-performance divisions of the U.S. Olympic Committee and USA Track & Field, this chapter reflects a science-based, athlete-centered, and coach-driven theme. It draws on the very best ideas from the fields of sport psychology, positive psychology, and traditional coaching theory.

Being a coach means far more than just coaching the sport. Coaching is about the relationship with another (or several others),

© Human Kinetics

Coaching encompasses more than simply strategies and tactics.

in which the intention is to teach, share, and mentor to help people to be better. Coaching is about teaching, guiding, encouraging, building, believing, caring, sharing, giving, forgiving, expecting, respecting, modeling, serving, and inspiring.

Philosophy

A person's philosophy is the unique framework of beliefs used to make decisions. A coaching philosophy is shaped by the coach's background, experiences, and education, and is a reflection of the coach's personal values.

Goals in Coaching Athletes

Coaches are teachers, trainers, and mentors to athletes. They teach skills and help athletes improve those skills so that, hopefully, athletes reach their potential. Coaching is also about helping athletes grow and develop psychologically and socially. The coaching process is one of collaboration and respect between coach and athlete. As athletes grow and develop in the coach–athlete relationship, they can, when ready, take on an increasing role in the process.

The coach should adopt an athlete-centered philosophy in which the athlete's well-being and development are the primary considerations. The slogan "athletes first, winning second" reflects this philosophy. Making decisions that affect athletes positively can result in winning and other forms of success. The coach should resist the temptation to compromise an athlete's safety, long-term personal development, or long-term athletic development for short-term gains. Personal values are reflected in the way someone coaches. A productive exercise for coaches is to ask the questions Why do I coach? and What values drive my coaching?

Instilling Positive Values

Participating in a good sport program can have many benefits. Regardless of any outside benefits, values are taught and reinforced in the athletic setting. The messages sent should be positive and supported by parents, coaches, and other interested parties. Because of the value of these experiences, coaches should find avenues of participation for many, including the disadvantaged. The following is a list of positive results from participating in sport:

- **Healthy physical development.** The physical development resulting from sport is a great benefit. The coach should administer the program and communicate in a way that fosters a positive attitude toward lifetime fitness that will prevail once the athlete's formal training has ceased.

- **Enhanced psychological development.** Much can be achieved in the realm of psychological development through sport participation. Sports provide environments in which young people learn to compete and accept the outcomes of competition. The establishment of healthy attitudes toward winning and losing provides an opportunity for character development. Winning should be considered a by-product of a positive sport experience, and losing should be seen as an opportunity for change, learning, and growth. The problem-solving process following a losing effort can be a valuable character-developing process. The coach should also assist athletes in applying all of these situations to other areas in their lives.

- **Positive social development.** The coach should use the sporting environment to foster social development. Sports present opportunities to teach honesty, respect for others, gracious winning and losing, and responsibility for one's actions.

- **Balance in life.** Sports provide balance for work and school demands while offering a healthy mechanism for challenging and improving oneself.

- **Fun.** In addition to the preceding attributes, sports can be positive pastimes and healthy sources of enjoyment for participants of all ages. If athletes enjoy their track and field practices, workouts, and competitions, they will be more likely to continue to participate and develop as they get older.

Fusing Sport Psychology and Positive Psychology

Athletes meet the sport at the coach, the environmental engineer who designs and delivers the sport experience to the athletes. Coaches shape the sport experience through everything they do or don't do, everything they say or don't say, and the behaviors they allow or don't allow. How athletes think is greatly influenced by the intentions, instructions, behaviors, and personal models of the coach. Positive coaching is about intentionally developing the athlete's mental and emotional skills and the physical, technical, and strategic capabilities they need to excel. For coaches whose intention is to get the very best performance from their athletes, positive coaching teaches them that how they coach is at least as important as what they coach.

Positive coaching develops competitive athletes and teams by teaching and modeling the process of building success, both inside and outside of sport. Positive coaching is about building the person up, never tearing the person down.

Positive coaches

- detect and correct errors,
- instruct constructively,
- are intense,
- are demanding, and
- expect focused attention and the athlete's best effort.

However, positive coaches never break an athlete's spirit. The primary goal of developing athletic competence and confidence requires that the coach build spirit in the athlete every day and in every way.

To be successful, coaches must understand two critical psychological concepts: intrinsic motivation and self-worth. Positive coaching is all about developing both in the athlete and

team consistently, persistently, and relentlessly. Building intrinsic motivation and self-worth must be the coach's primary intention.

Communication is a major element of coaching. Great coaches are great communicators. Positive coaches can be demanding without being demeaning, and they communicate with their athletes as they would wish to be communicated with.

Positive coaching is about the following:

- Striving for excellence
- Achieving optimal performance
- Teaching and modeling the process of success
- Leading a group to becoming a highly effective team
- Nurturing intrinsic motivation
- Communicating with athletes as one would want to be communicated with
- Respecting and protecting the self-worth of every athlete
- Being demanding without being demeaning
- Shaping athletes' will without breaking their spirits
- Realizing that winning does matter because every athlete should win in his or her life

Positive coaches don't rationalize; they actualize. They make every person they coach better. Following are descriptions of the key principles of the six stages of positive coaching.

Stage 1: Discover the Calling

Discovering the calling directs coaches inward, challenging them to explore their own essence, to reflect on their most fundamental values and personal principles, to consider and fully identify why they coach, and to then develop and write their own personal philosophy of coaching. This puts into words the calling to coach. It is crucial to take the time to reflect on the things that matter. The values and principles by which one lives heavily influence one's coaching style and impact on athletes.

Coaches would do well to take a few moments of quiet time to make a list of their most important personal values, and then to prioritize and reflect on them. A coaching philosophy is a reflection of the values that drive behaviors.

Just as the coach expects athletes to be highly motivated to become the very best they can be, they too should model humility and character by enthusiastically adopting the role of learner. Great teachers and coaches are those who continue to learn.

Coaches should reflect on how their coaching styles address each value they hold. Although winning the competition matters, winning the athlete first matters even more. Because coaches are the ultimate model for their athletes, they should model and develop positive character relentlessly.

Stage 2: Build the Foundation

It is important that athletes feel competent, experience achievement, and feel a sense of belonging. All of this is under the direction and control of the coach. The role of the coach is significant to every athlete, and the coach–athlete relationship is meaningful to both parties.

A healthy attitude toward competition is fundamental to competing at one's best, and the coach plays an important role in how the athlete views competition. The word *competition* comes from two Greek words that, when combined, mean "to strive with" or "to strive together." Competition brings out the best in both parties who are striving together. Unfortunately, many portray competition as a zero-sum process, defined only by winning and losing. When this is the case, the fear of failure becomes the driving motivation, which produces doubt, anxiety, worry, and, yes, actual fear. This manifests as a lack of confidence, distraction, a loss of focus, tension, and a loss of trust, all examples of wrong thinking.

Research has shown that having fun is a primary motivator for people participating in sport. Athletes experience fun when they have done well, delivered their very best effort, and given family and friends something to celebrate and feel proud of. It's hard to deny the power of these moments. Fun is what brings them back for more! The role of the coach is to develop the desire to have fun. An environment in which the focus is on mastery and improvement is conducive to both having fun and wanting to return for more.

Stage 3: Cultivate Positive and Caring Relationships

Positive coaching is about coaching people, not just athletes. Remember, coaches don't coach runners, jumpers, and throwers; they coach athletes who run, jump, and throw!

Cooperation is about giving and sharing oneself with others. Yet, so much of life, and certainly of sport life, is focused not on giving, but on getting. We don't always control what we get! On the other hand, people who are focused on giving and sharing themselves with others always have total control over their giving. They control to whom they give, what they give, how much they give, and how often they give. Most important, they control why they give. Whenever people give of themselves unconditionally, with no expectation of return, they feel better about themselves.

Respect is an important part of a coaching philosophy and is manifested in many ways: respect for the sport; respect for opportunity; respect for authority; respect for the rules; respect for the coach; respect for the team; respect for teammates; respect for health and keeping the body nutritionally fueled, rested, and in peak condition; respect for accountability; and respect for self. Respect should be expected and demanded of all, including the coach! No situation merits a coach being disrespectful to another person, especially an athlete. Being disrespectful undermines and ultimately kills respect, trust, belief, accountability, and intrinsic motivation, all of which are keys to great performance and athletic success. Being respectful of athletes builds respect, trust, belief, accountability, and intrinsic motivation.

Positive, constructive instruction creates an environment of construction, not destruction. Here are some suggestions for applying positive, constructive instruction when coaching:

- Always approach instruction positively.
- Always emphasize how to do something correctly.
- Focus on right, not wrong.
- Emphasize the importance of consistent, persistent, relentless, repetitive practice.
- Teach that practice does not make perfect. Planned, purposeful, perfect practice gives everyone the chance to make it perfect!
- Communicate and demonstrate confidence, belief, and trust that the athletes can and will develop the desired knowledge, skill, and capability.
- Affirm and encourage often.
- Celebrate improvement. Recognize and applaud the small steps along the way to the big prize.

Respond and *react* are different, yet related, terms. Reacting implies an instantaneous reaction with little or no thought. Responding implies deliberate consideration of something seen, heard, or sensed before beginning to speak. Positive coaches model responding and not reacting by doing the following:

- Listening carefully and attentively
- Observing carefully and attentively
- Catching athletes doing something right and then celebrating it
- Balancing positive and negative feedback
- Maintaining composure and controlling emotions

Stage 4: Empower Growth Mind-Sets

Having a growth mind-set is about approaching both sport and life with the understanding that everyone can get better every day. A growth mind-set is built on the tenet that every athlete can be better tomorrow than she was yesterday, as a result of the investment she made today.

An irrefutable truth in sport is that the athlete's performance always occurs before the outcome. The athlete has control over preparation and performance. Focusing on best performance (process), not winning (result), gives the athlete the very best chance for a positive outcome. Being a success and winning are closely related, but they are not the same thing! Success comes from engagement in a functional process.

Consider the things gained from the sport experience: positive memories; lessons learned; personal pride, satisfaction, and fulfillment; lifetime skills. These things are gained only through consistent, persistent, and dedicated engagement in a quality process of training and development!

Research shows that the strongest and most lasting and enduring motivation is intrinsic. Intrinsically motivated athletes focus on success (as opposed to avoiding failure and punishment) and are positive, not negative. Athletes who are self-confident and self-determining can make good decisions in critical moments and then deliver great performances when they are needed. That can happen only if they have had opportunities to make important decisions. Athletes must be instructed, encouraged, and allowed to make decisions for, about, and by themselves. Autonomy results when athletes have the confidence, control, and courage to make important, hard, and good decisions for, about, and by themselves.

Coaches like to have control. But that control often reduces athlete autonomy and opportunities to make decisions. Coaching athletes is much like raising children. As they get older, they should have more say in the decision-making process. Such a dependence-to-independence model is what teaches autonomy and self-sufficiency.

Stage 5: Inspire Passionate Hearts

The coach's role is to contribute to athletes' experiences in such a way that helps them to improve and grow. In that regard, a primary role is to inspire. Personal excellence is not limited to those who are the best and brightest. It is available to everybody. Every athlete can improve. Everybody can achieve personal excellence. But excellence is something that must be strived for. The coach's role is to cultivate in the athlete a desire for excellence.

When attention is focused on correcting what is being done wrong, everyone's attention is pulled away from what is being done right. If time and attention are consistently diverted from those things done well, performance in those areas may erode. Coaches should identify and build on every athlete's strengths, finding a balance between correcting faults and reinforcing strengths.

Coaches are the definers, shapers, and deliverers of the sport experience. It follows that they must model, reflect, encourage, and promote positive emotions. All experiences, good and bad, are growth opportunities for future success in both sport and life. Positive coaching is built on modeling, promoting, and nurturing positive emotions. It is also about learning from negative experiences.

Optimism is about belief, trust, confidence, and hope. Both coaches and athletes have choices in what they think. Optimism is a conscious choice. Positive coaches choose to be optimistic.

Celebrating and savoring achievements should not be reserved for the big one. Every victory and success, however small, should be celebrated and savored. Positive coaches promote, recognize, and celebrate not just wins, but also good plays, great effort, improvement, good decisions, and personal growth. Recognizing and celebrating smaller victories plants the seeds for later, larger victories.

Stage 6: Produce and Achieve Optimal Performances

Once a coach has heard the calling, built the foundation, cultivated positive and caring relationships, empowered growth mind-sets, and inspired passion, it is time to put it all together and deliver optimal performances. Thinking right in sport is a simple concept, yet for many it is an elusive one. All coaches and athletes recognize that wrong thoughts hurt sport performance. Negative and distracting thoughts get in the way of optimal performance.

Track coaches teach skills, and thinking right is a very important skill! It is learned through proper instruction, correct modeling, direct personal experiences, and consistent, persistent repetition. Following are three realities of the athlete's thought process:

1. You choose what you think about.
2. You can think about only one thing at a time.
3. You can change a negative thought to a positive one.

The mind is the gatekeeper of the body. Thoughts control actions and behaviors. Wrong thoughts block best performance, whereas right thoughts facilitate best performance.

Being focused is a perfect example of thinking right. All coaches want athletes to be focused and have the intention to deliver their very best performance. On competition day, athletes will display the focus they have practiced daily. Focus is about thoughts, and we choose our thoughts. Because thoughts are a result of choice, focus can be completely controlled.

Here are the five elements of focus:

1. **Time orientation.** Where are you? Right here, right now.
2. **Positive self-talk.** Develop the habit of strong, positive affirmations.
3. **Composure.** Not too high, not too low. Just right.
4. **Concentration.** Find what matters and pay attention to that.
5. **Confidence.** Confidence is not just a thought; it's a choice.

Coaches are master teachers. They often are brilliant at delivering passionate, constructive instruction, designing repeatable drills, and organizing practice sessions into efficient and effective learning experiences. Much of what coaches do is teach the movement skills of running, jumping, and throwing. However, focus may be the ultimate sport skill, a skill developed through constructive instruction; modeling; meaningful, repeatable experiences; time and attention to task; and lots of repetition.

Following are the seven Cs of success:

Confidence. The athlete's self-belief.

Concentration. The athlete's control of focus.

Composure. The athlete's control of physiological and emotional arousal.

Courage. Desire and confidence are greater than fear. Courage is learned.

Commitment. The athlete makes the final decision before meeting the challenge.

Control. The athlete takes it.

Choice. The athlete makes it.

Each of the seven Cs is crucial to success, and each begins with a thought. The athlete chooses the thought and thus controls confidence, concentration, composure, courage, and commitment.

Developing mental toughness is certainly an important component of coaching athletes to success. Mental toughness is available to every athlete. It is illustrated when athletes face significant challenges, struggles, and adversity and still deliver their best performances. Mental toughness is certainly about thinking right, but there is a misconception that it is a special, unique quality or perhaps even a genetic trait carried only by the lucky few. Nothing could be less true! Engaging in thorough preparation, giving the greatest possible effort, and having the will to choose to keep going, again and again, is what forges mental toughness. Mental toughness is about maintaining self-control and making the choice or choices necessary to take control and keep delivering the very best performance possible. Mental toughness is about being consistent, persistent, insistent, and relentless. It is both learned and earned.

Principles of Positive Coaching

Discover the Calling

- Reflect on personal values and foundational beliefs.
- Identify the goals and purposes of the sport experience.
- Develop and shape a coaching philosophy.
- Adopt the role of the learner.
- Choose to model and develop positive character relentlessly.

Build the Foundation

- Create and nurture each athlete's feelings of self-worth and self-esteem.
- Promote and protect the priority of each athlete's well-being and happiness.
- Develop and foster a sense of meaning and purpose.
- Develop a healthy attitude toward competition.
- Develop the desire to have fun.

Cultivate Positive and Caring Relationships

- Develop a spirit of cooperation.
- Communicate respectfully with those whom you lead, just as you would wish to be communicated with by those who lead you.
- Demonstrate and use positive constructive instruction.
- Demonstrate and use active constructive responding.
- Develop and model the regular sharing of gratitude.

Empower Growth Mind-Sets

- Develop and model a positive approach to achieving success; emphasizing engaging in the process.
- Emphasize that nothing of any real value is achieved without quality practice.
- Help athletes develop intrinsic motivation, internal motivation, approach motivation, and positive motivation.
- Develop personal autonomy, self-confidence, and self-determination in athletes by letting them make decisions for, about, and by themselves.

Inspire Passionate Hearts

- Develop the desire to strive wholeheartedly toward personal excellence.
- Identify and build on each athlete's strengths.
- Model, promote, and nurture positive emotions.
- Develop the perspective of optimism as defining sport culture.
- Celebrate and savor experiences in and outside of sport.

Produce and Achieve Optimal Performances

- Develop and model thinking right in sport.
- Develop and model focus and self-control.
- Develop and model the seven Cs of success.
- Develop and model mental toughness.
- Develop and nurture an environment that supports flow experiences.

Adapted, by permission, from *Winning Kids With Sport! Teach...Model...Practice...Inspire,* by Dr. Rick McGuire, 2012, Ames, IA: Championship Productions, www.ChampionshipProductions.com.

Conclusion

Positive coaching is about creating relationships and an environment that allows athletes to find flow in their sport experiences. Flow is about being in the zone in which one is capable of delivering a peak performance. Positive coaching is about helping the athlete achieve the flow state.

Positive coaching is about teaching athletes to perform better and achieve more so they can be prouder, happier, healthier, and more fulfilled. The result? They are motivated to come back for more. It is also about helping athletes build self-confidence and skills that will positively influence their life after sport. This ultimately is why we coach! It's not just about creating better athletes; it's about building stronger people.

Coaches will hopefully enjoy and learn from the chapters that follow. But first, they should commit to writing (or rewriting) their own personal philosophies of coaching. It's the first step, and perhaps the most important one, toward becoming a positive coach.

2

Ethics and Risk Management

Will Freeman

The coach is responsible for providing a balance between developing the athlete and enhancing the well-being of the person. A healthy working relationship of mutual trust between coach and athlete is the goal. Providing a safe environment that minimizes risk is conducive to improvement and enjoyment, and it helps develop coach–athlete trust.

Ethical Behavior

The coach, by the very nature of the position, is a role model for athletes and a representative of an entire profession and sport. The coach's dress, behavior, and relationship with others should be professional. Because of the position of authority and responsibility, the coach's personal life should also be held to high standards.

Coach–Athlete Relationship

A professional boundary must exist between the coach and the athlete, and the coach is responsible for setting that boundary. If physical contact is necessary as part of the coaching process, it must not be interpreted by the athlete or others as anything more than that. When meetings with individual athletes are needed, these meetings should be held in view of others or with an open office door.

No amount of coaching knowledge will guarantee success without a good relationship with the athlete. Athletic competence and confidence rely on a functional, effective coach–athlete relationship. Athletes are unique and need different things from their coaches. Effective coaching involves meeting the needs of every athlete.

The coach–athlete relationship must be professional. The coach should understand that although certain obligations should be met, the nature of the relationship is limited. It is the coach's role to define the limits of the relationship. Although respect is necessary, the coach and the athlete should not be considered peers.

A coach and an athlete may have a close working relationship, but a certain amount of space should remain between them. This is especially true in situations in which the possibility of inappropriate sexual contact may exist or be presumed to exist. The nature of coaching requires paying much attention to the athlete, but this attention should have limits based on the comfort of the athlete. Moreover, the beginning and ending of the coach–athlete relationship should be a matter of agreement.

The nature of the coach–athlete relationship dictates that the coach place demands on the athlete. These demands should be communicated with respect. When reprimand and criticism are necessary, they should be restricted to the athletic domain and administered professionally, privately, immediately, and tactfully without the use of insulting or personal tones.

Coach's Relationships With Others

The coach should demonstrate respect and ethical conduct in interactions with officials, other coaches, opponents, and all others in the athletic setting. The coach should exhibit self-control in disagreements and in emotional situations. Public criticism of other coaches, officials, or athletes is inappropriate.

Coach's Respect for the Rules

The coach should respect the rules and help the athlete develop a respect for the rules as well. Many sets of rules govern any athletic situation. Rules govern not only play, but also participation, eligibility, recruiting, performance-enhancing substances, and other areas. These rules must be respected and followed. When in disagreement, the coach should seek change or protest professionally through the proper channels. Team rules should be simple, easily and fairly enforced, and developed with input from athletes.

Professional Competencies

The coach should work to develop and maintain competence in the duties athletes expect and deserve from coaches. This section discusses such competencies.

Maintenance of a Safe Environment

It is the coach's obligation to make the sport as safe as reasonably possible for those participating. Maintaining safe practice and competition environments is the number one responsibility of the coach. Equipment must be safe, properly fit, and legally maintained. Facilities should be well kept. The coach should be versed in adapting the training program when dangerous climatic factors such as excessive heat, excessive cold, lightning, humidity, rain, and snow so dictate.

Injury Prevention and Management

Injury prevention and initial injury care are the responsibilities of the coach. The coach should be capable of providing first aid, and first-aid materials and equipment should be kept at the practice and competition sites. The coach should work with other professionals such as certified trainers, physical therapists, and medical doctors in the areas of injury management and rehabilitation.

Sound and Appropriate Training and Teaching

The coach should understand the demands and techniques of track and field skills and events. Also, the coach should be versed in developing training programs for track and field events and sound teaching progressions for all skills. An understanding of basic sport sciences will help in this process. The training program should be viewed as a planned path to success. Every athlete is at a unique place on that path, and each demonstrates a unique rate of improvement. Testing and competitions provide feedback the coach can use to evaluate the training and the progress of each athlete. At no time should training be used for the purpose of punishment.

Professional Development and Involvement

The coach has an obligation to improve professionally and continually work through available channels for self-improvement. The coach should consider joining professional organizations and taking a role in the activities of the sport's governing body, USA Track & Field (www.usatf.org). Coaches have a responsibility to assist in developing and improving the sport of track and field, much in the same way they develop their athletes and teams.

Commitment

Success in coaching requires a significant level of commitment. A person should not enter the coaching profession if a willingness to take the time and expend the effort needed to meet the needs of the athletes is lacking. At the same time, even the most dedicated coach has limited time and resources. A coach should be available for coaching or consulting only to a realistic level of commitment.

Risk Management

Although risk cannot be totally avoided in sport, it can be managed in a way that minimizes threats to athletes. Understanding risks and their impacts, and communicating those risks to athletes, is part of the coach's duties.

Legal Duties of the Coach

Every coach, by virtue of the title and position,

assumes certain legal duties. The most important of these are listed here:

- **Properly planning activities.** Coaches are held to certain standards of competency when planning activities. Teaching progressions must be reasonable, sound, and well administered. Practice activities should be reasonable, effective, safe, and appropriate to the athletes' ability levels.

- **Properly supervising activities.** Coaches need to know when supervision is imperative and how to supply it. Every athletic program should have adequate numbers of properly located, competent supervisors.

- **Providing proper instruction.** Coaches must be able to provide instruction that is pedagogically sound and consistent.

- **Maintaining current competencies.** Coaches are responsible for seeking professional development and improvement, and must be aware of and implement improvements and innovations in coaching techniques.

- **Providing a safe environment.** Teaching practices and procedures should be chosen and designed with safety in mind. Teaching progressions should be safe and pedagogically sound. Although overload is an important part of training, the increase of training loads should be gradual, progressive, and well planned. Coaches should subject athletes to training activities and competition opportunities that are appropriate to their ability levels and current states of fitness.

- **Warning people of dangers.** Coaches have a responsibility to alert athletes and others to dangers, particularly novices who may not recognize these dangers.

- **Providing emergency medical procedures.** Coaches should be able to handle medical emergencies and have general knowledge of athletic injuries and care. Training in first aid and CPR is necessary, and certification is preferred.

A plan should be in place for handling accidents and contacting parents and emergency personnel in the event of such occurrences. A well-stocked first-aid kit should be kept on the training and competition premises, and it should include materials needed for the handling of blood-borne pathogens. It should be noted that although these competencies are important, situations beyond the coach's level of expertise should be referred to the proper professionals.

- **Managing the rehabilitation of injuries.** Coaches should be competent in the rehabilitation of common sport injuries. They should be able to administer rehabilitation programs, keep records, and communicate the goals and processes involved to the athlete, parents, and other interested parties. Coaches should also protect injured athletes from further harm and refer them to those with more expertise when situations so dictate.

- **Keeping records.** Coaches need to keep accurate records of many types. These include personal and parental information, records of physical examinations, emergency notification information, attendance records, and training records.

Liability

Liability may occur when a coach fails to meet his legal obligation or responsibility by acting or failing to act in a way that results in real or perceived harm. When a coach is accused of being responsible for an athlete's injuries or neglecting his duties, a number of defenses are available, as described here:

- **Assumption of risk.** This defense maintains that athletes assume a certain amount of risk and liability for their injuries when they choose to engage in sporting activities because of commonly known and accepted incidental risks associated with such activities.

- **Comparative negligence.** This defense maintains that coaches can be held partially responsible, rather than completely at fault, when athletes become injured. A certain percentage of the fault is assigned to the coach. The remainder is assigned to the athlete as a result of the athlete's own action or inaction.

- **Volunteer statutes.** Some states provide coaches with immunity, provided they have satisfied certain requirements and demonstrated certain competencies.

- **Waivers, releases, exculpatory agreements, and consent.** Coaches may be able to take advantage of waivers and releases signed by athletes or their parent to attain some degree of immunity. Some courts, however, do not honor, or limit, the scope of these documents.

- **Sovereign immunity.** This defense can be used by a public or government institution that may not be held liable by law. Some coaches can use this defense because of their status as government employees.

Negligence

Negligence is defined as a failure to exercise a certain standard of care to ensure the safety and welfare of others when the law imposes or implies a duty of care. The following four conditions must be met to establish negligence:

1. **Duty.** The coach must have a legal duty to the injured person.

2. **Breach of duty.** The coach must have failed to fulfill this duty.

3. **Damages or injuries.** The purported incident of negligence must have resulted in measurable harm to the person to whom duty was owed.

4. **Proximate cause between breach of duty and damage.** The damage or injuries must have been caused by the coach's breach of duty.

Conclusion

A safe and healthy coach–athlete relationship is one of trust and mutual respect. Coaches who behave ethically provide positive modeling for the athletes they serve. The goal is athlete independence through a healthy process, not dependence on the coach.

Coaches must be able to identify and manage risks to athletes. Providing a safe learning environment, combined with a functional teaching process, minimizes such risks.

PART II

Science of Coaching

3

Sport Psychology

Will Freeman

Sport psychology is the study of the behavior of athletes and coaches in both practice and competition settings. Understanding psychology is important to good coaching because it provides the rationale and reason for understanding communication, motivation, and how athletes feel about themselves and others.

Physical–Mental Interface and Why the Coach Matters

Sport performance is a complicated interaction between mind and body and between athlete and coach. Effective training results in the healthy adaptation of the athlete. Appropriate loading and recovery, applied progressively, results in positive adaptation and improved performance. Yet physical preparation is only part of a larger process. What motivates the athlete, how the athlete approaches competition, and how the athlete's mental state influences performance in training and competitions are factors that all influence performance. The athlete meets the sport at the coach; thus, the coach needs to be well versed in psychology.

When training is functional and progressive, the athlete is likely to show improvement. When performance improves, the athlete's self-efficacy (the belief that one has the ability to perform the skill or event well) is likely to increase. Thus, functional and progressive training is crucial to the athlete's positive mental state. Coaches can influence behavior, but they lack authority over how athletes feel and react to others. Good coaching inspires and directs the athlete without being con-

trolling. The coach's respect for the athlete develops athlete–coach trust. The coach must exhibit both knowledge of the sport and a commitment to the well-being and development of the athlete.

From Dependence to Independence

Just as athletes grow physically and technically in training, they also need to grow psychologically. The relationship between coach and athlete is crucial to that process. As teacher, coach, and mentor, the coach provides guidance throughout the training process. As athletes grow and develop, it is appropriate to give them more input in the process. A dependence-to-independence model is important to developing self-responsibility and self-discipline in the athlete. Most importantly, such a model empowers athletes to take charge of their lives.

Self-Image

Self-image is the way athletes view or feel about themselves based on perceptions of personal strengths and weaknesses. It is acquired through life experiences and is affected greatly by others' reactions. Those most influential in the establishment of athletes' self-image are parents, peers, and coaches. It should be the highest priority of coaches to be positive and supportive of the athletes they serve.

An athlete's self-image is subject to change and is affected, both positively and negatively, by events and people. The coach must understand that a positive self-image and feelings of self-worth are often sources of motivation.

Self-image is extremely important both on and off the sport field and affects the athlete in the following ways:

- **Motivation.** The athlete's desire and drive to pursue and accomplish a goal can affect or be affected by self-image. Lack of self-belief can be a significant hurdle for the coach to overcome. Positive reinforcement and a progressive, functional training program can go a long way in building confidence and changing an athlete's negative self-image.

- **Learning.** Acquiring knowledge and skills can affect or be affected by self-image. A functional and rational training design provides for consistent improvement, thus positively enhancing self-confidence and self-efficacy (the belief that one can perform a skill well).

- **Athletic performance.** The level of performance in practice and competition can affect or be affected by self-image.

- **Personal relationships.** Self-image decides to a great degree whom an athlete likes or feels comfortable with, and the degree to which the athlete is liked and accepted by others.

- **Life and personal satisfaction.** The ability to realize personal goals and achieve happiness is affected by self-image.

Communication Skills

Effective communication is the cornerstone of good coaching and teaching. Understanding the communication process is the first step toward developing effective communication skills. The best planned practice experiences can fail if communication is ineffective. This section explains several aspects of communication pertinent to the coaching profession.

Any form of communication can be classified according to the following four dimensions:

1. **Sending and receiving.** The coach and athlete are both senders and receivers of information. The coach should be effective not only at sending messages but also at receiving them, via listening and comprehension.

2. **Verbal and nonverbal.** Verbal communication involves the spoken word. Although only one of many forms of communication, it is generally the form most frequently used and misused. Nonverbal communication is done with resources other than words. Demonstrations, signs, gestures, body language, and even one's presence are significant means of nonverbal communication. How something is said is as important as what is said.

3. **Content and emotion.** Effective communicators differentiate between the message and the sender's feeling about the message. Frequently, coaches must send negative messages, but they must strive to do so while still relating positive feelings about the recipient. Again, the way something is said is often as important as what is said.

4. **Direct or indirect.** Messages can be sent directly to the athlete or to others who may have contact with or influence over the athlete.

Quality and Quantity of Communication

The quality and quantity of communication are key variables governing the effectiveness of the communication process. Communication must be of high quality. All communication should be clear and precise and have meaning to both coach and athlete. For learning to take place, the quantity of communication should be limited. Every person has a finite capacity to grasp and use information at a given time; therefore, communication should be selective and concise. Breakdowns in communication on the part of coaches occur when messages are sent poorly, are not received by the athlete, or are misinterpreted by the athlete.

Coach-to-Athlete Communication

To determine the quality of communication in their relationships with athletes, coaches can ask the following questions: Do the athletes have confidence in me and the training plan? Do the athletes feel comfortable speaking openly? A coach's primary goal is to help athletes develop self-trust. This can occur only if coach–athlete trust occurs first. A training progression that manifests improvement will establish the credibility of the coach and build self-trust and self-confidence in the athlete. Open communication is crucial to that process.

The ability to communicate ideas and concepts to athletes is a crucial coaching skill. Good communication can take many forms. Coaches should be adept at the following frequently used forms:

- **Verbal explanations.** Verbal explanations involve the use of words to convey concepts to the athlete. The most common are movement concepts and background information to place a movement in the correct context. Verbal explanations should be clear and concise. They also should be meaningful to the athlete through the use of terms and concepts with which the athlete is familiar. Verbal explanations also should be somewhat limited in quantity, because people can process only a limited amount of information at one time.

- **Cues and cue systems.** Both temporal (timing) cues and spatial (position) cues are verbal directions a coach gives an athlete to elicit a motor response. A group of related cues using common terminology to adjust an athlete's movement patterns is called a *cue system.* Like verbal explanations, cues should be clear and concise, and use only pertinent information.

- **Demonstrations.** Demonstrations are performances of skills, in person or on video, for athletes to watch to learn desired movements. Good teaching programs include frequent and accurate demonstrations. Because most athletes are visual learners, seeing skills performed is very effective.

- **Feedback.** Sport feedback is typically seen as communication from coach to athlete after a trial, relaying information about the performance to help the athlete perfect the skill. Feedback is usually verbal and is often related to some cue or cue system. It can also take the form of a demonstration (e.g., video) or can be a combination of the two. Feedback can be substantial or minimal, depending on the situation. The athlete can also give intrinsic feedback to the coach, which is often prompted by the coach's questions, such as, How did that feel?

© Human Kinetics

Functional communication between coach and athlete is crucial.

Athlete-to-Coach Communication

Communication from athlete to coach is a crucial part of the communication process and necessary for collaboration. An athlete who is skilled at communication can learn faster and avoid many hours of misunderstanding. However, because not every athlete is a good communicator, part of the teaching process is helping the athlete communicate information the coach needs. A coach can foster athlete-to-coach communication by doing the following:

- **Listening.** The coach should convey openness and empathy to the athlete. This creates a learning environment in which the athlete is comfortable conveying information to the coach and is assured that it is valued, respected, and considered. Empathy is the ability to recognize and understand the feelings of others. The more time spent with athletes, the more empathic coaches tend to be.

- **Requesting intrinsic feedback from the athlete.** Sensations that athletes experience during performance can offer very important clues to the problem-solving coach. The coach should create a learning environment in which, within reason, this type of information is solicited and valued.

- **Questioning the athlete.** Coaches should be skilled at asking athletes direct, clear questions. This helps athletes become better communicators.

Guidelines for Sending Messages

1. Be direct. Be straightforward in your message.
2. Own your message. Use "I" or "my" not "we" or "the team."
3. Be complete and specific. Give the listener all he or she needs to fully understand your message.
4. Be clear and consistent. Don't confuse with double messages such as "I think you are a fine athlete, but you'll just have to be patient." This is an example of both acceptance and rejection.
5. State your needs and feelings clearly.
6. Separate fact from fiction. State what you see, hear, and know, and then clearly identify any opinions and conclusions you have based on the facts.
7. Focus on one thing at a time. Organize your thoughts before speaking.
8. Deliver messages immediately. Responding immediately makes for more effective feedback.
9. Make sure the message does not include a hidden agenda. Is the stated purpose of the message the same as the real purpose?
10. Be supportive. Does your message contain threats, sarcasm, negative comparisons, or judgments?
11. Be consistent with your nonverbal messages. Do your nonverbal messages reflect the verbal message?
12. Reinforce with repetition. Repeat key points. Consider using video and pictures to reinforce the message.
13. Make your message appropriate to the receiver's frame of reference by tailoring it to the experience and age of the receiver.
14. Look for feedback that your message was received and accurately interpreted. If there is no visible feedback, ask "Do you understand what I am telling you?"

Adapted, by permission, from R. Martens, 1987, *Coaches guide to sport psychology* (Champaign, IL: Human Kinetics), 50-53.

Self-Talk

Athletes constantly receive messages about themselves from the outside world. Feedback from the coach and significant others provides information that helps them form opinions of themselves. Athletes decide the importance of the messages depending on the respect they have for the sender.

Athletes also send messages to themselves. Humans show a remarkable tendency to be self-negative. This learned phenomenon manifests in self-esteem. The most salient messages an athlete receives do not come from the outside world but from self-talk. These self-messages have a significant effect on self-esteem. Many athletes sabotage themselves with negative self-talk, especially when training or competitions are going poorly. Table 3.1 highlights examples of negative and positive self-talk messages and the resulting behaviors of a high jumper.

TABLE 3.1   Self-Talk Examples for a High Jumper

Self-talk statement	Resulting behavior
"I can't believe I missed that jump. I'll never win this."	Anger, lack of focus, helplessness, increased tension
"I'm fine. Adjust my step. I'll make this next jump."	Improved concentration, positive feelings, calmness

Athletes have a choice about whether to send positive or negative messages to themselves. Coaches should help them construct positive messages and practice changing negative thoughts to positive ones. Just as with physical training, the skill of sending positive self-talk messages is trainable. We are creatures of habit. Changing a deep-seated habit of negative self-talk is possible, but it takes both repetition and time. Practicing the following steps of thought stoppage in practice situations can train this useful tool:

1. Recognize the negative thought or self-talk message when it happens.
2. Use a trigger such as the word *stop* or a snap of your fingers to stop the thought and clear your mental screen.
3. Replace the negative thought or self-talk message with a positive one.

Motivation

One of the underlying principles of human behavior is that people are motivated to fulfill their needs. Coaches should understand athletes' motivations and be sensitive to their needs. This does not mean giving athletes everything they want; rather, it is about using what motivates them to help them succeed. Because athletes' needs differ, coaches need to structure the training environment to best meet all of their needs.

Both internal and external motivations influence sport performance. Internal motivations are driven by a person's values and come from within. External motivations come from people and things outside the person, such as social comparisons, the desire to prove oneself to others, awards, and avoiding punishment. Internal motivations are more powerful over the long term than external motivations. Maintaining a healthy balance between the two is important to create a positive and healthy sporting experience.

All people are motivated by a positive self-image and feelings of self-worth. This includes the need to feel competent and experience reasonable degrees of success. Improving self-worth is directly related to developing self-confidence and improving as an athlete. The training environment can have a significant impact on the development of both competence and confidence in the athlete.

Goal Setting

Goal setting is a powerful process for motivating and providing direction. Success can be identified as achieving a performance goal, improving one's skill level, or surpassing the performance of others. The coach and athlete begin the training process by determining two points: (A) the initial level of skill and fitness and (B) the ultimate performance or competition goal. If the coach has sufficient knowledge and teaching skills, and the athlete has sufficient motivation and support, a plan can be created to bring the athlete along the path from A to B. Goals can be set for various points along the way. It is crucial that expectations be challenging, but also reflective of the athlete's potential.

Incorporating goals into a training plan can be very motivating. Goals provide direction, enhance motivation, provide organization, clarify expectations, focus energy on the task, and create standards. The coach and athlete should work together to set outcome and performance goals that are specific and appropriate for the athlete based on skill level. Performance markers during training provide the coach the information needed for adjusting the goals to ensure that the athlete is progressing optimally.

Types of Goals

The athlete should be able to differentiate among the following types of goals:

- **Outcome goals.** Outcome goals are related to the results, such as achieving particular performance marks or winning. Although these goals provide direction and motivation, the focus on outcome goals before and during competition often results in increased anxiety.

- **Process goals.** Process goals relate to the strategies and techniques used to achieve outcome goals. These performance objectives tend to be more short term than outcome goals, quantifiable, and related to the training process. Process goals are related to the athlete's skill improvement and tend to be within the athlete's control.

- **Attitudinal goals.** Attitudinal goals are more abstract and have to do with

effort, passion, direction, and focus. The attitude of the athlete has a direct bearing on achieving progress and outcome goals.

Coaches' Role in Goal Setting

Coaches should encourage athletes to evaluate their self-worth on the basis of improvement and effort and not on winning or losing. They should collaborate with athletes in setting realistic performance goals. Unrealistic goals set the athlete up for failure and the emotional trauma associated with it. Unrealistically high goals can be a result of competitive pressure, the input of other people, or simply misinformation about typical rates of progress or performance patterns. There is no formula or guide in this process except common sense and good judgment. Problems arise when goals are too numerous, not achievable, not adjusted based on the situation, too general, or focused only on the outcome.

Guidelines for Setting Goals

- **Goals should be realistic, yet challenging.** All athletes like and need to be challenged. High performance implies that athletes must get out of their comfort zones. Communication with the athlete and common sense can aid the coach in setting goals that challenge but are attainable.

- **Goals should be specific.** Telling the athlete, "Do your best," is not specific enough.

- **Goals should be measurable.** Setting and achieving quantifiable goals is important both as a motivator and to help the coach assess the training process.

- **Goals should consider the personality, motivation, and skill level of the athlete.** Athletes are unique and progress at different rates in the training process.

- **Goals should be committed in writing.** Sharing goals with teammates can motivate athletes to follow through with the process.

- **Goals should be associated with a planned time frame.** They may be immediate, short term, long term, or career oriented.

Learning Environment

The learning environment the coach creates during practice sessions determines the effectiveness of both teaching and learning. A practice environment in which a work ethic and good effort are expected and appreciated fosters fast improvement. A healthy social interaction between the coach and athletes and among the athletes makes each athlete more comfortable and allows learning to progress faster. Positively toned feedback and reinforcement, good communication, an emphasis on self-improvement, and the opportunity to have fun should all exist in the practice environment.

The coach must establish and maintain integrity in the training process to foster success. Integrity can be defined as doing the right things for the right reasons. At the highest level of sport, all athletes are talented. So what separates athletes at the top? Successful

Regular goal-setting meetings with input from both athlete and coach can be a powerful motivational tool.

© Human Kinetics

athletes do little things well. Those with this level of integrity are more self-motivated, responsible, and confident than those who cut corners in training.

Informational rewards (positive verbal feedback) from the coach are a powerful reinforcement to athletes who demonstrate integrity in training. A primary goal of training is for the athlete to develop self-trust in the competitive environment. Athlete self-trust occurs best after coach–athlete trust is achieved. Although the coach must convey expectations of the athlete through the training process, the athlete, not the coach, has the final say in the integrity of training.

Performance Environment

Competition should be focused on improvement and fun. The competition environment has much to do with the athlete's level of performance. The coach should convey confidence in and trust of the athlete when merited, encouraging maximal efforts and self-responsibility as well as good decision making in competition situations. A progressive and logical warm-up process should be used to prepare athletes physiologically for the effort and also to help them focus on the task ahead.

Arousal and Performance

Arousal is a physiological response to a stimulus. *Stress* is an imbalance between demand and response capability, especially if the consequences of failing to meet the demand are important to the person. Because people view stressors differently, their reactions differ. When athletes believe they may not have what it takes to measure up to a challenge, a stress response follows. *Anxiety* is a significant stress reaction that can be motivated by an event (state anxiety) or be a function of a predisposition to be anxious (trait anxiety).

Social comparison and competition, expectations of significant others (coach and parents), low confidence level, low training quality, and lack of trust and communication between coach and athlete can increase stress and anxiety levels. Other causes include safety issues, fear of rejection, and fear of discomfort. Successful athletes tend to view physical discomfort as a challenge to be overcome, not as pain. Excellence results from doing the right things, doing them often, and being persistent through adversity.

The widely supported inverted-U model shown in figure 3.1 illustrates an optimal arousal level for achieving optimal performance. With too little arousal, athletes will not be ready to perform optimally. With too much arousal, performance will suffer. The key is to find each athlete's window of optimal performance. Precompetition routines can aid the athlete in finding that level. Coaches need to keep in mind that athletes differ and that events require different levels of arousal.

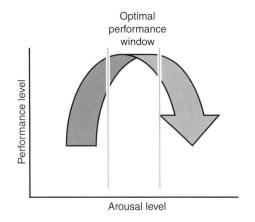

FIGURE 3.1   The performance–arousal curve.

Managing Arousal and Stress

The physical symptoms of arousal and stress include increased heart rate, butterflies in the stomach, sweating, and general nervousness. Psychologically, fear of failure, lack of confidence, and self-doubt have a huge impact on performance by tightening muscles, disrupting rhythms, and creating negative thoughts. Progressive muscle relaxation, relaxing music, and positive imagery and self-talk can help minimize the effects of stress and arousal.

Fear of Failure and Fear of Success

The pressure to win is imposed early on children. Many grow up viewing anything less than winning as a failure. Such a dysfunctional view of the athletic process increases stress and anxiety in athletes. They are motivated not just to win, but to avoid losing or disappointing significant others. This fear of failure is a primary cause of competitive trait anxiety. Many withdraw from the challenge rather than face failure. Successful athletes tend to attribute failures internally (not blaming them on outside factors); they see them as opportunities to learn and improve.

The athlete's perception of the event creates the stress, not the event itself. Asking the question, "What is the worst that can happen?" can often help athletes understand that their perceptions of the event may be flawed or unrealistic. A rational assessment of the event can help to keep things in perspective, thus lowering stress levels.

Fear of success can also be an issue. Familiarity breeds a certain level of comfort. Anything that takes athletes out of their comfort zones can be stressful. Achieving success, especially when it is unexpected, can be uncomfortable to some, stressful to others. Moving out of one's comfort zone always has the potential to provoke stress. Coaches must teach athletes that improvement in sport requires that they get out of their comfort zones. Success, like failure, is associated with a level of discomfort. Helping athletes accept and even look forward to being out of their comfort zones will help them improve.

Athlete Burnout, Overreaching, and Overtraining

How the athlete adapts to training stresses ultimately determines whether a positive training experience will result or staleness, overtraining, or burnout will result. Athlete burnout can ruin a season or even lead an athlete to leave the sport. Among the causes are loss of fun, boredom in training, overtraining, lack of improvement, problems with relationships (with the team or coach), and the inability to balance sport with other elements of life. By recognizing the issues and intervening, the coach may be able to keep the athlete on a healthy training progression.

Athletes in a progressive training model are consistently in a state of fatigue and partial recovery. Although appropriate loading balances load and recovery in a manner that promotes a positive training effect, it is not uncommon for athletes to overreach in training. Overreaching can be the result of overloading, under recovering, or both. Common sense, communication with the athlete, and the recognition that different energy systems require different recovery times help the coach develop an appropriate load–recovery cycle. What is overtraining for one athlete may be optimal for another, which is why individualized training progressions are needed.

The physiological response to training occurs during recovery, not during the loading phase. This demonstrates the need for the coach to understand recovery. When recovery is not ample to allow for adaptation, and another stimulus is applied, the risk of overreaching increases. Overreaching regularly can develop into overtraining. Whereas overreaching can be alleviated relatively quickly with ample recovery and other restorative modalities such as massage and hot–cold baths, overtraining is more serious. If an athlete overtrains, the recovery needed likely will disrupt the training progression, often forcing the cessation of training for a significant period of time.

The psychological implications of overreaching and overtraining also can be serious. Athletes who overreach show consistent levels of high fatigue. Training too much, especially technical and high-velocity work, can result in a depressed mental state. When indications warrant, the coach must modify training by decreasing the total work load and increasing recovery. This can be a challenge to athletes who are schooled in the more-is-better mentality of training.

Physiological symptoms of burnout include increased resting heart rate, increased blood pressure, consistent soreness that does not abate, sleep loss, decreased body weight, and decreased appetite and libido.

Psychologically, burnout can manifest as general mental fatigue, lethargy, depression, irritability, and an inability to concentrate. Coaches need to be aware of outside influences and the psychology of their athletes by asking questions such as these: Is the athlete enjoying the experience? Is there a balance between the time spent in athletics and that spent in other areas of the athlete's life? Are outside pressures negatively influencing the training process? The mantra for all coaches should be know the athlete!

Athletes make a significant investment of time and energy in training. They see it as a cost–benefit process. If the benefits outweigh the cost, they stay motivated and involved. Overtraining, however, results in a serious cost with little benefit. A coach who suspects overtraining must quickly assess the training, specifically looking at the relationship between load and recovery. Feedback from the athlete is crucial for identifying and avoiding training balance issues.

Both coach and athlete should view training as a 24-hour process, not just as the two or three hours spent in training each day. The hours outside of training are those over which the coach has little control. Educating the athlete on nutrition, rest and recovery, and healthy lifestyle choices will pay dividends.

Coach Burnout

The demands on the coach are many; thus, coaches are prime candidates for burnout.

A coach takes on many roles, including the following:

- Teacher
- Coach

- Mentor
- Administrator
- Counselor
- Marketer
- Meet manager
- Problem solver

Performing all of these coaching roles requires time that is spent away from home. Coach burnout can result from many things, including the following:

- Taking the job too seriously
- Feeling the pressure to win (often self-imposed)
- Dealing with problem parents and athletes
- Becoming disenchanted (i.e., the thrill is gone)
- Perceiving a lack of support (from family, friends, administration)

Balancing family and work is key to making the job enjoyable. Attracting and accepting help from parents and assistant coaches allows the coach to delegate some responsibilities, thus spreading out the work.

Burnout often prompts coaches to wonder why they are in coaching. Coaching, too, is a cost–benefit process. When the costs outweigh the benefits, coaches need to ask the following questions:

- Why am I feeling burned out?
- Can I manipulate those causes in a way that gives me more benefit at less cost?
- Can I enlist help in carrying the load (from captains, parents, assistant coaches, administration, family)?
- Am I a control freak? Do I try to do it all? How can I delegate?
- What is my definition of success? Is it a healthy definition for me and my athletes?
- Am I process or results oriented? What are the implications of each?
- Am I seeing improvement in the program? If not, what are the causes?

- Should I take a break to regenerate and reflect?

Identifying the causes of the problem are only part of the answer. Reflecting on these causes can aid in creating a healthy work environment for the coach.

Conclusion

The goal of all coaches should be to create an environment that builds competence and confidence in the athlete. The importance of the interface between the training model and the athlete's psychology should not be underestimated. When the training is functional and progressive, the athlete improves. Athletes who are improving and who exhibit strong self-esteem do not tend to be problem athletes.

Coaches must provide the tools and the guidance to build the athlete and the person. They must also adopt a dependence-to-independence model in which the athlete takes an increasing role in the process.

Creating a healthy sport environment is a big piece of the coach's job. Setting goals gives direction, but that is only the start of a long collaborative process with the athlete. The coach must ask the following questions:

- Am I able to meet the athlete's needs?
- Are athletes participating for the right reasons? What motivates them?
- Do the athletes have the motivation and maturity to develop in a dependence-to-independence model of sport?
- Is communication with the athletes functional and two-way?
- Can my athletes keep sport in a healthy perspective and balance it with nonsport elements of their lives?
- Does the design of my program (and the training) build competence and confidence in the athletes?

Coaches clearly make a difference in the psychology of athletes, and athletes know when their coaches are invested in them.

4

Sport Biomechanics

Robert Chapman, PhD

Biomechanics is the study of how physics interplays with anatomy and physiology to affect human performance. As such, an understanding of biomechanics is very important to success in coaching track and field. Often, the best performers in many events are not the strongest or the ones who can move their arms or legs the quickest. Think of throwing a paper airplane. You could throw the plane very hard, and it might land just in front of you. However, if you throw it with a light flick of the wrist, but using ideal technique and mechanics, the plane may sail. This principle applies to track and field as well. Moreover, proper technique is also important for injury prevention, because most of the events in track and field require the application of significant amounts of force either to the ground or to an object.

Much of the study of biomechanics is devoted to the study of physics and the laws of mechanics. This chapter begins by examining these fields and then progresses to an examination of the interplay between these fields and the biological sciences.

Fundamental Biomechanics Terms and Concepts

To communicate, athletes, coaches, medical professionals, and clinicians need a common terminology. This section defines several fundamental terms and concepts that are critical for understanding the scientific nature of biomechanics and the application of these principles to human movement.

Force

Forces cause a change in the state of motion of a body. They can move a body from rest (as in a sprint start), slow or stop a body that is moving (as in the blocking motion that occurs in the throwing events), or accelerate a body that is already moving. Forces are measured in Newtons metrically and in pounds in the British system.

Mass

A body's mass is the amount of matter it possesses. Mass and weight are not the same. Weight is the force gravity exerts on a body. A convenient way to clarify this concept is to think of an astronaut in space. Removed from the influence of gravity, the astronaut's weight changes, but the mass remains the same. The units used for measuring mass are the gram metrically and the slug in the British system.

Center of Mass

The center of mass, as it relates to the human body, is the point at which all the mass of that body is assumed to be located when examining that body's behavior. The center of mass can be thought of as the balancing point for the body or as the average location of a body. The following are the key points regarding center of mass:

- Rigid objects have a fixed location of the center of mass.
- The center of mass of a person standing lies in the vicinity of the hips.

- Because people are capable of changing body position, the center of mass can move if the body is in contact with the ground. For example, a standing person who lifts the arms raises the center of mass.

- The center of mass of the body can actually lie outside of the body itself. A person can move the center of mass outside the body by assuming a pike or reverse pike position. This strategy is often employed by high jumpers (figure 4.1) and pole vaulters to clear the bar.

Linear Motion and Angular Motion

Linear motion is the motion of a body along a straight path. Angular motion is rotational, meaning that the path of the body is circular—the body or system rotates around an axis. In athletics, we seldom see pure cases of linear or angular motion because most athletic movements are a combination of the two (figure 4.2). For example, a high hurdler is moving down the track linearly, but each jump over the hurdle involves angular motion of the torso relative to the legs. For the sake of simplicity, linear motion and angular motion are studied separately, but every concept pertaining to linear motion has a corresponding angular concept. The study of biomechanics can be greatly simplified by associating corresponding linear and angular concepts.

Kinematic Parameters

Kinematic parameters describe the appearance of movement, such as the position of the body at any given time in a movement. The three key kinematic parameters are displacement, velocity, and acceleration. The following sections describe these parameters first in a linear sense and then in an angular sense.

Linear Kinematic Parameters

Displacement is defined as the change in position of a body with respect to a particular starting point and direction. Displacement is measured in units of length such as feet and meters.

Velocity is defined as displacement per unit of time with respect to a specified direction. It describes the speed of a body. Velocity is measured in units expressing distance and time, such as miles per hour or meters per second.

Acceleration is defined as the change in velocity per unit of time with respect to a specified direction. It describes the change in speed of a body. Increasing velocity constitutes a positive acceleration, whereas slowing or decelerating constitutes a negative acceleration. Acceleration is measured in units expressing velocity (distance/time) over time. It is commonly expressed in mathematical arrangement as distance/time^2. For example, acceleration may be expressed as meters/second^2 or miles/hour^2. Velocity and acceleration are different concepts; a sprinter at a constant top speed may have a velocity of 10 m/sec, but because he is at a constant speed, his acceleration is zero.

Angular Kinematic Parameters

Angular displacement is defined as the change in position of a rotating body with respect to some direction of rotation. In angular terms, the change is measured in position by the size of the

FIGURE 4.1 The athlete's center of mass can be outside the body in certain situations, such as when clearing a crossbar in the high jump.

© Human Kinetics

FIGURE 4.2   A sprinter running at a high velocity demonstrates both linear motion and angular motion.

angle or number of revolutions it has rotated through. Angular displacement is measured in units of circular measure such as degrees or revolutions.

Angular velocity is defined as angular displacement per unit of time with respect to some direction of rotation. It describes the speed of rotation of a body. Angular velocity is expressed in units of angular displacement over time; for example, degrees/second or revolutions/minute.

Angular acceleration is defined as the change in angular velocity per unit of time with respect to some direction of rotation. It describes the change in speed of rotation of a body. These changes may be positive or negative. Angular acceleration is expressed in units of angular displacement/time^2; for example, degrees/second^2 or revolutions/second^2.

Newton's Laws

Sir Isaac Newton postulated three laws of motion in the 1600s, and they form the basis for all studies of movement. As in the previous section, the laws are covered in this section first in a linear sense and then in an angular sense.

Linear Applications of Newton's Laws

Newton's first law states that an object will retain its state of motion until it is acted on by some outside force. In other words, an object at rest tends to stay at rest, and an object in motion tends to stay in motion. A resting object's tendency to remain at rest is called inertia. A moving object's tendency to keep moving is called momentum. Mass is a measure of a resting body's inertia and has much to do with a moving object's momentum values.

Newton's second law describes the relationships among force, acceleration, and mass. This law states that a force applied to an object tends to accelerate it in the direction of the force, and that the acceleration produced is proportional to the force and inversely proportional to the object's mass. Mathematically, Newton's second law can be expressed as $F = M \times a$, where F represents the force applied; M, the mass of the object; and a, the acceleration.

Newton's third law is commonly called the law of action and reaction. More precisely, for every force exerted, there is an equal force exerted in the opposite direction. In other words, all forces occur in pairs. Downward forces produce upward reactive forces; backward forces produce forward reactive forces. A special example of Newton's third law is that of ground reaction force. When force is applied to the ground, the ground exerts force back. If this force is sufficient, displacement of the body occurs.

Angular Applications of Newton's Laws

In an angular sense, Newton's first law states that a rotating system will retain its state of motion until it is acted on by some outside force. An object's tendency to resist rotation is called angular inertia. A rotating object's tendency to remain in rotation is called angular momentum. Factors determining angular inertia and momentum values are discussed in a later section.

In an angular sense, Newton's second law expresses the relationships among force, acceleration, and mass in rotating bodies. The law states that a rotation-producing force (called a torque) applied to an object tends to accelerate the object into rotation in the direction of the torque, and that the angular acceleration produced is proportional to the torque and inversely proportional to the angular inertia of the object. Mathematically, Newton's second law can be expressed in angular form as $T = I\alpha$, where T represents the torque; I, the angular inertia; and α, the angular acceleration.

In an angular sense, Newton's third law states that for every torque exerted, there is an equal torque exerted in the opposite direction. Rotational forces occur in pairs, conserving equilibrium. Clockwise forces yield counter-clockwise reaction forces, and vice versa.

Kinetic Parameters

Kinetic parameters describe the forces involved in movement. As an example, think of a sprinter in the starting blocks. Kinetics can be used to describe the forces applied by the feet to the block pedals and the hands to the ground. Kinematics, as defined earlier, describes the joint angles and position of the hands and feet relative to each other. The proper execution of both kinetic and kinematic parameters is important to performance. Two key kinetic parameters are momentum and impulse. These are explained in this section first in a linear sense and then in an angular sense.

Linear Kinetic Parameters

Momentum, the quantity of motion of a body, can be expressed mathematically as the product of mass and velocity. Momentum and velocity are related, but they are not the same. The proper development of momentum is as important as the development of velocity

and is usually prerequisite to it. Developing momentum is an important part of good technique in all events, and failure to develop momentum properly leads to numerous technical faults.

Impulse, the momentum change produced in a body, can be expressed mathematically as the product of force and time. Thus, the two factors that determine impulse are the amount of force applied and the time over which it is applied. Momentum development, then, requires large forces applied for longer periods of time (figure 4.3).

In the initial movements of a track and field event, velocity is low, and therefore the body has an opportunity to apply large forces over longer periods of time to produce impulse and develop momentum that will help later in the event. Later, when maximal velocities are achieved, the amount of time available for force production is limited. Therefore, impulse generation and momentum development are of concern when acceleration is taking place, but not at high velocity.

Angular Kinetic Parameters

Angular momentum, the quantity of motion imparted to a rotating body, can be expressed mathematically as the product of angular iner-

FIGURE 4.3   The sprinter demonstrates a change in impulse and momentum with acceleration.

tia and angular velocity. Angular momentum and angular velocity are related, but they are not the same. The proper development of angular momentum is as important as the development of angular velocity and is usually prerequisite to it. Developing angular momentum is an important part of good technique in all rotational events, and failure to develop angular momentum properly leads to numerous technical faults.

Angular impulse, the momentum change produced in a rotating body, can be expressed mathematically as the product of torque and time. Thus, the two factors that determine angular impulse are the amount of torque applied and the time over which that torque is applied. Angular momentum development thus requires large torques applied for longer periods of time.

In the initial movements of a rotational event, velocity is low (figure 4.4*a*), and therefore the body has an opportunity to apply large forces over a longer period of time to produce angular impulse and develop momentum that will help later in the event. Later, when maximal velocities are achieved (figure 4.4*b*), the amount of time available for force production is limited. Therefore, angular impulse generation and angular momentum development are of concern when acceleration is taking place, but not at high velocity.

Transfer of Momentum and the Hinged Moment

A transfer of momentum occurs when the momentum of a system is imparted to a part of that system. This requires stopping a part of the system. For example, abruptly stopping a car can cause an object to be thrown from the seat. The momentum of the object is conserved in spite of the car's stopping. In the same way, when the horizontal movement is stopped in a throwing event, the momentum is passed on to the implement. In some situations the momentum of parts of the system is conveyed to the entire system. For example, many field events use an arm action called blocking. This occurs when a swinging limb's movement is stopped, and the momentum of the segment is transferred to the entire system. An example of blocking is the arm action in the high jump, in which the

FIGURE 4.4 Discus windup: *(a)* initial turn; *(b)* final turn.

upward swing of one or both arms is stopped quickly, enhancing the lift achieved at takeoff (figure 4.5).

When a body is in linear motion and one end of the body is stopped, the other end continues to move, rotating about the axis formed at the stopped end. This is called a hinged moment. When a hinged moment occurs, the uppermost points in the body accelerate into rotation, while the lower points decelerate.

People are subjected to hinged moments anytime the foot is planted in a jump or throw. Another example is a thrower who blocks, pulling the nonthrowing arm in close to the body just prior to release. This stops the rotation of the nonthrowing side and accelerates the throwing side. The hinged moment can aid the acceleration of an implement in a throw or harm performance in any event by introducing excessive forward rotation.

Bodies in Flight

Flight is an important part of track and field athletics. An implement is projected into flight in throwing events, the body is projected into

FIGURE 4.5 Transference of momentum at high jump takeoff.

flight in jumping events, and flight is experienced between the strides of a race. This section examines the special circumstances objects and bodies are subject to during flight.

Gravity

When a body is in flight, gravity serves as a force to accelerate it toward the ground. Gravity acts on every object in proportion to its mass, so all objects (barring special aerodynamic situations) fall at the same rate. The rate of gravitational acceleration is labeled g, and is valued at 9.81 meters/second^2. The acceleration due to gravity is nearly the same all over the world, varying only slightly because of differences in elevation.

Aerodynamics

Certain objects, because of their shape and rotation in flight, can stay airborne longer than other objects of comparable mass. This is because, through the principles of fluid dynamics, they are buoyed by the flow of air around them. The javelin and discus are two such objects. A complete discussion of aerodynamics is beyond the scope of this chapter, but proper rotations and release angles for these two implements are important to using their aerodynamic qualities to improve performance.

Predetermined Flight Path and Rotations

The center of mass of any object that is projected into flight (again, barring special aerodynamic situations) uses a parabolic curve as a path. This flight path is predetermined and unalterable. So, for example, once a long jumper leaves the ground, there is nothing she can do to alter her flight path. Any rotations of the body (desired or undesired) that occur in flight are predetermined as well. This path and these rotations are produced by forces prior to flight. Obviously, all of the flight characteristics of an implement are established during the throw. In a jump, all of the flight characteristics are established during approach and takeoff. As such, the majority of coaching time is devoted to movements that happen while the athlete is still on the ground.

Flight and the Center of Mass

Because the path of the center of mass in flight is predetermined, the location of the center of mass in flight is fixed at any instant. Yet, changing body positions can change the relative location of the body's center of mass. This permits an athlete to rearrange his body into different positions about the fixed location of his center of mass in flight (figure 4.6). For example, jumpers can use their ability to manipulate body parts about the center of

mass to achieve better landing and bar clearance positions. However, they can do nothing to alter the flight path itself.

Special Considerations for Rotating Systems

Rotation is an important part of track and field athletics. This section examines special circumstances of objects and systems in rotation.

Axes of Rotation

Rotation occurs about an imaginary line called an axis (figure 4.7). For rotation to be stable

FIGURE 4.6 Elongating the body to slow forward rotation in long jump flight.

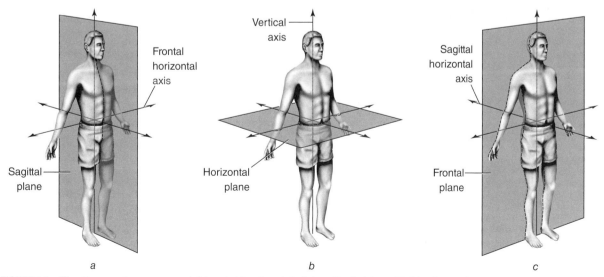

FIGURE 4.7 The three primary axes: *(a)* frontal horizontal; *(b)* vertical; *(c)* sagittal horizontal.

and continued, the axis of rotation must pass though the body's center of mass. When a body experiences flight and rotation simultaneously, the axis of rotation always passes through the center of mass. This is true for each plane in which rotation occurs.

Angular Velocity Versus Curvilinear Velocity

All parts of a rigid rotating body have the same angular velocity because they rotate through the same angle in a given period of time. However, all points on a rotating body do not exhibit the same velocity in a curvilinear sense.

Velocity is measured as distance covered per unit of time, and the points farther from the axis actually cover more distance in a given period of time than do the points closer to the axis. For this reason, discus and hammer throwers should keep their implements away from their bodies, so they can move them faster without increasing angular velocity (figure 4.8).

Tangential and Axial Acceleration

Systems in rotation are in a constant state of acceleration. Consider a hammer thrower.

FIGURE 4.8   A discus thrower with a long arm pull can move the discus faster but cannot increase angular velocity.

Once released, the hammer does not continue on its circular path. Rather, it travels in a straight line tangent to the curve. The tendency of the ball to leave the curve and travel in a straight line is the result of tangential acceleration. At the same time, the hands are constantly pulling on the handle. This constitutes a force directed toward the axis of rotation. This force produces an axial acceleration. The constant interplay of these tangential and axial accelerations keeps the hammer on its circular path. A similar interplay of tangential and axial accelerations exists in curve running.

Conservation of Angular Momentum

The two factors that determine the amount of momentum a rotating system possesses are the radius of the system and the angular velocity of the system. The law of conservation of angular momentum states that a rotating system's angular momentum values remain constant unless acted on by an outside force. Any internal alteration of the system produces another compensating alteration. A decrease in radius causes a system to spin faster, whereas an increase in radius causes it to spin slower; momentum values remain constant in both cases. Similarly, changes in angular velocity produce changes in the radius of the system.

Consider a discus thrower. When a right-handed thrower blocks by pulling her left arm in close to her body, the radius of rotation decreases and the speed of rotation of the right arm increases. On the other hand, extending the arms slows the speed of rotation, which is what the discus thrower does at the beginning of the movement at the back of the ring. The slower rotation in this beginning part of the throw helps the athlete maintain her balance while creating angular momentum.

Clearly, athletes can use body positions to manipulate the radius of a rotating body to slow or speed rotation. There are numerous examples in which radii are decreased by joint flexion to increase angular velocity. For example, the knee flexion observed during the recovery phase of each running stride effectively shortens the leg so that it can move forward more quickly. The flexed trail leg of a hurdler helps him pull the leg through faster to be in proper position for the next step. There are just as many examples of athletes extending their limbs to slow rotation. Long jumpers extend their limbs in flight in the hang style to slow forward rotation and achieve better landing positions. Throwers use extended free arms and legs at times to maintain high momentum values without high angular velocities. Pole vaulters extend their bodies after takeoff to slow their swing (figure 4.9).

FIGURE 4.9 The vaulter extends the body early in the swing to slow rotation.

Transfers of Angular Momentum

An athlete in rotation may slow, stop, or even reverse that rotation by rotating the body parts in the same direction. These secondary axes of rotation give the body a tool to absorb the rotation of the entire body. An example is a long jumper using the hitch-kick style (figure 4.10), who rotates the arms and legs in a clockwise direction to absorb the body's clockwise rotation. Of course, this can be done only temporarily. As landing nears, the athlete stops the secondary rotations in preparation for landing, and the rotation returns.

Summations of Force

This section examines various aspects of force production in athletic performance and how the application of force can be improved.

Proximal and Distal Joints

Proximal is a term that means "close to the center of the body." *Distal* means "away from the core of the body." Every joint in the body is uniquely constructed. Because bone, muscle, and connective tissue differ in the way they are arranged, they also differ in their ability to produce force and in the speeds at which they can produce force. Generally speaking, proximal joints are heavily muscled and capable of producing large forces, yet operate somewhat

FIGURE 4.10   Long jumper using the hitch-kick style.

slowly. Distal joints are less heavily muscled and are poorer at force production, yet operate more quickly.

Firing Orders

To produce large forces, joints must be used in the correct order and at the appropriate times. A particular sequence of joint usage is called a firing order. The characteristics of a joint determine the best point for that joint to contribute to the entire motion. Large muscles contribute early to overcome inertia, and smaller, faster muscles contribute later, after inertia is overcome. Generally speaking, an athlete should use proximal-to-distal firing orders to maximize performance. In throwing events, the athlete employs the large muscles of the trunk to overcome inertia, then the shoulder, then the elbow, and finally the wrist. In running and jumping, the athlete uses the hip first, then the knee, and finally the ankle. Of course, in these arrangements, each joint does not complete its action before the next joint acts; their actions overlap somewhat.

Using All Available Joints

In most track and field events, the body should attempt to produce as much force as possible in the time available. Because every joint is capable of producing some force, it is logical that all the joints capable of producing force should be used in the intended direction. Faulty techniques may put joints in positions that limit or negate their ability to contribute to force production.

Stability and Posture

This section examines the mechanics of stability, issues related to human posture in performance, and the relationships between them.

Stability and Dynamic Stability

The stability of an object is its degree of resistance to toppling over. Two factors affect the stability of an object. The first is the height of the object's center of mass. The higher the center of mass is located, the less stability the object exhibits and the more likely it is to topple. The second factor affecting stability is the horizontal distance between the center of mass and the base of support. The closer the center of mass is to the edge of the base of support, the more likely the object is to topple. A body cannot be stable when the center of mass lies outside the base of support.

In humans, the feet provide the base of support. In double-support situations, both feet are in contact with the ground, so the base of support is sufficiently wide to minimize instability. At other times, in single-support situations, only one foot contacts the ground, so instability increases. Humans move by repeatedly losing and regaining stability. This condition is called dynamic stability. Although we must experience some instability to move, excessive instability may lead to technical breakdowns and errors.

Posture

Posture is the functional state of the core of the body. It is one of the most important, yet most neglected variables in athletic performance. In all athletic events, proper posture (figure 4.11) is a prerequisite to efficiency, high performance, stability, and elastic energy production. Posture can be considered from the standpoint of stability and alignment, as follows:

- **Postural stability.** Athletes constantly apply force during performance to receive reaction forces that create displacement. If the core of the body is not stable, distortion and angular movements occur as these forces are absorbed and wasted. Forces must be applied from a stable base to produce efficient displacements.
- **Postural alignment.** The alignment of the core of the body, particularly of the head and pelvis, is as important as postural stability. Improper alignment of the head can impair the function of the shoulders and arms, hinder balance, and prevent relaxation. Pelvic misalignment decreases the efficiency

FIGURE 4.11   Good running posture makes movement more efficient, conserves energy, and leads to optimal performance.

of the legs, prevents rotation in events in which rotation is desired, and reduces elastic energy production.

Conclusion

An understanding of biomechanics is critical to coaching success in track and field. Performance in many events is based on the proper application of force, and the best teachers of this skill are often those with a firm understanding of the biomechanical principles involved. Proper mechanics can not only help optimize performance but also minimize injury. In many cases, good athletes are born with incredible talent for the sport, but great athletes are often made by refining their biomechanical skills through great coaching and technical practice.

5

Sport Physiology

Robert Chapman, PhD

Physiology is the study of how systems within the human body function. An understanding of physiology is important to success in coaching, because physiology provides the rationale for the development of training programs. This chapter outlines the functions of body systems important to performance, including the neuromuscular system, the energy systems, and the cardiovascular system. Human growth and development and their effects on training are also addressed. The chapter ends with a discussion of the effects of lifestyle factors such as nutrition, hydration, and sleep on the athlete's health and ability to perform.

Neuromuscular System

The neuromuscular system includes the components of the nervous system responsible for controlling skeletal muscle activity and the muscle tissue involved in force production during performance. Because the effectiveness of the neuromuscular system is possibly the most important factor in speed and power events, training this system may be the most important goal of training for these events.

Nervous System

The nervous system is primarily responsible for movement control. The function of a neuron (nerve cell) is to conduct a neural impulse to muscle tissue or to another neuron. The nerve cell is composed of a soma (cell body), an axon, and a dendrite. The axon conducts the neural impulse away from the cell body, and the dendrite conducts the impulse toward the cell body. Motor neurons are types of neurons

that innervate muscle tissue. They are capable of activating muscle fibers, which affects motor activity.

The neural impulse itself is basically composed of electrical pulses. If a neuron receives these pulses, and the pulses are of sufficient magnitude, the neuron is stimulated to conduct the impulse. There are no degrees of conduction. This is referred to as the all or none principle.

The nervous system is composed of a central nervous system (CNS) and a peripheral nervous system. The CNS consists of the brain and the spinal cord. The peripheral nervous system (PNS) consists of the branch nerves and the neuromuscular junctions.

Contractile Mechanisms

Contractile mechanisms are the structures in the muscle tissue responsible for producing movement. This section examines topics involving the anatomy and function of the contractile mechanisms.

The sarcomere (figure 5.1) is the smallest unit of contractile tissue. Many sarcomeres combine to form muscle fibers and entire muscles. The sarcomere consists of noncontractile proteins (proteins not involved in the contraction process) that provide structure to the muscle tissue and contractile proteins (proteins involved in contraction).

The two types of contractile protein filaments are thick and thin. Thin filaments are primarily composed of the protein actin. They are attached to the ends of the sarcomere and extend toward the middle of the sarcomere. Thick filaments are composed of the protein

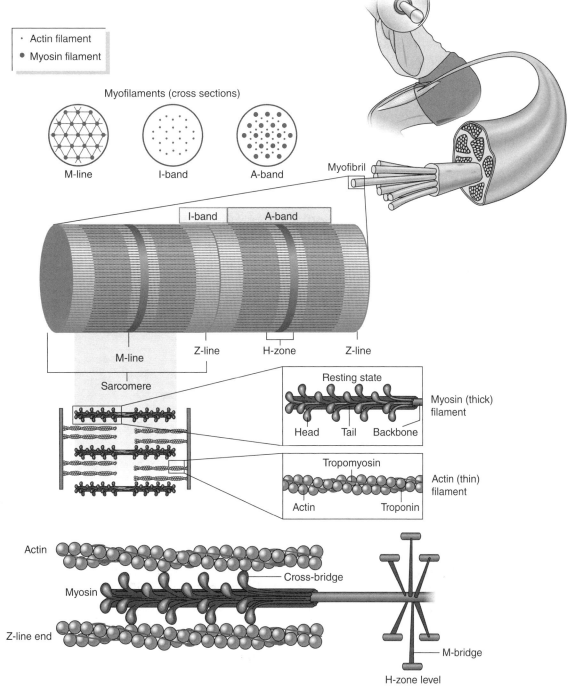

Actin filament
Myosin filament

Myofilaments (cross sections)

M-line   I-band   A-band

Myofibril

I-band   A-band

M-line   Z-line   H-zone   Z-line

Sarcomere

Resting state

Head   Tail   Backbone

Myosin (thick) filament

Tropomyosin

Actin   Troponin

Actin (thin) filament

Actin

Cross-bridge

Myosin

Z-line end

M-bridge

H-zone level

FIGURE 5.1   The sarcomere.

myosin. They are found in the middle of the sarcomere and lie between the thin filaments.

Each thick fiber possesses many cross-bridges, which extend toward the thin filaments. A head at the end of each crossbridge contains an enzyme that can hydrolyze (i.e.,

break down) adenosine triphosphate (ATP) to create energy for the muscle to contract.

Actin and myosin have a chemical affinity for each other, but when ATP is broken down, they cannot bond because the bonding sites are blocked. When contraction is signaled by a neural impulse to the neuromuscular junction, the crossbridge on the thick myosin filaments attaches to the thin actin filaments. When ATP is hydrolyzed in the myosin head, the crossbridge ratchets, causing the filaments to slide past each other, shortening the muscle and causing movement. The steps of this process are as follows:

1. The neurotransmitter acetylcholine is released at the neuromuscular junction.
2. Acetylcholine triggers the release of calcium ions into the sarcomere.
3. The calcium ions make actin binding sites available to the myosin crossbridge heads.
4. The crossbridge heads bind to the thin filaments and swivel, producing movement.

Motor Unit

A motor unit consists of a motor neuron and all the muscle fibers it innervates (figure 5.2). This particular group of fibers is called a pool of fibers and is normally scattered throughout a muscle. There are different types of motor units, which vary in their force-producing capabilities, speeds of contraction, and methods of fueling. Motor units may function in the following two ways.

1. **Volitional function.** In this type of operation, cognitive activity sends the impulses to the motor neuron, which then activates its pool of fibers. The person consciously decides to create movement.
2. **Reflex arc.** In this type of operation, a signal generated by some sensory organ is sent to the motor neuron, activating it and causing contraction in its pool of fibers. The brain is left out of the loop, because no conscious decision is made to effect movement. This type of function is used in all reflex actions.

Muscle Fiber Types

Skeletal muscle differs, both in terms of the mechanism of action and gross physical struc-

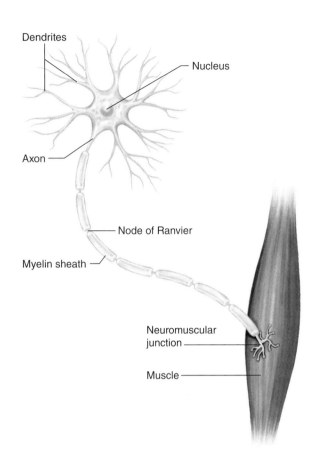

FIGURE 5.2 The motor unit. The motor neuron innervates the muscle fibers.

ture. Generally, there are three skeletal muscle fiber types: type 1, type IIa, and type IIx.

Type I fibers are often called slow-twitch (ST) fibers, because the process of going from a relaxed state to full tension takes about twice as long (about 100 milliseconds) as the same process in type II, or fast-twitch (FT), fibers (about 60 milliseconds). ST fibers primarily use the oxidative (i.e., aerobic) energy system to make ATP for muscular contraction. They have a large number of mitochondria to produce energy and a large number of capillaries to bring in oxygen-rich blood. As such, they do not fatigue as quickly as FT fibers do. Elite endurance athletes typically have a high percentage of ST fibers, often more than 80 percent of their total.

FT fibers come in multiple forms, but the vast majority are either type IIa (FTa) or type IIx (FTx). FTx fibers are low in mitochondria and capillaries, so they fatigue much more quickly than ST fibers do. However, because the time to peak tension of FT fibers is short compared to that of ST fibers, they can produce more force. FTa fibers are unique in that they have many characteristics of both ST and FT fibers. For example, the time to peak tension of FTa fibers is the same as that of FTx fibers, but they have more mitochondria and capillaries, and therefore are more fatigue resistant than FTx fibers are. As such, FTa fibers are often called intermediate fibers. Power, explosive, and sprint athletes often have a high percentage of FT fibers, often 70 percent or more of their total. A typical nonathlete usually has close to 50 percent ST fibers and 50 percent FT fibers.

Many coaches wonder whether training can cause skeletal muscle fibers to change their type. For example, could prolonged endurance training cause FT fibers to become ST fibers? Or in the alternative, can prolonged sprint or strength training cause ST fibers to become FT fibers? In general, the answer is no. For the most part, the percentage of ST and FT fibers is genetically determined. Any changes between the two that may happen with training are extremely small (on the order of about 1 to 2 percent). However, with prolonged training (or detraining), FT fibers can change between the a and x subtypes. Training improves speed or endurance not by changing fiber type, but by improving the function of the fibers.

Energy Systems

The energy systems are responsible for providing adenosine triphosphate (ATP), an energy-rich compound that fuels the work and recovery of cells and is the basic fuel for muscle contraction. The purpose of all energy systems is to produce ATP from various substrates. ATP releases energy from the breaking of a chemical bond, separating ATP into adenosine diphosphate (ADP) and inorganic phosphate (Pi).

Regardless of the energy system employed, energy is created by the chemical breakdown of some fuel source. These fuel sources are called substrates, and the most important ones are glucose, glycogen, and fatty acids. The intensity of effort generally dictates the substrate employed.

- Glucose is a form of sugar. Normally, certain levels of glucose are found in the bloodstream. Glucose plays a critical role in the body's chemical processes.
- Glycogen is a sugar stored in muscle tissue and the liver. It can be converted to glucose and moved into the bloodstream and then used as fuel.
- Fatty acids are mobilized fats that circulate in the bloodstream. They are basically building blocks for fat molecules. Fatty acids are normally the primary fuel source used at rest; however, exercise at certain levels causes the body to use stored fat as well.

The three energy systems are the ATP-PC (or alactic) system, the glycolytic system, and the oxidative (or aerobic) system. The ATP-PC system and the glycolytic system operate anaerobically, which means without the presence of oxygen. The oxidative system operates aerobically, which means with oxygen. The glycolytic and oxidative systems require some type of substrate.

Anaerobic Energy Systems

The ATP-PC energy system often is referred to as the alactic energy system because lactic acid is not produced as a by-product as it is in the glycolytic energy system. It uses the small amount of ATP stored and available in muscle for immediate energy and synthesizes additional ATP from ADP and the donation of a high-energy phosphate from phosphocreatine (PC). PC's sole role is to serve as a storage form of high-energy phosphate, which is donated to ADP to make ATP during initial movement. This process gives the other energy systems time to turn on their ATP production during times of high energy demand, such as sprinting. This system requires no substrate, but at intense workloads it can provide energy for approximately 3 to 15 seconds, depending on the athlete and his training status. The time is limited because the body can store only a limited amount of ATP and PC in the muscle.

The glycolytic energy system makes ATP available for muscle contractions and other purposes using glucose and glycogen as substrates. This anaerobic system can provide energy rather quickly for very intense work. However, lactic acid is produced as a by-product, and the hydrogen ion associated with lactic acid promotes a fatigued state that limits performance. The hydrogen ion with lactic acid is believed to cause fatigue via two mechanisms. One is that high acid levels impair the function of a key enzyme of the glycolytic energy system, thereby reducing the rate of ATP production. The second mechanism is that high acid levels appear to block part of the actual contractile mechanism in skeletal muscle, which leads to the sensation of the muscle tying up.

The glycolytic energy system is thought to be able to produce ATP during an all-out or near-maximal exercise bout for approximately 45 seconds, with some variation on this time limit due to training and other factors. Unlike the ATP-PC energy system, which has a time limit depending on the amount of stored energy (i.e., ATP and PC) in the muscle, the body does not run out of glucose or glycogen in 45 seconds. The time limit depends on the rate of lactic acid formation, the body's ability to remove lactic acid from the muscle, and the ability of the body to tolerate high levels of lactic acid, all of which can be affected by training.

Aerobic Energy System

The aerobic (or oxidative) energy system produces ATP for muscle contractions and other purposes using fat or glucose and glycogen as substrates. The oxidative system, as its name implies, uses oxygen as part of this process in producing ATP. The advantages of producing ATP from the aerobic energy system are that the body can easily deal with the by-products of this energy system (carbon dioxide and water) and that the capacity of this energy system to produce ATP is extremely large. The disadvantage of ATP production by the aerobic energy system is that, compared to the other two energy systems, the rate of ATP production is very slow. The aerobic system is very efficient at producing energy, but it cannot keep up with the demand for ATP when the body is operating at high intensity. Increasing exercise intensity beyond a threshold value causes increased activation of the anaerobic systems.

It is important to keep in mind that all three energy systems are always on and are constantly producing ATP. It is not that one energy system turns on and runs until it is exhausted, and then the next one turns on. The contribution of each of the three systems to the overall ATP production depends on several factors, such as the intensity of the exercise, the training state of the athlete, and the environmental conditions (e.g., heat, altitude).

The amount of energy each system contributes during events of varying distances can be found in table 5.1. This chart first appeared in the 1970s, and it has undergone several revisions as newer techniques for measuring energy expenditure have been developed. This more recent table shows that many events are much more aerobic than originally theorized in the 1970s.

TABLE 5.1   Energy Source Comparisons for Training for the Middle and Distance Events

Energy source (%)	400 m	800 m	1,500 m	5,000 m	10,000 m	Marathon
Aerobic	43	66	84	88	90	97.5
Anaerobic	57	34	16	12	10	2.5

Adapted from P.B. Gastin, 2001, "Energy system interaction and relative contribution during maximal exercise," *Sports Medicine* 31(10): 725-741.

Cardiovascular System

The cardiovascular system is responsible for delivering oxygen and other needed materials to tissues throughout the body. Although numerous organs comprise this system, this discussion concentrates on the heart, lungs, blood, and blood vessels.

Diffusion is a key term in our discussion of cardiovascular function. It refers to the random movement of molecules across tissue membranes. This process is driven when a gas, such as oxygen, is highly concentrated on one side of the membrane and scarce on the other. Molecules of the gas tend to move across the membrane from the side with the higher concentration to the side with the lower concentration. Diffusion is the process by which oxygen moves from the lung across the lung wall and into the blood, following its pressure gradient. Similarly, oxygen moves from the capillary in the muscle to the mitochondria via diffusion. Diffusion occurs for carbon dioxide in the opposite direction, from muscle to blood and from blood into the lung.

Heart

The heart serves as a pump, creating a pressure head for moving blood into various organs throughout the body and creating an effective delivery system for oxygen and other materials needed by the tissues. The heart actually operates as two pumps. The right side pumps blood into the lungs for oxygenation (figure 5.3). After oxygenation, the blood returns to the heart, where the left side of the heart pumps the oxygen-rich blood throughout the body.

Heart rate is the frequency of heartbeats, or pumping cycles. Increased oxygen demand by the tissues requires the heart to beat faster; therefore, heart rate is a good indicator of the level of demands being placed on the body. Stroke volume refers to the amount of blood the heart pumps in a single beat. Cardiac output refers to the amount of blood the heart pumps per unit of time. Mathematically, it can be expressed as the product of heart rate and stroke volume.

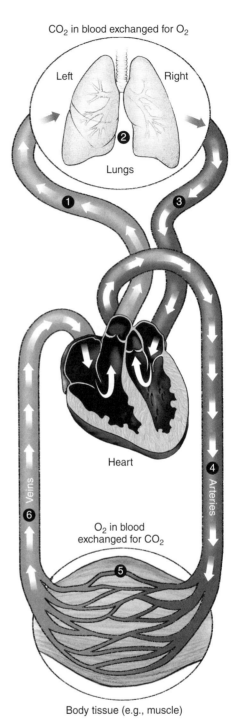

FIGURE 5.3 The blood circulates through the heart, lungs, and muscles.

Lungs

The process of ventilation moves air into and out of the lungs, allowing oxygen to diffuse into the bloodstream for circulation and distribution throughout the body and facilitating the removal of carbon dioxide. Diffusion occurs in the lungs as oxygen moves from lung tissues called alveoli into the capillaries and blood for transport. Carbon dioxide diffuses in the opposite direction.

Blood

Blood is a protein-containing liquid that circulates throughout the body delivering oxygen and other needed materials to the cells, delivering carbon dioxide to the lungs for removal via ventilation, and transporting various components between body tissues.

Oxygen is transported in the blood, primarily by hemoglobin, an iron-containing protein found inside red blood cells. A very small amount of oxygen (about 1 to 2 percent) can be transported dissolved in plasma, the watery portion of the blood.

The arteriovenous oxygen content difference, or A-$\dot{V}O_2$ difference, is an important concept in the study of the cardiovascular system. It refers to the difference in the amount of oxygen carried by the blood after it leaves the lungs and the amount of oxygen carried in the blood after oxygen is extracted by the tissues. The A-$\dot{V}O_2$ difference is a good measure of the volume of oxygen extraction by the tissues per unit of blood. It is important to note that even during maximal exercise, the tissues cannot fully extract all of the oxygen from the blood.

Blood Vessels

The three types of blood vessels are arteries, veins, and capillaries. Arteries transport oxygen-rich blood to tissues throughout the body. Veins return oxygen-depleted blood to the heart. Capillaries are small vessels found between arteries and veins. Capillaries allow oxygen to be extracted by the tissues. Diffusion occurs as oxygen moves from the capillaries across the membrane and into the cells.

Growth and Development

To best assist young athletes in their physical development, coaches must understand the natural process of adolescent growth and development. The training program for the young athlete must be designed to work in concert with the natural maturation process. This section examines some of the factors that vary as maturation takes place, factors that affect the maturation process, and factors to consider when designing training.

Age

Age may be the most important variable to consider when determining the appropriateness of training activities. Athletes in late childhood (6 to 10 years old) should be taught only very basic skills, be subjected to interest-awakening activities, and be allowed to play and have fun.

Athletes in early adolescence (11 to 14 years old) should be subjected to a variety of activities, taught a variety of skills, and prepared for an increase in training in the years to come. Energy system fitness training can be introduced at this time, particularly aerobic training and limited interval work. Team-oriented activities are important because of the social nature of children at these ages, and are the best way to train fitness.

Athletes in late adolescence (15 to 19 years old) are ready for more specific and demanding training, as well as higher training volumes. Boys and girls are both developing quickly at these ages and are capable of performing more complex activities. More advanced anaerobic training can be done at these ages.

Growth and Maturation

In late childhood (6 to 10 years old), boys and girls grow at about the same rate. Typically, they grow 2 to 3 inches (5 to 7.6 cm) and gain 3 to 6 pounds (1.4 to 2.7 kg) per year.

In early adolescence (11 to 14 years old), puberty brings on hormonal changes that cause rapid growth and gains in body fat. This is normal and helps the body meet the caloric needs to fuel growth. Children of both genders experience a spurt of rapid growth. Girls typically experience this growth spurt at an earlier age than boys do, but the response is highly individualistic.

In late adolescence (15 to 19 years old), growth continues, often rapidly. The growth process typically continues longer for boys than it does for girls, largely because of the influence of testosterone.

Young athletes mature at different rates, so it is wise for the coach to ascertain the degree of readiness of each athlete to undertake each type of activity. This is important to prevent injuries and the mental fatigue or burnout often seen in young athletes who are trained at very high levels. It is not uncommon for highly successful athletes at the youth level to be early maturers, ones who have reached puberty at an earlier age, and thus have more muscle mass for select activities. As a result, these early-maturing athletes may also receive more focused instruction in sports at a younger age than later-maturing youth, and thus develop more technical skill earlier. However, when it comes to success in elite-level athletics as adults, research indicates that most elite adult athletes were later maturers physiologically. Whether this phenomenon is due to physiological, sociological, or psychological factors is not known. The take-home point is that all young athletes, whether more or less mature physically for their age, should receive quality instruction and development as they pursue the sport of track and field.

Gender

There is little difference between age-appropriate training for young male and young female athletes. However, as puberty approaches, there are great social differences between the genders that affect athletes' motivation for participation. The coach should provide equal opportunities for athletes of both genders to participate and be sensitive to these differences.

Heredity

Genetics can influence a variety of the physical features of children and adolescents. Those who are more talented, provided they have an aptitude for the chosen activity, will respond and progress better with training.

Health Status

The primary goal for any coach is to keep the athlete healthy and injury free. Coaches should err on the side of caution and adapt training programs for athletes who are ill or injured. With young athletes, the coach should be especially careful to avoid and prevent overuse injuries. Promoting recovery from training is just as important as prescribing the training stimulus.

Iron Deficiency Issues

Iron is a key element in hemoglobin and myoglobin, substances involved in the delivery of oxygen to the working muscle. Iron-deficient athletes commonly experience fatigue, poor recovery between workouts, and impaired performances. It is not uncommon for actively training track and field athletes to be iron deficient, and the occurrence of deficiency is slightly higher in distance runners and females in all events.

Iron deficiency needs to be determined by a clinician via a measure of serum ferritin. Ferritin is a protein involved in iron transport and storage, and the level of ferritin closely mirrors the amount of iron stored in bone marrow. Simple measures of hemoglobin concentration or hematocrit levels, although easier and less costly than a serum ferritin test, are poor indicators of iron deficiency in athletes, because these levels can vary greatly depending on hydration status or the degree of acclimatization to hot weather training. Although a normal serum ferritin level for the general population can range from as low as 15 ng/ml (nanogram per milliliter), for athletes a common bottom-of-normal value is 20 ng/ml for women and 30 ng/ml for men.

Athletes should not take iron supplements without knowing their serum ferritin level, because a very small percentage of people have a condition called hemochromatosis, which is characterized by extremely high (greater than 500 ng/ml) ferritin levels. In these people, supplemental iron can be harmful to organs such as the liver, and iron overload in general can be toxic. It is best to follow a physician's recommendation when supplementing with iron.

Lifestyle Issues

This section examines how lifestyle issues affect the training program and suggests guidelines for improving these aspects of life.

Sleep

Good sleep habits are crucial to the success of the training plan. Adequate sleep (8 to 10 hours per day) is essential to permit regeneration. Also, adequate sleep, especially in the hours before midnight, is necessary to allow recovery from exercise.

Nutrition

A proper nutritional plan is essential to top athletic performance. Athletes should eat a variety of nutritious foods and avoid unhealthy choices. The coach should have a general understanding of essential nutrients.

Protein is a compound that builds and repairs body tissues. It is also involved in many of the body's chemical processes. Protein is made of smaller units called amino acids, some of which cannot be made by the body in sufficient quantities to maintain health. These amino acids are considered essential and must be obtained from food. Animal-derived protein from eggs, dairy products, and meat is considered complete because it contains all the essential amino acids. Plant-derived protein comes from nuts, grains, and legumes and lacks one or more of the essential amino acids.

Carbohydrate is an energy-providing organic compound that is broken down by the body to produce glucose. This glucose may be immediately used as fuel, or it may make its way to the liver and muscles (where it is stored as glycogen) and to fat cells (where it is stored as fat). Starch and sugar are the major forms of carbohydrate. Foods such as grains, legumes, vegetables, and fruits that contain starch and naturally occurring sugar are referred to as complex carbohydrates because their molecular complexity requires the body to break them down into simpler forms to obtain glucose. In contrast, simple sugar, refined from naturally occurring sugar and added to foods, requires little digestion and is quickly absorbed by the body.

Fat consists of fatty acids attached to a substance called glycerol. Fat is the most concentrated of the energy-producing nutrients. It also plays an important role in the body's chemical processes. Dietary fat is classified as saturated, monounsaturated, or polyunsaturated according to the structure of its fatty acids. Animal-derived fat is high in saturated fat. Plant-derived fat is rich in monounsaturated and polyunsaturated fat. A high intake of saturated fat is considered unhealthy.

Minerals are minute amounts of elements that are vital for the healthy growth of teeth and bones. They also facilitate the body's chemical processes. Mineral nutrients are classified as major elements (calcium, chlorine, magnesium, phosphorus, potassium, sodium, and sulfur) and trace elements (chromium, copper, fluoride, iodine, iron, selenium, and zinc).

Vitamins are organic substances needed for normal metabolism that cannot be synthesized by the body in adequate amounts. Vitamins are classified as fat soluble or water soluble. Fat-soluble vitamins (vitamins A, D, E, and K) are absorbed and can be stored in the body, so they do not need to be consumed every day to meet the body's needs. Water-soluble vitamins (C, B_1, B_2, B_3, B_6, B_{12}, and folic acid) cannot be stored in adequate amounts and need to be eaten daily to meet the body's needs.

In addition to these nutrients, fiber and water are also essential. Although fiber provides no energy or building material, it is vital to good health. It is needed for proper digestive function. Water and hydration are examined in detail later.

Nutritional status plays a supporting role in training and helps the athlete handle training loads. Weight loss or weight gain should be undertaken carefully and only after much examination and planning and with extreme patience and expert guidance.

Choosing from and balancing the traditional four food groups (fruits and vegetables, dairy, meats, and grains) is a simple, effective way to meet general nutrition needs. Often, the healthiest diet is a balanced diet. Excessive amounts of highly processed and refined foods such as sugars, oils, and flours should be avoided. In general, athletes in training should aim for a target of 70 percent of their calories from carbohydrate, 15 percent from protein, and 15 percent from fat.

A proper diet pre- and postworkout can substantially affect the quality of the session. The current recommendation is to consume approximately 50 grams of carbohydrate within 30 minutes after completing a training session to maximize glycogen resynthesis in the muscle. Some data suggest that postexercise drinks or meals should have a four-to-one carbohydrate-to-protein ratio to maximize glycogen resynthesis.

Simply cooked meals and raw foods are nutritionally superior to complex preparations. Ideally, eating several small meals throughout the day is best for athletes. Breakfast is extremely important and should contain some protein-rich food. Eating a variety of foods improves nutrition and enhances immune system function.

Hydration

Sufficient water intake is crucial for maintaining efficiency in nearly all body functions. It is equally important for ensuring adaptations to training. Hydration status has a dramatic effect on performance. A 1 percent reduction in body weight due to dehydration leads to an average 6 percent decline in performance, depending on the event.

The best way for an athlete to monitor hydration status is to use the pee test. The color of the urine is a simple indication of hydration status. Several color-coded charts are available online (for example, see the USOC handout at www.teamusa.org/~/media/TeamUSA/sport%20performance/pdf%20handouts/Hydration_2011.pdf). Note that some medications and B-complex vitamins can darken the color of the urine.

A focus on hydration should start well before the workout and continue during the workout. Increased water intake may be necessary during hot or dry weather, especially if it's windy. A coach should never withhold water during a practice as a form of punishment. Air travel tends to dehydrate the body quickly, so increasing water intake prior to and during such trips is advised.

It is possible for athletes to overhydrate with water. This rare condition, called hyponatremia, is a dangerous condition in which extreme water intake flushes out the body's sodium stores, leading to muscle and cardiac issues. This is a very rare phenomenon, and normally, athletes are underhydrated for the tasks they perform in practice or competition. However, coaches should be aware of athletes who obsess about hydrating, because they may be at risk of overhydrating.

Coaches should also be aware of young athletes who use caffeine-containing energy drinks. These substances can affect heart rate, nervous system function, breathing rate, and thermoregulation abilities.

Conclusion

Knowledge of proper physiological concepts can help the coach prepare athletes for performing at their best. Although much of the information in this chapter is common sense, a lot of misinformation, as well as gimmicks and superstition, is attached to many principles of sport science. At the end of the day, the coach is responsible for helping the athlete determine what information is useful, how to apply it, and how to get the most out of it. Proper training is the cornerstone of athletic development; however, the proper application of sport physiology principles can often be the small edge many athletes need to move from second place to first place.

6

Training Design

Vern Gambetta

Periodization is simply planning. Planning gives direction and purpose to training. It also provides a context in which to evaluate performance aside from wins and losses or personal records. Periodization is a systematic attempt to gain control of the adaptive response to training in preparation for competition. It is based mostly on scientific inferences rather than hard scientific evidence. On the other hand, an immense body of coaching evidence going back into the early 20th century underscores the following key elements of what eventually became known as periodization:

- Systematic approach
- Strategy to distribute training loads in relation to competition goals
- Defined structure for progression
- Sequential building-block approach
- Set time frame for execution of the plan
- All components of training addressed
- Pursuit of specific competition goals
- Reflection of the undulatory nature of the adaptive process
- Systematic manipulation of the variables of volume, intensity, and density
- Method for monitoring training and evaluating competition results

Effective long- and short-term planning is the cornerstone of the athletic development process. As a concept, the periodization process is an educated attempt to anticipate future performance based on an evaluation of previous competition, training results, and scientific knowledge about the body's adaptive response to stress. Periodization addresses the timing, sequence, and interaction of the training stimuli to maximize adaptive response in pursuit of specific competitive goals. It is achieved by planning and organizing training in a cyclic structure to develop all global motor qualities in a systematic, sequential, and progressive manner for optimal athlete development.

Planning is essential to performance regardless of the level of competition. Long-term planning should focus on global themes and training priorities based on competition performance, training, and testing data from previous years. It is helpful to conceptualize it as the table of contents of a book. The plan directs the reader to each chapter for more detail.

Training is the manipulation of the application of stress and the body's subsequent adaptation to that stress to maintain homeostasis. Because the body always seeks to maintain a state of homeostasis, it works constantly to adapt to stresses. The adaptation that occurs is predictable. In training, the desired adaptive response is called supercompensation (figure 6.1).

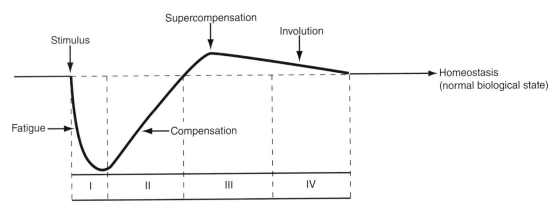

FIGURE 6.1 Supercompensation model.

Reprinted, by permission, from T.O. Bompa, 1983, *Theory and methodology of training: The key to athletic performance*, 3rd ed. (Dubuque: Kendall Hunt). Modified from N. Yakovlev, 1967, *Sports biochemistry* (Leipzig: Deutsche Hochschule für Körperkultur).

Supercompensation is a four-stage process. The first stage involves the application of a training stress and the body's reaction to this training stress, which is fatigue. There is a predictable drop-off in performance due to that stress. The next stage is the recovery phase, during which the energy stores and performance return to baseline (state of homeostasis) as represented by the point of the application of the original training stress. The next stage is the supercompensation phase. This is the adaptive rebound response above the baseline. It is very important to understand that physical qualities respond and adapt at different rates, so it is misleading to think that one generalized supercompensation curve exists.

Essentially, each physical quality has its own supercompensation curve. The art is designing these curves of adaptation so that they coincide at the proper time. "These differences in timing for supercompensation are due to the duration of the various biological regeneration processes that take place during the recovery phase. While the replenishment of creatine phosphate will take only a few seconds to a couple of minutes to return to normal levels, the reloading of the muscle with glycogen may last up to 24 hours or in some cases, even longer. The production of new enzymes or proteins may also take hours, sometimes even days to complete" (Olbrecht 2000, 6). Adaptation is an ongoing undulatory process (figure 6.2). If all the variables are manipulated correctly and the proper ratio of work to recovery is achieved, the result is a continually rising sinusoidal curve pointed toward higher-level performance.

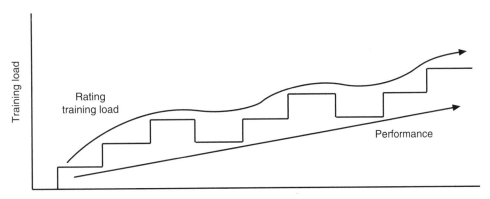

FIGURE 6.2 Undulation chart.

Reprinted, by permission, from T.O. Bompa, 1999, *Periodization: Theory and methodology of training*, 4th ed. (Champaign, IL: Human Kinetics), 48.

The last step in the process is the decline of the supercompensation effect. This is a natural result of the application of a new training stress, which should be applied at the peak of supercompensation. If no training stress is applied, there will also be a decline; this is the so-called detraining phenomenon.

Training volume, intensity, and frequency must be appropriate for the athlete. If training is too hard, the athlete will struggle to get back to baseline and no supercompensation will occur. If training is too easy, there will be very little adaptive response. If this is continued over several training cycles, then the law of reversibility will take effect. Simply stated, the law of reversibility is use or lose it. If the training load is adequate and the timing of the application of the training stress is correct, then a supercompensation effect will occur.

The other theory regarding the process of adaptation to the stress of training is the two-factor, or fitness fatigue, theory. It is a logical extension of the supercompensation model. The basic premise is that the fitness effect of training is slow changing and long lasting, whereas the fatigue effect of training is of shorter duration but greater magnitude. The two factors, fitness and fatigue, are the immediate training effect of every workout. The most immediate effect of any workout is fatigue, but the long-term effect is the adaptive changes in the targeted motor qualities over time. "According to the two-factor theory of training, the time intervals between consecutive training sessions should be selected so that all the negative traces of the preceding workout pass out of existence but the positive fitness gain persists" (Zatsiorsky 1995, 15). As with the supercompensation model, the key to applying the two-factor model is understanding that motor qualities and physical capacities adapt at different rates.

To predict each athlete's adaptive response, the coach must manipulate the training load to ensure supercompensation. A training load consists of three interdependent variables: volume, intensity, and frequency (sometimes called density). Volume is the amount of work, intensity is the quality of work, and frequency is how often the training stress is applied. To adapt, athletes must be stressed to a level beyond what they are accustomed to. This is called overload. The overload can be manipulated by changing volume, intensity, or frequency. Not overloading all the variables at the same time ensures a positive adaptive response. There is a reciprocal relationship between volume and intensity; if one rises, the other should fall.

Foundational Training Principles

A sound training program is based on foundational principles. The following principles do not stand alone; they are interdependent and allow for no shortcuts or deviations. Coaches must carefully follow them to design and implement quality training program.

Principle of Progression

In its simplest form, progression moves from simple to complex, easy to hard, and general to specific work. These simple steps give way to complex interactions. Training variables do not progress at the same rate; nor do people.

Proper progression requires clearly defining each step and articulating goals and objectives for each step. Progression is not linear. It should start with a clear picture of what the athlete should achieve or look like at the end of a training program. However, that progression toward the ultimate objective will, in all probability, proceed in a staircase-like fashion. Constant progress should continue toward the goal, but some of the steps along the way will be smaller than others. Plateaus and occasional regressions should be expected and factored in.

Within a career and also within a training year, progression in its broadest sense should occur in the following steps:

1. **Basic conditioning.** This step addresses the development of the global motor qualities in a systematic manner.
2. **Basic technical model.** This step is about teaching and mastering the basic techniques of the events.

3. **Specific advanced conditioning.** This incorporates more advanced training methods to meet the individual athlete's needs.

4. **Advanced technical model.** This step refines the basic technical model and builds on it to improve the repertoire of the athlete's technical skills.

Principle of Accumulation

Adaptation to the stress of training is a cumulative process. Athletes do not do a workout and gain an immediate positive training response unless it is a relatively small technical adjustment. The effect of training accumulates over time, provided training has been consistent and the athlete has been injury free. This also relates closely to the principle of context. If everything is kept in context, then the training effect will accumulate and progress at a predictable rate. Remember, adaptation to different training demands occurs at different rates, and the ultimate training adaptation is the synergistic accumulation of the collective training responses. One workout cannot make an athlete, but one workout can break an athlete. Thus, athletes must be patient and allow time for training to take effect. Getting caught up in a constant quest for positive reinforcement from workouts is ultimately self-defeating.

Principle of Variation

Training volume, intensity, frequency, and sometimes exercise selection must be constantly varied in a systematic manner to ensure continual adaptation. This variation should be planned to measure the effect of the variation. If training is not varied, the body will adapt quite rapidly, and the training effect will quickly be dulled. No variation results in a significant risk of staleness and possibly overtraining.

The principle of variation, or variability, has a basis in the time course of biological adaptation. The body's response to training stress is predictable. During the first 7 to 14 days of a new training program, the body adapts

quickly. Rapid gains in training or technical breakthroughs often occur. After this initial period, the athlete begins to level off. Olbrecht (2000) termed this the fast adaptation phase. The second phase, stabilization, is usually about three weeks long. At the end of this time frame, the body is much less responsive to the same training stimulus, so the training needs to be modified to ensure continued adaptation. This is the rationale for the length of the mesocycle.

A logical, sensible combination of the following actions ensures a continued adaptive response:

- **Increase volume.** In many ways, volume is the easiest and simplest variable to manipulate.
- **Increase intensity.** This involves changing the quality of work, and is more viable in speed and power events.
- **Change frequency.** Add or reduce the number of training sessions. Also consider multiple sessions in a training day to address different components.
- **Change the actual composition of the workouts.** Sometimes this can be as simple as a change in rest intervals; at other times it may be a change in the sequence of exercises. Monotony in workouts can dull the adaptive response.
- **Increase the difficulty of training.** This can be done by changing the environment (e.g., sea level to altitude or moderate to hot climate) or simply performing two hard sessions consecutively.

Principle of Context

Context establishes the nature of the relationship of the training components within the system. What is done today in training should fit with yesterday's workout and must flow into tomorrow's workout. The same is true for the components of training. Before something new is incorporated into training, it needs to fit into the context of what is already being done and what is planned. Perhaps the biggest violation of the principle of context is to take one component (e.g., speed or strength) and train it to the exclusion of all others. This is fundamentally unsound. A component may be emphasized for a phase, but it should be kept in proportion to the other components and put into the context of the whole training plan. If the principle of context is not observed, the components of training will get out of proportion and adaptation will not occur at the predicted level.

Principle of Overload

To progress, athletes must be subjected to a load beyond that to which they have adapted. Overload is achieved by manipulating volume (the amount of work), intensity (the quality of the work), and frequency (how often training sessions are applied). Because a reciprocal relationship exists between volume and intensity, athletes must be careful about increasing both at the same time.

Principle of Recovery

Recovering from a workload, in both the short and long term, is crucial to create a positive adaptation to the training stimulus. If the athlete is unable to recover from the training stress, then the load is not appropriate. No two athletes are the same in ability, nor are they the same in the ability to recover.

SAID Principle

SAID is an acronym for *specific adaptation to imposed demands.* You are what you train to be. It is more than just doing work. The work must be directed and have a purpose that relates to the event and be specific to the person. The training adaptation depends on the type of overload imposed on the athlete. "Simply stated, specific exercise elicits specific adaptations creating specific training effects" (McArdle, Katch, and Katch 2001, 460).

The highest degree of specificity is the actual event. Coaches must use their knowledge of biomechanics to design drills and exercises that result in maximal return for the time invested. Doing so makes good use of training time and results in more direct transfer.

For effective planning, coaches must do the following:

- Clearly define training goals. Goals must be measurable and observable.
- Identify key training areas (KTAs) relative to athletes' current competitive status and state of fitness. Prioritize what the athletes need to work on. It is impossible to do everything.
- Clearly separate the need to do from the nice to do. Focus, focus, focus!
- Plan to prepare athletes for optimal performance improvement with a definite climax to the season or a peak performance, if needed or appropriate.
- Stress long-term career preparation so that short-term goals do not compromise long-term development.
- Create a plan to help evaluate progress toward goals. A good plan is like a road map; it shows where the athlete is at all times relative to the final destination.

Essentially, a sound training program is analogous to a mosaic consisting of the global motor qualities of speed, strength, stamina, suppleness, and skill plus recovery. Even though a synergistic relationship exists among all biomotor qualities, they are not equally emphasized in a training program. The emphasis varies from athlete to athlete and event to event. All components must be trained during all phases of the year, but the proportion changes significantly with training age and the priorities of the particular training period.

Adaptation time changes with the quality being trained and the system being stressed. For optimal adaptive response to occur, some training tasks require complete recovery before they can be repeated (i.e., activities of high neural demand such as maximal strength, speed, and speed strength workouts). Conversely, some training tasks can be trained with incomplete recovery (i.e., activities of high metabolic demand such as basic endurance, speed endurance, and strength endurance workouts).

Each training component has its own time to adaptation. Flexibility improves and adapts from day to day. Strength improves and adapts from week to week. Speed improves and adapts from month to month. Work capacity improves and adapts from year to year. Without emphasis, those qualities decline at the same rates at which they adapt.

There is a natural tendency to focus on the immediate training effect, the response to training from a single workout. However, the focus should be on the cumulative training effect, which reflects the adaptive changes and level of improvement of technical abilities from a series of workouts (Issurin 2008, 79). Therefore, it is imperative to carefully plan the sequence of training sessions from day to day and within the session itself, as well as to project the potential effect of training on subsequent days. Where does the workout fit within the microcycle plan? Coaches need to keep in mind that the workout is only one component of a very big picture.

Careful consideration of the complementary nature of training units is necessary for achieving positive training adaptations both within and between workouts. Complementary training units are just that, components that work together to enhance each other. The following training units are complementary: speed and strength; strength and elastic strength; endurance and strength endurance; and skill, speed, and elastic strength. Ultimately, the units have more than a complementary relationship. They should enhance each other and mesh with the ultimate effect being *synergistic!* It is important to point out that certain units are contradictory. Quite simply, high-neural-demand activities contradict high-metabolic-demand activities.

The coach must have command of the long-term buildup of training for the athlete to ensure an athlete's optimal progress throughout his or her career. The long-term plan has the following three stages, which overlap somewhat:

1. **Basic training phase.** Typically, this phase lasts four years, but in some cases it can extend to six years. The goals are general physical development, the establishment of the foundations of technique, and the establishment of sound training routines and training habits. The frequency of training during this phase increases from three sessions a week in the first years to five sessions a week at the end of the phase.

2. **Buildup training phase.** This phase, which usually lasts three years, involves a gradual change to more specific and higher-intensity, concentrated training loads. There is a greater emphasis on competition, although competitions are designed to provide objective feedback on the progress of training. The number of sessions can be as high as 12 in a seven-day microcycle. The length of each training session is increased. In the later stages, multiple daily training sessions may be added.

3. **High-performance phase.** The duration of this phase is open ended. Training is directed by the specific needs of the athlete relative to competition goals. Competition is the focus, and training is of high intensity and much more specific.

Planning is the preparatory work the coach must do to structure training systematically in alignment with the themes and objectives of training and the athlete's level of conditioning. Following are basic factors coaches should consider when developing a plan:

- The demands of the event should dictate all training.
- The qualities of the athlete must be carefully considered to ensure that the plan fits.
- Considering the pattern of injuries relative to the event allows for planning a remedial injury prevention component.
- The 24-hour athlete concept takes into consideration the demands and stresses the athlete faces outside of training.
- The gender of the athlete is important. Females have different needs than males, which affects the training plan. Strength training assumes a more significant part of training during all phases of the training year.
- The time frame available for executing the plan is important. Is it a scholastic

situation, in which the athlete will be in a program for four years? Is it a short-term preparation for one competition or test?

- The specific goals of the plan must be considered. The goals should be as detailed, specific, and measurable as possible. Coaches need to remember that the goals define the target.

- The developmental level of the athlete should dictate the direction and content of the plan. The coach must carefully consider the athlete's current state of fitness and current level of technical development.

- The competitive schedule ultimately is what drives the plan. Everything should point toward improvement in competition.

- Coaches must carefully consider the athlete's ability to recover from the work.

Coaches should consider the following questions when developing a plan: What is the performance objective? When is the performance objective to be met? What are the major components needed to fulfill the objective? What means are available to meet the objective? What are possible obstacles—physical, psychological, financial, spiritual, and relational? Does technique need to be altered? If so, how much time do I need (have) to effect change? What motivational obstacles might occur throughout the year? How many competitions are needed to prepare for the championship? Does the work planned suit the athlete in terms of likes, dislikes, and adaptive ability?

Breaking Down the Training Year or Season

The long-term plan, or the macrocycle, is a general guide; the training is organized into periods or phases. The macrocycle can be as long as 12 months in a single periodized year or as short as four months in a double periodized year. Each macrocycle is divided into periods—usually, a preparation period, a competition period, and a transition or

recovery period. The periods are divided into mesocycles. Each mesocycle should have a general theme and a list of the major and minor training emphases.

The preparation period is, as the name implies, a time of preparation. There are no competitions during this period. The emphasis is on general work to raise work capacity or more specific work to address deficiencies. This period often is split into a general preparation phase and a more specific preparation phase in which the athlete begins to address event-specific needs.

In the competition period, the focus is on results in competition. There are two types of competition periods, competition I and competition II. Competition I is the time for developmental competitions. The goal during this period is adaptation based on what was done in a preceding preparatory period. Competition I is also an opportunity to develop competition skills. The competition II period encompasses the important and crucial competitions of the macrocycle. The emphasis is highly specific application work based on what was done in the competition I period.

The transition period is devoted to bridging competition and training periods. This is an active period that allows no detraining. The goals are to regenerate, rehabilitate, and remediate. Remedial work addresses any fundamental deficiencies.

The training within each of the aforementioned periods is broken down into mesocycles, which usually vary in length from two to six weeks, although the most common length is four weeks. The mesocycle generally consists of microcycles that can vary in length from 7 to 14 days.

Daily training is based on a thematic approach; each day has a specific theme that determines the direction and content of that day's training. The themes are carefully chosen to direct the flow of training from day to day to ensure that the training and competition targets are met. The daily themes do not vary significantly from phase to phase to ensure a consistent approach.

The training session, which is a collection of training units, is the cornerstone of the training plan. A long-term plan is a succession of linked training sessions in pursuit of specific objectives. The training session should have the greatest emphasis in planning and execution. Each session must be carefully evaluated to adjust the following sessions accordingly. It is especially important to have contingency plans ready for individual training sessions.

Each training session should have a general theme supported by objectives for each component in the training session. The components should be very specific and measurable. The coach should make sure the planned session fits with the time available that day for training, taking into account the difficulty of the skill if it is a skill session. Proper equipment should be available and in working order, and the training area should be safe. The coach should always keep the training session in the context of the long-term plan.

When planning a specific workout, coaches would do well to run through this checklist of questions:

- What should the athletes do? What equipment do they need?
- When in the workout should the highest-intensity neural demand activities occur?
- What is the time of the training year? What is the total volume?
- What is the number of exercises or drills? What is the work-to-rest ratio?
- What is the intra-exercise and intrasegment recovery?

Each training session should have a teaching emphasis, a training emphasis, or a stabilization emphasis. In a teaching emphasis session, the coach must make sure to teach correctly the first time. The coach should not be in a hurry, but rather, take the time to attend to details and individual needs. The ultimate goal of the teaching session is skill mastery.

The training emphasis workout is the refining process. This involves more repetition. It may not take more time, but it does demand constant attention to detail. The stabilization emphasis workout is used once the main competitive season begins or emphasis changes in a training cycle. The general theme in stabilizing is to maintain what has been done before.

Teaching and training emphasis sessions occupy significantly more time than stabilization sessions. When designing the session, coaches should carefully consider the following:

- Progression and sequence
- Training time available and time allocation
- Integration with skill workouts
- Size of the facility or training area relative to the number of athletes training
- Equipment needed and available
- Coaching personnel available
- Number of athletes participating in the training session

Every workout should have a remedial injury prevention component. This is most easily addressed in the warm-up. This component should be designed to meet the athlete's needs and should take no more than 20 minutes. It is important that coaches consider intraworkout recovery when planning the training session. This can take the form of self-massage, shaking, and stretching. Intraworkout nutrition in the form of hydration is the most basic and practical form of recovery.

As the athlete progresses in training age, multiple workouts in a day provide a sharper focus. Multiple sessions are a necessity for the elite athlete; this is not an option. It is preferable to keep such sessions to 60 minutes or less. Each session should flow or lead into the next session, and sessions should be structured so that the work is compatible.

The ultimate goal of planning is to prepare the athlete to be at the optimal state of readiness for the most important competitions of the year. This entails understanding the concepts of tapering and peaking. Mujika and Padilla (2003) defined a taper as "a progressive non-linear reduction of training load during a variable period of time, in an attempt to reduce the physiological and psychological stress of daily training and optimize sports performance." A systematic taper leads to an increase in power and neuromuscular function, improvement in various blood measures, and a positive psychological state. All of this leads to improved performance. This process must be systematic and a key part of the overall plan.

All gains from training should be achieved by the start of the taper. This is not a time to improve fitness; it is a time to stabilize, sharpen, and fine-tune. The tapering process is both an art and a science, and it is highly individual. There are as many psychological factors in the peaking process as there are physiological. Peaking is the culmination of the buildup of training. It is imperative that the coach emphasize throughout the training year that all the training is pointing toward a peak. This reinforces confidence in preparation. Peak performance is a logical extension of the cumulative effects of training and competition periods.

Proper peaking can result in a 2 to 6 percent improvement in performance. Of course, this depends somewhat on the level of athlete development. A prime consideration is how long an athlete can maintain peak performance, how many competitions it takes to achieve that peak, and how many times in a training year can peak performance be attained.

Training intensity must not be cut to maintain the effects of the acquired physiological and performance adaptations. This seems to be true with both developing and high-level athletes. Volume must be significantly reduced. Studies have shown that volume decreases in the range of 60 to 90 percent can be effective, depending on the sport and the level of the athlete. The frequency of training must be maintained, especially in technique-oriented events (Mujika and Padilla 2003, 1184).

The time of the taper can be as short as 4 days and as long as 28 days. However, planning the peaking process requires some basic considerations. There must be a detailed plan for the unloading with a daily postworkout assessment. Research has shown that "Progressive, nonlinear tapering techniques seem to have a more pronounced positive impact on performance than step-taper strategies" (Mujika and Padilla 2003, 1186). Athletes should use only recovery techniques that restore and invigorate, not those that tear down. They should also avoid the overuse of massage and vigorous recovery methods because they can be very fatiguing. A psychological game plan is also a must, as is an increase in mental practice during this time of reduced training. Athletes should visualize peak performance and rehearse all aspects of the competitive environment so that, in the competition, they feel as though they have been there before. Because visualization is highly individual, coaches should be sure to get input from the athletes. Now is also the time for their favorite workouts. The qualification procedure and championship format play huge roles in determining the peaking process and the beginning of the taper.

A mini taper is beneficial for determining how the athlete responds to a taper. This should be at least 12 weeks out from the planned taper to ensure adequate buildup again. This is especially beneficial with athletes of younger training ages. The female athlete's taper must take into consideration the menstrual cycle; for some females this is a very difficult time. Also, the female athlete must continue to strength train up to the competition or risk significant loss of power.

The role of competition leading into the taper and peak must be considered. If competition sharpens the athlete, then it is beneficial. This is highly individual and depends on the level of the athlete. The diet must be carefully controlled during the taper because the reduction in workload can result in a tendency to put on weight. Athletes should also keep neural stimuli up during the taper weeks. They need to sharpen, not deaden.

Functional Warm-Up Routine

A functional warm-up process for track and field athletes accomplishes the following:

- Prepares the athlete physiologically for the high-demand work of the session and competition.
- Minimizes the risk of injury.
- Develops a large range of motion at the hips, thus eliciting the stretch reflex mechanisms needed in high-velocity sprinting and jumping.

- Develops and trains the neuromuscular templates needed for sprinting, jumping, and throwing.
- Trains fitness and develops the biomotor abilities of speed, strength, coordination, flexibility, and endurance.

Table 6.1 offers the coach a variety of movements and exercises to use to design a warm-up routine. The theme of training for a given day will dictate the choice of exercises and length of the warm-up. All warm-up routines follow this logic in the choice of exercises: simple to complex, easy to hard.

Cool-downs bring the athlete back to homeostasis. Thus, they follow the opposite progression of hard to easy, complex to simple.

TABLE 6.1 Warm-Up and Cool-Down Exercises

	Exercise	Demand	Speed	Complexity	Warm-up	Cool-down
	TRACK EXERCISES					
1	Low-level skipping	Low	Slow	Easy	X	X
2	Proprioceptive walk	Low	Slow	Moderate	X	
3	Leg cradle	Low	Slow	Moderate	X	
4	Easy skip with arm circles	Low	Medium	Moderate	X	X
5	Inverted hamstring	Low	Slow	Moderate	X	X
6	A skip	Medium	Medium	Moderate	X	X
7	B skip	Medium	Medium	Moderate to high	X	X
8	Squat side step	High	Slow	Moderate	X	
9	High-knee jog	Low	Medium	Moderate	X	X
10	Piston step	Medium	Fast	Moderate	X	
11	Carioca	Medium	Medium	Moderate	X	X
12	Jog, jog, quick step	Medium	Medium	Moderate	X	
13	Straight-leg bound	Medium	Medium	Moderate	X	
14	Ankling	Low	Slow	Moderate	X	X
15	Alternate toe-touch walk	Low	Slow	Moderate	X	
16	Walk with arm circles	Low	Slow	Moderate	X	X

(continued)

Table 6.1 *(continued)*

	Exercise	Demand	Speed	Complexity	Warm-up	Cool-down
17	Quick-step running	High	Fast	Moderate	X	X
18	Single-leg quick step	Medium	Fast	Moderate	X	X
19	Increasing quick step 1-5	High	Fast	Moderate	X	X
20	Knee hug lunge, elbow to instep	Low	Medium	Complex	X	
21	Knee hug lunge, step with twist	Medium	Slow	Complex	X	X
22	Side run with arms crossing	Medium	Medium	Complex	X	X
23	Static walk (drive/hold, step)	Medium	Slow	Complex	X	X
24	Skip with arm circles	Medium	Medium	Complex	X	X
25	Backward run	High	Medium	Complex	X	
26	A-C skip	High	Fast	Complex	X	
WALL EXERCISES						
	Exercise	Demand	Speed	Complexity	Warm-up	Cool-down
27	Wall swing facing wall	Medium	Medium	Moderate	X	
28	Wall swing sagittal	Medium	Medium	Moderate	X	
29	Trail leg circle	Medium	Medium	Moderate	X	
30	Wall lead leg lunge facing wall	Low	Medium	Moderate	X	
START PROGRESSIONS						
	Exercise	Demand	Speed	Complexity	Warm-up	Cool-down
31	Standing start	Medium	Fast	Moderate	X	
32	Falling start	Medium	Fast	Moderate	X	
33	Touch and go	High	Fast	Complex	X	
34	Four-point start	High	Fast	Complex	X	

ACCELERATIONS						
	Exercise	Demand	Speed	Complexity	Warm-up	Cool-down
35	Walk-in 40 m acceleration	Medium	Fast	Moderate	X	X
36	Standing 40 m acceleration	Medium	Fast	Moderate	X	
37	Touch and go, 40 m	High	Fast	Complex	X	
38	Four-point start, 40 m	High	Fast	Complex	X	

Conclusion

Coaches must understand and apply training principles to give direction and purpose to training. The application of the principles obviously occurs in the day-to-day training sessions. To have meaning, those sessions must be part of a plan. The plan directs the work and provides a context for evaluating the training. That being said, plans must be flexible and adaptable based on the athlete's response to training.

7

Biomotor Training for Speed and Power Events

Vern Gambetta

Training programs for the speed and power events differ slightly, although they share many elements. This chapter addresses the abilities needed for success in speed and power events, outlines activities for developing them, and provides organizational guidelines for developing effective training programs.

The following primary biomotor abilities must be addressed in training:

- Speed
- Strength
- Endurance
- Flexibility
- Coordination

In addition, these primary abilities have subcategories. For example, power is a combination of speed and strength, agility is a combination of speed and coordination, and mobility is a combination of flexibility and coordination.

Training that develops all the biomotor abilities in a balanced way throughout the season is called multilateral training. Balance is essential to long-term progress and the avoidance of injury. These abilities are interdependent and must be trained consistently to achieve desired results. Specialization may call for the proportional increase of one or more of these abilities, with a consequent decrease in others to balance out the training load. Essentially, all components of training are trained throughout the training year with different emphases depending on the time of the year and athlete level.

Strength-Related Abilities

Of all the biomotor qualities, strength is the most all-encompassing. There is no event in track and field that does not require some expression of force; therefore, all events benefit from event-appropriate strength training. Strength is a highly interdependent motor quality that profoundly interacts with and affects all other biomotor qualities. Proper development of strength results in the following benefits:

- Improved ability to reduce and produce force
- Increased ability to express explosive power
- Increased joint stability
- Injury prevention and rehabilitation

Strength is the ability to exert force with no time constraints; it is simply the degree to which force can be applied. In contrast, power is the ability to express force in the shortest amount of time. Power is broken down into speed-dominated power and strength-dominated power. Strength-dominated power is characterized by the expression of high force against external resistance, as exhibited in the shot put, discus, and hammer events. Speed-dominated power is the production of high force expressed at high speed with restricted resistance, as exhibited in the sprints and jumps.

The acquisition of strength is governed by neuromuscular, muscular, biochemical, structural, and biomechanical factors, which are highly interdependent. The nervous system, in response to the demands of a specific task, governs recruitment order and sequence. The brain does not recognize individual muscles; rather, it recognizes patterns of movement. Therefore, it is imperative to train movements, not muscles. The initial adaptation to strength training is neural through increased firing rate and motor unit recruitment, and improved motor unit synchronization. The body essentially learns to engage the appropriate movers and stabilizers to reduce and produce force.

The two broad classifications of muscle fibers are slow-twitch (type I fibers) and fast-twitch (type II fibers, of which there are two subtypes, IIa and IIb). Type I fibers are fatigue resistant and do not have the force-producing potential. Type II fibers produce high force but fatigue rapidly. Their potential peak power output is four times that of type I fibers, and they respond differently to training. As muscle tension increases, motor units are recruited based on size. The larger, slower type I motor units are recruited first, and then the smaller, more powerful type II fibers are recruited. This is called the size theory of motor unit recruitment.

There are four types of muscle actions. In isometric (static) muscle action, there is no movement or change in the length of the muscle but high tension. Concentric (shortening) action occurs when the muscle shortens to overcome resistance. Eccentric (lengthening) action occurs when the muscle lengthens against resistance. Elastic, or reactive, action (the stretch–shortening cycle) occurs when the muscle is stretched to enhance the subsequent concentric action.

Strength training is defined as coordination training with appropriate resistance to handle body weight, project an implement, resist gravity, and optimize ground reaction forces. To apply this definition appropriately, we need to look closely at how each element relates to track and field events.

- **Handling body weight.** The emphasis is on relative strength working with various percentages of body weight resistances.

- **Projecting an implement.** In the throws, the weight of the implement determines the resistance needed to develop strength to move that implement at the desired release speed.
- **Resisting gravity.** Events that demand work against gravity necessitate a more eccentric and isometric emphasis to express the necessary force.
- **Optimizing ground reaction forces.** Events that require high ground reaction forces demand realistic reactive strength.

Strength exercises are classified in the following three categories:

1. **General strength.** Exercises to develop general strength focus on the force component. They are characterized by slower speeds and higher force movements. Traditional weight training exercises and other resistance methods do not seek to imitate sport-specific skills. Speed is of little or no concern. This is all about force, not speed.

2. **Special strength.** The purpose of exercises in this category is to convert general strength to specific strength. They involve movements that are similar to, but not the same as, the specific event movements. They incorporate movement with resistance that incorporates the joint dynamics of the skill. Olympic-style weightlifting, medicine ball work, stretch cord work, and plyometric training fit into this category. A significant force component is present, but the speed component is much more prominent. The exercises are more specific than general strength exercises.

3. **Specific strength.** These exercises are characterized by movement with resistance that imitates the joint action of the sport skill. There is a high degree of specificity in terms of mechanics, skill, and above all, speed. This obviously has the highest degree of transfer to a specific event.

Both special strength and specific strength are categories of functional strength. Specific strength exercises are specific to the technical movements of the event being trained for.

Speed-Related Abilities

Speed is the ability to move the body or parts of the body through the greatest range of motion in the least amount of time. Speed, a function of strength, is a motor skill that is enhanced through the application of sound motor learning principles in training. To train speed, coaches must understand its components.

Starting involves overcoming inertia to get the body moving from a stationary position and into a good position from which to accelerate. Acceleration is the rate of change of velocity with respect to time, and is typically reported in meters per second per second (m/s^2). Most athletes accelerate to maximal speed in four to six seconds. Absolute speed, also called maximal speed, is the ability to move the body at the highest velocity possible. Speed endurance is the ability to maintain speed in a climate of fatigue.

Endurance-Related Abilities

Endurance-related abilities incorporate both aerobic (with oxygen) and anaerobic (without oxygen) elements. Track and field events have vastly different endurance requirements based on duration. For speed and power events, it is sometime best to use work capacity as an umbrella term to define the type and direction of endurance work necessary. Work capacity is the ability to tolerate and recover from a workload. The goal is to build a strong foundation of general fitness that has specific transfer to the demands of the event and considers individual needs. Following are the three components of work capacity:

1. **The ability to tolerate a high workload.** The key word here is *tolerate.* Many athletes can perform an occasional high workload, but cannot do so on a regular basis.

2. **The ability to recover from the workload before the next training session or competition.** This is closely tied to the first concept of workload tolerance. An athlete who cannot recover is risking overuse injuries or overtraining and will not be able to adapt to the training stress.

3. **The capacity to resist fatigue whatever the source.** Fatigue is more than metabolic. An athlete must be able to resist both neural and mental fatigue as well.

Energy for work can be derived anaerobically or aerobically. The anaerobic system produces energy very rapidly, resulting in large but brief power outputs for brief, intense activities. However, it is limited in the amount of energy it can produce. The anaerobic system causes a lactic acid buildup, a rapid depletion of phosphocreatine (PC) stores (which results in rapid power reduction), and a significant drop in speed. The aerobic system is just the opposite; it can produce large amounts of energy. Unfortunately, this energy cannot be produced rapidly. It is limited by the body's ability to break down carbohydrate and fat with the help of oxygen and to deliver oxygen to the muscles.

Flexibility-Related Abilities

Flexibility is a measure of the controlled range of motion around a joint. Different activities demand varying degrees and types of flexibility. Flexibility is closely related to strength and posture. Functional flexibility is defined as the dynamic, three-dimensional range of motion of body parts. Flexibility is highly individual and somewhat event specific.

Static flexibility is the ability to attain a large range of motion at a joint without accompanying movement. Static flexibility training activities involve moving into positions that challenge flexibility limits. Static flexibility exercises are best used as part of a postworkout cool-down.

Dynamic flexibility is the ability to attain a large range of motion at a joint with accompanying movement. Dynamic flexibility training normally consists of simple movements that require large ranges of motion. According to Thomas Kurz, "Flexibility training is speed-specific because there are two kinds of stretch receptors, one detecting the magnitude and the speed of stretching, the other detecting magnitude only. Static stretches improve static flexibility and dynamic stretches improve dynamic flexibility, which is why it does not make sense to use static stretches as a warm-up for dynamic action" (Kurz 2001, 236). Progressive dynamic flexibility exercises should be part of the warm-up routine for all speed–power events.

Coordination-Related Abilities

Coordinative abilities relate to the ability to efficiently connect, link, and sync to reduce force, produce force, or stabilize at the appropriate time in the appropriate plane at the correct time in milliseconds. According to Drabik (1996), the coordinative abilities are as follows:

- **Balance.** Maintenance of the center of gravity over the base of support, balance is both a static and a dynamic quality.
- **Kinesthetic differentiation.** This is the ability to feel tension in movement to achieve the desired movement.
- **Spatial orientation.** This is the control of the body in space.
- **Reaction to signals.** This is the ability to respond quickly to auditory, visual, and kinesthetic cues.
- **Sense of rhythm.** This is the ability to match movement to time.
- **Synchronization of movements in time.** This concerns synchronizing unrelated limb movements.
- **Movement adequacy.** This is the ability to choose movements appropriate to the task.

Coordinative abilities never work in isolation. They are all closely related and are the underlying foundation and the prerequisite for technical skills. Technical execution is highly dependent on coordinative abilities. Without mastery of these abilities, technical proficiency in the various events is difficult to achieve. The development of general coordination abilities should precede the development of event-specific abilities. Early multilateral development of young athletes can aid in event-specific development later.

Organizing Training and Classifying the Demands of Work

Aerobic capacity is the maximal amount of oxygen the body can consume in a minute. Aerobic power is expressed as a percentage of the aerobic capacity that can be used. The higher this percentage is, the greater the aerobic power is. Anaerobic capacity is the maximal amount of lactate a person can produce. Lactate is both a by-product of anaerobic metabolism and a fuel for exercise. Anaerobic power is simply the percentage of the anaerobic capacity that can be used.

Training for endurance requires an understanding of training the energy systems. Conceptually, the energy systems are intensity dependent, not time dependent. The contribution of each system varies with the intensity and duration of the effort.

Adenosine triphosphate (ATP) is necessary for movement; it is manufactured aerobically or anaerobically depending on the intensity of the exercise. Furthermore, the energy systems must interact with the other systems of the body to ensure an efficient, smooth, and coordinated action. Consideration should always be given to the dominant energy system demands of the training activities relative to the demands of the event. Although this should guide coaches, it is not the sole objective of a workout.

Training Methods for Biomotor Ability Development

This section provides training program activities for speed and power events. These activities may be applicable in any training program.

Flexibility Training Methods

Range of motion is a crucial part of elastic force generation in track and field events. Consistency is key to improving flexibility. A daily commitment to flexibility and range of motion work pays long-term dividends. Following are a number of options for developing and improving flexibility.

Static stretching refers to traditional stretching exercises. These exercises place a joint in a position that challenges range of motion, usually using gravity or other muscle groups to increase tension levels. Static stretching is best used in cool-down settings.

Facilitated stretching routines are more sophisticated and include proprioceptive neuromuscular facilitation (PNF) techniques, elastic band stretching, and yoga techniques. These can be used daily, most commonly as part of a warm-up routine.

Dynamic flexibility exercises are simple movements that move joints through large ranges of motion (figure 7.1). Leg swings, trunk twists, and arm circles are examples of this type of work. These exercises are used as the core piece of a well-developed and logical warm-up progression. The choice of exercises should follow a format of low demand to high demand and simple to complex.

Hurdle mobility exercises force joints to move through large ranges of motion. They improve mobility, flexibility, and coordination. Following are examples of these exercises:

FIGURE 7.1   Skip with arm circles is an example of a dynamic flexibility exercise.

Hurdle Overs

- Hurdle walkover (alternate lead leg; figure 7.2)
- Hurdle walkover (same lead leg; figure 7.3)
- Side (straight leg)
- Side (bent leg)
- Forward and back
- Swing step
- Walkover skip
- Shuttle

FIGURE 7.2 Hurdle walkover (alternate lead leg): *(a)* step over hurdle with left leg; *(b)* step over next hurdle with right leg; *(c)* step over next hurdle with left leg.

FIGURE 7.3 Hurdle walkover (same lead leg): *(a)* step over hurdle with right leg and follow with left leg; *(b)* step over next hurdle with right leg; *(c)* follow with left leg.

Hurdle Over-Unders
- Over/under (right over, left under; figure 7.4)
- Over/under (left over, right under)
- Side under (right lead; figure 7.5)
- Side under (left lead)

FIGURE 7.4 Hurdle unders, over/under (right over, left under): *(a)* step over low hurdle with right leg; *(b)* follow with left leg over low hurdle; *(c)* leading with left foot, move under the high hurdle; *(d)* step over the next low hurdle with right leg.

FIGURE 7.5 Hurdle unders, side under (right lead): *(a)* leading with the right side, move under the high hurdle; *(b)* stay perpendicular to hurdles, right side leading, and step out from under the high hurdle; *(c)* face low hurdle and prepare to step over with right leg.

Strength Training Methods

Maximal strength training covers a wide spectrum of exercises, the goal of which is to raise explosive power. Traditional weight exercises include body weight exercises, free-weight training with kettlebells, dumbbells, and bars, and machine exercises. Olympic weightlifting methods use the traditional competitive Olympic lifts of the snatch and the clean and jerk and various derivatives and modifications.

Powerlifting uses the squat, deadlift, and bench press and various derivatives. The goal of powerlifting is to improve strength without the concern for speed of movement.

Elastic equivalent training combines an explosive weight exercise with a similar plyometric movement. It is very high-neural-demand training that increases explosive power. Following are some examples: In each pairing, the athlete performs 4 to 6 repetitions of weight exercises and 8 to 12 repetitions of elastic equivalent exercises.

> **Squat** (6 at 75 to 80 percent 1RM) and jump squat (10 repetitions)
>
> **Bench press** (6 at 75 to 80 percent 1RM) and medicine ball chest pass (10 repetitions)
>
> **Hang clean** (6 at 75 to 80 percent 1RM) and stair jumps (10 repetitions)

Maximal power training exercises should allow for the production of the highest forces possible throughout the whole range of movement. To achieve maximal power, the bar or the implement must accelerate throughout the entire movement. Multithrow routines are excellent for maximal power training. Multithrows are high-intensity throws performed from various positions using a shot or heavy medicine ball. Examples include overhead back throws, underhand forward throws, and rotational throws. These develop power and coordination. Following is a sample program:

Multithrows

- Overhead back throw (figure 7.6) × 6
- Forward throw through the legs (figure 7.7) × 6
- Squat and chest pass throw (figure 7.8) × 6
- Over-the-shoulder throw, right (figure 7.9) and left × 6
- Hop-hop-throw (overhead or underhand) (figure 7.10) × 6

FIGURE 7.6 Overhead back throw: *(a)* squat and move medicine ball between legs; *(b)* rise from squat and swing arms overhead to throw ball back.

FIGURE 7.7 Forward throw through the legs: *(a)* squat and move medicine ball between legs; *(b)* rise from squat and swing arms up to throw ball forward.

FIGURE 7.8 Squat and chest pass throw: *(a)* rise from squat with medicine ball near chest height; *(b)* press ball up and toss overhead

FIGURE 7.9 Over-the-shoulder throw, right: *(a)* with medicine ball in both hands, swing ball near chest height toward right shoulder; *(b)* release ball over right shoulder.

FIGURE 7.10 Hop-hop-throw (overhead or underhand): *(a)* stand with medicine ball in both hands, feet together; *(b)* hop forward; *(c)* sink into squat with ball between legs; *(d)* swing ball underhanded and release.

Circuit training is essentially interval strength training. The athlete performs a strength exercise for a certain number of repetitions or amount of time followed by a prescribed rest interval; then progresses to the next exercise. The goal of circuit training is to develop muscular endurance, which has the added benefit of improving work capacity.

The circuit can be constructed in several ways. Perhaps the most common is a repetition-based circuit in which the athlete performs a set number of repetitions of a particular exercise and then moves on to the next exercise. Another option is a time-based circuit, in which the exercises are performed for a certain amount of time with a fixed rest interval. The load or exercise has to be carefully chosen so the athlete can work for the entire time prescribed. Progress is judged by the number of repetitions achieved. This training method can significantly improve work capacity and result in significant body composition changes. Following is a sample circuit:

Basic Strength Circuit

Work with a partner on a one-to-one work-to-rest ratio. One partner does the complete circuit and then rests as the other partner works. Continue for the prescribed repetitions.

- Pull-up x 5
- Push-up x 5
- Squat x 15
- Two-position sit-up x 5

Elastic and Reactive Training Methods

Plyometrics train the stretch–shortening cycle of muscle action to enhance the subsequent concentric action. The goals are to raise explosive power, increase the tolerance of greater stretch loads and improve stiffness, and attenuate ground reaction forces. Plyometric training is classified based on the projection of the center of gravity.

In-place response is characterized by vertical displacement of the center of gravity. Following are examples of in-place plyometric exercises:

Jumps in Place
- Forward/back
- Side to side
- Rotational (90 degrees)

Hops in Place
- Forward/back
- Side to side
- Rotational (90 degrees)

Bounds in Place
- Forward/back
- Side to side
- Rotational (off one foot onto the opposite foot)

The short response is characterized by horizontal displacement of the center of gravity with 10 contacts or fewer. The tuck jump, standing long jump, and standing triple jump are examples of short-response plyometric exercises.

The long response is characterized by horizontal displacement of the center of gravity, with speed, and with more than 10 contacts. Bounds, hops, and skips are examples of long-response plyometric exercises.

The plyometric demand matrix (table 7.1) was developed to govern progression (Radcliffe and Farentinos 1999) while developing a program. The variables can be manipulated moving down or across the columns. A suggested range of sets, repetitions, and distances appears in each box.

Postural (Core) Strength Training Methods

Medicine ball exercises use a medicine ball as the load. Coaches should choose exercises that work the core in all planes of motion: trunk flexion and extension (sagittal plane), lateral flexion (frontal plane), trunk rotation (transverse plane), combinations (tri-plane), and catching (dynamic stabilization in all three planes). Examples include various catch and throw combinations, abdominal and spinal exercises with a medicine ball, and callisthenic

TABLE 7.1 Plyometric Demand Matrix

	Low impact	Medium impact	High impact	Shock
In-place response	3 or 4 sets 10 to 20 reps	3 sets 10 to 12 reps	2 or 3 sets 8 to 10 reps	2 sets 10 reps
Short response	3 sets 10 to 12 reps 10 to 20 meters	3 sets 10 reps 10 to 20 meters	2 or 3 sets 8 to 10 reps 10 to 20 meters	2 sets 10 reps
Long response	3 sets 10 to 20 reps 20 to 40 meters	2 or 3 sets 10 to 15 reps 20 to 40 meters	2 or 3 sets 10 to 12 reps 20 to 40 meters	NA

exercises using the ball as a light load. Additionally, medicine ball work can be used to enhance postural strength and the ability to withstand impact by having the athlete catch a thrown ball.

Basic Core

- Wide rotation x 10 each side
- Big circle x 10 each direction
- Over the top x 10 each side
- Rotate and step x 10 each side
- Chop and step x 10 each side

Medicine Ball Rotations and Twists

- Standing full twist x 10 each direction
- Standing half twist x 10 each direction
- Wide rotation with partner push x 10 each way
- Half chop with a push x 10 each way
- V-sit throw x 20
- Seated side throw x 10 each side

Medicine Ball Wall or Partner Throw Series

- Overhead throw x 20
- Soccer throw x 20
- Chest pass x 20
- Standing side to side (cross in front) x 10 each side
- Down the side (standing facing the wall) x 10 each side
- Around the back (standing back to the wall) x 10 each side

Speed Development Training Methods

Examples of interval work with recoveries are provided in chapter 8. This section offers an abbreviated description of some speed development training methods. Many others may also be appropriate. The key in applying these to speed development workouts is to remember that intensity and quality—not volume—are the stimuli to speed development. Coaches need to know their athletes and carefully select appropriate methods based on their level of development and the time of the training year.

Acceleration Development

Acceleration work normally takes one of the forms described in this section. In all of these activities, intensities should be high and recoveries long enough to ensure good-quality work, usually one to two minutes.

- **Rollover start.** From a rolling start position, allow the hips to fall forward until the desired shin angle is achieved. Push off both feet and fully extend the front leg until there is a full extension of the limb from hip to toe. Place the next step under to behind the hips, and repeat the extension. Use a strong arm action and violent attack of the ground with each step. Drive for five to eight steps, and then accelerate to a normal run for another 10 meters.
- **Acceleration development sprints.** Short sprints, up to 40 meters long, are

used to isolate acceleration abilities and mechanics. These are usually executed from a standing or a block start and are volitional.

- **Acceleration ladder.** Start by placing the forefoot of the front leg just in front of the first rung of the ladder. Lean forward until the desired shin angle is achieved, and then accelerate through the ladder, placing each step just in front of each rung.
- **Resisted runs.** Resisted runs are sprints performed with some type of resistance, such as harness runs, hill sprints, and sled pulls. Because loading places the body in acceleration-type positions and requires the use of mechanics that are used in acceleration, resisted runs are often used to improve acceleration. These runs are usually 20 to 50 meters long.
- **Harness resistance runs.** These runs are performed with a harness from a rollover start position. Place a harness around your waist, and have someone provide resistance for you to pull against. This exercise introduces driving by helping you feel the force application. Drive with the harness for five to eight steps before releasing it and accelerating for another 10 meters.

Speed Development

Speed development work should place the athlete in situations of maximal velocity for periods of time not exceeding three seconds. Normally, this work falls into one of four categories: speed development, variable speed, assisted speed, and mach speed.

Speed development runs are sprints of 40 to 60 meters that bring the athlete to maximal velocity for a short period of time at the end of the run. Variable speed runs are complex runs involving alternating periods of relaxed running and maximal-velocity running. Examples are ins and outs and sprint-float-sprint runs. Variable runs should provide two or three short maximal-velocity situations and are typically 60 to 100 meters long.

Assisted speed drills are sprints in which athletes use assistive devices that enable them to run faster than normal. Examples are towed sprints, downhill running, and wind-assisted sprinting.

Mach sprint drills strengthen the muscles in postures and actions that are similar to those that occur during the sprint action to improved technique. Mach drills are categorized into posture drills, specific strength drills, and functional flexibility drills. This work develops strength, postures, and firing orders specific to sprinting, as well as specific technical sprint skills. Here are some examples:

- Knee lift, which includes A1 (marching), A2 (skipping), and A3 (running)
- Foreleg action, which includes B1 (marching), B2 (skipping), and B3 (running)
- Backside drive and extension

In all of these activities, intensities should be high and recoveries long enough to ensure good-quality work.

Speed-Endurance Development

Speed-endurance work improves both speed endurance and anaerobic fitness. This work usually consists of high-intensity sprints of 80 to 300 meters, with recoveries long enough to guarantee a high quality of work. Typical sessions include three to six runs. Various set–repetition combinations can be used depending on the time of the training year and athlete level. This type of training is very demanding and should be done carefully and only by experienced, advanced athletes.

Lactate-tolerance work improves anaerobic fitness and the ability to run in the discomfort of oxygen debt, acidosis, and lactic acid buildup. This work consists of high-intensity runs of 300 to 600 meters followed by very long recoveries. Typical sessions consist of only one or two runs. This type of training is very demanding and should be done carefully and only by experienced, advanced athletes who compete in events in which anaerobic fitness is crucial to performance.

Tempo runs are performed at submaximal velocities and intensities. Tempo running for speed and power athletes normally consists of repetitions of 100 to 300 meters performed at 70 to 90 percent intensity. Recoveries vary from one to four minutes long. Tempo running improves aerobic and anaerobic fitness in an introductory, safe manner. Here are four examples of tempo runs:

- Repeat 100s or 120s (one-minute recovery)
- 6 to 8 x 300 meters (two-minute recovery)
- 6 to 8 x 200 meters (two-minute recovery)
- 8 x 150 meters (90-second recovery)

Technical and Coordination Training Methods

Technical training teaches the specific movements and skills involved in an event, and may involve drills, teaching progressions, or event rehearsals. Technical training follows a general-to-specific, simple-to-complex progression.

Competition

Competitions are the most intense activities of all. For this reason, they have a significant impact on the total training load. Coaches should consider competitions part of the program, not an addition to it, and should figure them into athletes' total training volumes.

Training Design Considerations for Speed and Power Events

Many training design issues are addressed in chapter 6. This section provides additional considerations and guidelines for the development of the biomotor qualities needed in speed and power events.

Overload should be planned carefully. Coaches must be careful not to load the ath-

lete indiscriminately. In the speed and power events, the main stimulus for adaptation is not volume, but intensity. Although overload is necessary for progress, planning rest and recovery is just as important; the balance of overload and rest and recovery is the key factor.

Because adaptation to training is specific, coaches need to ensure that the demands of the event are addressed in training. For example, to train speed, athletes must run fast in training. To become explosive, they must train explosively. Periodic shifts in training emphasis and activities should be done each mesocycle. This enhances adaptation, speeds progress, and prevents staleness.

Speed and power development depends on the effective training of the neuromuscular system. Speed and power are best developed by high-intensity, low-volume, and long-recovery methods. To become faster and more powerful, athletes must experience high intensity in training. Runs must be fast; jumps, explosive. At the same time, lower volumes of training and long recovery periods ensure that the intensity of training stays high. Athletes are better off doing less work with longer rests between repetitions than poor-quality work.

Guidelines for Developing Individual Biomotor Abilities

To develop the most complete athlete possible, coaches must blend the biomotor qualities in the training plan. No component of training can or should be developed in isolation. How they are blended is the key to successful program design.

Organizing Speed Training

In a speed development program, athletes should develop acceleration and absolute speed first. Speed-endurance and lactate-tolerance work interfere with speed development. Although these types of work are necessary, they should be scheduled later in the training year, after athletes have improved their acceleration and speed. Sample workouts for the three types of speed work are included in chapter 8. Speed development should follow the thematic progression of acceleration to speed to speed endurance.

Organizing Strength Training

General strength and strength endurance should be the initial focus of young athletes. Elastic strength, power, and absolute strength should be trained in a remedial way until they have attained sufficient gains and proficiency in general strength and strength endurance. Advanced absolute strength, power, and elastic strength work should only be attempted by experienced, advanced athletes. Strength development should follow the thematic progression of general strength to explosive power to maintenance.

Organizing Endurance Training

Overemphasizing the endurance portion of the program is a common error in the training for speed and power events. Although endurance training is useful to a smaller degree, overemphasizing it is not a good use of training time and also can hinder strength, speed, and coordination development. Coaches must understand the basic premises of speed and power training and the value of such training. An increase in training load implies that endurance is being trained through increased volumes.

Organizing Flexibility Training

Flexibility training of all types is normally administered fairly consistently throughout the macrocycle. Some aspect of flexibility should be trained daily.

Organizing Coordination Training

Constant attention should be given to developing coordination in all athletes. Improvements in coordination are the key to improvements in technique. Coordination improvements also are crucial to improving speed. The development of coordination follows the thematic progression of general to specific, and simple to complex.

Grouping Training Elements

Much care should be given to the grouping choices made within a training session. Each session should have a common theme to enhance adaptation. For example, a session may be made up of speed and power–related activities. Another may be made up of energy system fitness components. One workout may feature explosive activities of short duration, and another may feature more extensive activities. All units of the session should reflect the theme of that day.

Contrasting Training

Contrast between successive training sessions is important as well. The themes of succeeding sessions should vary to enhance adaptation, avoid staleness, and prevent injury. A general rule is that the days before and after a high-demand day should be of lower demand.

Event-Specific Training

Although the activities and guidelines in this chapter have a part in the training programs of sprinters, hurdlers, jumpers, and throwers, to some degree the program for each event area should be individualized. For example, although run training is a part of many successful throwing programs, run volumes and distances should be considerably less than those of sprinters. At the same time, the throwers' weight routines would likely be more extensive. Moreover, the lactate-tolerance work done by a 400 runner is not needed by a jumper. A single program and training philosophy could be successful for all speed and power events areas, provided wise modifications are made for the various events and the athletes participating in them.

Record Keeping in Training

Record keeping is an important part of the training process. Records of the volumes and intensities of all types of training should be kept as accurately as possible. This enables the coach to monitor training loads accurately and to modify training from cycle to cycle and year to year. Although intensity evaluation is subjective, intensities of certain parts of training can be accurately charted.

Testing and Evaluation

Testing—the periodic, planned, physical testing of biomotor abilities—is an important part of the training plan. As such, it should be considered part of the program, not an addition to it, and should be figured into the total training volume. To be accurate and objective, testing must occur in controlled environments.

Testing can be used to do the following:

- **Identify talent.** A functional predictive testing procedure can aid the coach in determining both the potential and the event choice of the athlete.
- **Analyze the training program.** Improvement over time through multiple, repeated testing procedures helps the coach determine whether the training is working.
- **Evaluate athletes' strengths and weaknesses.** All athletes have strengths and weaknesses. Shoring up weaknesses can maximize improvement and minimize injuries.
- **Predict performance.** Test results are immediate indicators of what an athlete is capable of at any given time in the training cycle.

Testing should be administered consistently. The same tests should be administered on the same day of each succeeding mesocycle and microcycle and in the same manner each time. Information gained through haphazard testing cannot be used with any reliability. Tests should be valid and should test the qualities the coach wishes to measure. An example is using a 600-meter test for long sprinters. It would be improper to use the same test with throwers, who do not benefit from training speed endurance.

The testing environment should be controlled as much as possible. This includes testing at the same site and using standardized measurements and the same number of trials, equipment, and warm-up practices. The day of testing should be consistent and should follow a recovery day.

For the sake of safety, very complex or intense tests should be avoided with young athletes and all athletes in the early stages of training. Note that the skill level of the athlete will affect results. An example is teaching an athlete to do the standing triple jump test. Initial tests may show poor results simply because the athlete has not developed the skill template. Over time, and assuming the athlete is practicing the movement regularly in training, the test results would likely show significant improvement and be more reflective of what the test is measuring.

Biomotor Test

The following biomotor test is excellent for testing speed and power athletes. Scoring is shown in table 7.2.

Test Protocol

30 m: Run of 30 meters from a standing start. The clock starts when the rear foot leaves the ground. Best of two attempts.

SLJ: Standing long jump from a squat position into a sandpit. Best of two attempts.

UHF: Underhand forward throw with a shot off a toe board (16 lb [7.3 kg] for men, 8.8 lb [4 kg] for women). Best of two attempts.

STJ: Standing triple jump from a runway into a sandpit. Begin from double support. Best of two attempts.

OHB: Overhead back toss with a shot off a toe board (16 lb [7.3 kg] for men, 8.8 lb [4 kg] for women). Best of two attempts.

150 m: One maximal-effort 150-meter sprint on a track.

600 m: One maximal-effort 600-meter trial on a track.

TABLE 7.2 **Scoring for Biomotor Test Battery**

Points	30 m	SLJ	OHB	STJ	UHF	150 m	600 m
1000	3.60	3.60	22.80	10.50	17.00	16.00	01:20.0
990	3.61	3.58	22.57		16.88	16.10	01:20.7
980	3.62	3.56	22.34	10.35	16.76	16.20	01:21.4
970	3.63	3.54	22.11		16.64	16.30	01:22.1
960	3.64	3.52	21.88	10.20	16.52	16.40	01:22.8
950	3.65	3.50	21.65		16.40	16.50	01:23.5
940	3.66	3.48	21.42	10.05	16.28	16.60	01:24.2
930	3.67	3.46	21.19		16.16	16.70	01:24.9
920	3.68	3.44	20.96	9.90	16.04	16.80	01:25.6
910	3.69	3.42	20.73		15.92	16.90	01:26.3
900	3.70	3.40	20.50	9.75	15.80	17.00	01:27.0
890	3.71	3.38	20.27		15.68	17.10	01:27.7
880	3.72	3.36	20.04	9.60	15.56	17.20	01:28.4
870	3.73	3.34	19.81		15.44	17.30	01:29.1
860	3.74	3.32	19.58	9.45	15.32	17.40	01:29.8
850	3.75	3.30	19.35		15.20	17.50	01:30.5
840	3.76	3.28	19.12	9.30	15.08	17.60	01:31.2
830	3.77	3.26	18.89		14.96	17.70	01:31.9
820	3.78	3.24	18.66	9.15	14.84	17.80	01:32.6
810	3.79	3.22	18.43		14.72	17.90	01:33.3
800	3.80	3.20	18.20	9.00	14.60	18.00	01:34.0
790	3.81	3.18	17.97		14.48	18.10	01:34.7
780	3.82	3.16	17.74	8.85	14.36	18.20	01:35.4
770	3.83	3.14	17.51		14.24	18.30	01:36.1
760	3.84	3.12	17.28	8.70	14.12	18.40	01:36.8
750	3.85	3.10	17.05		14.00	18.50	01:37.5
740	3.86	3.08	16.82	8.55	13.88	18.60	01:38.2
730	3.87	3.06	16.59		13.76	18.70	01:38.9
720	3.88	3.04	16.36	8.40	13.64	18.80	01:39.6
710	3.89	3.02	16.13		13.52	18.90	01:40.3
700	3.90	3.00	15.90	8.25	13.40	19.00	01:41.0
690	3.91	2.98	15.67		13.28	19.10	01:41.7
680	3.92	2.96	15.44	8.10	13.16	19.20	01:42.4
670	3.93	2.94	15.21		13.04	19.30	01:43.1
660	3.94	2.92	14.98	7.95	12.92	19.40	01:43.8
650	3.95	2.90	14.75		12.80	19.50	01:44.5

(continued)

Table 7.2 *(continued)*

Points	30 m	SLJ	OHB	STJ	UHF	150 m	600 m
640	3.96	2.88	14.52	7.80	12.68	19.60	01:45.2
630	3.97	2.86	14.29		12.56	19.70	01:45.9
620	3.98	2.84	14.06	7.65	12.44	19.80	01:46.6
610	3.99	2.82	13.83		12.32	19.90	01:47.3
600	4.00	2.80	13.60	7.50	12.20	20.00	01:48.0
590	4.01	2.78	13.37		12.08	20.10	01:48.7
580	4.02	2.76	13.14	7.35	11.96	20.20	01:49.4
570	4.03	2.74	12.91		11.84	20.30	01:50.1
560	4.04	2.72	12.68	7.20	11.72	20.40	01:50.8
550	4.05	2.70	12.45		11.60	20.50	01:51.5
540	4.06	2.68	12.22	7.05	11.48	20.60	01:52.2
530	4.07	2.66	11.99		11.36	20.70	01:52.9
520	4.08	2.64	11.76	6.90	11.24	20.80	01:53.6
510	4.09	2.62	11.53		11.12	20.90	01:54.3
500	4.10	2.60	11.30	6.75	11.00	21.00	01:55.0
490	4.11	2.58	11.07		10.88	21.10	01:55.7
480	4.12	2.56	10.84	6.60	10.76	21.20	01:56.4
470	4.13	2.54	10.61		10.64	21.30	01:57.1
460	4.14	2.52	10.38	6.45	10.52	21.40	01:57.8
450	4.15	2.50	10.15		10.40	21.50	01:58.5
440	4.16	2.48	9.92	6.30	10.28	21.60	01:59.2
430	4.17	2.46	9.69		10.16	21.70	01:59.9
420	4.18	2.44	9.46	6.15	10.04	21.80	02:00.6
410	4.19	2.42	9.23		9.92	21.90	02:01.3
400	4.20	2.40	9.00	6.00	9.80	22.00	02:02.0
390	4.21	2.38	8.77		9.68	22.10	02:02.7
380	4.22	2.36	8.54	5.85	9.56	22.20	02:03.4
370	4.23	2.34	8.31		9.44	22.30	02:04.1
360	4.24	2.32	8.08	5.70	9.32	22.40	02:04.8
350	4.25	2.30	7.85		9.20	22.50	02:05.5
340	4.26	2.28	7.62	5.55	9.08	22.60	02:06.2
330	4.27	2.26	7.39		8.96	22.70	02:06.9
320	4.28	2.24	7.16	5.40	8.84	22.80	02:07.6
310	4.29	2.22	6.93		8.72	22.90	02:08.3
300	4.30	2.20	6.70	5.25	8.60	23.00	02:09.0
290	4.31	2.18	6.47		8.48	23.10	02:09.7
280	4.32	2.16	6.24	5.10	8.36	23.20	02:10.4

Points	30 m	SLJ	OHB	STJ	UHF	150 m	600 m
270	4.33	2.14	6.01		8.24	23.30	02:11.1
260	4.34	2.12	5.78	4.95	8.12	23.40	02:11.8
250	4.35	2.10	5.55		8.00	23.50	02:12.5
240	4.36	2.08	5.32	4.80	7.88	23.60	02:13.2
230	4.37	2.06	5.09		7.76	23.70	02:13.9
220	4.38	2.04	4.86	4.65	7.64	23.80	02:14.6
210	4.39	2.02	4.63		7.52	23.90	02:15.3
200	4.40	2.00	4.40	4.50	7.40	24.00	02:16.0
190	4.41	1.98	4.17		7.28	24.10	02:16.7
180	4.42	1.96	3.94	4.35	7.16	24.20	02:17.4
170	4.43	1.94	3.71		7.04	24.30	02:18.1
160	4.44	1.92	3.48	4.20	6.92	24.40	02:18.8
150	4.45	1.90	3.25		6.80	24.50	02:19.5
140	4.46	1.88	3.02	4.05	6.68	24.60	02:20.2
130	4.47	1.86	2.79		6.56	24.70	02:20.9
120	4.48	1.84	2.56	3.90	6.44	24.80	02:21.6
110	4.49	1.82	2.33		6.32	24.90	02:22.3
100	4.50	1.80	2.10	3.75	6.20	25.00	02:23.0
90	4.51	1.78	1.87		6.08	25.10	02:23.7
80	4.52	1.76	1.64	3.60	5.96	25.20	02:24.4
70	4.53	1.74	1.41		5.84	25.30	02:25.1
60	4.54	1.72	1.18	3.45	5.72	25.40	02:25.8
50	4.55	1.70	0.95		5.60	25.50	02:26.5
40	4.56	1.68	0.72	3.30	5.48	25.60	02:27.2
30	4.57	1.66	0.49		5.36	25.70	02:27.9
20	4.58	1.64	0.26	3.15	5.24	25.80	02:28.6
10	4.59	1.62	0.03		5.12	25.90	02:29.3

General Strength Tests

These are tests of general strength, coordination, and body control. The athlete performs as many repetitions as possible in a certain period of time. A 30-second sit-up test is an example.

Weight Exercise Maximum Tests

These are tests of absolute strength and power. Various protocols can be used, and safety should be a priority. It is recommended that the coach not use a 1-repetition maximum (1RM) test, but use a table, such as table 7.3, to determine an athlete's 1RM.

Rest and Restoration

Restoring the body is an important part of training. It not only assists in injury prevention and increases general comfort, but also enhances the effectiveness and quality of training and makes an athlete able to handle larger training loads. Restoration can be scheduled at any time, but it is most frequently scheduled after intense work. At high levels, coaches and athletes must consider restoration a part of training, not an addition to it. Restoration can take the form of rest, active rest, restoration, or restorative training, as described here:

TABLE 7.3   Maximum Lift Based on Repetitions

The weights provided are given in pounds. Divide pounds by 2.2 to convert to kilograms.

% of 1RM	100	95	90	85	80	75
Repetitions	1	2	4	6	8	10
Pounds lifted	500.00	475.00	450.00	425.00	400.00	375.00
	495.00	470.25	445.50	420.75	396.00	371.25
	490.00	465.50	441.00	416.50	392.00	367.50
	485.00	460.75	436.50	412.25	388.00	363.75
	480.00	456.00	432.00	408.50	384.00	360.00
	475.00	451.25	427.50	403.75	380.00	356.25
	470.00	446.50	423.00	399.50	376.00	352.50
	465.00	441.75	418.50	395.25	372.00	348.75
	460.00	437.00	414.00	391.00	368.00	345.00
	455.00	432.75	409.50	386.75	364.00	341.25
	450.00	427.50	405.00	382.50	360.00	337.50
	445.00	422.75	400.50	378.25	356.00	333.75
	440.00	418.00	396.00	374.00	352.00	330.00
	435.00	413.25	391.50	369.75	348.00	326.25
	430.00	408.50	387.00	365.50	344.00	322.50
	425.00	403.75	382.00	361.25	340.00	318.75
	420.00	399.00	378.00	357.00	336.00	315.00
	415.00	394.25	373.50	352.75	332.00	311.25
	410.00	389.50	369.00	348.50	328.00	307.50
	405.00	384.75	364.50	344.25	324.00	303.75
	400.00	380.00	360.00	340.00	320.00	300.00
	395.00	375.25	355.50	335.75	316.00	296.25
	390.00	370.50	351.00	331.50	312.00	292.50
	385.00	365.76	346.50	327.25	308.00	288.75
	380.00	361.00	342.00	323.00	304.00	285.00
	375.00	356.25	337.50	318.75	300.00	281.25

% of 1RM	100	95	90	85	80	75
Repetitions	1	2	4	6	8	10
Pounds lifted	370.00	351.50	330.00	314.50	296.00	277.50
	365.00	346.75	328.50	310.25	292.00	273.75
	360.00	342.00	324.00	306.00	288.00	270.00
	355.00	337.25	319.50	301.75	284.00	266.25
	350.00	332.50	315.00	297.50	280.00	262.50
	345.00	327.75	310.50	293.25	276.00	258.75
	340.00	323.00	306.00	289.00	272.00	255.00
	335.00	318.25	301.50	284.75	268.00	251.25
	330.00	313.50	297.00	280.50	264.00	247.50
	325.00	308.75	292.50	276.25	260.00	243.75
	320.00	304.00	288.00	272.00	256.00	240.00
	315.00	299.25	283.50	267.75	252.00	236.25
	310.00	294.50	279.00	263.50	248.00	232.50
	305.00	289.75	274.50	259.25	244.00	228.75
	300.00	285.00	270.00	255.00	240.00	225.00
	295.00	280.25	265.50	250.75	236.00	221.25
	290.00	275.50	261.00	246.50	232.00	217.50
	285.00	270.75	256.50	242.25	228.00	213.75
	280.00	266.00	252.00	238.00	224.00	210.00
	275.00	261.25	247.50	233.75	220.00	206.25
	270.00	256.50	243.00	229.50	216.00	202.50
	265.00	251.75	238.50	225.25	212.00	198.75
	260.00	247.00	234.00	221.00	208.00	195.00
	255.00	242.25	229.50	216.75	204.00	191.25
	250.00	237.50	225.00	212.50	200.00	187.50
	245.00	232.75	220.50	208.25	196.00	183.75
	240.00	228.00	216.00	204.00	192.00	180.00
	235.00	223.25	211.50	199.75	188.00	176.25
	230.00	218.50	207.00	195.50	184.00	172.50
	225.00	213.75	202.50	191.25	180.00	168.75
	220.00	209.00	198.00	187.00	176.00	165.00
	215.00	204.25	193.50	182.75	172.00	161.25
	210.00	199.50	189.00	178.50	168.00	157.50
	205.00	194.75	184.50	174.25	164.00	153.75
	200.00	190.00	180.00	170.00	160.00	150.00
	195.00	185.25	175.50	165.75	156.00	146.25
	190.00	180.50	171.00	161.50	152.00	142.50

(continued)

Table 7.3 (continued)

% of 1RM	100	95	90	85	80	75
Repetitions	1	2	4	6	8	10
Pounds lifted	185.00	175.75	166.50	157.25	148.00	138.75
	180.00	171.00	162.00	153.00	144.00	135.00
	175.00	166.25	157.50	148.75	140.00	131.25
	170.00	161.50	153.00	144.50	136.00	127.50
	165.00	156.75	148.50	140.25	132.00	123.75
	160.00	152.00	144.00	136.00	128.00	120.00
	155.00	147.25	139.50	131.75	124.00	116.25
	150.00	142.50	135.00	127.50	120.00	112.50
	145.00	137.75	130.50	123.25	116.00	108.75
	140.00	133.00	126.00	119.00	112.00	105.00
	135.00	128.25	121.50	114.75	108.00	101.25
	130.00	123.50	117.00	110.50	104.00	97.50
	125.00	118.75	112.50	106.25	100.00	93.75
	120.00	114.00	108.00	102.00	96.00	90.00
	115.00	109.25	10 3.50	97.75	92.00	86.25
	110.00	104.50	99.00	93.50	88.00	82.50
	105.00	99.75	94.50	89.25	84.00	78.75

Reprinted, by permission, from T.O. Bompa, 1996, *Periodization of strength*, 4th ed. (Toronto: Veritas).

- Rest is the total absence of training activity.
- Active rest is activity that is different from traditional training, such as participation in another sport.
- Restoration activities help to eliminate soreness and accelerate recovery from exercise. They include whirlpools, ice baths, saunas, and massage.
- Restorative training activities aid recovery from the negative effects of training. General strength, medicine ball, and hurdle mobility activities, and even bodybuilding lifts, can serve this purpose and are often used on days before and after a high-demand training day.

Conclusion

Effective preparation blends the training of the various physical capacities to help athletes achieve peak competition readiness. Careful consideration must be given to the appropriate combination of all the biomotor abilities coupled with necessary rest and recovery to help the athlete achieve peak performance at the time of the most important competitions.

PART III

Running Events and Relays

8

Sprints

Joe Rogers

This chapter examines technical and training considerations for the sprint events. The events covered are the 60 meters, 100 meters, 200 meters, and 400 meters. It begins with a brief outline of rules, safety practices, and talent demands for the sprints. General concepts of the sprint events and the skills required for them are then covered. Next, each event is examined individually with regard to techniques and demands. The chapter ends with training guidelines and drill progressions for the skill of sprinting.

Rules of the Sprint Events

The rules of the sprint events are relatively simple. All of the races are run in lanes, with the exception of the indoor 400-meter race. A three-command start is used whenever the athletes use starting blocks. At most levels, the sprinter is disqualified after only one false start, so focus should be on starting mechanics and reacting to the sound of the gun. The athlete should react and not anticipate the sound. Rules also dictate that the athlete be motionless after achieving the set position and until the gun is fired. There also are rules for the assignment of heats and lanes and the arrangement of trial rounds in many meets. Rules may differ slightly at the youth, high school, collegiate, and USATF national levels. Coaches should acquire the appropriate rulebooks and become thoroughly familiar with the rules corresponding to the levels at which their athletes are competing. Space does not permit a full discussion of these procedures in this chapter. A thorough knowledge of the rules of competition gives the coach a distinct competitive advantage.

Safety in Sprinting

Proper safety practices should be used when teaching the sprints. Equipment and surfaces should be kept in good order, and athletes should wear proper footwear. Traffic control around the training areas must be adequately monitored to prevent mishaps. A vigorous pretraining and preracing warm-up is important to avoid injury resulting from explosive muscular action. The warm-up should move progressively from easy to complex movements. Dynamic flexibility exercises are preferred over static exercises, and the process should be gradual and progressive. However, static stretching can be effective when done at the end of the training or racing session.

The coach should be aware of any muscular or neurological fatigue the athletes are experiencing. Allowing for adequate recovery between training sessions is important to protect against injury and to maximize learning and adaptation.

Talent Demands for the Sprints

The ability to move limbs at high rates of angular velocity is an indication of potential for the sprint events. The athlete must be capable of learning to express this high frequency rate through large ranges of motion. Because successful sprinters come in various body types, the coach should not give up too quickly on an athlete who doesn't meet the perceived ideal body type. All athletes, regardless of the events they pursue, can benefit from sprint training. The development of strength in the sprinter is crucial to success. Because speed is a subset of strength, speed capabilities surface only after strength and power are developed.

General Analysis of Sprint Events

To assess the potential of sprint candidates, the coach must have a good understanding of basic sprinting mechanics, including the technical skills important for achieving a high level of performance as well as those that inhibit good performance. A good knowledge of the difference between acceleration and high-speed running is vital. The coach should also develop a keen eye for identifying movements that indicate a breakdown of mechanical form and posture.

Once coaches know the faults to correct, they must implement learning drills and exercises to teach the correct technical model.

Mechanical Considerations

The sprint cycle has both a support phase, during which force is applied to the ground, and a flight phase, during which the nonsupport leg is recovered in preparation for the next ground contact. The sprint cycle can also be seen as exhibiting front-side mechanics (everything that occurs in front of the center of mass) and backside mechanics (all actions that occur behind the center of mass).

Contact with the ground occurs on the ball of the foot, slightly in front of the center of mass, and with limited amortization at the hip, knee, and ankle joints. If ground contact occurs too far in front of the center of mass, braking forces will slow the athlete. The recovery and preparation of the foot for ground contact is very active and is often referred to as negative foot speed. The body is moving forward in a positive direction while the foot is moving backward in a negative direction. At high velocity, the action on the front side of the cycle is elastic and nonvolitional. At high velocity, athletes are often overcued by coaches to claw the ground instead of strike the ground in a piston-type action. The goal is a strong impulse into the ground over a short time. This implies a significant vertical application of force.

An aggressive extension of the support leg is how force application occurs during ground contact. As the runner's velocity increases, ground contact time decreases. Minimal ground contact time at high velocity is crucial to success. When ground contact time is too long, an imbalance between front- and backside mechanics occurs. The result is a disruption of elastic force generation and postural breakdown, both of which are highly detrimental. An effective coaching cue is not to fully extend the knee joint at the moment of toe-off. Such full extension is a common result of fatigue, especially late in the longer sprint races. It is also common in sprinters who have not yet developed speed-endurance ability.

Training the sprinter well involves significant technical drilling and execution. Both coach and athlete should understand that the proper distribution of effort in a race considers different race phases; athletes must develop and repeat their effort distribution among the phases until they combine into a smooth progressive process. The acceleration process has its own unique harmonic of decreasing ground contact times, changing body angles, and increasing stride length. Acceleration phase mechanics dictate what happens once the athlete is at high velocity.

Good high-velocity mechanics also require good posture, large ranges of motion at the hips to create needed stretch reflexes, and the ability to apply great force to the ground over a short period of time (power). The ability to maintain high velocity is a function of adaptation to training. A functional thematic sprint training model should follow this progression: acceleration mechanics to high-speed mechanics to high-speed mechanics for longer periods.

Phases of Sprinting

The initial phase that the sprinter must master is the drive phase, or acceleration. This requires a very large force moving the athlete's center of mass forward. The coach should evaluate the athlete's strength for applying a large horizontal force. Strength training has its greatest advantage for the sprinter in this phase of sprinting. Exercises and drills that develop strength and balance are critical in developing good acceleration skills. The next step is to develop the athlete's ability to transition from acceleration to maximal-velocity sprinting.

The use of the arms in sprinting is another important developmental consideration. Although the arms do not in themselves produce any force either horizontally or vertically, they play a very important role in balance, posture, and rhythm.

The final consideration of sprint racing is avoiding deceleration as fatigue sets in. The coach must plan a proper sequence of training to achieve the most efficient speed endurance for the competitor.

Acceleration

The acceleration phase (figure 8.1), or drive phase, reflects the sprinter's change from zero to maximal or near-maximal velocity. Acceleration is an expression of *positive change in speed* over time. The greatest amount of acceleration occurs in the first stride out of the blocks. While the athlete is increasing speed with each subsequent step, the rate of acceleration is diminishing and velocity is increasing. During this early phase of the race, ground contact time is high, because large horizontal forces are required to get the body moving. As the athlete approaches maximal velocity, a primary goal is to make a smooth transition from an aggressive, volitional cyclic mechanic to a more elastic, nonvolitional cyclic mechanic. The smoother and more efficient the transition is, the easier it is for the athlete to sustain maximal-velocity efforts.

Maximal Velocity

Maximal-velocity sprinting logically begins at the point at which no more acceleration can be

FIGURE 8.1 The acceleration phase demonstrates changing ground contact times, body lean, and arm length.

achieved. Usually, maximal velocity is reached between 50 and 60 meters for high-level, fit athletes. Athletes commonly have achieved 80 percent of maximal speed by the first 20 meters, thus demonstrating the explosive nature of the first steps. Through the acceleration process, ground contact times decrease until maximal velocity is achieved. Along with decreasing ground contact times, forward trunk lean (which is initially considerable) decreases as the sprinter transitions to higher-velocity mechanics. At maximal velocity, the sprinter is upright and tall, with the head in line with the spine. Stride frequency increases through the acceleration process and stabilizes at maximal velocity. A common problem with young sprinters is trying to increase stride frequency too quickly, thus inhibiting functional acceleration rhythms and elastic processes.

Acceleration mechanics have a direct bearing on high-velocity mechanics, and cannot be overemphasized. Once the athlete is at maximal velocity, the repeating sprint cycle is occurring at a very high rate of speed with ground contact times that are very short. Any attempt to make changes in the cyclic mechanic at high velocity is next to impossible, thus the need for a functional acceleration process preceding it. Once at maximal, controlled velocity, the athlete must run with mechanical efficiency to maintain maximal-velocity mechanics and elastic force generation. Technical breakdown that occurs at high velocity is most often blamed on fatigue, but often a poor acceleration process is the real culprit.

Proper posture is extremely important to the mechanics of sprinting. The athlete's trunk and shoulders should be aligned vertically, with the head and neck in line with the spine (figure 8.2). The alignment of the pelvis is a primary

FIGURE 8.2 Ground contact times are short and posture is tall at maximal velocity in the sprints.

determiner of sprint mechanics. A forward tilt of the pelvis results in a decreased range of motion at the hip joint and a disruption of front-side mechanics (and accompanying stretch reflex cycles), and can contribute to hamstring and other injuries.

The arms are driven forcefully in opposition to the legs. During the acceleration phase, ground contact times are longer, and arm actions mirror that by being long and powerful. As the athlete accelerates and ground contact time decreases, the arms must move faster around the shoulder joint, necessitating flexion at the elbow to speed up the arm rotations to match the increasing speed of the leg rotations.

The hand of the recovery (forward-moving) arm should rise to near chin level. The hand of the drive (backward-moving) arm extends to a position just behind the hip. It is crucial to teach the athlete to move the arms from the shoulder joints and not just the elbows. As the arm moves backward, the elbow extends slightly to increase leverage, creating a larger moment of inertia. The recovery arm flexes at the elbow to speed recovery of the limb. As backside movement ends and the foot leaves the ground, the knee joint is slightly bent (not at full extension).

At toe-off, the foot dorsiflexes, the knee flexes, and the heel moves directly toward the hip. The ability to recover the leg quickly is with a hallmark of all great sprinters. The shortened lever from knee and hip flexion promotes a faster recovery. The recovery height of the heel and foot is a consequence of the force applied to the ground. Improper recovery mechanics are usually a result of improper or weak force application to the ground.

A quick and high heel recovery is crucial to the speed of the recovery phase. The ankle of the recovery leg should cross at or above the knee of the support leg. As the recovery leg moves to the front side, the thigh continues up to a position parallel to the ground. Stretch reflexes in the extensor muscles of the hip then fire to begin pulling the leg down and back. Once ground contact is made, force should be applied very quickly over a short time. At high velocity, the athlete should not try to pull or push horizontally (clawing), but instead drive into the ground with a piston action. Too high a horizontal component creates a delay in free-leg recovery, contributes to forward lean, and thus affects balance, posture, and elastic force production.

For longer sprint events, maximal velocity refers to the maximal *desired* velocity. The 200- and 400-meter events require a distribution of effort over a longer time. The desired velocity is slightly slower than absolute maximal velocity. As an example, athletes run the first 200 meters of a 400-meter race about 1.5 seconds slower than they run their best 200 meters.

Table 8.1 summarizes some common errors sprinters make and provides ways to correct the problems.

Deceleration

Deceleration occurs with fatigue. The deceleration phase is defined as the time at which maximal-velocity effort is no longer possible to sustain. Fatigue can manifest as increased ground contact times and increased backside

TABLE 8.1   Common Errors and Corrections for Sprints

Fault	Reasons	Corrections
Forward pelvic position while sprinting as evidenced by backside heavy actions and an inability to lift the knees	• Weak abdominal core musculature • Postural issues	• Train the core for strength and stability every day. • Volitionally set the appropriate neutral pelvic tilt before each effort.
Low heel recovery (below the other knee) during the sprint cycle	• Clawing the ground rather than using a piston action to apply force to the ground • Lack of amplitude at the hip joint • General fatigue or lack of fitness to sustain good mechanics	• Pop the ground; don't claw it. • Develop skill using sprint drills. • Do fitness training runs of varying distances while maintaining good elastic sprint mechanics.
Tightening up before the end of the race	• Dysfunctional acceleration or race distribution pattern • Not sufficiently fit for the race demand	• Develop proper acceleration mechanics. • Use an acceleration ladder or stick drills to practice increasing stride length during the acceleration process. • Build necessary strength and speed endurance for the race demand.
Instability in the set position	• Weakness in the shoulders, wrists, or fingers and an inability to support weight on the hand bridge while in the set position • Leaning too far forward over the hands in the set position • Anticipating the firing of the gun	• Strengthen the shoulders, arms, wrists, and fingers with fingertip push-ups, shoulder presses with dumbbells or barbells, dips, and handstands. • Keep the shoulders on top of the hands in the set position until enough strength is developed to allow a more forward lean. • Practice starts with variations of the hold time during the set position. This develops the ability to react to the sound.

(continued)

Table 8.1 *(continued)*

Fault	Reasons	Corrections
Stumbling at the first step from the blocks	• Shoulders too far over the hands in the set position • Being too weak to drive adequately from the blocks • Insufficient foot pressure on the rear pedal	• Keep the shoulders on top of the hands in the set position. • Drive aggressively against both blocks. • Strengthen the legs, especially during the general preparation period.
Standing up at the start	• A strength deficit that manifests as an inability to drive out at the appropriate angle (The athlete must stand up to avoid falling.) • Failing to push adequately from both blocks	• Develop strength through weight training, hill runs, harness pull resistance runs, stadium step runs, and plyometrics. • Learn the appropriate starting technique and how to apply forces to the blocks. Technique modifications are often necessary to address strength deficits.

dynamics. Although deceleration is not desired, it is a reality in sprinting that must be addressed in training. To minimize deceleration, the athlete must focus on maintaining functional sprint mechanics and posture throughout the late stages of the race. Maintaining elastic reflexes, especially hip oscillations, is crucial to delaying the effects of fatigue. In training, speed-endurance and lactate-tolerance work can improve the ability to delay and manage deceleration.

Skills of the Sprint Events

The start is a very important aspect of sprint racing. However, because the start is connected to the acceleration process, they must be developed in conjunction with each other.

The best starting position sets up the drive phase. Therefore, hesitation or loss of balance from the start position leads to a very poor start and acceleration pattern. The set position in the blocks must place the athlete in a balanced state but ready to instantly drive forward. The athlete must have adequate leg extension strength to produce a powerful start. Drills and exercises that mimic the start action and increase leg strength are valuable.

Starting

In determining block settings for the start, the athlete should evaluate which leg has the most

power. One way to test this is to execute a single-leg vertical jump test on each leg. Most athletes place the most powerful leg in the forward position. The front block should be set approximately two foot lengths behind the line as a starting reference point. The pedal should be adjusted so that the knee of the front leg rests just behind the starting line in the kneeling position. The rear block should be placed approximately 12 inches (about 30 cm) behind the front block. The athlete can make adjustments as needed to ensure the best position from which to apply forces to the blocks. The key point is that the athlete must feel pressure on both feet when rising to the set position.

The athlete should back into the blocks on the command "On your marks." This helps ensure that the blocks are firmly set and without slippage at the start. The hands are positioned at shoulder width, and so the fingers and thumb form a bridge just behind the line. The shoulders should line up directly above the hands, and most of the weight should be on the feet and rear knee. The head should be relaxed and in line with the spine as the athlete awaits the command to move to the set position.

On the command "Set," the athlete immediately raises the hips to a level slightly higher than the shoulders. The front knee should be at 90 to 100 degrees, and the rear knee at 120 to 130 degrees. In the set position, younger sprinters often balance their weight between the hands and feet, whereas stronger, higher-level sprinters place 70 to 80 percent of their weight on the hands. If the athlete drives off the blocks and either stumbles or stands up, the coach should evaluate whether the athlete is too far forward over the hands. Weight distribution in the set position or block placement can be adjusted as needed. The shin angles of the two legs in the set position should be nearly parallel and at very acute angles to the ground. The athlete should feel pressure against both blocks. The force against the rear block is very intense but short in duration; the force against the front block is slightly less intense, but applied for a longer time. Aggressive, long arm actions off the blocks help with achieving big amplitudes in the initial strides, thus initiating needed stretch reflexes quickly.

When in the set position (figure 8.3), the athlete's mental focus should be on reacting to the

FIGURE 8.3   Sprint start sequence.

gun rather than anticipating it. The first action on the sound is to drive both feet hard against the block pedals, pushing the shoulders forward and upward. As the body's center of mass moves forward, the rear foot releases from the rear pedal while the front leg continues to drive to full extension. As the rear knee moves forward, the opposite arm drives forward aggressively, similar to an uppercut punch. The opposite arm drives backward equally forcefully.

The hips and the knee of the front leg extend, creating a straight line from the foot through the knee, hip, and shoulder in a forward and upward direction that is approximately 45 degrees at toe-off. The head remains in a neutral position in line with the spine. As the free leg swings forward early in the acceleration process, the foot recovers low to the ground quickly to catch the runner before falling. Initial low heel recoveries change to higher recoveries with each step of the acceleration process as the athlete moves to a more upright position.

Running the Curve

For a race on the curve, it is advisable to set the blocks in the outer portion of the lane and direct the line of the blocks toward the inside edge of the lane to a point approximately 8 inches (20 cm) outside the inner lane line. This permits the athlete to take the first two or three steps in a straight line and apply greater force efficiently. As the athlete accelerates on the turn, an inward lean occurs out of necessity (figure 8.4). The degree of inward lean is a function of the turn radius and velocity of the runner. As the acceleration process unfolds, an increasing vertical force application occurs, and force is also directed out to maintain the inward lean. Arm action will vary slightly from that of a runner sprinting on the straight, because the outside arm must be brought somewhat across the body. Running the curve is a skill that must be developed and practiced, and it is a significant factor to consider when choosing relay runners to run turn legs of the 4 x 100.

Finishing

The athlete finishes when any part of the torso touches the plane of the finish line. Because

FIGURE 8.4 A sprinter running on a curve must lean inward and push out to counter centrifugal forces.

sprint races are short and finishes between athletes often close, how athletes finish often decides the results. Leaning at the finish line is very helpful, but only if timed properly. Leaning too early inhibits cyclic rhythms and elastic reflexes. One technique is to turn the shoulder of the arm that is moving forward into the line (figure 8.5). The most commonly used technique involves driving both arms back while dipping the head and shoulders forward through the finish line. Finishing is a skill that athletes should practice during workouts.

Event-Specific Technical Considerations

Although races from 50 to 400 meters are all considered sprints, they have unique energy demands. Training for all of them requires developing the best maximal-velocity running possible. They all have similar acceleration patterns except that the longer races may extend the length of acceleration to achieve

FIGURE 8.5   Turning the shoulder at the finish.

a more efficient period of energy expenditure to sustain a longer duration of effort. The big difference is that the long sprint races require a greater effort to avoid deceleration. All sprint training requires the use of a variety of speeds to teach the body to relax and learn to transition from one phase to the next.

60 Meters and 100 Meters

Speed endurance is addressed minimally in 100-meters training, because energy system fitness is not the contributing factor it is in longer races. Race fatigue in the 100 meters is more the result of neurological fatigue than metabolic fatigue. A contributing factor to coordination breakdown is an inefficient acceleration phase. In the 100-meter race, approximately 80 percent of maximal speed is achieved in the first 20 meters. By 30 meters, the sprinter has achieved over 90 percent of maximal speed. An athlete with an efficient acceleration pattern continues to accelerate through 50 to 60 meters. An erratic applica-

tion of force through this phase is a significant contributor to neurological fatigue. A significant amount of skill practice should be devoted to addressing both acceleration mechanics and maximal-velocity mechanics. After an appropriate time is spent developing acceleration and high-speed mechanics, speed endurance can be introduced. Introducing too much speed endurance too early is a common mistake coaches make.

200 Meters

Because the 200-meter race lasts less than 30 seconds, lactate tolerance is not a large concern. However, the issue of speed endurance is more critical for this race than it is for the 100 meters. The 200-meter athlete often loses good sprint mechanics as coordination falters. Proper posture and mechanics is crucial while finishing the 200-meter race. A progressive plan of intervals can aid the runner in delaying and managing the effects of fatigue late in the race. For all sprint races, athletes should train at a variety of speeds while focusing on good posture and good cyclic mechanics. The 200-meter distance demands the maintenance of stretch reflexes and stride amplitude throughout the effort. Multiple-pace training also helps to prevent a neurological imprint (pace block), which can inhibit optimal development. High-speed curve-running mechanics are unique to the 200 meters and require significant focus in training.

Time differentials between the first and second 100 meters of the 200-meter race help the coach analyze the quality of the race distribution. The second 100 meters has a fly-in start and is run on the straight; thus, the fitter athlete will demonstrate a faster second 100 meters.

400 Meters

The 400-meter race is unique in that the athlete must conserve energy to sustain a high-level effort for more than 40 seconds. Therefore, lactate tolerance becomes an essential part of the mature athlete's preparation. When considering this aspect of training, coaches must recognize that excessive lactate-tolerance training can have a detrimental effect on the nervous system and can create significant fatigue in the athlete. The athlete must have developed the necessary strength levels and acceleration and speed skills before taking on the high demand of lactate-tolerance training. Coaches developing training plans for very young athletes should emphasize acceleration, speed, strength, and coordination as opposed to lactate-tolerance work. This will help them avoid excessive fatigue and keep them enthused for sprinting the longer race.

Because the start of the 400 meters is on the curve, athletes use virtually the same starting mechanics as those used in the 200-meter race. The first 4 to 5 seconds of the race is alactic in demand; thus, the athlete does not have to conserve energy for those first seconds. After about 25 meters or so, the 400-meter sprinter builds acceleration at a more gradual rate than sprinters in the shorter sprint races do. Athletes should run the first 200 meters approximately 1.5 to 2 seconds slower than their best 200-meter time (93 to 95 percent of best effort). As a result of the onset of fatigue, the second 200 meters will be 2 to 3 seconds slower than the best 200-meter time. Falling off more than 3 seconds in the second half of the race indicates a fitness issue that must be addressed, or that the first half of the race was run too fast.

Fatigue can cause the breakdown of sprint mechanics, posture, and pelvic alignment late in the 400-meter race. Sprinters must be conscious of what they are doing as fatigue sets in. A primary goal of 400-meter training is to maintain elastic mechanics late in the race. Although speed-endurance work is crucial to training the 400-meter sprinter, coaches must also stress the development of acceleration and maximal speed during training, because these are the foundations of success in all sprint races.

Additional Guidelines and Teaching Principles

A functional sprint training program focuses on a balance of biomotor qualities. In addition to the obvious need for speed-related skills, various types of strength, power, flexibility, mobility, and energy fitness are crucial to high performance in the long sprints. Coaches should refer to chapters 6 and 7 on training design and biomotor development for speed and power athletes.

The development of speed should follow a logical training progression. A large part of sprinting skill is neurological and elastic. Running fast in competition requires that the athlete run fast in training. Every speed development program should focus early on acceleration mechanics. The coach cannot expect good high-velocity mechanics (speed) unless the athlete is trained in how to get up to speed properly (acceleration). Most annual plans address these abilities, which should be developed prior to introducing speed-endurance training. Too much speed-endurance training prior to developing the ability to run well at maximal velocity is counterproductive.

Sprinting is a technical, elastic event. Therefore, posture, high amplitude at the hips, and proper sprint mechanics must be emphasized within the available training time. The repetition of drills and sprint-specific movements imprint the necessary firing orders and neuromuscular patterns.

Athletes should learn the following four start skills progressively as part of a sound acceleration process that accompanies the start:

1. Rolling start
2. Three-point crouch start
3. Four-point crouch start without blocks
4. Four-point start in blocks

Although there is a proper technical model for the sprint start, the strength and skill levels of athletes differ. Start mechanics may need to be modified until athletes have reached appropriate strength levels.

Drill Progressions for Sprint Skills

When coaching and correcting sprinters' mechanical faults, coaches should use both whole actions and drills. Because sprinting is a cyclic activity, the value of developing and practicing the entire rhythm should not be underestimated.

Start Drills

Before introducing starts from blocks, coaches can use the following drills to help athletes develop their starting and acceleration abilities.

ROLLING START

1. Take a stance with one foot forward and one to the rear.
2. Bend at the waist to about a 90-degree angle.
3. Push the body forward over the front foot until balance is lost.
4. Drive the rear leg forward as the foot recovers close to the ground.
5. As the rear knee moves forward, continue to push hard with the front foot.
6. Drive the arms in opposition to the legs.
7. Continue driving with each step to maintain balance.

THREE-POINT CROUCH START

1. Stand at the line.
2. Reach down with the hand on the rear-foot side and support the torso over that hand.
3. Extend the arm on the front-foot side and hold it high above the body.
4. Keep the shoulders on top of the down hand.
5. With a push from both feet, drive the shoulders upward and forward.
6. Vigorously drive the arms in opposition to the legs.
7. Recover with the rear foot while continuing to push with the front foot.
8. Become more upright with each stride (trunk angle).

FOUR-POINT CROUCH START WITHOUT BLOCKS

1. Start as in the three-point crouch start.
2. Place two hands on the ground and form a bridge between the thumbs and fingers.
3. Keep the shoulders on top of the hands.
4. Proceed as in the three-point crouch start.

FOUR-POINT START IN BLOCKS

1. Set the blocks as described in the earlier section on starting.
2. Get in position with the hips above the shoulders and the head aligned with the spine.
3. Feel pressure on both feet in the pedals.
4. Balance among all points of contact.
5. At the sound of the gun, drive the shoulders forward and up from both feet.
6. Clear the rear block quickly while continuing to drive against the front block.
7. Obtain full extension of the front leg at block release.
8. Vigorous arm actions reflect ground contact times.
9. Use a lower heel recovery in the first steps.

Acceleration Drills

The following drills strengthen the athlete's ability to increase the drive phase of running. They overload the musculature in a way that creates large horizontal forces and improves the capacity to do that. These exercises can be enhanced with a strong weight training regimen.

WALL DRILL

1. Stand 1 meter from and facing the wall.
2. Place the hands on the wall with full arm extension.
3. The angle of the trunk should be approximately 45 degrees to the wall.
4. On the "Go" command, pump the legs as if running out of the blocks while attempting to push the wall.
5. Execute the drill for 10 to 20 seconds as vigorously as possible.

STICK DRILL

1. Place sticks that are flat and small, such as yardsticks, on the ground past the starting line.
2. Place the first stick 0.5 meters past the starting line (18 to 20 in.).
3. Place each subsequent stick a progressive additional distance of 15 to 20 centimeters (e.g. 0.5, 0.7, 0.9, 1.1, 1.3, 1.5, 1.7, 1.9 or 0.5, 0.65, 0.8, 0.95, 1.1, 1.25, 1.4, 1.55 m). The distance increments should be determined by your maturity and strength.
4. Start from behind the line. Drive each foot down and back so the heel steps on each stick. This develops the sense of a gradual increase in stride.

ACCELERATION RUN

1. This drill can be done with or without sticks. If sticks are used, place them in the same way as in the stick drill.
2. Build up runs of distances from 20 to 60 meters. The shorter runs help beginners understand the initial drive action.
3. As the correct patterns develop, add 10, 20, and 30 additional meters.
4. This drill can be done from a rollover, crouch, or block start.

RESISTANCE RUN

1. Pull a sled or use a harness to pull another athlete 20 to 30 meters.
2. Your strength and ability level will dictate the amount of resistance used. The amount of resistance should not negatively affect your mechanics.
3. This drill is especially good for general preparation period training.

HILL RUN

1. Run uphill using hills of varying degrees of grade.
2. Lean into the hill and focus on the driving action.
3. Add more resistance by wearing a weight vest.

STADIUM STEP RUN

1. Take one step at a time
2. Run with very quick, driving steps.
3. Cease the run when you can no longer maintain quickness.
4. Run two or more steps at a time, emphasizing driving action.

Maximal-Velocity Development Drills

The following drills teach correct sprinting posture as well as proper sprint mechanics.

An important principle of motor learning is incorporating the drill action into the regular performance of the skill. Athletes should follow the drill activity with actual sprinting to tie them together.

LEARNING THE A POSITION

1. Stand on one leg.
2. Lift the heel of the raised leg as close as possible to the hip on that side (figure 8.6).
3. Dorsiflex the ankle of the raised leg (toe-up position).
4. The knee will rise to the appropriate level with this action.
5. Move the arms in opposition to the legs.
6. Align the head with the spine.
7. Keep the shoulders on top of the hips.
8. Keep the pelvis in a neutral position.

FIGURE 8.6   Learning the A position.

A DRILL

1. In this drill, march, jog, or run forward.
2. Step forward, bringing one side to the A position (figure 8.7).
3. Alternate legs to that position while marching, jogging, or running forward.
4. In the A position, have the toe up (dorsiflex the ankle), the heel up (heel to hip), and the knee up (it will come up automatically).
5. Step over the knee of the supporting leg. The ankle of the raised leg crosses the supporting leg at or above the knee.
6. As the foot comes off the ground with each step, it moves immediately to the hip. Do not let the foot kick backward.

FIGURE 8.7   A drill.

B DRILL

1. Execute by marching, jogging, or running.
2. Start the action as in the A drill.
3. As the free leg moves forward, extend at the knee as if to reach out (figure 8.8).
4. Just prior to ground contact, pull the foot back under the center of mass.
5. As in the A drill, recovery of the heel must be directly to the hip with no backward direction. Think, "Step over the other knee."
6. Foot contact is on the ball of the foot.

This drill fires hip extension to develop negative foot speed action. It is excellent for strengthening the gluteals and hamstrings. However, be cautious with this drill if you have sore hamstring muscles.

FIGURE 8.8 B drill.

STANDING CYCLE

1. Stand on one leg while holding on to a support structure on the same side of the body.
2. Start from a static A position.
3. Drive the foot of the free leg forward and downward toward the ground as in the B drill.
4. Snap the ball of the foot in a horizontal movement, just scraping the ground under the body.
5. The momentum of this action must cause the foot of the free leg to recover to the hip by its own momentum, moving upward and back to the starting position.
6. Execute the action repeatedly.
7. Start and finish each execution from the A position.
8. As the foot moves off the ground, continue to emphasize a motion directly toward the hip, not backward.
9. Maintain a toe-up position throughout.

HIP POP

This drill strengthens the iliopsoas muscle, a major hip flexor involved in sprinting.

1. Get in a standing position.
2. Using the hip punch, kick a foot forward as if to kick a ball. Execute the punch in a very short, quick manner. The punch will move you forward about a foot (30 cm).
3. Follow the punch with another on the opposite leg.
4. Repeat, alternating legs, as you move forward.
5. Commonly, the drill is done for about 10 meters.

ACCELERATION RUN

Repeat runs of varying distances up to 50 meters. Focus on the kinesthetic feel of the correct acceleration mechanics.

1. Use long arms to start.
2. Decrease body lean with each step.
3. Keep toe up, heel up, knee up.
4. Use big amplitude at the hip joint.
5. Step over the knee on the side of the support leg.
6. Make sure foot strike position is under the body.
7. Contact the ground with the ball of the foot.
8. Balance arm action with the opposite leg action.
9. Maintain a tall posture; avoid leaning forward or backward.
10. Keep pelvic position neutral (no forward tilt).

Speed Development Runs

The following training exercises increase maximal-velocity running. Most of them incorporate an activity that lasts no longer than four or five seconds at maximal velocity. The reason for this is that people cannot sustain maximal-velocity runs for longer than this. Sprinting maximally for longer periods makes the workout one of speed endurance rather than speed development. Remember, athletes must develop speed before speed endurance.

INS AND OUTS

This drill includes variations of runs with changing tempos, with some segments at high velocity. Ins and outs teach high-velocity relaxation and the ability to change speeds. Make sure you understand changing tempos before the run begins.

Design

- Acceleration segment
- Float segment
- Maximal-velocity segment
- Float segment
- Maximal-velocity segment
- Deceleration segment

Segments can vary based on the goals of the session. The distance of each segment can be adapted to your needs. Here are some samples:

- Sample 1: 30-20-30-20-30 meters
- Sample 2: 30-30-30-30-30 meters
- Sample 3: 30-20-30-40-30 meters

FLYING SPRINT

1. Set cones or markers to indicate where the maximal sprint starts and finishes. The acceleration zone should be long enough to allow a gradual acceleration to get to top speed.
2. Accelerate for 20 to 30 meters; then run at maximal velocity for approximately three to four seconds.
3. Recover amply between sprints. This is high-quality work.

ASSISTED RUN

These are overspeed exercises for training. Care must be used when doing these runs. This is demanding work and requires ample recovery.

Following are examples of assisted runs:

- Sprints with the wind at your back
- Harness assist runs
- Runs that use a pulley system to tow you slightly faster than you can sprint on your own
- Downhill runs on a slight grade of around 1 to 2 percent

Sprinting Menu

As mentioned previously, the training of speed is a progressive process that moves from an acceleration focus to a speed focus over time. Only after these two abilities are developed does the athlete take on speed endurance. It is logical that the athlete should learn to accelerate before learning to run at maximal velocity. Likewise, coaches should not focus on speed endurance until they are confident the athlete can first run fast. This section provides a progressive menu of workouts for training acceleration, speed, and speed endurance.

Acceleration Drills

These drills emphasize the development of the drive action of starting. The progressive use of longer acceleration intervals from the starting blocks develops the sense of gradual acceleration and transition to top speed.

SPRINT LADDER

Set up a ladder that gradually increases step length by 6 inches (15 cm) per step from the starting blocks. The emphasis is on increasing velocity and stride length, changing body angles, and changing arm action. This drill is an excellent tool for learning to increase stride length. Recovery is important. Perform 10 to 15 repetitions with three-minute rests between them.

20-METER BLOCK RUN

Perform five repetitions of 20-meter runs from the starting blocks. Perform two to five sets. Allow three minutes for recovery between repetitions and six minutes for recovery between sets. Total volume: 200 meters building to 500 meters.

30-METER BLOCK OR ROCKER START RUN

Perform five repetitions of 30-meter runs from the starting blocks or runs from a rocker start (rollover position three-point start). Perform two to four sets. Allow three minutes of recovery between repetitions and seven minutes of recovery between sets. Total volume: 300 to 600 meters.

40-METER BLOCK OR ROCKER START RUN

Perform four repetitions of 40-meter runs from the starting blocks or runs from a rocker start (rollover position three-point start). Perform three sets. Allow three minutes of recovery between repetitions and nine minutes of recovery between sets. Total volume: 480 meters.

50-METER BLOCK RUN

Perform three repetitions of 50-meter runs from the starting blocks. Perform two or three sets. Allow four minutes of recovery between repetitions and seven minutes of recovery between sets. Total volume: 300 to 450 meters; this is a very high-quality effort.

Speed Drills

The following speed development drills are examples of short runs of maximal speed that have a buildup period to achieve maximal velocity. They incorporate three to five seconds of maximal effort with a minimum of three minutes of recovery between repetitions. Recovery should be longer between sets.

20-METER RUN WITH 15-METER ACCELERATION ZONE

Perform five repetitions of 20-meter runs using a 15-meter acceleration zone. Perform three or four sets. Time the 20-meter segments only. Allow three minutes of recovery between repetitions and six minutes of recovery between sets. Total volume: 300 to 400 meters.

40-60-METER RUNS

Perform five repetitions of 40-60-meter runs. Perform two to five sets. Allow four minutes of recovery between repetitions and eight minutes of recovery between sets. Total volume: 200 to 240 meters.

VARYING TEMPO DRILL I

Run at varying tempos. Perform three repetitions of the following: 15 meters of acceleration, 10 meters at maximal velocity, 15 meters of float, 10 meters at maximal velocity, and 20 meters of float. Perform two to four sets. Allow four minutes of recovery between repetitions and eight minutes of recovery between sets. Total volume: 420 to 840 meters.

VARYING TEMPO DRILL II

Run at varying tempos. Perform three repetitions of the following: 20 meters of acceleration, 10 meters at maximal velocity, 15 meters of float, 10 meters at maximal velocity, 15 meters of float, and 10 meters at maximal velocity. Perform two or three sets. Allow 5 minutes of recovery between repetitions and 10 minutes of recovery between sets. Total volume: 480 to 720 meters.

VARYING TEMPO DRILL III

Run at varying tempos. Perform three repetitions of the following: 40 meters of acceleration, 20 meters of relaxed running, and 30 meters at maximal velocity. Perform three sets. Allow three to five minutes of recovery between repetitions and five to eight minutes of recovery between sets. Total volume: 810 meters.

Short Speed Endurance Drills

The following runs are primarily used to develop speed endurance. The shorter runs include less full recovery time between repetitions, which makes them short speed-endurance efforts.

75-METER RUN

Perform four repetitions of 75-meter runs at 90 to 95 percent effort. Perform one or two sets. Allow three minutes of recovery between repetitions and six minutes of recovery between sets. Total volume: 300 to 600 meters.

60-METER RUN

This is more of a short speed-endurance effort. Perform four repetitions of 60-meter runs at 95 percent of maximal effort. Perform three sets. Allow two minutes of recovery between repetitions and four minutes of recovery between sets. Total volume: 720 meters.

150-METER RUN

Perform three to six repetitions of a 150-meter run at 90 percent of maximal effort. Allow five minutes of recovery between repetitions. Total volume: 450 to 900 meters.

SHORT SPEED ENDURANCE VARYING TEMPO DRILL

Run at varying tempos. Perform three repetitions of the following: 50 meters of acceleration, 50 meters of float, and 50 meters of lift. Perform two sets. Allow 5 minutes of recovery between repetitions and 10 minutes of recovery between sets. Total volume: 900 meters.

100-METER RUN

Perform three repetitions of a 100-meter run at 95 percent or more. Perform two or three sets. Allow 5 minutes of recovery between repetitions and 10 minutes of recovery between sets. Total volume: 600 to 900 meters.

Long Speed Endurance Drills

Long speed-endurance runs are primarily emphasized in the general preparation period of conditioning. This type of training should be introduced progressively. The purpose is to increase the physical work capacity of the athlete and then later add training of greater intensity.

200-METER RUN

Perform three to six repetitions of a 200-meter run at 95 percent. Allow 10 to 12 minutes of recovery between repetitions. Total volume: 600 to 900 meters for sprinters who run the 100 to 200 meters; 1,200 meters for sprinters who run the 400 meters.

300- AND 200-METER RUN

Perform one repetition of a 300-meter run; then perform three repetitions of a 200-meter run. Perform both runs at 90 percent of maximal effort. Allow eight minutes of recovery after the 300-meter run and six minutes of recovery between repetitions of the 200-meter runs. Total volume: 900 meters.

300-METER RUN

Perform two or three repetitions of a 300-meter run at 90 percent of maximal effort. Allow 12 to 15 minutes of recovery between repetitions. Total volume: 600 meters for sprinters who run the 100 or 200 meters; 900 meters for sprinters who run the 400 meters.

400-200-400 DRILL

Run one repetition of 400 meters at 95 percent effort or more, one repetition of 200 meters at 95 percent effort or more, and one repetition of 400 meters at 95 percent effort or more. Allow full recoveries between runs. Total volume: 1,000 meters. This drill mimics a typical meet scenario for a 400-meter runner who runs three events.

300/100 DRILL

Run 300 meters at 95 percent of maximal effort. Slow down and return walk to the 300 mark. Finish the 400 with a hard 100 meters. Record your total 400-meter time. Perform two sets. Allow 15 minutes of recovery between sets. Total volume: 800 meters.

Microcycles for the Sprints

The microcycle plans in this section cover a week of training and are a suggested guideline for a high school–age athlete. The difference between this level and a collegiate or post-collegiate level is volume and intensity. For a young, developing athlete of pre–high school age, the focus would be more on skill development and less on high-intensity and energy system training.

The first phase is the general preparation phase (figure 8.9). The primary emphasis in this phase is preparing the athlete for training by progressively improving all biomotor abilities. The intensities are low, and the goal is to prepare the skeleton, joints, ligaments, and muscles to handle the increased loads that will follow. The plan should involve a gradual increase in volume and a moderate increase in intensity.

Microcycle #	Dates:	Event group: Sprints
Phase: General preparation	Comments: Focus on fitness and building acceleration to speed	
Sunday	Monday	Tuesday
Active rest	Dynamic warm-up Hurdle walkover flexibility drills Technical sprint drills Tempo endurance runs Core strengthening Cool-down	Dynamic warm-up Sprint technical drills Acceleration runs General strength training circuit Medicine ball throws Cool-down
Wednesday	Thursday	Friday
Extended dynamic warm-up Hurdle walkover flexibility exercise Rollover starts Interval training Harness resistance runs Core and abdominal strength Cool-down	Extended recovery day warm-up Technical sprint drills Speed development runs Plyometric jumps Extended cool-down	Extended dynamic warm-up Hurdle walkover exercises Start mechanics Hill runs General strength circuit Cool-down
Saturday	Intensity of load by day	Post-workout comments
Extensive warm-up Technical sprint drills Rollover starts with acceleration Repetition runs Medicine ball throws Cool-down	(see intensity table below)	

	Su	M	Tu	W	Th	F	Sa
Hard			x		x		
Medium		x				x	x
Easy				x			
Rest	x						

FIGURE 8.9 Sample seven-day microcycle for the sprints: general preparation phase of training.

The second phase is the special preparation phase (figure 8.10). As the athlete moves into this phase from the general preparation phase, the focus shifts toward developing the biomotor abilities that are most involved in performing the sprint events. Strength, power, and explosiveness are key.

Neurologically, this phase addresses the technical model for acceleration and maximal-velocity running. The level of intensity is gradually increased, and high demands

Microcycle #	Dates:	Event group: Sprints
Phase: Specific preparation	Comments: Continued development of speed; introduce speed endurance	
Sunday	Monday	Tuesday
Active rest	Dynamic warm-up Accelerations from three-point start Sprint drills, technical work Tempo endurance runs Core strengthening Cool-down	Dynamic warm-up Hurdle walkover flexibility Speed development runs Plyometric drills Medicine ball core exercises Weight training, strength development Cool-down
Wednesday	Thursday	Friday
Extended dynamic warm-up Falling accelerations Sprint drills General strength Cool-down	Extended recovery day warm-up Sprint drills Harness resistance runs or hill runs Plyometric drills or speed Weight training, power development Extended cool-down	Extended dynamic warm-up Hurdle walkover flexibility Technical rehearsal Cool-down
Saturday	Intensity of load by day	Post-workout comments
Competition		

	Su	M	Tu	W	Th	F	Sa
Hard			x		x		x
Medium		x				x	
Easy				x			
Rest	x						

* If there is a competition on Tuesday, consider a lighter day on Wednesday and do weight training on Monday/Wednesday or Monday/Thursday.

FIGURE 8.10 Sample seven-day microcycle for the sprints: specific preparation phase of training.

are placed on the components of fitness that contribute to sprinting. As intensity increases, athletes need adequate recovery periods to allow their bodies to adapt and grow stronger.

The third phase is the competition phase (figure 8.11). This usually falls at the end of the season, and some call it the championship season. This is the phase in which the most important competitions fall. The most critical aspect of this period is adequate rest. The volume of work begins to lessen while intensity remains high. Extra time for recovery is often included.

Microcycle # Phase: Competitive	Dates: Comments: Focus on competition and race mimicry and fine tuning	Event group: Sprints
Sunday	**Monday**	**Tuesday**
Active rest	Dynamic warm-up Hurdle walkovers flexibility Long speed endurance Weight training, power Cool-down	Dynamic warm-up Sprint drills Accelerations Starts through 40 to 60 meters Moderate plyometric work Cool-down
Wednesday	**Thursday**	**Friday**
Extended dynamic warm-up Accelerations Repetition runs at 3/4 race distance 400 m sprinters run race segments at race rhythm Weight training, power (2 or 3 sets of 1 to 3 reps) Cool-down	Extended recovery day warm-up Hurdle walkovers flexibility Starts with acceleration transition Sprint drills Extended cool-down	Race day warm-up mimicry Sprint flexibility Start mechanics rehearsal Accelerations Cool-down
Saturday	**Intensity of load by day**	**Post-workout comments**
Race-day warm-up Major competition Race-day cool-down	(see intensity table below)	

Intensity of load by day:

	Su	M	Tu	W	Th	F	Sa
Hard			x				x
Medium		x			x		
Easy				x		x	
Rest	x						

FIGURE 8.11 Sample seven-day microcycle for the sprints: competitive phase of training.

Conclusion

This chapter addressed the technical models of both acceleration and maximal velocity for quality sprinting. In preparing athletes for the sprint events, the coach must develop and train all aspects of motor development. The biomotor abilities of strength, speed, speed endurance, flexibility, and explosive power must all be addressed throughout the training year. Of course, a high priority should be on the components that are most involved in performance, but some coaches ignore some of the nonspecific qualities. There needs to be balance in the training approach. The plan should include activities and drills that address the correct technical model throughout the training year.

A key difference in training the 400-meter sprinter versus the 100-meter sprinter is the need to develop lactate tolerance. The 400-meter athlete must be able to sustain high levels of speed for much longer. Although this higher endurance requirement necessitates more lactate tolerance, caution must be emphasized when including this type of training. Most athletes need 48 hours of recovery after addressing lactate tolerance before repeating it.

Athletes are unique in how they respond to the demands of the various components of training. What is a moderate load for some may be extremely high for others. Coaches should pay attention to how athletes respond to their training loads while working out and be ready to adjust workout plans when athletes exhibit fatigue. Although physiology is the same for everyone, athletes have their own strengths as well as weaknesses that may result in physical breakdowns. Maturity also plays a role in adaptation and recovery.

9

Relays

Joe Rogers

Relay racing, one of the most exciting track and field events, is also the most team oriented. All members of the relay team must coordinate to move the baton around the track as fast as possible. Of course, the speeds of the individual athletes contribute significantly to the effort, but the biggest challenge is passing the baton with maximal efficiency. The coach must arrange for athletes to practice the exchange so that their speeds and accelerations are adjusted to accomplish this goal. The more familiar the athletes are with each other's abilities, the greater will be their confidence in making baton passes.

Rules of Relay Racing

The rules governing the start of running events govern the relay events as well. Four runners carry the baton in turn around the track, and baton exchanges are made within a 20-meter exchange zone. Either runner may be outside the zone when the pass is made, but the baton must be inside at the moment of the exchange. This chapter focuses on the 4 x 100 and 4 x 400 events. Other rules dictate matching uniforms and baton design.

For relay races with legs of 200 meters or less, the outgoing runner may line up in a 10-meter fly zone that precedes the exchange zone. Although the outgoing runner may accelerate in this zone, the baton exchange may take place only in the 20-meter exchange zone.

The coach should acquire the appropriate rulebook and become thoroughly familiar with the rules. This provides a distinct competitive advantage.

Safety in Relay Racing

Safety concerns in the relays are the same as those in the sprints, with one notable addition. Quality relay exchange work is a demanding activity, and its physical toll should not be taken lightly. Relay exchange work can turn an easy day into a hard day, so coaches should take care in the scheduling and loading of this type of work. When planning for speed training volumes, all relay work should be counted as high-velocity training in both sessions and microcycles.

Talent Demands for Relay Racing

Good sprinters make good relay runners. Hurdlers and jumpers can be good candidates for the relay events as well. Often, an athlete who does not excel in any individual sprint event may be of help in the relay because of a unique strength, such as starting, curve running, or baton handling.

Acceleration skills are important for all relay legs, but the first leg presents two special demands: coming out of the blocks and running on a curve. If an athlete has the speed to be on the relay team but is not reliable in receiving the baton, the first leg might be the best choice. If the fastest athlete is also very good at speed endurance, she may be the best candidate for the second leg of the 4 x 100 relay. The rationale is that the second-leg runner can take the baton early and hand it off late. For the anchor leg, the sprinter who likes to run from behind or who is a strong competitor might be a good candidate.

Repetition in training is a key to success in relay running. The longer athletes work together, the better their chance for success will be.

General Analysis of Relay Racing

The 4 x 100 relay is one of the most exciting of all the relays. Because of the high velocity of the athletes, there is greater risk for error in coordinating the exchanges. The exchanges require very precise timing of the movements through the exchange zone. In determining who should run each leg of the race, coaches should consider the individual qualities of the athletes. Who is the best starter? Who runs the curve well? Who has the least or most experience in the exchange? What is the best position for the weakest leg?

The 4 x 400 relay is a little more forgiving if the timing is not efficient. Because the race is much longer, there is more time to adjust to exchange errors. However, efficiency in baton passing and the speed of the baton through the passing zone still have a large impact on how well the race goes.

4 x 100 Relay

In the 4 x 100-meter relay, or any relay with legs of 200 meters or less, the outgoing runners have the advantage of using the 10-meter acceleration zone that precedes the 20-meter exchange zone. This gives the outgoing runner more distance in which to accelerate before receiving the baton. The outgoing runner may use this zone to accelerate, but the baton may not be passed until it is inside the 20-meter exchange zone.

The entire 4 x 100 race is run in lanes. The challenge of this relay is to maintain high velocity while passing the baton. The key to achieving maximal baton speed lies in timing the outgoing runner's start and acceleration to match the incoming runner's speed at the moment they make the handoff. The process of determining this timing is discussed later in this chapter.

Table 9.1 summarizes errors relay racers sometimes make and the best ways to correct them.

TABLE 9.1 Common Errors and Corrections for Relay Racing

Fault	Reasons	Corrections
The outgoing relay runner slows down in the passing zone.	• Nervous anticipation or lack of confidence in completing the exchange • Leaving before the incoming runner reaches the go-mark • Reacting to the command of another team	• Perform speed and speed-endurance work to improve endurance. • Perform repetition after repetition to develop trust.
The incoming runner does not reach the outgoing runner.	• The outgoing runner leaves too soon. • The incoming runner is fatigued. • The outgoing runner reacts to the command of another team.	Repeat the pass enough times so the outgoing runner can start at the right time and judge and adjust to the incoming runner's speed as needed.

(continued)

Table 9.1 *(continued)*

Fault	Reasons	Corrections
The incoming runner slows down for the pass.	• The runner is not fit enough to maintain speed through the passing zone. • The act of passing the baton disrupts the sprint cycle, causing the runner to slow down. • The incoming runner is not on the appropriate side of the lane.	• Develop fitness through speed-endurance training. • Attack the passing zone and continue to sprint until after pass is made. • Remember that the task of securing the blind pass always lies with the incoming runner. • Practice staying on the appropriate side of the lane (both incoming and outgoing runners).
The outgoing relay runner fails to give a steady target.	• Running with an extended arm causes hand movement. • The receiving athlete grabs for the baton.	• Through stationary and running drills, establish the feel of the exact high hand position desired. • Practice a continuous high hand reach position while running during practice. • Drill a steady hand position while the incoming runner secures the pass.

4 x 400 Relay

In the 4 x 400-meter relay, or any relay legs of 400 meters or more, there is no acceleration zone. Each runner must line up inside the exchange zone. The 4 x 400 race is usually run with a three-turn stagger; thus, three full turns of the race must be run in lanes. The first exchange is made in lanes, whereas athlete position for the second and third exchanges are determined by the positions of the incoming runners.

The first-leg runners run the entire leg in the assigned lane and pass to the second-leg runners in staggered lanes. The second-leg runners run the first curve in the assigned lane. At the end of the first curve, the second-leg runners can break to the inside lane. No runner may interfere with any other runner.

Because the incoming athlete in this relay is fatigued, a visual pass is the preferred method of exchange. The outgoing runner should take the baton in the left hand so that he is facing the inside of the track.

Skills of Relay Racing

Some skills affect relay efficiency. Although speed is the overriding consideration in selecting members for relay teams, an aggressive attitude is an important quality for all members of the team. Thinking "Attack!" when approaching the exchange can contribute to an aggressive mental attitude. Being comfortable carrying the baton while maintaining good sprint mechanics as well as starting with the baton must be learned though repetitive practice with correction.

Starting With the Baton

The runner who starts the relay race should use a conventional block start (figure 9.1).

FIGURE 9.1   Starting with the baton.

Rules allow the baton to extend beyond the starting line, so it should be gripped with the middle and ring fingers. The weight should rest on the bridge of the thumb, forefinger, and little finger. The block should be lined up toward the outside of the lane on a tangent to the curve. This technique is discussed in chapter 8.

Passing the Baton

Maintaining speed through the passing zone is very important. The incoming athlete must continue to sprint even after passing the baton. Speed-endurance training plays an important role in achieving top zone speed. The athlete must be prepared to adjust to the teammate who may start late or early. Knowing how to maintain lane position (inside or out) is also extremely important in the exchange process. The athlete usually needs to hold her position on the track after completing the pass to avoid interfering with other relay teams. Once the other teams have moved through, athletes should always move off the track to the inside.

All outgoing baton receivers must develop an efficient acceleration pattern to achieve a high speed at the moment of exchange. An additional principle in baton passing is that the higher the hands are at the moment of the exchange, the easier it is to maintain excellent sprint mechanics. Additionally, the high hand position creates ample free space between the athletes.

4 × 100 Relay

Athletes running the second, third, and fourth legs of the relay use some form of modified start. Often, these are different for blind and visual exchanges. For the 4 × 100 relay, a blind exchange is necessary to maintain the high velocities that occur in the race. The most effective blind exchange starts are the modified crouch start and the three-point start. The outgoing runner lines up in a starting position but raises the arm on the front-leg side and looks back underneath it to see the incoming runner. The path of the baton around the track is in the middle of the lane, thus dictating in which hand the baton is held. Runners 1 and 3 (the curve runners) are on the inside of the lane and thus carry the baton in the right hand, whereas runners 2 and 4 are on the outside of the lane and carry the baton in the left hand. The exchanges are made as follows: right-to-left, left-to-right, and right-to-left.

4 × 400 Relay

For the 4 × 400 relay, the start for each runner is the same as with any 400-meter race. The visual exchange is the preferred method. The best start for the outgoing runner is a crouch start. The runner lines up with the body turned inside toward the curb for improved visibility. The pass is made right-to-left at each exchange, which necessitates the changing of hands with the baton. This change is usually done as soon as the exchange is made and the runner is accelerating out of the zone. In the case of the visual pass, the outgoing runner needs to determine a target point; when the incoming runner hits the target, the outgoing runner goes.

Starting each leg with a minimal loss of baton speed is a skill that runners must practice at various speeds. If the incoming runner is slowing down because of fatigue, the outgoing runner must adjust his speed accordingly to avoid getting away too quickly. A good technique is to take off when the incoming runner hits the go-mark, take two or three driving strides to accelerate, turn back, look at the teammate, and reach to the rear with a high and open hand to receive the pass. Of the two runners involved in the pass, the outgoing runner is the one who must make adjustments to make the pass work. The coach should emphasize to all incoming athletes to run through the zone with an attack mentality. The incoming runner's effort does not stop until the baton is safely passed.

Calculating the Go-Mark for Sprint Relays

The procedure outlined here is a method for determining where to place the go-mark to cue the outgoing relay athlete to start to sprint into the exchange. This process is reasonably accurate and can be tweaked to gain more accuracy. It gives the athlete a good starting point to work from.

1. Runners take a flying start of 20 or 30 meters, depending on whether they are running 4 x 100 or 4 x 400. Time all potential relay-leg runners through the exchange zone (20 meters long). Start the stopwatch as soon as the athlete reaches the front edge and stop it as soon as the torso hits the end of it. T_i = time of incoming runner to cover the 20 meters.

2. 20 divided by T_i = the speed (S_i) of the incoming runner in meters per second.

3. Line up all receiving athletes at the starting point position of the fly zone. On the command of "Go," time them until they reach the point inside the zone where you want the exchange to take place. T_o = time of outgoing runner in seconds.

4. Multiply T_o x S_i = distance traveled by the incoming runner from the go mark to the point of exchange.

5. Measure from where the incoming runner will be positioned at the point of exchange back from the distance calculated in step 4. That is a good go-mark starting point.

6. Adjust the mark as the proficiency of the athlete develops.

7. Have the outgoing runner (wearing competitive spikes) step off the number of shoe lengths from the edge of the fly zone to the go-mark. This provides a benchmark measure to use without having to use a tape measure.

Blind Exchange

The blind exchange is so named because there is no visual contact between the runners during the exchange. Typically, it is used in the 4 x 100 relay. This section explains the techniques of both the outgoing and incoming runners.

The outgoing runner takes off at full speed at the instant the incoming runner hits the go-mark. It is important that the outgoing runner focus on the incoming runner's feet and not be distracted. The outgoing runner should stay in his half of the lane, depending on which hand will receive the baton (inner half for right-hand target, outer half for left-hand target). The carry side should always be in the middle of the lane. At the verbal signal or at some predetermined mark, the outgoing runner extends the arm back and presents the open hand, trying to establish a high, stable target. The outgoing runner should trust the incoming runner to deliver the baton and not feel for it.

Because the outgoing runner is blind to the pass, the incoming runner has the responsibility for making the pass. The incoming runner should run in the inner or outer half of the lane, depending on which hand holds the baton. The carry side should always be in the middle of the lane. It is very important that both runners position themselves so the exchange can be made in the middle of the lane. This is a common mistake of runners who lose focus in the excitement of the moment. The incoming runner should continue to run strongly through the zone without decelerating until the outgoing runner is safely carrying the baton. The incoming runner may give a verbal command when ready to pass the baton, which the outgoing runner responds to by raising the receiving arm.

Because there are eight lanes, eight verbal commands may be happening at the same time. This can be confusing. It is helpful to have a unique command that no one else uses. Another option is to not use a verbal command, but have the outgoing runner raise the receiving arm and hand at a designated spot in the exchange zone. If the timing of the run is coordinated correctly in response to the incoming runner hitting the go-mark, this spot should be consistently at the same point. The baton is forcefully placed in the outgoing runner's hand using a snap of the wrist and forearm.

The two primary methods of executing the blind pass are the upsweep method and the push pass. In both methods, the incoming athlete uses a firm action of the wrist to firmly place the baton in the receiver's grasp. The receiver should firmly grip the baton as soon as it is felt in the hand. The critical technique for the receiver to focus on is to give a steady target hand, making it easy for the passer to hit the target. If a pass is not completed as quickly as expected, the receiver must not panic and start reaching and grabbing for the baton. A stable target is crucial.

Upsweep Method

The upsweep method is a pass used by less-experienced athletes because it is very simple to do and easy to learn. However, it has also been used by international teams. In this technique, the receiver extends the receiving arm backward and forms a V between the thumb and index finger of the receiving hand. The fingers point downward. Although the arm and hand should be raised as high as possible, they are lower than in the push pass.

As the incoming runner approaches the target, she raises the passing arm in a forward and upward motion to fit the end of the baton into the V of the receiver's hand. The passer should keep a relaxed grip to allow the receiver to take the baton from the hand but with enough control to avoid dropping the baton. As the receiver grasps the baton and swings the arm back into a sprinting motion, the baton is held with the free end below the hand. This requires the athlete to shift the baton upward into the hand to have the top of the baton available to pass to the next receiver.

Push Pass

The push pass has several advantages. The motion of pushing the baton into the receiver's hand is more in rhythm with normal sprint arm motion. The outgoing runner extends the receiving arm back and keeps the shoulder high. To maintain a high position, the arm swings more laterally than it does with the upsweep method. The receiver spreads the fingers of the hand in a similar manner to the upsweep, but the wrist is flexed so that the passer sees the flat palm of the receiver's hand. Rather than lifting the baton into the V of the thumb and index finger, the passer pushes the baton onto the flat palm of the receiver's hand (figure 9.2). Because the motion of pushing the baton into the palm is an extension of the swinging sprint arm action, disruption of a good acceleration rhythm is minimal. Another advantage of this pass technique is that the level of the exchange allows both athletes to remain in a tall sprint posture, thus conserving velocity through the exchange.

FIGURE 9.2 Push pass.

Visual Exchange

The visual exchange is used for relays with legs of 400 meters or more. This pass places the responsibility on the outgoing runner. Because the incoming athlete is fatigued, deceleration can be a factor. If the fatigue varies from race to race, the outgoing athlete may sometimes be running away from the passer. A receiver who watches the pass can control her speed to make sure the pass is completed.

While practicing the exchange, the receiver should determine a go-mark. When the incoming runner hits this mark, the receiver knows it is the best time to take off to have the best match of both runners' speed to facilitate the exchange. Typically, that mark falls somewhere between 3 and 10 meters in front of the zone. With talented athletes, it could be farther. The distance depends on the speed of the incoming athlete. The slower the runner is, the longer the receiver must wait before taking off. The faster the runner is, the sooner the receiver may leave.

The recommended technique is for the outgoing athlete to watch the teammate's feet closely as she approaches the predetermined go-mark (figure 9.3). As soon as the receiving athlete sees the teammate reach the go-mark, she turns in the direction of the run and executes three driving steps to accelerate through the passing zone. After the three strides, the receiver turns to the rear, looking back at the passer and extending the receiving arm back while maintaining the forward running momentum. The open hand of the receiver spreads with the fingers and thumb open to take the baton. The receiver must keep the hand in a shoulder-high position to maintain a tall sprint position during the exchange.

The incoming passer should make every effort to press the baton into the receiver's hand. She should avoid deceleration and press the run through the zone so as not to force the receiver to slow down or come back to get the baton. Mentally envisioning passing the baton in the second half of the zone is helpful.

FIGURE 9.3   The outgoing runner watches the incoming runner's feet to the go-mark.

Another consideration is how the other receiving athletes line up after the first exchange has been completed. The officials position all subsequent receiving athletes in line along the back edge of the exchange zone in the same order as the incoming teammates. The first team in gets the pole position, the second team gets the second position, and so on.

Teaching and Training Guidelines for Relay Racing

Relay practice can be either supplemental to sprint training or incorporated into it. The addition of baton-passing drills to a regular sprint training session is essential to developing skill, confidence, and coordination among relay teammates.

Technical skill development is best worked on in the early portion of practice when athletes are fresh. Jogging while doing repeated passing drills could easily be incorporated into the prepractice warm-up.

It is wise to practice multiple combinations of team members at different legs of the relay. This can help the coach determine which combinations are most effective. Also, in the event of injuries, substitutions may be needed. Larger meets often have multiple rounds, making it logical to rest some athletes who may be competing in other events, and then reassembling the best team for the final round.

Often, during practice sessions, athletes have difficulty running at speeds achieved in competition. This can make judging the go-mark a challenge. Therefore, evaluating go-mark adjustments is best done in competition. Filming exchanges is invaluable to the coach.

Start With a Baton

Relay start development from the blocks is no different from that for all sprinters. However, athletes should practice to get used to holding the baton at the line. The baton should be grasped in the appropriate hand (the right hand for the first leg of the 4 × 100) and at the bottom end. The two middle fingers wrap around the baton while the index finger and thumb form a bridge just behind the starting line. The small finger should be placed on the ground to give the sprinter a balanced position. The baton may extend beyond the starting line. All other aspects of the initial drive phase of acceleration are the same as for the block start.

Starts for legs 2, 3, and 4 can be done with a modified standing start or a three-point crouch. The three-point crouch is recommended for achieving a consistent drive phase. A description of this start is provided in chapter 8.

Blind Exchange

The standing blind pass is the best drill for practicing the blind exchange. Two athletes stand one behind the other so their exchange arms are directly in line. Each athlete extends the exchange-side arm so the baton touches the palm of the receiver's hand, determining the distance between them. The athletes swing their arms from the shoulder, as in running. At a command of "Pass," or any verbal command, the receiver moves his arm, extending it to the rear with an open palm. The passer reaches forward and taps the palm of the receiver's hand with the baton. If the upsweep method is used, the passer executes that action and touches the V between the thumb and index finger. The baton is not exchanged yet. As soon as contact is made, the athletes return to arm-swinging action. This drill is repeated multiple times on command.

The next step adds a baton pass to the action. The receiver then passes the baton back and the athletes repeat the action. The receiver does not look back and must learn to offer a high, steady target.

After learning the standing drill, the athletes progress to carrying out the drill while jogging in single file. Eventually, four athletes execute the drill in single file.

As with all technical skills in track and field, the coach should teach rhythm before speed in relay passing. The practice of handoffs in the zone should begin at slower speeds. As speeds increase, the start and go-marks should be changed accordingly.

Conclusion

Relay racing is one of the most enjoyable experiences in track and field. Achieving a high level of performance with others can be exhilarating. Team members often perform at higher levels when other teammates are relying on their efforts because they do not want to let teammates down. Correct practice of the skill of baton exchanging is essential to gain proficiency and confidence in each other as relay partners.

Coaches should incorporate relay skill practice into normal sprint training. Training all sprinters on the team with relay drills is a good idea because coaches never know when they may need to substitute a relay leg. In most championship meets with qualifying rounds, the coach may substitute relay legs for the early rounds to allow more recovery for some of the athletes who may be running multiple races.

10

Endurance Running and Racewalking

Joe Vigil, PhD, and Andrew Allden

The endurance events are both simple and complex. On one hand, these events are a simple matter of one athlete covering a specific distance faster than another. However, on a physiological level, they employ the widest range of energy systems and heart-rate zones. Athletes in these events are most affected by nutrition and hydration before, during, and after the event. Psychologically, both the coach and the athlete experience the full gamut of emotional states and conditions. Biomechanic skills in the endurance events range from racewalking to hurdling (steeplechase) to sprinting.

The endurance events discussed in this chapter are the 800 meters, 1,500 meters, 3,000-meter steeplechase, 5,000 meters, 10,000 meters, marathon, and racewalk. The chapter begins with a brief discussion of rules, safety practices, and talent demands for endurance events. This is followed by a general analysis of the events and the skills required for success. Finally, training guidelines and teaching progressions for these events are provided.

Rules of the Endurance Events

The rules of the endurance events are relatively simple. Starting from a standing position is imperative. A two-command start is used. At some levels of competition, the international start is used, in which runners are required to move up to the starting line on the first command. Rules also dictate the assignment of heats and lanes and the arrangement of trial rounds in certain meets.

Because endurance races are seldom run in lanes, the rules govern the obstruction of other runners—most notably, that a runner may not cross the path of another runner unless she has sufficient space to avoid impeding the crossed runner's progress. Jostling, cutting across, or obstructing another competitor in a way that impedes his progress may result in disqualification. Direct contact is not necessary. Veering right or left in the finish straight and forcing through other competitors are also grounds for disqualification.

Rules differ slightly at the high school, collegiate, USATF, and IAAF levels. The coach should acquire an appropriate rulebook and become thoroughly familiar with the rules. This provides a distinct competitive advantage.

Safety in the Endurance Events

Good safety practices should be used when training endurance athletes. Because of the high volume of work, special problems arise. A proper training program balances intensity and volume and provides event-specific flexibility, strength, and drill training. Coaches should give thought to the training surface and appropriate footwear for the athletes given the conditions.

Because most endurance training programs include a great deal of training off the track, safety when running near traffic and other hazards is an important consideration. Over-training and heat-related problems are significant issues in these events; avoiding these situations is an important part of safety and injury prevention. Hydration, environmental conditions, and nutrition are also more significant in the endurance events because of their longer duration.

Dehydration

Dehydration thickens the blood and makes it harder to pump (think water versus molasses). On average, males can lose 2.0 liters (or quarts) per hour through sweating; females, 1.1 liters per hour. In warm weather athletes should restrict their fluid loss to 1 to 2 percent of their total body weight. Each pound (about 0.5 kg) of fluid loss needs to be replaced by 16 to 24 ounces (473 to 710 ml) of water. Runners should consume 16 to 24 ounces (473 to 710 ml) of fluid containing electrolytes per pound (about 0.5 kg) of body weight lost during exercise. These figures are estimates; there is great variability among individuals and environmental conditions. In addition, for optimal performance for events lasting longer than one hour, athletes should consume 120 to 400 calories per hour during the event either as fluids or in addition to fluids.

Heat

Performance in endurance events can be significantly affected by extremes in climate. In regard to heat, the longer the event, the greater the impact. In the case of the marathon, for every 5 degrees the temperature rises above 50 degrees Fahrenheit (or about 3 degrees it rises above 10 °C), the athlete's final time typically increases by about 0.5 percent. If the temperature is above 98.6 degrees Fahrenheit (37 °C) and the humidity is above 70 percent, running outside should be avoided. The body sheds heat through the evaporation of sweat. When humidity is high, evaporative cooling is inhibited, and so is the body's ability to shed heat.

Great care needs to be taken when an athlete travels from a cooler climate to a warmer climate or when the daily temperature rises significantly. The body takes 5 to 8 days to significantly acclimatize to warmer conditions, and 14 days to reach near-maximal acclimatization.

Heatstroke is a medical emergency and should be treated immediately by getting the runner into an air-conditioned, or at least cooler and shaded, environment. Attempts to bring down the athlete's body temperature through the use of water and ice should begin immediately while medical assistance is sought.

Iron

Inadequate body iron reserves affect the athlete's adaptation to training. Low iron limits the quality and quantity of high-level endurance work output. Fitness is built by the athlete adapting to the training stimulus, and this adaptation requires iron.

Iron deficiency, which is more common in female athletes, can cause overtraining symptoms. A decrease in iron stores can cause a decrease in aerobic capacity since iron is part of hemoglobin, which carries 98.5 percent of blood's oxygen, and more than half of the enzymes of aerobic metabolism contain iron.

Excessive impact stress can cause hemolysis due to extravascular compression and intravascular acidosis, which can cause the following to occur:

- Increase in blood acidity
- Increase in red blood cell transit velocity
- Decrease of the mean life of red blood cells from a normal 120 days to approximately 80 days

Iron depletion is a decrease in serum ferritin levels, which inhibits erythrocyte and hemoglobin levels in the blood. An athlete's ferritin level is the most accurate indicator of his or her iron stores. Distance athletes who run 60 miles or more per week should have their ferritin levels monitored at least twice a year. If blood tests reveal an iron deficiency, the athlete should reduce training volume and consult a sport science doctor or nutritionist to begin a program designed to increase iron stores through good nutrition and iron supplementation.

Talent Demands for the Endurance Events

Obviously, high levels of endurance are required for these events, but it is important to recognize the need for good absolute speed. This is a must for athletes at the highest levels. Typically, endurance athletes have slim builds and are often diminutive, especially those who run in longer races. However, successful endurance athletes come in all shapes and sizes.

Skills of the Endurance Events

The endurance events are not often thought of as skill events, but athletes must master basic skills to optimize performance. Elements such as starting and passing often trip up both skilled and novice runners. Both athlete and the coach need to be mindful of the risks and rewards of modifying running technique. Doing so without building the physical infrastructure to support it is a recipe for injury. Additionally, intentional modifications of form do not always lead to the intended results because of the limitations of the coach's naked eye and knowledge. Because some so-called flaws may be adaptations of the athlete's body and subsequent mechanics, modifying them may not lead to improved performance or decreased injury risk.

Start

Endurance events begin with a standing start (figure 10.1). The torso is erect and the arms are near the sides in the set position.

The three common starting arrangements in endurance events are the waterfall start, the one-turn stagger, and the alley start.

1. **Waterfall start.** Most distance races begin with a waterfall start, in which all competitors are placed on a curved starting line and are permitted to move to the curb immediately once the race begins, provided no obstruction takes place. Typically, runners move toward the curb to save distance, but they should do so on a path that marks a tangent to the inside of the curve. Runners positioned on the inside of the track should run aggressively to avoid being boxed in by other runners.

2. **One-turn stagger.** Some distance races begin with a one-turn stagger, in which each runner is assigned a lane and must run the entire first turn in that lane. After exiting this turn and crossing the breakline, runners may move to the inside as they wish, provided no obstruction takes place. A runner in an outside or middle lane should take advantage of the tangents and move toward the curb gradually to reach lane 1 or 2 just prior to entering the curve. This is also true for a runner who draws the middle to outside position in the waterfall start in the 1500 meters.

3. **Alley start.** Some distance races are started in alleys. In this type of start, runners line up on multiple waterfalls

FIGURE 10.1 Standing start.

© Human Kinetics

(generally two) and are allowed to break immediately to a designated inside lane line. After the runners break to this line, the race is run like a one-turn stagger, with runners in the outside alleys permitted to break inside after crossing the breakline.

General Running Mechanics

The endurance runner must be proficient in the skills of sprinting. Running mechanics greatly influence aerobic efficiency, anaerobic efficiency, and running economy. Improvements in economy lead to improvements in training and race performance. Specificity dictates that changes in running mechanics developed through training relate to the running speed employed in training. Training at the variety of speeds used in multiple training regimes improves running economy at all of these speeds.

The best way to improve mechanics is through the correct application of sprint drills and hill running. Additionally, the infrastructure, range of motion, and specific muscular strength must be in place to support any form adjustments. With a few exceptions, the running mechanics exhibited in distance and middle distance races resemble maximal-velocity mechanics. Also, although the features are not as pronounced, the mechanics of the acceleration process can be found at the start and in race surges.

Proper alignment of the core of the body is important for efficiency and injury prevention. The head should be kept in a constant neutral position with respect to the spine (figure 10.2). Lordotic, or butt-out, postures, reflective of forward pelvic tilt, also are inherently inefficient. The pelvis should move slightly but never deviate greatly from a neutral position. Flexibility and mobility in the hip and low back region are essential to proper posture.

Ground contact occurs under the body's center of mass. Hip extension drives the foot into the ground. The ankle should be stabilized in a dorsiflexed position prior to contact, but the foot strike should be more full footed than in sprinting. Overstriding, in which the foot lands substantially in front of the center of mass, should be avoided by increasing knee lift, push-off, and stride frequency.

The relaxed movements of the upper body counter and balance the movements of the lower body. The upper-body action differs from sprinting in that generally the arms are held close to the sides, with slight movements of the shoulder axis in the transverse plane. Keeping the head and chest erect contributes greatly to effective arm action.

Adjustments in form and foot strike should be undertaken with caution, because the naked eye cannot fully appreciate the domino effect of even the most minor form modification. Foot strike is a function of the speed at which the athlete is traveling, and modifying natural foot strike in the belief that it will improve speed or decrease the chance of injury generally is not recommended.

FIGURE 10.2 In proper body alignment, the head is in a neutral position, aligned with the spine.

© Human Kinetics

Race-Pace Preparation and Distribution

The runner should have a good sense of pace and understand the paces required to execute the race as planned. Developing a series of target splits for various points in the race based on goals and training performances is common practice and an important part of race preparation. With the exception of the 800 meters, an optimal time is typically produced by an even or negative split (the second half slightly faster than the first). Because of its unique demands, the 800 meters requires a slightly faster first half to achieve an optimal time.

Race Positioning and Tactics

The runner must become skilled at gaining good positioning at all times. Although running close to the curb shortens the distance run, it places the runner in jeopardy of being boxed in by other runners. In most instances, in heavy traffic, runners should run directly behind the outside shoulder of the runner in front to prevent being boxed in. Drafting (running behind another runner so that runner splits the air) uses less energy to achieve the same pace. Sometimes settling in behind a runner or taking the lead are good strategies, but the coach should prepare the athlete to react correctly to a variety of situations that may occur in the race. Surging is the act of increasing speed to gain a competitive advantage. Kicking is an increase in speed at the end of the race in an attempt to win or improve position. Both show mechanical shifts that resemble those seen in acceleration. The runner should also be prepared to lean at the tape in the event of a close race.

Foundations of Endurance Event Training

The foundations of endurance event training are the adaptations produced in the infrastructure of the body. Endurance training programs must develop the neuromuscular system and elicit changes in blood chemistry just as training programs for the speed and power events do. However, endurance training programs must also produce radical changes and improvements in the energy and blood delivery systems.

In all endurance event training programs, much importance is placed on developing the energy systems. Each event has specific aerobic and anaerobic energy demands that depend to some degree on the athlete. The training for each event should be specific to the demands of the event. The aerobic and anaerobic energy systems must be trained together and in harmony.

Endurance training programs also must develop the blood delivery systems. Although this normally occurs as a consequence of good energy system development, at times cardiorespiratory system development may be a goal in itself.

The marathon has unique energy system demands compared to the other endurance events because of its duration (120 minutes or more). This duration dictates that training address the body's greater reliance on fatty acids as fuel. Easy, long runs and marathon-pace runs train the body to metabolize fatty acids and spare the body's limited glycogen stores. The body has about a 90-minute supply of glycogen; this is why marathoners may hit the wall at around two hours or at 18 to 20 miles. Fatty acids are very concentrated, and even a very lean runner has a sufficient amount for hours of continuous activity.

Runners derive energy from carbohydrate aerobically and anaerobically. A runner who paces the marathon correctly has a fuel consumption ratio of about three to one, carbohydrate to fatty acids. As the race progresses and carbohydrate stores are depleted, the ratio changes to rely more on fatty acids. Running at too rapid a pace early in the race forces the runner to operate anaerobically and thus burn glycogen that will be needed later. Remember, fat is burned in a carbohydrate (glycogen) oven. Anaerobic metabolism is dramatically less fuel efficient than aerobic metabolism. In addition, hydrogen ions accumulate and inhibit the enzymes that control glycogen metabolism. Fatty acid metabolism needs glycogen, so if the runner has metabolized all of the available glycogen, none will remain to prime the fatty acid energy pump. Burning fatty acids requires plenty of oxygen, so as fatty acid metabolism increases, the marathon runner's heart must work harder to pump more oxygenated blood to the muscles. This increase in effort to increase fatty acid metabolism can be made more difficult by dehydration.

Energy Systems

Every endurance event uses aerobically and anaerobically produced energy in varying proportions. A key concept of training design for endurance events is that an appropriate training stimulus targets the correct proportion of anaerobic and aerobic system development to allow the athlete to favorably compete at a specific distance. It is equally important to understand that these systems are not black and white; they are more shades of gray. All of the systems function all of the time. The intensity and duration of the effort determines the degrees to which each system is employed to produce energy.

The approximate percentages of aerobically and anaerobically produced energy for each endurance running event are listed in table 10.1, illustrating the differences among the events. However, variations from this table may be found, and these numbers differ for individual athletes of various levels. The faster the runner, the greater the anaerobic contribution.

Regardless of the energy system employed, energy is created from the chemical break-down of fuel sources called substrates. The most important substrates are fatty acids and glycogen. The intensity of effort generally dictates the substrate employed.

Aerobic and Lactate-Threshold Training

Aerobic development depends on training without the negative effects of acidosis on the cells. For this reason, racing and training should be well planned and follow specific guidelines. In aerobic training, either glycogen or fatty acids are used as fuel.

The level of work intensity—specifically, the speed of the run—determines the substrate used. Heart rate increases as the level of work and speed of running increase. Therefore, heart rate can be used as an indicator of the intensity of the effort. For this reason, most of the training intensities and levels of work referred to are defined by heart-rate zones. When heart-rate zones are used to establish training intensity, it is best to use an actual rather an estimated maximal heart rate (MHR). If MHR is not known, an estimated MHR can be calculated using the following formula:

$$208 - (0.7 \times age) = MHR$$

Once an estimated or actual MHR is determined, the Karvonen formula can be used to calculate heart rates at different intensities of training such as recovery, lactate threshold, and $\dot{V}O_2$max:

Karvonen formula

Maximal heart rate – resting heart rate
= heart-rate reserve

(Heart-rate reserve x % desired) + resting heart rate = % for top or bottom of zone

---

TABLE 10.1   Energy Source Comparisons for Training for the Middle and Distance Events

Energy source (%)	400 m	800 m	1,500 m	5,000 m	10,000 m	Marathon
Aerobic	43	66	84	88	90	97.5
Anaerobic	57	34	16	12	10	2.5

Adapted from P.B. Gastin, 2001, "Energy system interaction and relative contribution during maximal exercise," *Sports Medicine* 31(10): 725-741.

Two levels of work intensity define the aerobic training regimens used to develop a runner's endurance base: the aerobic threshold and the lactate threshold. The speed or pace of running as well as heart rate may also be used to define these and other training intensities. The amount of rest allowed between bouts of intense work has a significant impact on the energy systems involved.

When athletes train higher than their targeted intensity and push the workout into a higher-intensity zone than intended, they incur all of the fatigue and risk of the higher zone but get only the training benefit of the lower zone—and often less because they may be unable to complete the workout. Consider an athlete who pushes the lactate threshold workout to a higher level of intensity so that she runs at a 5K race pace or at $\dot{V}O_2$max effort instead of slower than that. What she should have done is stay below her lactate threshold to train her body to process lactate as fuel. By running too hard, the athlete may actually decrease the effectiveness of the workout and increase the wear and tear on her body at the same time.

The aerobic threshold is the level of work at which the primary fuel source shifts from fatty acids to glycogen. Aerobic threshold training involves running at this intensity. Running at this level of work trains the runner's aerobic system to use fatty acids as the chief energy source, sparing glycogen for faster paces. This level of work is about 65 percent (plus or minus 5 percent) of a runner's $\dot{V}O_2$max pace, or about 65 percent of MHR at the current level of fitness.

It is important to understand the role of oxygen in the metabolism of substrates. The availability of oxygen determines whether the breakdown of substrate is complete or limited.

The term *aerobic metabolism* signifies the presence of oxygen. Its supply determines whether movement will use carbohydrate or fatty acids. If the supply of oxygen is limited, movement will also be limited, although the energy will come from another source.

Aerobic threshold training is the best form of aerobic development and therefore the development of endurance. A runner's goal must be to continuously increase the oxygen available for aerobic metabolism. Endurance is defined as the capacity to sustain a given speed of work rate for the longest period of time. The majority of the energy supplied during exercise greater than 60 to 120 seconds is derived through oxidative metabolism; therefore, performance in endurance sports depends heavily on aerobic threshold training.

The relationship between heart rate and substrate is illustrated in table 10.2.

Above the aerobic threshold, the runner must rely more on the anaerobic system to aid the aerobic system. Training just below the lactate threshold makes more efficient use of glycogen. This spares glycogen and delays the involvement of the anaerobic system.

Lactate-threshold (LT) training prepares the body to use lactate as fuel. It also raises the pace or the effort point at which these products are produced. Lactate threshold is an important determinant of distance running performance because it represents the fastest speed a runner can sustain aerobically without a significant anaerobic contribution. This level of work is about 85 to 90 percent of a runner's $\dot{V}O_2$max pace at the current level of fitness, and about 88 to 90 percent of a runner's MHR. LT runs are designed to improve a runner's lactate threshold. The goal of this training is to run at a faster pace for a longer period of time.

TABLE 10.2 **Heart Rate Necessary for Aerobic Metabolism of Two Substrates**

Substrate	Heart-rate zone	Storage sites
Fatty acids	60 to 75 percent MHR	Muscle cells
Glycogen	75 percent or more of MHR	Muscle cells, liver

Ideally, runners should train at the lactate threshold but not faster. LT pace typically is a 5K race pace plus 25 to 30 seconds per mile (1.6 km), or the pace at which the runner could race for one hour. LT intervals can be performed at a slightly faster pace (1 to 5 seconds per mile, or per 1.6 km) than a continuous LT run, but it is important that they remain at LT effort. LT intervals should never be faster than a 10K race pace. Recovery for LT intervals should be 20 percent of the duration of the interval. LT pace should be decreased very gradually, typically when a race performance indicates an improvement in fitness.

LT is the best predictor of long-distance running performance. All running speeds have an anaerobic contribution. LT is the transition between running that is almost purely aerobic and running that includes significant anaerobic metabolism. When an athlete is running slower than lactate-threshold pace, the anaerobic contribution is negligible. The goal of training must be to increase an athlete's $\dot{V}O_2$max as much as possible to inhibit lactate production, acidosis, and an increase in hydrogen ions. The process shifts the lactate curve to the right (figure 10.3) and allows the athlete to run at a faster pace longer. Ultimately, this is the goal of all distance runners.

Anaerobic Training

The two anaerobic energy systems are the anaerobic alactic system and the anaerobic glycolytic system (table 10.3). Both produce energy without the presence of cellular oxygen. The difference in the two is the fuel substrate used to create adenosine triphosphate (ATP) energy for cellular use.

The alactic system produces energy using readily available phosphocreatine (PC). The human cell holds enough PC to produce energy at high levels for 6 to 10 seconds. Although short lived, this system is very efficient. Improvements in velocity result from training this energy system. However, we cannot extend the time of energy production beyond these few seconds. This system is used for starts and during surges. Despite it being a very small percentage of endurance performance (5 percent or less), endurance athletes who want to reach their full potential should not neglect or ignore this system.

The glycolytic system produces energy using the slower process of breaking down carbohydrate (figure 10.4). It is the primary fueling system for running at near-maximal velocities from approximately 7 seconds after the onset of work until 90 seconds later. The factor that eventually limits performance in this

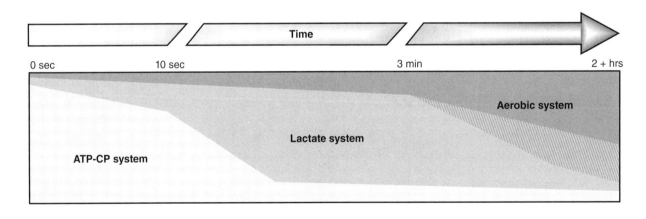

Lactate system producing lactate to utilize as preferred aerobic system fuel

FIGURE 10.3 Contribution of the three energy systems over time.

© P.J.L. Thompson, 1994, 2005, 2011. Used with permission.

TABLE 10.3   Metabolism Time Duration and By-Products of Anabolic Metabolism

Anaerobic system	Substrate	Duration	By-products
Alactic	Phosphocreatine	6 to 10 seconds	None
Glycolytic	Glycogen	10 to 90 seconds	Hydrogen ions

system is severe acidosis. Training in this zone improves the velocity an endurance runner can attain. It also improves the runner's ability to delay the onset of acidosis. This coping ability is called lactate tolerance Lactic acid does not exist in the blood; as soon as it is produced, it disassociates into lactate and hydrogen ions. Lactate does not cause fatigue. Its clearance depends on the body's ability to use it as fuel. Lactate production increases progressively as running intensity increases. The ability to use lactate as fuel varies from runner to runner, depending on fitness level, nutritional status, and rested state. This is why a fixed lactate concentration may not be a reliable predictor of performance.

$\dot{V}O_2$max Training

$\dot{V}O_2max$ is a term frequently used in discussions of endurance training. It refers to the maximal rate at which the body is capable of taking in and consuming oxygen, and is the best indicator of aerobic power. Because of the involvement of both aerobic and anaerobic energy in running, $\dot{V}O_2$max training best develops runners. $\dot{V}O_2$max training employs a level of work approximately 90 to 100 percent of MHR. This level of work also can be measured as 95 to 100 percent of $\dot{V}O_2$max at the runner's current state of fitness. One of the primary adaptations resulting from this type of work is enlargement and strengthening of the left ventricle. This improves its ability to operate as a living pump and transport blood and oxygen to the working muscles. The intensities associated with this level of work are comparable to those found in an all-out running effort of 10 to 15 minutes. For most women and young male runners, it correlates closely to their performance at 3,000 or 3,200 meters. For older, more experienced males

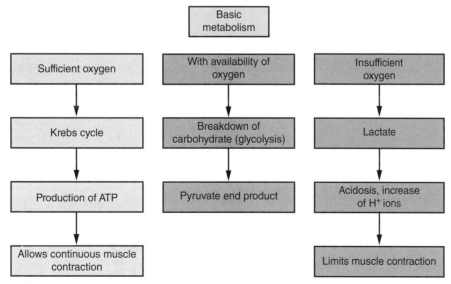

FIGURE 10.4   Normal paths for energy production.

and some elite women, it correlates closely to their best performance at 5,000 meters. Table 10.4 shows the relationship of $\dot{V}O_2$max to specific endurance running events.

Teaching and Training Guidelines for the Endurance Events

In general, the first concern when increasing endurance capabilities is developing the aerobic base. After this has been achieved, the primary concern turns toward developing race-specific energy sources. This progression results in increased aerobic power and $\dot{V}O_2$max. After a period that emphasizes aerobic development and $\dot{V}O_2$max, intervals and then repetitions establish the buffering in the blood needed to tolerate acidosis.

Although much of the training for endurance events focuses on energy system development, other biomotor abilities have a great bearing on performance. Acceleration, speed, power, mobility, strength (relative to body weight), and other abilities are important for high performance in these events, especially in middle-distance races. Although these are not the primary focus of training, a certain portion of the training program should address them.

800 Meters

The 800 meters is an unforgiving endurance event because it provides little time in which to correct errors. In training, the 800-meter

TABLE 10.4   Percentage of Oxygen Use by Event

$\dot{V}O_2$max	% $\dot{V}O_2$max
800 meters	120%
1,500 to 1,600 meters	110%
3,000 to 3,200 meters	102 to 100%
5,000 meters	97%
10,000 meters	92%

runner must develop a strong endurance base and $\dot{V}O_2$max. The anaerobic component is also vital because of the high proportion of anaerobic energy required and the acidosis that accompanies the effort. Lactate tolerance must be developed. Intervals with short recoveries early in the training macrocycle followed by repetitions late in the training year will help improve lactate tolerance.

With regard to race distribution, the athlete's 400-meter capability is a limiting factor. An optimal performance typically is achieved by running the first lap three to four seconds slower than the athlete's best 400 meters, and the second lap two to four seconds slower than the first one. Another way to look at this is to say that the athlete will slow about one second every 200 meters. The biomotor abilities of acceleration, speed, strength, power, and mobility are required for optimal performance in the 800 meters.

1,500 Meters

The 1,500-meter run offers one of the widest variants on what and how much to train because of its great demand for aerobic and anaerobic energy. Aerobic power is more important than in the 800 meters, so the development of $\dot{V}O_2$max capabilities is essential. Training at the lactate threshold also is more important because glycogen storage sites become a factor in this race. Lactate tolerance is vital and, as in the 800 meters, is established with intervals early in the training year and repetitions late in the training year. Total training mileage typically is 25 percent higher than for the 800 meters, but may be much higher depending on the athlete. This additional mileage may be accomplished by using longer aerobic threshold runs.

The 1,500-meter race model is more forgiving than that of the 800 meters. Physiologically, a steady pace is the most economical. Typically, an athlete's fastest time is produced by running slightly faster for the first and last 400 meters but otherwise at an even pace throughout. Athletes should not neglect the development of the biomotor abilities required for the 800 meters and all middle-distance events.

3,000-Meter Steeplechase

The 3,000-meter steeplechase is trained, metabolically, similar to the 5,000 meters. Many advocate training the aerobic contribution in a way similar to that of the 5,000 meters, and training the anaerobic component similar to that of the 1,500 meters. Good hurdling technique is a must, but it does not compensate for a lack of proper aerobic and anaerobic training. Advanced steeplechasers should be able to run the event within 35 seconds of their best 3,000-meter time without barriers. A 50-second differential is a good goal for an emerging steeplechaser.

Steeplechase training creates early fatigue as a result of the barrier clearances and rhythmic disruptions. Consequently, interval training over barriers should be limited to once per week, although technique and drill work can be done more frequently. The race requires good tactical awareness because the runner needs to constantly evaluate where he is in relation to the barriers and other runners.

Even pacing produces the best overall performance in the steeplechase. Energy distribution is particularly important in this race because of the horizontal velocity required to hurdle well. A steeplechaser who goes out too fast and slows significantly in the second half may struggle to accelerate at each barrier or have to resort to a step technique.

5,000 Meters

The 5,000-meter run is a classic $\dot{V}O_2$max race. Because it is run at 95 to 97 percent of $\dot{V}O_2$max pace, this is the key system to develop. Racing at this distance requires long training runs; marathon-pace runs also may be helpful. Lactate-threshold runs and lactate-threshold intervals are a large, important part of the 5,000-meter training program. The anaerobic energy contribution for this event dictates the need for repetitions and intervals. Intervals should be set up similarly to those in 1,500-meter training programs, although less frequently. Anaerobic alactic training should be included in every training program.

There are two key components to the racing model for the 5,000 meters. In general, optimal performance is achieved using a relatively even pace with a slightly faster first and fifth kilometer.

10,000 Meters

The 10,000-meter race requires both volume and intensity. A common error when designing training programs for this event is overlooking the anaerobic energy contribution. Total mileage in the microcycle is greater than that in training for shorter endurance events. The longest runs may approach 20 miles (32 km), or two hours. Marathon-pace runs also are beneficial. Lactate-threshold runs and lactate-threshold intervals are of benefit and may be longer and of higher volume than those used for the 5,000 meters. $\dot{V}O_2$max should be developed by designing a least one workout per microcycle for this purpose. Repetitions are longer than in programs designed for other distance events.

The racing model for the 10,000 meters can be considered an expansion of the 5,000-meter model. The 10,000 meters is run at approximately 92 percent of $\dot{V}O_2$max, so the early laps can seem easy. At this time, the runner should be patient. For this reason, mental and physical rest before competition is essential for the 10,000 meters, and races are generally scheduled much less frequently than other distance events. Climate is an important factor in this race and should be addressed from the outset. In general, optimal performance is achieved by using a relatively even pace with a slightly faster first and tenth kilometer.

Marathon

Training for the marathon is dictated by its particular energy system demands. High volume is important, but equally important is using targeted higher-intensity work to properly stress the appropriate energy systems. The marathon's heavier reliance on the fatty acid energy system requires stressing that system to gain the appropriate training effect.

The objective of marathon training is to train the body to make the best use of fuel. Long-duration, easy runs are important, but they do not provide all the training needed to optimize marathon performance. Marathon-pace runs and long runs with segments at marathon pace are important in training because the energy systems are, in part, intensity specific. Because lactate threshold is also very important in marathon performance, lactate-threshold runs and intervals are key training methods. By raising lactate threshold, the athlete improves her fuel efficiency, thus sparing valuable glycogen for later in the race. Although the anaerobic component is not as significant as it is in shorter events, it still exists. Typical training programs include at least one workout per microcycle stressing $\dot{V}O_2$max. Such sessions typically mirror the longer interval or repetition sessions used by 10,000-meter runners.

In a general reversal of standard training progressions, some marathon training programs emphasize speed development early in the program and then progressively focus on more endurance-oriented activities later to address the specific energy system demands of the event. Also in a reversal of the standard training theory model, volume rises and typically levels off as long runs get longer but reach a point of diminishing return. At that point, the intensity of the long run increases to provide the specific training stimulus required to best prepare for the event. The long run is a major training component, and athletes should complete one per microcycle. The duration of long runs need not exceed two and a half hours regardless of the athlete's ability level, although one run longer than this may be beneficial during the macrocycle.

Because of the duration of the event, fluids (including electrolytes) and carbohydrate must be consumed during the race. Consuming and processing these is a learned skill that needs to be tested and practiced on long runs, because gastrointestinal problems are one of the top reasons runners do not finish marathons.

Running Inventories for Endurance Events

Table 10.5 provides an inventory for aerobic training, and table 10.6 provides an inventory for anaerobic training.

Hill work is an excellent means of anaerobic training for endurance runners. It can be used to train both the anaerobic glycolytic and the anaerobic alactic energy systems. It has been shown to improve running economy by forcing proper running mechanics (running uphill with poor mechanics is difficult if not impossible). Hill sessions should be done on softer surfaces; treadmills are an option. The risk for injury is highest during the downhill recovery. Sessions can use the same formats as those listed in tables 10.5 and 10.6. Alactic hill repetitions may be done on an incline of 5 to 10 percent and 20 to 60 meters long followed by a near-complete recovery. Glycolytic hill repetitions may be done on an incline of 3 to 5 percent and 60 to 600 meters long

TABLE 10.5 Aerobic Training

Type of work	Pace	Heart rate (% MHR)	Recovery	Example
Recovery run; easy run	5K race pace + 1:30	60 to 75	NA	30 to 90 min
Long run; continuous run	5K race pace + 1:30	60 to 75	NA	70 to 150 min
Marathon-pace run, long tempo	5K race pace + 0:45 to 1:00, or marathon race pace	75 to 85	NA	40 to 60 min alone, or as part of a 70 min to 150 min run
Lactate threshold run; tempo run; anaerobic threshold run	5K race pace + 0:25 to 0:30, or pace for one-hour race	88 to 90	20 percent of total run time	20 to 30 min, or 2 or 3 × 10 min, or 4 × 5 min
$\dot{V}O_2$max interval; $\dot{V}O_2$ interval	3K to 5K race pace	90 to 100	50 to 100 percent of run time	3,000- to 8,000-meter volume; repeat efforts of 2 to 5 min

TABLE 10.6 Anaerobic Training

Type	Intensity (% MHR)	Extent	Reps per set	Sets	Session volume
Alactic	95 to 100	30 to 60 m	2 to 4	2 to 4	360 to 600 m
Speed endurance	90 to 100	60 to 150 m	2 to 5	2 or 3	300 to 1,200 m
Speed endurance 1	90 to 100	150 to 300 m	1 to 4	1	300 to 1,000 m
Speed endurance 2	90 to 100	300 to 600 m	1 to 5	1	300 to 1,800 m
1,500 to 1,600 m pace interval	100+	200 to 500 m	4 or 5	2	3,000 to 4,000 m
800 m pace interval	100+	100 to 300 m	3 to 5	2	1,000 to 2,000 m

followed by a near-complete recovery. Longer repetitions or repetitions with less-than-complete recovery may be done as $\dot{V}O_2$max training. Repetitions of 600 to 1,000 meters or repetitions of 200 to 600 meters are excellent examples of this work. They should be done on an incline of 3 to 5 percent.

Microcycles for the Endurance Events

Figures 10.5 and 10.6 are examples of one-week microcycle plans for both precompetitive and competitive phases of training.

Microcycle # Phase: Precompetitive	Dates: Comments:	Event group: Endurance
Sunday	Monday	Tuesday
Warm-up and stretch Long run (preferably on flat) High school 60-90 min College 90-120 min Post collegiate 90-150 min at 70% of $\dot{V}O_2$max Cool-down and stretch	Warm-up and cool-down for each run Recovery run of 45 to 60 min at 60% $\dot{V}O_2$max Running drills 10 min Plyometrics: 3 × 10 hurdle bounds, 3 × 50 bounds up 3% grade, 10 min Core work with emphasis on bilateral activities Cool-down and stretch	Warm-up and stretch Intervals faster than race pace, 1 to 1.5 times race distance in volume Can vary from 60 m to 1k in length, depending on goal of the season Cool-down and stretch
Wednesday	Thursday	Friday
Warm-up and cool down for each run Recovery run of 45 to 60 min at 60% $\dot{V}O_2$max Running drills 10 min Pylometrics: 3 × 10 bounds, 3 × 50 bounds up 3% grade, 10 min Core work with emphasis on bilateral activities Cool-down and stretch	Warm-up run of 20 min Long intervals at race pace or faster, 1 to 1.5 times race distance Cool-down and stretch	If not racing: Warm-up and cool-down for each run Recovery run of 45 to 60 min at 60% $\dot{V}O_2$max Running drills 10 min Plyometrics: 3 × 10 hurdle bounds, 3 × 50 m bounds up 3% grade, 10 min Core work with emphasis on bilateral activities Cool-down and stretch If racing: Warm-up Recovery run Short session of running drills Light core work Cool-down
Saturday	Intensity of load by day	Post-workout comments
If not racing: Warm-up and stretch Lactate threshold run 2 at 83-88% $\dot{V}O_2$max High school: up to 25 min Collegiate: up to 35-40 min Post collegiate up to 60-70 min Marathoners: up to 80-90min Cool-down and stretch or race		

	Su	M	Tu	W	Th	F	Sa
Hard			x		x		x
Medium	x						
Easy		x		x		x	
Rest							

FIGURE 10.5   Sample seven-day microcycle for endurance events: precompetitive phase of training.

Microcycle # Phase: Competitive	Dates: Comments:	Event group: Endurance
Sunday	**Monday**	**Tuesday**
Warm-up and stretch Special endurance 1 Long run (preferably on flat) 60-150 min Cool-down and stretch	Warm-up, cool-down, and stretch for each run AM Special endurance 2 Run 30-40 min PM Special endurance 2 Run 30-40 min Running drills Plyometrics 3 × 10 hurdle bounds, 3 × 50 bounds up a 3% grade Core work with emphasis on bilateral activities	Warm-up and stretch Special endurance 1 Long run (preferably on flat) 60-150 min Cool-down and stretch
Wednesday	**Thursday**	**Friday**

Warm-up and stretch
Fartlek run of 45 to 60 min
Running drills
Plyometrics: 3 × 10 hurdle bounds, 3 × 50 m
  bounds up 3% grade
Cool-down and stretch
	Warm-up run of 20 min
	Lactate threshold run
	1 mile at 85%; add 1 mile per week up to 4 for
	  high school, 6 for college
	Cool-down and stretch
		Warm-up, cool-down, and stretch for each run
		AM
		Special endurance 2
		Run 30-40 min
		PM
		Special endurance 2
		Run 30-40 min
		Running drills
		Plyometrics 3 × 10 hurdle bounds, 3 × 50 bounds
		  up a 3% grade
		Core work with emphasis on bilateral activities

Saturday	**Intensity of load by day**	**Post-workout comments**
Warm-up and stretch 60 min run on undulatory terrain; practice uphill and downhill mechanics Cool-down and stretch	(intensity chart)	

Intensity of load by day:

	Su	M	Tu	W	Th	F	Sa
Hard		x			x		x
Medium				x		x	
Easy	x		x				
Rest							

FIGURE 10.6 Sample seven-day microcycle for endurance events: competitive phase of training.

Steeplechase

The steeplechase is unique among the endurance events because the barriers and water jumps add a highly technical challenge. The standard steeplechase race is 3,000 meters and includes 28 barriers and seven water jumps evenly distributed over seven and a half laps. The common junior distance is 2,000 meters, with a proportional number of barriers and water jumps. The start and finish lines may vary, and the water jumps may be on either the inside or the outside of the track. The steeplechase barriers, or hurdles, are significantly heavier and less flexible than standard hurdles and are a significant impediment to forward motion and the runner's health if they are hit. The barriers are 36 and 30 inches (91 and 76 cm) high, for men and women, respectively.

The steeplechase is a distance hurdling race. Excellent sprint hurdling technique is not essential to success in the steeplechase, but efficient hurdle clearance must be a goal of any training program. This can be developed through practicing the skills and drills of the sprint hurdler as well as steeplechase-specific drills. The steeplechase runner should learn to use either leg as the leading leg because race circumstance may require this ability. Because of the absence of a predetermined hurdle step pattern in this race, the athlete must approach the hurdles aggressively and visually locate them well in advance so she can adjust her stride lengths efficiently in anticipation of takeoff.

Water barrier clearance in the steeplechase should be initiated by taking off as in hurdling (figure 10.7). The leading foot should be planted firmly on the barrier and the body propelled forward while passing the barrier. Takeoff occurs relatively close to the barrier as in hurdling.

Ideally, the foot should be placed on the barrier so the toe can push off the front of the barrier as the foot rocks forward. To conserve

horizontal velocity and momentum, the runner should keep the body's center of mass as low as possible throughout the clearance of the barrier. The runner aggressively pushes off in a forward motion so that the body advances well beyond the barrier before losing contact with it. The objective is to propel the body horizontally, not vertically. Because the landing should provide a smooth transition to the next running step, jumping the farthest possible distance may not be advantageous because it may lead to a two-footed landing.

The steeplechase is a dangerous event without proper preparation. The typical steeplechase training program includes flexibility work, drills, and interval work over hurdles. Athletes, especially those new to the event, should practice over conventional hurdles and not steeplechase barriers to minimize the risk

FIGURE 10.7 Water barrier clearance.

of injury. The full water jump should be used minimally in practice; it may be simulated by placing a steeplechase barrier in front of a sandpit or on a grass infield. Because of the unique stress on the body caused by the barriers and the water jump, the steeplechase should not be run too often. Athletes should therefore identify a secondary event, generally either the 1,500 meters or the 5,000 meters.

A common error in athlete selection for the steeplechase is selecting slower athletes. Because of the horizontal velocity requirements of hurdling, at slower running speeds hurdling becomes inefficient and even dangerous. Athletes attempting the steeplechase at these slower rates are better off using a quick step on–off technique. The ideal athlete for the steeplechase has the speed of a 1,500-meter runner and the endurance of a 5,000-meter runner. General athleticism and a high degree of coordination are also helpful. Former soccer players often make good steeplechase runners because of their great lower-extremity dexterity.

Table 10.7 summarizes some common errors in the steeplechase.

TABLE 10.7 Common Errors and Corrections for Steeplechase

Fault	Reasons	Corrections
Clearance over the barriers is too high	• The takeoff is too close, leading to a greater takeoff angle to avoid hitting the barrier. • Approach velocity is too low, which leads to a greater time needed above the barrier. • The athlete does not push aggressively forward off the hurdle.	• Move the takeoff position farther back by focusing on it earlier in the approach. • Increase approach velocity even if it is significantly faster than race pace. Otherwise, speed will be lost during the hurdle and extra energy will be required.
Landing too deep in the water at the water barrier	• Approach velocity is too low. • The direction of the takeoff is too steep, leading to a loss of horizontal velocity. The landing is also at a steep angle when this mistake is made, causing significant braking on landing.	• Increase velocity into takeoff. • Take off farther back to keep the motion forward rather than upward.
Raised arms at landing	• Raising the arms brings the body closer to the ground and provides a safer, but slower landing and stops forward momentum.	• Push off the barrier with the goal of moving forward at a high speed rather than upward to get the distance required. This lowers the trajectory so there is less need to cushion the landing with arm movement.
Landing in the water on both feet	• Fear of injury from the impact when landing off the water barrier as a result of coming in slowly and jumping higher to get greater distance, which means dropping from a greater height	• Increase approach velocity to land farther from the barrier. • Do practice over a steeple hurdle placed at the sandpit. Take off from the runway onto the hurdle, push off, land on a single leg, and run out of the pit.

Racewalking

Internationally contested racewalking events are 20 kilometers and 50 kilometers (12.4 and 31 miles) long. Younger athletes race from 1,500 meters to 10 kilometers. Racewalking differs from running in the two rules that govern form. A common analogy is that running is like freestyle swimming, whereas racewalking is like the butterfly. Both are competitions to cover a set distance as quickly as possible either without restriction or with specified step or stroke mechanics.

Rules of Racewalking

The rules that govern racewalking basically are the same as those that govern endurance running events, with two additional rules about stride mechanics. Racewalkers must keep one foot on the ground at all times, as judged by the human eye without recourse to photography or recording devices. This limits flight time to less than that which is perceptible to a trained judge, about 30 milliseconds per step. Further, the knee of the advancing leg must be straightened from the instant of foot contact with the ground until the leg has reached vertical.

If an athlete is seen to be close to breaking either rule, officials provide visual warnings by way of yellow paddles with symbols indicating loss of contact or failure to straighten the leg. The yellow paddle is accompanied by an oral warning. A walker is disqualified when three separate judges write red cards recommending disqualification. The type of infraction is irrelevant to the card count. At the side of the track or road course for the competition, a board displays competitors' numbers and a tally of red cards written for each. Competitors are required to stop only when shown a red disqualification paddle by the chief judge to indicate that they have received three red cards.

Talent Demands for Racewalking

Racewalking is a typical endurance event. Athletes with high levels of endurance, core strength, and flexibility, the ability to acquire new motor skills, and the capacity to maintain a high cadence for extended periods are good candidates for racewalking.

Skills of Racewalking

Racewalking events place high demands on the energy systems. At the same time, technical efficiency is equally crucial. Good training programs emphasize the development of legal and energetically economical biomechanics, provide physiological preparation to increase base endurance, raise $\dot{V}O_2max$, increase velocity at lactate threshold, maximize efficiency at race pace, prepare athletes psychologically for optimal performance even under the added stress of being judged during competition, and help athletes identify best practices to suit their individual needs, such as nutrition before and during races, sleep, recovery strategies, and periodization.

Biomechanics of Racewalking

In racewalking (figure 10.8) the leading leg straightens at the knee as the heel strikes the ground approximately 14 inches (about 36 cm) in front of the torso. Posture is upright and relaxed. Shoulders are low, and the arms are flexed at 90 to 80 degrees throughout the action. Most racewalking technique flaws arise from a lack of knowledge of optimal mechanics or a lack of kinesthetic awareness.

The trailing foot is driven close to vertical at toe-off. The hands, gently closed, reach their maximal swing points. The back hand comes just behind the waist of the shorts, and the front hand comes up to the level of the sternum and is directly above the leading heel.

The supporting leg remains straight at the knee as it begins to pass under the body. The foot of the supporting leg rolls from heel to toe throughout ground contact. Note that the toes of the front foot have not yet contacted the ground. There is no vertical hip drop. The foot of the swinging leg is kept close to the ground. The arm angle is unchanged, and the arm swings from the shoulder without any hunching action. The hand and forearm pass close to the iliac crest (the top of the hip bone) and thus assist hip rotation.

The supporting leg reaches vertical and is still straight at the knee. The hips are rotated in a plane parallel to the ground without any side-to-side sway or drop. The head is upright

FIGURE 10.8 Racewalking technique.

throughout the stride, with the eyes on the horizon. There is no forward or backward lean from the waist, and a lordotic (butt-out) position is avoided.

Hip rotation brings the far side of the shorts into view. The trailing leg continues to drive, starting to roll up onto the toes. Care is taken not to lift the knee of the swinging leg high in front of the body, a common flaw in runners as they learn correct form.

The leading leg rapidly straightens to the point of heel contact without increasing foot height above the ground. The rear foot continues to roll up onto the toes as the knee starts to bend slightly.

The knee of the rear leg bends to assist with forward propulsion of the leg into the swing phase. This is further enhanced by the rapid drawing back of the leading arm. The hips are flat from side to side, although they are rotated to allow a clear view to the far iliac crest.

The motion is cyclical and, once learned, automatic. The steps of the left and right legs should mirror one another. The feet are aligned with the direction of travel, splaying neither in nor out. The inside borders of the shoes land along an imaginary line in the direction of travel.

Table 10.8 on the following page describes some errors made by racewalkers and provides solutions to fix the problems.

Energy Systems for Racewalking

The metabolic requirements for racewalking are the same as those for running events of similar duration. A rough guide is to treat kilometers walked as equivalent to miles run. Thus, the energy systems used in a 20-kilometer racewalk are those used to run 20 miles. This equivalence breaks down below 3 kilometers and above 35 kilometers of walking because of the mechanical limitations imposed by the rules of racewalking. Elite runners and racewalkers competing in a one-hour event use similar percentages of $\dot{V}O_2$max and lactate-threshold velocity.

TABLE 10.8　Common Errors and Corrections for Racewalking

Fault	Reasons	Corrections
Reaching too far in front of the body with the swinging leg	• Lack of knowledge of correct biomechanics • Lack of kinesthetic awareness • Attempting to lengthen the stride	• Study videos of elite racewalkers to learn proper biomechanics. • Obtain visual feedback in real time by setting up cameras around a treadmill with a TV monitor. Get slower feedback with video played back after each of a series of 100-meter walks at race pace. • Restrict the heel strike to no more than 18 inches (about 46 cm) in front of the navel.
The hip of the swinging leg drops as the swinging leg passes under the body.	• Lack of knowledge of correct biomechanics • Lack of kinesthetic awareness • Lack of core strength	• Study videos of elite racewalkers to learn proper biomechanics. • Obtain visual feedback in real time by setting up cameras around a treadmill with a TV monitor. Get slower feedback with video played back after each of a series of 100-meter walks at race pace. • Perform a routine of dynamic and static core exercises at least three times per week.
Receiving several bent-knee yellow paddles or red cards in competition	• Lack of knowledge of correct biomechanics • Lack of kinesthetic awareness • Overstriding in front of the body • Lack of quadriceps strength through the last degrees of leg straightening • Tight hip flexors or hamstrings	• Study videos of elite racewalkers to learn proper biomechanics. • Obtain visual feedback in real time by setting up cameras around a treadmill with a TV monitor. Get slower feedback with video played back after each of a series of 100-meter walks at race pace. • Restrict the heel strike to no more than 18 inches (about 46 cm) in front of the navel. • Add strength training for the quadriceps, working through the last 10 to 15 degrees of straightening while standing. • Add static and dynamic stretching for the tight areas. Use a foam roller to loosen the hamstrings.

Stride Cadence

Racewalking at high levels requires a stride rate of at least 210 steps per minute. An important goal of the training program is to develop the ability to attain and maintain this rate or higher.

Teaching and Training Racewalking Biomechanics

The two methods used to teach racewalking technique to beginners are the imitation method and the template method. Coaches should avoid explaining the rules when athletes are first learning because excess focus on what must not be done interferes with skill acquisition. An athlete who has learned correct technique will also have adopted legal technique. Prior to the first competition, the coach should teach the athlete the rules and also the procedures for judging, such as the use of yellow paddles and the disqualification board.

Imitation Method

The imitation method involves displaying a model for the learner to imitate. The availability of video on the Internet has made this approach easy. Once an athlete has some semblance of racewalking form, the coach should work to correct faults by instruction and demonstration or by video feedback. The coach can show an athlete a film of her technique and explain how it may be improved. The shorter the feedback time the better the results. The best results are achieved by having the athlete racewalk on a treadmill with multiple camera angles showing form on a monitor directly ahead of the athlete. The coach indicates flaws on the screen, and the racewalker endeavors to correct them, watching the results of these changes in real time.

Template Method

The template method involves taking a familiar movement pattern and modifying it systematically until a good technical model for racewalking is achieved. This process starts by using running as a familiar motor pattern. One modification is made at a time to the movement until racewalking technique is perfected. The coach needs to be patient, modifying only one technical feature at a time. Again, a real-time feedback system on a treadmill is a useful tool in this process.

Training Guidelines for Racewalking

The coach should structure the development of a racewalker, as with any endurance athlete, with the added goal of refining racewalking technique. Physiological development must be combined with the development of efficient stride mechanics.

Training programs for endurance running can be adapted for use by racewalkers by expressing workouts in terms of time and effort (heart rate). For example, a runner might be required to cover 5 x 1,500 meters with three minutes of rest between them, aiming to reach 95 to 98 percent of MHR. The equivalent workout for a racewalker differs only in the distance covered in each work interval. If the expected work period for the runner is five minutes, the distance for the racewalker might be 1 kilometer (0.6 mile). In the same fashion, a 90-minute run at an easy conversational pace results in a greater distance covered but has similar physiological benefits as a 90-minute racewalk at the same perceived level of exertion. A 20-minute tempo run and a 20-minute tempo racewalk play the same roll in improved performance, although the runner covers more ground in the allotted time.

Core work to improve stability, especially of the hips to prevent dropping at each heel strike, is important in preparing a racewalker. The inclusion of running in a racewalking program is fine for fitness, but the coach must watch for any gait changes that may affect the legality or economy of the racewalking technique.

Conclusion

The importance of individualizing workouts to match the training and developmental needs of the athlete is one of the big challenges of endurance coaching. The challenge of individualizing is further complicated by the fact that most coaches work with teams or groups. This chapter provides a foundation to help coaches meet each athlete's needs. Within the team or group setting, individualizing workouts is possible by modifying the volume, recovery, and intensity or pace. In this manner, the coach can meet both team and individual needs. As with all events, the knowledge base for endurance events is always expanding. This chapter should help coaches evaluate new ideas and decide whether they are worthy of consideration as they develop their training models.

11

Hurdles

Joe Rogers

The hurdle events discussed in this chapter are the 100-meter hurdles for women, the 110-meter hurdles for men, and the 400-meter hurdles for men and women. The chapter begins with a brief discussion of rules, safety practices, and talent demands for the hurdles. A general overview of the events and the skills they require follows. Next, each event is discussed individually with regard to technique and demands. The chapter ends with an outline of training guidelines and drill progressions for these events.

foul in the 400-meter hurdles is allowing the trail leg to pass outside the hurdle. Rules also dictate the assignment of heats and lanes and the arrangement of trial rounds in most meets. Rules differ slightly at the high school, collegiate, USATF, and IAAF levels. Coaches should acquire the appropriate rulebooks and become thoroughly familiar with the rules. This provides a distinct competitive advantage.

Table 11.1 outlines specifications for the hurdle races addressed in this chapter.

Rules of Hurdling

The rules of hurdling are relatively simple. The hurdle races are run in lanes, with rules governing the start the same as in sprint events. The hurdler must make an attempt to leap each barrier; knocking the hurdle down intentionally is illegal. Also, the hurdler's entire body must pass over the hurdle. A common

Safety in Hurdling

Good safety practices should be used when teaching hurdling. Equipment and surfaces should be kept in good order, and athletes should wear proper footwear. Traffic control around the hurdling area should be adequate to prevent mishaps. With beginners, the coach should use modified hurdling to create a pro-

TABLE 11.1   Hurdle Spacing and Height

Race	Distance to first hurdle	Distance between hurdles	Run in distance	Hurdle height
Women's 100-meter hurdles	13m	8.5m	10.5m	33 in. (84 cm)
Men's 110-meter hurdles	13.72m (45 ft.)	9.14m (30 ft.)	14.02m (46 ft.)	42 in. (107 cm)
Women's 400-meter hurdles	45m	35m	40m	30 in. (76 cm)
Men's 400-meter hurdles	45m	35m	40m	36 in. (91 cm)

ductive atmosphere. Both padded and short hurdles make practice safer and accelerate learning. Coaches should avoid the phrase *Jump the hurdle.* That concept leads to inefficient hurdling and creates safety issues for the athlete as well as others in adjacent lanes. Beginners should start with low, nonthreatening barriers to ensure proper running rhythm, safe skill acquisition, and the development of confidence. Athletes should progress to higher hurdles only when skill and confidence warrant it.

Talent Demands for the Hurdles

Hurdlers should be chosen from athletes who are capable sprinters. Abilities needed in hurdling are very similar to those needed in the sprint events; thus, sprinting skills should be developed accordingly. Good hurdling candidates demonstrate the following:

- Speed (a must)
- Coordination (clearing the hurdle efficiently and quickly returning to the sprint is crucial)
- Elastic capability (hurdlers are sprinters first)
- High levels of power (the ability to apply a high level of force over a short time)
- Flexibility and mobility at the hip (crucial to an efficient and elastic hurdling action)
- Long leg length (preferred, but not required)

General Analysis of the Hurdle Events

Hurdling is sprint racing with 10 obstacles. The athlete must adjust his sprint technique to negotiate those obstacles. Because the hurdles are spaced evenly, the athlete establishes a specific rhythm with the stride pattern between and over the hurdles.

Hurdle races can be divided into cyclical units. For the 100 and 110 hurdles, there should be three steps between the hurdles and one stride over the hurdle. Therefore, each cyclical unit consists of four strides. Those four strides create a specific rhythm that is repeated throughout the race. The key to successful racing is developing that rhythm with great quickness.

Although the same three phases of sprinting—acceleration, maximal velocity, and deceleration—apply to the hurdle race, the unique rhythm changes the nature of the sprint mechanics. The athlete must adjust her mechanics to create the needed step pattern to clear the hurdles.

For the 300 and 400 hurdle races, the number of strides between the hurdles varies depending on maturity and gender. The goal, however, is to develop a consistent step pattern that allows the athlete to maintain high velocity into and over the hurdles.

Phases of Hurdle Races

The acceleration phase is the first phase of a hurdle race. As in sprinting, the athlete accelerates from zero velocity to maximal, controlled velocity. The athlete must maximize acceleration and achieve a tall posture before the first hurdle. To negotiate the first hurdle with maximal efficiency, the athlete needs to be moving at a high rate of speed; maximal velocity is achieved by the third or fourth hurdle. To properly negotiate each hurdle, the athlete must accelerate into the takeoff before each hurdle. Because of the rhythmic nature of hurdling the 100-meter or 110-meter races, the process of acceleration involves quickening that rhythm to achieve and maintain maximal rhythm.

The maximal-velocity phase begins when the athlete reaches maximal, controlled rhythm. Because the distance between the hurdles is fixed, the athlete cannot increase stride length to increase speed. Rather, she needs to increase stride frequency between hurdles. For the 400-meter hurdler, the maximal-velocity phase refers to maximal desired speed, not attainable speed. To conserve energy and achieve best performance for the 400-meter hurdles, the athlete needs to achieve a balance between the times of each half of the race.

The deceleration phase is the last phase. As in all sprint races, metabolic fatigue reduces racing speed as a result of a loss of coordination in the 100- or 110-meter hurdle races. Metabolic fatigue also reduces racing speed in the 400-meter hurdles. In the 100- and 110-meter hurdles, the athlete must manage fatigue by training speed endurance, with and without hurdles. In the 400-meter hurdles, the athlete must develop both lactate tolerance and muscular endurance to maintain good posture and efficient sprint mechanics in the late stages of the race.

The distribution of race phases in the 400-meter hurdles is slightly different. Distribution refers to the relative lengths of the three race phases. In the 400-meter hurdles, much consideration and planning must be given to the distribution of the phases. Most top 400-meter hurdlers show a 5 percent decline in speed over the second half of the race, resulting in not more than a three-second differential between the first and second 200 meters. It is common for the novice to experience a high state of fatigue around the 300-meter mark, which is often the result of running the first half of the race too fast. The price of exhaustion is much higher than that experienced in the 400-meter flat race because of the added energy expenditure of hurdling.

Modifying Sprint Mechanics for the 100- and 110-Meter Hurdles

The hurdler should be proficient in all the skills of sprinting. The nature of hurdle racing is very rhythmic. This event is divided into equal spaces between the hurdles. For the 100- and 110-meter hurdle events, the athlete takes three steps between the hurdles and one step over them. Therefore, each unit in these events is divided into four steps. The athlete should attempt to apply the quickest rhythm possible throughout the race while maximizing hip amplitude and stretch reflexes. The negotiation of the hurdle step must deviate from normal sprint mechanics to raise the athlete's center of mass over the hurdle. The goal is to minimize this deviation from sprint mechanics and recover quickly to the ground to apply force and return to performing sprint mechanics.

Minimizing Airtime

Acceleration occurs only when the hurdler is on the ground. It makes sense that getting over the barrier, onto the ground, and into sprinting mechanics as quickly as possible should be the hurdler's goal. Drill selection for training the hurdling action should emphasize efficient, balanced, and fast movements, and training should occur regularly. Time in the air is time lost in applying force to the track surface.

Skills of the Hurdle Events

The uniqueness of racing with obstacles adds to the biomotor ability demands of the hurdle events. It is helpful for the athlete to have long legs to minimize the need to raise the center of mass to cross the barrier. Flexibility is also very important, especially excellent hamstring flexibility. A shorter athlete can compensate for a height disadvantage by having great explosive leg power along with flexibility. Natural running speed is a great quality for all athletes, and hurdlers benefit from this as well. However, many successful hurdlers do not have the top sprint ability, yet they combine good speed with flexibility, quickness, power, and rhythm to be superior over the hurdles. In assessing potential hurdlers from the athlete pool, coaches should look for speed, good size, the ability to learn new skills, and an aggressive and fearless attitude toward competition.

Approach to the First Hurdle

To a large degree, the acceleration phase constitutes the approach run to the first hurdle. The approach consists of a specific number of steps developed for consistency. The approach is discussed in greater detail in the sections covering the individual hurdle races. Most hurdlers use eight steps to the first hurdle in the 100- and 110-meter events, although several contemporary hurdlers have moved to a seven-step pattern based on the idea that seven steps creates better amplitude at the hips and elicits stretch reflexes more effectively. The seven-step method also requires great strength.

For the 400-meter event, most male hurdlers use 20 to 22 steps to the first hurdle, and most female hurdlers use 24 to 26 steps. In the 400-meter hurdles, most acceleration occurs before the first hurdle. For shorter hurdle races, a greater vertical component of ground force is applied during acceleration to the first hurdle, because the hurdler needs to come to a more erect posture in preparation to negotiate the first hurdle.

Table 11.2 summarizes common errors made by athletes in the hurdles.

TABLE 11.2 Common Errors and Corrections for Hurdles

Fault	Reasons	Corrections
Not running aggressively to the first hurdle	• Fear of the hurdle • Lack of comfort with the step pattern • Lack of the needed explosive power for the hurdle start	• Practice with training hurdles or lowered hurdles to build confidence • Develop the necessary strength
Being too far from the first hurdle	• Lack of strength and speed • Ineffective acceleration • Taking too few steps to the first hurdle	• If there is a lack of contractile leg strength, focus on strength development, especially in the general preparation training period • Consider switching legs in the blocks to add one more step • Lengthen the arm action and increase the amplitude of the movement during acceleration
Bounding between the hurdles	• Strength or speed deficit • Inefficient flight and landing mechanics, causing slowing	• Develop explosive power • Lower the hurdles and decrease the spacing between the hurdles
Being too high over the hurdle	• Taking off too close to the hurdle • Jumping the hurdles instead of running the hurdles • Fear of the hurdle	• Take a cut step at the takeoff • Develop the rhythm of running hurdles by using shorter hurdles and closer spacing. This also builds confidence • Develop rhythm before speed
Descending onto the top of the hurdle.	• Taking off too far from the hurdle • Decelerating into the hurdle • Fatigue	• Develop speed endurance and explosive power • Develop aggressiveness and work to attack each barrier. One-step drills are recommended
Being off-balance when landing after the hurdle	• Lead leg not following a straight path • Center of mass not over the foot on landing • Lack of flexibility and mobility	• Train the path of the lead leg to be straight forward over the hurdle • Be sure the opposite arm is balancing the trail leg • Perform wall drills with the lead leg • Work regularly on mobility and flexibility

Between the Hurdles

The run between the hurdles resembles maximal-velocity mechanics. Between-hurdles running is discussed in greater detail in the sections covering the individual hurdle races. If the hurdle step is completed quickly and rhythmically, the hurdler can return to sprinting quickly with minimal energy loss.

Hurdle Takeoff

The hurdle takeoff is a modification of maximal-velocity mechanics. The takeoff step is grounded as close under the body's center of mass as possible. The athlete senses this as a cut step (shortened step). The shin angle at touchdown is nearly vertical, consistent with the vertical push-off present in the steps prior to the takeoff. The hips extend forcefully, driving the foot down and back to increase backside action and create acceleration into the hurdle.

As this occurs, there is considerable displacement of the hips forward past the takeoff foot before flight is achieved. This displacement is initiated in the core (the trunk and hips) as opposed to the limbs. The lead-leg action is initiated by the displacement of the hips toward the hurdle. This helps conserve posture in flight, counters the forward rotation associated with the displacement, and improves the efficiency of the hurdle clearance. Body lean may be needed to aid clearance, especially for shorter men, but any body lean achieved during hurdle takeoff should not result in poor posture.

Hurdle Clearance and Landing

Hurdle clearance is a modification of maximal-velocity mechanics to allow efficient clearance while maintaining as much speed as possible (figure 11.1). The forward displacement of the hips is essential for the clearance

FIGURE 11.1   Proper hurdle mechanics creates the least disruption to the sprint cycle.

to take place. The lead-leg action is initiated by the displacement of the hips at takeoff. The extension of the lead leg is proximal to distal; the athlete leads with the knee and then extends the leg. The extension sequence should be hip to knee, then knee to foot, in that order.

The objective is to negotiate the hurdle with minimal deviation from good sprint technique. To minimize the need to raise the center of mass any higher than necessary, the athlete can lean well forward into and over the hurdle. The athlete looks through the eyebrows at the next hurdle to keep a low profile while clearing the trail leg. The arms act as a balance to maintain good forward momentum and a tight body action to avoid too much lateral movement. The arm opposite the lead leg reaches forward to balance the shoulders, leading with the elbow upward and forward. This keeps the shoulder joint in the most favorable position to achieve greater freedom of movement.

Proper timing of trail-leg recovery depends on the proper displacement of the hips beyond the foot at takeoff. Relaxing and stretching the hip flexors of the trail leg is key for proper timing to occur. Relaxing and stretching the hip flexors delays the trail leg, but it is recovered tight to the body. Recovery is very fast once initiated.

Although most trail-leg recovery is reflexive and natural, the athlete must abduct the hip and evert the foot to clear the trail leg over the hurdle. Abduction at the hip joint lifts the leg to the side while the knee remains well flexed. The eversion of the ankle joint prevents the trail foot from dangling down and catching the crossbar as it passes over the hurdle. The trail leg is flexed tightly at the knee throughout its recovery, creating a shorter, faster movement.

Upper-body actions counter lower-body actions to allow the athlete to efficiently cross the barrier. A greater split of the arms at takeoff matches the extended displacement of the legs

c

d

g

h

at takeoff. A wider sweep of the arm on the trail-leg side counters the wider path of the trail leg. Although a shorter recovery radius of this arm would be faster, the need to balance the mass of the moving trail leg requires a wider arm recovery. The tighter the trail leg is, the better the balance of these forces will be.

As the lead leg moves forward, a slightly bent knee and a dorsiflexed foot aids in accelerating the foot down. The athlete must actively work to pull down the foot as close to the hurdle as possible. On landing, the key is a vertical shin angle and active foot action on foot contact. This prevents braking and aids the hurdler in quickly returning to sprinting mechanics between the hurdles. The efficiency of the hurdle landing and getaway step is directly related to the efficiency of takeoff.

Cues for Hurdlers

- Attack the hurdle.
- Be fearless.
- Sprint through the hurdle.
- Use a cut step at takeoff.
- Maintain a tight trail leg.
- Have the toe up on top of the barrier (dorsiflexion).
- Use a vigorous arm action.
- Lead the arm with the elbow.
- Perform an active landing off the hurdle.
- Move the lead leg under the center of mass.
- Remain tall off the hurdle.
- Sprint off the hurdle.

Event-Specific Technical Considerations

The shorter hurdle races have demands similar to those of the other short sprint races with adjustments made to achieve specific step patterns. Depending on which step pattern is used to the first hurdle, the athlete may have to learn to start from the blocks with the feet

switched from the normal pedal position. This may require some accommodation to learn a new feel to starting.

The block clearance should be very much the same as with other sprint races, but the acceleration pattern requires a move to a taller posture much sooner to be ready to hurdle. New hurdlers should work on the step pattern to the first hurdle with a very low obstacle in place of the hurdle. Using an actual hurdle may be intimidating, preventing the athlete from running aggressively enough to develop the correct feel of the start. When the athlete is developing a feel for good hurdle rhythm, learning takes place more quickly with hurdle heights and spacings that promote success. A coach should adjust the hurdles to the athlete's ability rather than force the athlete to adjust to the hurdle.

100- and 110-Meter Hurdles

Most developing hurdlers take eight steps to the first hurdle, although several elite hurdlers have switched to seven steps. With an eight-step approach, the lead foot is placed on the rear block pedal. For seven steps, the lead foot is on the front block pedal. The choice of a seven- or eight-step pattern is determined by which pattern gets the hurdler through the first hurdle the fastest and most efficiently. In theory, the seven-step pattern is faster, but it demands great strength and power.

An eight-step approach changes the progression of body angles more quickly as the athlete approaches the first hurdle. Heel recovery height in each stride to the first hurdle is low to accommodate the shorter steps of the eight-step approach. The need to be in a taller posture sooner is mandated by the need to address the first hurdle.

With seven steps, the progression to the first hurdle is more reflective of a sprint acceleration, yet it still requires a technical adjustment over a conventional sprint acceleration pattern. The decision to use a seven-step approach should be evaluated by answering the following questions:

- Does the athlete reach the appropriate takeoff spot without stretching the last stride?

- Is shin angle vertical at the plant of the takeoff step?
- Is the takeoff spot too far from the hurdle? (If so, the athlete may drop onto the hurdle before touchdown.)
- Which step pattern is faster? (This can be determined by timing the athlete's maximal efforts through the first and second hurdles using both patterns.)

The drive phase in the sprint hurdle race extends through the third hurdle. Although modifications of the acceleration process must be made to negotiate the barriers, some semblance of acceleration mechanics is sustained to at least the third hurdle.

Running between the hurdles in the 100- and 110-meter races requires a modification of maximal-velocity mechanics. Advanced hurdlers usually need to decrease stride length between hurdles to fit in three steps. This requires a lower heel recovery, limited time on the ground, and an incomplete extension of the supporting leg. All hurdlers should attempt to shorten the takeoff step to accommodate an efficient takeoff position into the hurdle. The steps of developing hurdlers often are not long enough to require a shortened stride pattern. As fatigue sets in, in the latter stages of the race, these athletes often stretch their steps, leading to a loss of speed and rhythm.

Force application to the track between hurdles is primarily vertical, just as in maximal-velocity sprinting. Sprinting between hurdles also reflects a shorter backside action. However, the hurdle step is different and requires a larger backside movement into the hurdle takeoff. Because the step pattern between hurdles is fixed, the athlete increases speed by increasing stride frequency. This often results in decreased stride length and the need to get the foot off the ground quickly to recover for the next step.

Displacement of the hips at takeoff is crucial to cover the distance necessary to get over the barrier. Often, athletes fail to displace into the hurdle adequately because they take off too close to the hurdle, encountering the hurdle too soon to complete the displacement process. For this reason, the takeoff point for each hurdle clearance should be monitored in training. Men should take off from a point approximately 7 feet (213 cm) in front of the hurdle, and women from a point approximately 6 1/2 feet (198 cm) in front of the hurdle.

In women's hurdling, the hurdles are placed about 2 feet (60 cm) closer together than in men's hurdling, and the hurdles are 33 inches (84 cm) high. In men's hurdles, the hurdles are 42 inches (107 cm) for seniors and 39 inches (99 cm) for high-school athletes. The men's hurdle height is much higher relative to their centers of mass than the women's hurdle height is. This requires male hurdlers to develop more forward lean and horizontal hip displacement. Female hurdlers have to deviate from normal sprint mechanics less than men do.

400-Meter Hurdles

The 400-meter hurdler starts with a drive phase much like a flat 400-meter runner would. The drive phase extends at least half the distance to the first hurdle. The first hurdle for both men and women is 45 meters from the start. Consistency to the first hurdle is crucial for developing a smooth rhythm over the first hurdle. It is best to establish a stride pattern as part of the race plan for the 400 hurdles. Male hurdlers typically take 20 to 22 steps to the first hurdle and 13 to 15 steps between hurdles. Female hurdlers typically take 24 to 26 steps to the first hurdle and 15 to 17 steps between hurdles.

It is advantageous to use a left lead leg for hurdling on the curve. A right lead leg requires a move to the outer portion of the lane at the hurdle to avoid dragging the trail leg inside the hurdle crossbar, a cause for disqualification. The 400-meter hurdler who can lead with either leg over the hurdles has a clear advantage. The coach needs to determine whether an even or odd step pattern is the most efficient for the athlete.

The first part of the 400-meter hurdles should be run aggressively but under control. Although the coach and athlete can develop a series of goal splits between hurdles, the 400-meter hurdle race has a unique rhythm that must be trained. This is a 400-meter race with 10 interruptions to the rhythm (the hurdles). Through various training runs at various distances, the athlete begins to learn the appropriate pace and stride pattern. Consistency is key to success in the 400-meter hurdles. Disruptions of well-trained rhythms and stride patterns create step issues leading into the hurdles.

Teaching and Training the Hurdles

The development of a variety of biomotor qualities is essential to improving hurdle performance. In addition to the obviously essential speed-related qualities, various types of strength, power, flexibility, and mobility are crucial to high performance. Refer to chapter 7 for more on these qualities.

100- and 110-Meter Hurdles

Because speed is an important aspect of hurdling, the training plan for hurdle development should follow guidelines similar to those for sprinters. Acceleration and speed development precede speed-endurance training.

Hurdling is a rhythmic event divided into units from hurdle to hurdle. An athlete who wants to understand hurdling must develop a feeling for and knowledge of the rhythmic action of the steps from hurdle to hurdle. The coach can learn a lot by listening to the hurdler run. The longest pause between foot contacts will be over the hurdle. The shortest will be the third step before takeoff. To help the hurdler establish a rhythm, the coach can set up a running lane with low training hurdles not more than 12 inches (30 cm) high spaced about 8 meters apart for males and 7 1/2 meters apart for females. Using short, choppy steps, the athlete runs through six to eight training hurdles. When approaching each hurdle, the athlete simply extends the stride over the hurdle while not thinking of jumping. The athlete will not be sprinting but simply trying to set up a quick running step pattern. This kind of rhythmic drill can help the young hurdler develop a feel for the hurdling pattern.

The development of hurdle technique can be practiced through various drills. Following are concepts to emphasize during practice:

- Maintain a tall posture.
- Lead with the knee rather than the foot.
- Remember that hurdle action is a quick action.
- Keep the forces lined up horizontally.
- Make sure the lead foot follows in line behind the knee and over the hurdle.
- Keep the trail leg folded tightly with the foot near the hip as it is abducted and brought through.
- Move the trail leg around and down under the center of mass.
- Exaggerate the arm action but keep it similar to a sprint action.
- Sprint off the hurdle.

As the athlete continues to learn, the hurdles should be low so as to be nonthreatening. This allows the athlete to develop confidence and fearlessness and encourages aggressive running. If the hurdles are threatening, the athlete will be reluctant to run aggressively and will learn improper techniques. As the athlete develops the motor skills needed for good hurdling, the barriers should be adjusted in both height and spacing as long as the athlete can run with the correct rhythm and technique. Practice done with hurdles that are too high or too far apart for the athlete's ability forces the athlete to adjust to get over the hurdle in a way that results in deceleration. This leads to incorrect motor patterns that delay skill development. As the athlete progresses, hurdles can be adjusted higher and closer to the normal racing spacing. Regardless of hurdle height or spacing, the athlete must achieve the correct running rhythm at all times. Even after achieving proficiency, practicing with modified hurdles can help the athlete race at quicker tempos.

Hurdle training for the 100- and 110-meter hurdles can be organized in the same way as sprint training: acceleration to maximal velocity to speed endurance. Most speed development activities are applicable to hurdle training. Many sprint activities can be done over hurdles, although sprint training without hurdles may also be appropriate. Speed work with and without hurdles is recommended.

Acceleration practice is applicable over the first three hurdles. Speed training is best done over hurdles 4 through 6, whereas speed endurance is trained over the last four hurdles. Another speed endurance plan involves moving hurdles closer by 1 foot (30 cm) and placing an 11th hurdle within the 110-meter distance.

To train maximal-velocity rhythm, the coach should incorporate maximal rhythmic speed training. This involves establishing goal split times (touchdown to touchdown between hurdles) needed to achieve the athlete's overall goal time and then placing four to six hurdles in a lane and adjusting the spacing so the athlete can achieve that split time. Usually, shortening the hurdle spacing by 1 or 2 feet (30 or 60 cm) works well. The hurdler then works over hurdles that are lowered by 3 to 6 inches (7.6 to 15.2 cm). This allows the hurdler to sprint more quickly and mimic the speed and rhythm of a race.

The field of motor learning uses a concept called contextual interference. This occurs when the hurdler adjusts her effort to changing circumstances (e.g., hurdles that are closer together) to become neurologically aware of correct performance. This process aids in the overall learning of correct technique. By developing a quicker rhythm, the hurdler develops new motor patterns that are imprinted neurologically.

A useful concept in hurdle coaching is the fact that stride length and stride frequency are inversely proportional. Increasing one tends to decrease the other. When a hurdler gets too close to the hurdles because his steps are too long, increasing the frequency helps shorten his stride length and solve the problem. Lowering the frequency can also move the athlete closer to the hurdle.

400-Meter Hurdles

The 400-meter hurdles pose unique demands. Portions of the training program for this event resemble those of the 100- and 110-meter hurdles, whereas other parts resemble training for the 400 or 800 meters. Although speed endurance is critical in preparing the 400-meter hurdler, acceleration, absolute speed, and power should not be ignored. A good athlete who runs the 100- or 110-meter hurdles well will not have great difficulty mastering hurdle technique with 30- or 36-inch (76 or 91 cm) hurdles. The 400-meter hurdler will not have to raise his center of mass as high in negotiating the barrier. However, the concept of driving through the hurdle and running off the barrier remains the same. The lead- and trail-leg movements are mechanically similar to those used in high hurdle mechanics.

Although leading with the left leg on the curve is preferable, the 400-meter hurdler should be able to lead with either leg. When the stride pattern between the barriers results in an even number of strides, the opposite lead leg will come up at each subsequent hurdle. An inability to use the opposite lead leg in this situation will force a significant adjustment in rhythm (usually by chopping strides) to facilitate the correct takeoff position into the hurdle. Such rhythmic disruption seriously disrupts cyclic elastic rhythms and leads to early fatigue.

An odd number of strides between the hurdles maintains the same lead leg through the hurdles. Most male hurdlers use 13 or 15 strides, and most female hurdlers use 15 or 17 strides. Training runs over barriers at various distances develops confidence for running through the barriers. Placing the barriers at varying spaces is a good way to teach the hurdler to steer well before arriving at the hurdle and to maintain velocity.

Training runs over the first three hurdles cover 150 meters and are good acceleration training. Running over the first five hurdles (200 meters) is good for learning to control the pace for the first half of the race. Runs of 300 to 350 meters over barriers help the athlete develop lactate tolerance. Running the first 200 meters without hurdles at a controlled pace and then finishing the last 200 meters over hurdles helps the athlete expend the necessary effort while fighting fatigue.

The timing of splits (touchdown times between hurdles) helps the coach and the athlete diagnose race-pace problems. This information also is extremely valuable in assessing the efficiency of the overall race. Splits can tell the coach where fitness needs improvement.

It is useful to have this information from both practice runs and competition.

Drill Progressions for the Hurdle Events

In developing the skill of hurdling, it is important to follow a sequence that leads from good sprint mechanics and posture toward hurdle running. Coaches should emphasize the concept of sprinting over the hurdles, never jumping. Walking and skipping drills can be used to teach exaggerated steps over low barriers. Athletes must keep the action in a straight, forward direction and have a sense of sprinting through the barrier. Along with these actions, drills of repetitive motion of the lead leg going straight to the hurdle and trail-leg movements emphasize correct position. As the athlete begins to show proficiency with these skills, the challenge can be increased with higher obstacles in a gradual progression toward actual racing spacings.

Approach to the First Hurdle

Each step of the learning process should be mastered before moving to the next. When introducing the approach to the first hurdle, the coach should start with the teaching progression used with sprinters. Once the athlete can start from a crouch position, the focus should be on developing good drive phase mechanics. After establishing a consistent eight-step pattern, the hurdler should practice starting and running through a box such as a pizza box that is approximately 6 feet (183 cm) beyond the eighth step mark.

As the athlete develops skill, the box can be gradually moved out to the first hurdle mark. When appropriate, an actual hurdle is used. This is a good time to use the stick drill to train the proper step progression to the first hurdle. Finally, actual block starts are introduced.

Running Between Hurdles

Hurdle racing is very rhythmic, and it is crucial to mimic proper rhythms in training. After the athlete demonstrates skill in the start to the first hurdle, the coach can introduce running between hurdles by placing a pizza box about 6 feet (183 cm) beyond the eighth step mark. The athlete runs from the blocks to the first box, clears the box, and continues for three more steps. The coach then places another box 6 feet (183 cm) past that point. The athlete practices the start over the two boxes. The process continues with more boxes as the athlete is ready. The athlete works on developing the correct rhythm over the boxes until good hurdle technique is established.

Once the athlete is ready, he moves on to actual hurdles. The hurdles should be spaced about 1 or 2 feet (30 or 60 cm) closer than normal. Even advanced athletes benefit from closer hurdles during training because it helps to train race-speed rhythms. Hurdles that are 3 inches (7.6 cm) lower than normal can be helpful as well. The lower hurdle allows the athlete to focus on speed and avoid excessive hurdle contact.

For male hurdlers, placement of the hurdles on the women's hurdle marks will move them 2 feet (about 60 cm) closer than normal. For female hurdlers, the coach (or athlete) can step off a 2-foot-closer (60 cm) mark for the second hurdle and then a 4-foot-closer (about 120 cm) mark for the third hurdle, and so on.

Additional Drills for Hurdle Skill Development

The drills in this section help the athlete focus on technique. They allow the athlete to repetitively perform correct technical movements to enhance the kinesthetic feel of the correct action. The five-step approach teaches the athlete to achieve higher running velocities into the barrier. The wall drills can be executed daily both as a warm-up activity and as a rehearsal of the proper technical feel. The half hurdle drills allow the athlete to focus on a single aspect of hurdle action. They are also nice progressions for warming up prior to whole hurdling. The one-step drill emphasizes the need to sprint off the hurdle to have momentum for subsequent hurdles. The drills can be done to reinforce correct technique, as part of a warm-up, alternated with whole hurdle practice, or to isolate individual motor learning patterns.

FIVE-STEP HURDLING

Begin with the first hurdle at its normal position; then measure and mark the other hurdles 11.5 to 12 meters apart for men and 11 to 11.5 meters apart for women. This spacing allows five strides between hurdles and makes it easier to establish speed to the next hurdle, thus building the neural patterns for faster hurdling.

You can also alternate three-step and five-step patterns. Here are two examples that include eight-step start rhythms:

- 8 steps, 5 steps, 3 steps, 5 steps, 3 steps, 5 steps, 3 steps, 5 steps
- 8 steps, 3 steps, 5 steps, 3 steps, 3 steps, 5 steps, 3 steps, 3 steps

Another option is to set up a lane with all three-step hurdle spacing (for speed) and next to it a lane with all five-step spacing (for rhythm). First run the lane with five steps, and then follow it with a run with three steps.

LEAD-LEG WALL DRILL

Place a hurdle against a wall so that the crossbar lies flat against the wall. Stand 4 to 5 feet away (122 to 152 cm), facing the hurdle. Lean forward from the ankle and lift the knee of the lead leg forward as if to take off into the hurdle. The foreleg extends so the sole of the foot moves above the crossbar and flat against the wall. The opposite forearm swings forward, leading with the elbow, to balance the motion. The head and chest continue forward to achieve a good layout position as in hurdling. The chest comes close to the thigh.

Now step back. Repeat this motion to improve flexibility and mobility. Balance the arm and leg action and lead with the knee. Execute multiple repetitions. This movement can be one element of a daily prehurdle warm-up.

TRAIL-LEG WALL DRILL

Set the hurdle to a height that allows you to lift the trail leg over an imaginary extension of the crossbar. Place the hurdle approximately 2 feet (about 60 cm) from a wall with the crossbar parallel to the wall. Stand to the side of the hurdle with the lead leg on the ground just past the hurdle crossbar. Reach forward with the hands, resting them on the wall. Lift the trail leg and bring it over an imaginary extension of the crossbar. The foot should be everted. Recover the trail knee toward the armpit, and keep the heel of the foot as tight to the leg and hip as possible. After passing over the crossbar, the foot drops to the ground. The leg moves to the rear of the hurdle and repeats the action. This action simulates the actual trail-leg action during hurdling. The goal is to improve the ability of the hip joint to abduct and cycle as close to the body as possible.

HALF HURDLE RUNS

Set up hurdles for warm-ups at normal spacing and at normal height or lower. Run at the hurdles with the center of mass directed toward the right or left edge of the hurdle, depending on whether you are going to cross the hurdle with the lead leg or the trail leg.

Half Hurdle Lead-Leg Drill

This drill allows you to clear the lead leg with good technique without worrying about raising your body high enough to clear the hurdle. This action is a common part of a progressive warm-up routine for hurdlers. The height of the hurdle is determined by your readiness for the activity. Start as low as necessary and gradually raise the hurdle. The number of hurdles can vary, and the hurdles should be set five steps apart.

Run at the hurdle with normal lead-leg action and take it over the end of the hurdle. The trail leg passes to the side of the hurdle and does not go over the crossbar. Make the trail-leg action as normal as possible.

Half Hurdle Trail-Leg Drill

This drill is done just like the half hurdle lead-leg drill, except that you move to the other end of the hurdle. The height of the hurdle is determined by your readiness to run through the hurdle with the correct trail-leg mechanics. As you warm up, the hurdle can be raised.

In this drill, the trail leg, not the lead leg, clears the crossbar. The lead leg must lead just as if it were hurdling the hurdle to put the trail leg in the correct position to clear the hurdle. This is a great way to train the trail leg to be aggressive off the ground.

HURDLE SKIPOVER

This drill is done over a series of low hurdles. Hurdles are spaced 5 to 6 feet (152 to 183 cm) apart. This drill can be executed either over the whole hurdle or in the half hurdle style. Approach the hurdle head on.

Standing 4 to 5 feet (122 to 152 cm) in front of the hurdle, skip with the takeoff leg and lift the lead knee up, bringing the lead foot above the hurdle. The lead foot then steps down and over the bar. Simultaneously, the foot of the trail leg is lifted up and over. The foot of the lead leg lands first, followed by the foot of the trail leg. Once the foot of the trail leg lands, immediately skip again on the trail foot and step over the next hurdle with the same action. Continue through a series of 8 to 10 hurdles.

STEPOVER AND SPRINT

Execute this drill over a low hurdle. Stand and face the hurdle with a bent lead leg extending over the hurdle crossbar. Once ready, lean forward and step off the trail foot, landing with the lead leg on the front side of the hurdle. As the lead leg lands, recover the trail leg and immediately sprint 10 meters. The key to a successful action is to keep the trail leg bent and move as quickly as possible into the next sprint step. This is a good drill for training both a quick trail-leg recovery and an active landing off the hurdle.

ALTERNATE LEAD-LEG DRILL

This drill develops the ability to lead with either leg in the 400-meter hurdles. Set hurdles 1 foot (30 cm) farther apart than normal high hurdle spacing (the second hurdle will be 1 foot [30 cm] farther, the third hurdle will be 2 feet [60 cm] farther, and so on). Begin with six hurdles and add as needed. Make sure the hurdle height is low enough to comfortably negotiate it with the trail leg. Run at about three-quarter speed, taking four strides between hurdles. Alternate the lead leg after each hurdle.

Another method is to space the hurdles 6 meters apart to accommodate two strides between the hurdles with alternate lead legs.

ONE-STRIDE HURDLING

Place six to eight hurdles 4 meters apart. Use low hurdles at first and gradually increase hurdle height as skill develops. Rarely is this drill done above intermediate hurdle height.

Approach the first hurdle using a normal eight-stride approach. Hurdle with only one step between barriers. The first time you try this drill, you will experience the sense of slowing as you cover more hurdles.

Focus on accelerating off each hurdle. This drill emphasizes how the trail-leg action is tied to the lead-leg action. A dynamic trail-leg action off the ground sets up a quick recovery and active landing of the lead leg. This drill reinforces the concept of sprinting off the hurdle.

Microcycles for the Hurdles

The microcycles (weekly training plans) outlined in this section are examples of the progression of work from the beginning to the end. The first microcycle (figure 11.2) addresses training in the general preparation phase, the early stage of training. The emphasis is to prepare the body for the harder training that will follow. The primary purpose is to strengthen the skeleton, joints, tendons, ligaments, and muscles. The loads are progressively increased with lower-intensity work. The training addresses the whole body in general.

As the athlete transitions into the early competitive season, the specific preparation phase begins (figure 11.3). In this phase, workouts primarily address the biomotor abilities

Microcycle #	Dates:	Event group: Hurdles
Phase: General preparation	Comments: Focus on fitness, building acceleration to speed, technical development	
Sunday	Monday	Tuesday
Active rest	Dynamic warm-up Acceleration drills Technical work on starts to hurdle 1 Core work Hurdle strength Lift (core): Clean, squat, step-up, snatch Cool-down	Dynamic warm-up Hurdle drills Rhythm work over hurdles (adjust spacing) Plyometrics Medicine ball throws Lift: Peripheral lifts Cool-down
Wednesday	Thursday	Friday
Extended dynamic warm-up Sprint drills Hurdle strength Bodyweight strength circuit Core work Cool-down	Extended recovery day warm-up Acceleration drills Hurdle drills Speed intervals (see menu) Multithrow Lift (core): Clean, squat, step-up, snatch Extended cool-down	Extended dynamic warm-up Sprint drills Hurdle strength Lift: Peripheral lifts Core work Cool-down
Saturday	Intensity of load by day	Post-workout comments
Extensive warm-up Tempo run or tempo intervals Core Cool-down	(table below)	

	Su	M	Tu	W	Th	F	Sa
Hard			x		x		
Medium		x					x
Easy				x		x	
Rest	x						

FIGURE 11.2   Sample seven-day microcycle for the hurdles: general preparation phase of training.

that help athletes perform in the events. Some general fitness work continues, but the focus is on increasing work capacity for the demands of the sprints. Although there will be some small increases in the amount of work, the biggest increase will be in the intensity of training. This all points toward improving the ability to sprint faster and maintain the speed longer.

The final phase, called the competition phase (figure 11.4), addresses the athlete's objectives of achieving top performance in the major championship events at the conclusion of the season. In this phase, the volume of training loads is reduced and recovery receives a greater emphasis. The intensity remains high, but the reduced volume promotes recovery between training sessions.

Microcycle #	Dates:	Event group: Hurdles
Phase: Specific preparation	Comments: Increased loads, focus on further conditioning and technical development	
Sunday	**Monday**	**Tuesday**
Active rest	Dynamic warm-up Acceleration drills Technical work over multiple hurdles (adjust height and spacing) Core work Hurdle strength Lift (core): Clean, squat, step-up, snatch Cool-down	Dynamic warm-up Hurdle drills Half race distance hurdle runs Plyometrics Medicine ball throws Lift: Peripheral lifts Cool-down
Wednesday	**Thursday**	**Friday**
Extended dynamic warm-up Sprint drills Hurdle strength Bodyweight strength circuit Core work Cool-down	Extended recovery day warm-up Acceleration drills Hurdle drills (one-step low hurdles, blocks over 2 or 3 hurdles) Speed intervals (see menu) Multithrow Lift (core): Clean, squat, step-up, snatch Extended cool-down	Extended dynamic warm-up Sprint drills Hurdle strength Lift: Peripheral lifts Core work Cool-down
Saturday	**Intensity of load by day**	**Post-workout comments**
Extensive warm-up Extensive easy run Core Cool-down	(see table below)	

	Su	M	Tu	W	Th	F	Sa
Hard			x		x		
Medium		x				x	
Easy				x			x
Rest	x						

FIGURE 11.3 Sample seven-day microcycle for the hurdles: specific preparation phase of training.

Microcycle # Phase: Competitive	Dates: Comments: Focus on competition, technical refinement, race mimicry, fine tuning	Event group: Hurdles
Sunday	**Monday**	**Tuesday**
Active rest	Dynamic warm-up Acceleration drills Technical work over multiple hurdles (adjust theight and spacing) Core work Hurdle strength Lift (core): Clean, squat, step-up, snatch Cool-down	Dynamic warm-up Hurdle drills Speed endurance intervals (see menu) Plyometrics Medicine ball throws Lift: peripheral lifts Cool-down
Wednesday	**Thursday**	**Friday**

Extended dynamic warm-up
Sprint drills
Hurdle strength
Bodyweight strength circuit
Core work
Cool-down
	Extended recovery day warm-up
	Acceleration drills
	Hurdle drills (1 step low hurdle runs, blocks
	  over 2 or 3 hurdles)
	Speed intervals (see menu) or starts over
	  3 to 5 hurdles
	Multithrow
	Lift (core): Clean, squat, step-up, snatch
	Extended cool-down
		Race day warm-up
		Sprint drills
		Core work
		Cool-down

Saturday	**Intensity of load by day**	**Post-workout comments**
Race day warm-up Meet Race day cool-down	(see table below)	

	Su	M	Tu	W	Th	F	Sa
Hard			x		x		x
Medium		x					
Easy				x		x	
Rest	x						

FIGURE 11.4 Sample seven-day microcycle for the hurdles: competitive phase of training.

Conclusion

The hurdle events are a highly specialized form of sprinting, although the phases of hurdling are the same as those in flat sprint races—start, acceleration, maximal velocity, and deceleration. The process of negotiating barriers forces the hurdler to adopt precise step patterns between the hurdles to cover the distance with speed. The hurdler cannot open up the stride the way a flat sprinter can. Because the length between the hurdles is fixed, the hurdler must instead increase stride frequency. Clearing the hurdle while maintaining a high speed requires exceptional flexibility and maneuverability. The goal is to deviate from normal sprint action as little as possible. This requires repeating the correct movements to learn the sprint motor pattern. Although training addresses strength, flexibility, power, speed, and speed endurance, it must also address neurological development to help the athlete achieve the balance and rhythm of hurdle racing.

PART IV

Jumps

12

Coaching Jumping Events

Jeremy Fischer

Before examining the specific jumping events—the long jump and triple jump in the horizontal jumps and the high jump and pole vault in the vertical jumps—it's important to discuss some general concepts. This chapter covers basic rules, safety practices, and talent demands for the jumps, followed by an analysis of the events and the necessary skills. The chapter ends with some general training guidelines and drills to help all jumpers.

Rules of the Jumping Events

The coach should acquire a rulebook, be familiar with all pertinent rules, and educate athletes in this regard. High school, collegiate, USATF, and IAAF rules differ somewhat and are updated annually. A thorough knowledge and understanding of the rules provides a distinct competitive advantage. Chapters 13 and 14 provide more detail on the rules governing the horizontal jumps and vertical jumps, respectively.

Talent Demands for the Jumps

Speed, power, and jumping ability are the primary skills required for success in the jumping events. Taller athletes may have an advantage, but smaller athletes with these abilities also can succeed in the jumps. Because speed may be the greatest determinant of success in these events, it is unwise to use unsuccessful sprinters in the jumps. Any athlete who is a candidate to be successful in the sprints should be considered a potential jumper as well.

General Analysis of the Jumping Events

This section addresses the basic technical models used in the jumping events. The events are similar in some respects. For example, creating takeoff is important in all jumping events; however, the degree and execution of the takeoff varies. All jumping events also have an approach separated into three phases. In all jumps, it is important to create horizontal velocity. For each of these parameters, teaching models have been created so that the coach can instruct the athlete step by step.

Horizontal and Vertical Velocity in the Jumps

Horizontal and vertical velocity combine to generate takeoff angles in the jumps. Horizontal velocity is developed in the approach run and is crucial to loading the takeoff leg and contributing to the distance jumped in the horizontal jumps. The takeoff also produces vertical velocity, enabling greater projection in flight. However, there is a trade-off between horizontal and vertical forces. Increasing vertical velocity at takeoff normally results in a decrease in horizontal velocity. The jumps require different relative horizontal and vertical forces for optimal projection at takeoff. The high jump has the greatest vertical component, the long jump and pole vault are next, and the triple jump has the least.

Creating Vertical Lift

At takeoff, vertical velocity is achieved in two ways:

1. The body's center of mass can be lowered in the penultimate step to increase the extension of the takeoff leg. This lowering occurs in the long and high jumps and to some degree in the pole vault. In the triple jump, lowering the center of mass should be avoided because of the low takeoff angle desired in the hop phase of that event.

2. The takeoff foot can be planted in front of the body's center of mass at takeoff. This is advantageous in the high jump, but only minimally in the other jumps, in which the potential for a loss of horizontal velocity due to braking is great.

General Mechanics of Sprinting and the Approach

Because the approach run in the jumps resembles a sprint race in its simplest form, the jumper must be proficient in the skills of sprinting. The approach run is a progres-

sion from acceleration to maximal velocity. A thorough understanding of both acceleration and maximal-velocity mechanics is essential to learning the jumping events. Coaches and athletes should review the skills of sprinting in chapter 8.

Jump Approach

The jump approach serves three purposes:

1. Achieving desired velocity at takeoff
2. Achieving accuracy in the takeoff location
3. Achieving functional body position at takeoff to maximize force application and conserve horizontal velocity

In the jump approach, a volitional drive phase is used to quickly build velocity in a relatively short time. The jumper actively pushes as the acceleration phase unfolds. The middle portion of the approach is more nonvolitional; the athlete allows speed to develop by using stretch reflexes to drive the process. The last steps are a transition into takeoff, with the goal of achieving appropriate takeoff positions while conserving horizontal velocity.

Start

The start of the jump approach (figure 12.1) should be as simple as possible to ensure

© Human Kinetics

FIGURE 12.1 Start of the jump approach.

consistency. For this reason, crouch starts and rolling starts are recommended in the jumping events. Walk-in and nonstatic starts require many repetitions to achieve consistency.

Posture

During the approach, the jumper should demonstrate good posture at all times. Neutral pelvic tilt and proper alignment of the spine and head help the jumper achieve an appropriate takeoff position, optimal force application, and takeoff accuracy.

The head should be in a constant neutral position with respect to the spine. Moving the head indiscriminately can disrupt acceleration and negatively influence posture. Abruptly lifting the head or torso at the start of the approach run is a common error. The legs should push the body gradually and completely into a tall running position as the jumper approaches maximal velocity.

The pelvis should also be in a constant neutral position with respect to the spine. Good posture and proper acceleration mechanics help to keep the pelvis in this position. Anterior pelvic tilt, or a forward rotation of the pelvis, is a common error that disrupts the elastic sprint cycle and interferes with proper takeoff mechanics.

Large ranges of motion at the hip should be established and maintained during the approach run. A common error occurs when the jumper, in a hurry to build speed, increases frequency at the expense of range of motion and good posture. During the early stages of acceleration, the vertical component of the strides progressively pushes the body into a tall, upright running position. Later, when maximal velocity is reached, the vertical push helps conserve stride length and set up good takeoff mechanics. Significant vertical push-off should occur in each step when at maximal velocity.

The trunk angle should progressively and consistently change from a significant forward lean at the start of the approach to a near-upright position at the point of highest velocity. Although the angle of body lean does indeed change, the alignment of the head, spine, and pelvis should remain constant with respect to each other.

Length of the Jump Approach

Generally, the approach ranges from 14 to 20 strides in the long jump, triple jump, and pole vault, to 8 to 10 strides in the high jump (figure 12.2). The approach length depends on the strength, ability, and maturity of the athlete. Beginning athletes should use shorter approaches until they develop the necessary foundation and skills.

When the athlete is establishing the length of the approach, the number of steps used is more important than the actual distance of the approach run. Approaches may use an even or odd number of steps, depending on the athlete's preferred takeoff foot. However, the starting mechanics remain the same. Teaching an even number of steps is recommended to ease skill acquisition.

Phases of the Approach

All phases of the approach, especially the start, should be practiced for consistency. Often, in the early stages of learning, athletes benefit from developing the approach on the track rather than on the runway, to eliminate the distraction of the board, box, and pit. One or more check marks can help both coach and athlete correct inconsistencies in the approach. The athlete places a check mark where the run begins and may use a second four-step mark to ensure consistency in the back of the approach run. Most coaches place at least one additional covert check mark four to six steps from the end of the run, again to check for consistency in the approach run.

Most step variance issues at takeoff (fouling or coming up short of the takeoff mark) are a result of inconsistencies in the first four to six steps. The technical execution of the approach run greatly determines the effectiveness of the takeoff in all jumping events. Both coach and athlete should pay attention to developing proper acceleration, high-velocity mechanics, and good posture during the approach. Achieving optimal approach velocity and takeoff mark consistency requires significant repetition in training.

Frequency and stride length are inversely proportional; increasing one decreases the other.

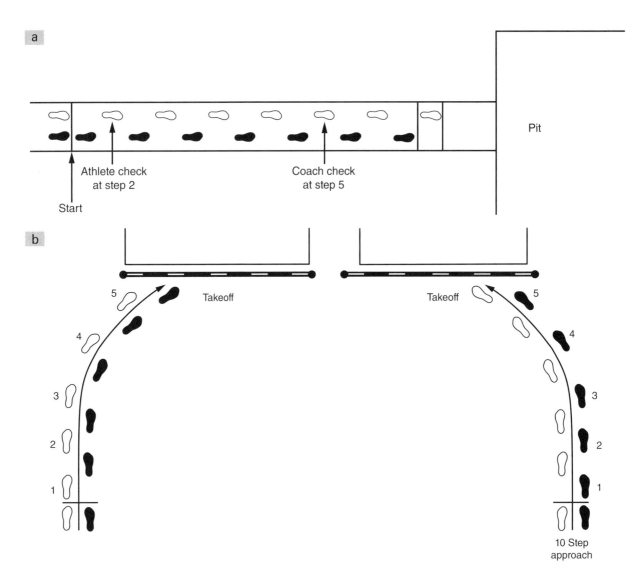

FIGURE 12.2 Approach steps for *(a)* the long jump, triple jump, and pole vault; and *(b)* the high jump.

This is an important concept for approach management. If frequency is too high at the start of the run, the athlete will fall short of the target or reach for the takeoff spot. The coach should not move the athlete's starting check mark indiscriminately. Errors in accuracy usually result from errors in execution, which most often occur in the first four steps.

Attaining high velocity is important to success in the horizontal jumps and pole vault, but speed should not be developed at the expense of good mechanics. Also, speed should not be so excessive that the jumper is out of control or unable to appropriately apply force at takeoff.

The five phases of the jump approach are the start, drive, high-velocity, preparation, and takeoff. These phases should blend into each other smoothly and without disruption.

The jump begins with the start. The simpler the start technique is, the more consistent the approach will be and the more accurate the takeoff will be. Starting from a standing position is recommended over a jog-in or walk-in start. The athlete should begin the approach with the same foot forward as would be forward in a block start.

The drive phase consists of the first six steps of the approach in the long jump, triple jump, and pole vault, and the first three to five steps in the high jump. This phase is volitional as the jumper is actively thinking "Push, push, push." It is a phase of pure acceleration, characterized by low frequency and high displacement. A functional drive phase helps the jumper overcome inertia and build momentum so that later phases can be performed easily and with correct posture.

The high-velocity phase is characterized by a transition from acceleration to maximal velocity and should occur gradually as velocity increases. The high-velocity phase is nonvolitional and is driven by stretch reflexes. An abrupt transition into this phase can lead to inaccuracy in the takeoff and form breakdown in the late stages of the run. Short ground contact times in this phase reflect a cyclic movement that is difficult to change mechanically. Therefore, a consistent and sound acceleration phase must precede it.

The preparation phase over the final four strides of the approach is a transition from approach mechanics to takeoff mechanics. In this phase the athlete demonstrates near-maximal-velocity sprint mechanics while maintaining a vertical body posture in preparation for takeoff. In the penultimate step, the athlete lowers the center of mass to create the vertical component needed at takeoff. Conserving both horizontal velocity and large ranges of motion at takeoff is necessary for optimal force application.

Takeoff posture is a key element for success in the jumps. Leaning forward or backward, dropping or throwing the head back, and sticking the butt out are all common errors in the final steps. An effective elastic takeoff is the result of a continuing large range of motion at the hips. Decreasing the range of motion at the hips in anticipation of the takeoff is a common error that results in both loss of elastic energy and braking. Conserving horizontal velocity is a primary goal as the athlete prepares for takeoff. The athlete must not compromise stride length while moving through these steps, because the displacement of the body after takeoff is proportional to the displacement occurring in the final strides. Deceleration should be minimized.

Foot strikes initially occur in front of the body in the drive phase of the approach. As the athlete accelerates and moves to a more upright position, foot strikes move under the body's center of mass. The takeoff step is a foot strike that is again in front of the body. This is a function of an active penultimate step and is what creates a catapult effect at takeoff (figure 12.3).

FIGURE 12.3   Catapult effect at takeoff.

Penultimate Step and Preparation to Jump

The penultimate step should be grounded under the body's center of mass to preserve horizontal velocity. The ankle should be stable in a dorsiflexed position prior to impact, and a heel-to-toe rolling action of the foot should occur on contact. While the penultimate step is grounded, the athlete slightly lowers the body by slightly flexing the penultimate leg. The lowering on the penultimate step should not produce deceleration or loss of posture, and it requires that the penultimate foot be active on landing. The body should move significantly past the penultimate foot before the foot leaves the ground. This helps to conserve velocity and set up an active knee drive at takeoff. This action also forces the takeoff foot into a position in front of the body, setting up a strong catapult action off the ground.

Takeoff

A good takeoff involves several factors that work in concert: body posture, the action of the takeoff leg, and the swinging movements of the other limbs. Takeoff foot placement depends on the jumping event. For the long jump, triple jump, and pole vault, foot placement slightly in front of the center of mass is ideal. For the high jump, which requires a higher level of vertical velocity, a foot placement well in front of the center of mass is ideal. The ankle should be stable in a dorsiflexed position prior to impact. Contact of the penultimate foot should resemble a heel-to-toe rolling action. There should be a very slight give in the joints of the takeoff leg to set up a stretch reflex. The takeoff leg should extend continually and completely during takeoff. A common problem with young jumpers is not fully firing the takeoff leg at takeoff. The jumper's body should displace forward and up as a result of both horizontal and vertical forces applied to the ground. Figure 12.4 shows the penultimate step for the long jump.

The takeoff leg action is accompanied by a powerful swinging motion of the free leg. It swings forward and upward through a full range of motion. The arms swing powerfully and progress through a large range of motion once the jumper is airborne.

General Teaching and Training Guidelines for the Jumps

Good advice for the coach is to never neglect safety considerations and always provide supervision. A safety check should be part of every day's setup time. The coach should monitor the event areas during practices to make sure equipment is in order and in place, and never leave athletes unsupervised.

The coach should address and demand good technique and efforts in everything done in training. All elements of the training program—running, multijumps, medicine ball work, multithrows, and even lifting— are opportunities to teach technical skills and movements that occur in the approach and takeoff actions. Specific information on strength and biomotor development can be found in chapter 7.

A useful concept in coaching the approach is that stride length and stride frequency are inversely proportional. Increasing one decreases the other, and vice versa. When a jumper is getting too close to the takeoff location because her steps are too long, increasing frequency (especially in the drive phase) will decrease stride length and solve the problem. Lowering frequency (especially in the drive phase) can lengthen the approach and put an athlete closer to the takeoff location.

Runway and approach work can be done without takeoffs or with modified takeoffs in all events. For example, long, high, and triple

FIGURE 12.4 The landing of the penultimate step for the long jump occurs with the knee over the ankle and the foot slightly in front of the center of mass.

jump approaches can be rehearsed with a modified takeoff and without the actual jump. Pole vault approaches can be performed on the track, with or without a sliding box.

The majority of technique work, especially in the horizontal jumps, should be done from runs shorter than those used in competition. This creates a better environment for learning skills, providing the opportunity for more repetitions in practice. The workout should be terminated when fatigue results in an inability to perform the skill technically well. The coach should break down movements into easily practiced and easily mastered parts in the early stages of learning, but also allow for rhythmic work that addresses the full rhythm of the event.

General Cyclic Drills for the Jumps

Skipping, hopping, bounding, and running drills are applicable for year-round use. These are especially good for early-season work when the training focus is on getting fit and building a foundation. Teaching these fundamental movements to beginners pays dividends later when jump-specific work is initiated.

Skipping Drills

Skipping involves a double contact on each foot before moving to the other leg to do the same. Skips are good exercises for warm-up and cool-down progressions and are typically done with repeats of 30 to 50 meters in length. This is a relatively low-demand activity.

LOW-LEVEL SKIPPING

Low-level skipping is remedial, with low heel recovery, and is done with a bouncy, elastic skip step. Be light on the feet and quick off the ground. Use short, quick arm actions with the elbows bent.

POWER SKIPPING

Power skipping is more dynamic and aggressive. Completely fire off the ground during the skip, fully extending the leg. Use long arms. The position during the nonsupport phase is like an extended lunge with big amplitude at the hip.

Hopping Drills

Hopping involves taking off and landing on the same foot. Athletes should learn hopping in place and then progress to hopping down the track or runway. This is a high-demand activity.

IN-PLACE HOPPING

In-place hopping is done with a large amplitude at the hip (big cycle). The heel recovers to the buttocks and cycles forward and down to the ground. Perform on each leg.

FORWARD HOPPING

Forward hopping is in-place hopping performed down the track. Perform on each leg. Use a big amplitude at the hip and a large range of motion. Strive for an elastic cycle and high heel recovery of the hopping foot. Learn to cycle the leg while standing in place; then move forward only when ready. Forward hop for 10 to 20 meters to start, increasing the length as strength and skill increase. Use arms actively in opposition of leg actions. The free-leg action actively counters the cyclic action of the support leg.

Bounding Drill

Bounding is a leaping-style running action that accentuates the knee drive and the extension motion. It requires a very aggressive ground force application. It is typically done for 20 to 40 meters, and can increase to nearly 100 meters for world-class athletes. This is a relatively high-demand activity.

BOUNDING

When bounding, aggressively drive into the ground. Use an aggressive arm action in opposition of the legs. Perform a full extension off the ground, creating a lunge position in the air (figure 12.5). Hold the knee up.

FIGURE 12.5   Bounding.

Running Drills

Running drills develop appropriate nervous system templates for sprinting. They emphasize fundamental technique and posture that allow for the elastic reflexes needed in sprinting.

Sprint drills are covered in chapter 8. These can be used in all phases of training, and are often part of the daily warm-up progression.

RUNNING OVER CONES OR BOXES

Use a three-stride rhythm between cones or boxes that are about 5 meters apart. This is a good rhythmic drill, and a good drill for learning the penultimate step.

ACCELERATION

Perform accelerations of 30 to 40 meters to achieve consistency in the drive phase and approach rhythm. Use long arms to counter long ground contact times. Keep the head in line with the trunk. Use a 45-degree trunk angle on the first step; then decrease the angle with each step so that the trunk is vertical by step 6. Step over the other knee. Let oscillation at the hip occur to maximize stretch reflexes. Use a large range of motion at the hip.

Conclusion

In the jumping events, coaches should teach the progressions of the approach, penultimate step, and takeoff. The most common theme for success in all jumping events is horizontal velocity. With increased speed, the athlete also increases the chances of injury if the body is not prepared for the extra forces created. Preparing the body technically and physiologically by slowly progressing through the teaching progressions and using correct technique in the drills is important. Maintaining postural integrity and the correct body alignment also helps the athlete achieve technical success.

13

Horizontal Jumps

Jeremy Fischer

This chapter addresses the rules and technical teaching models for the two horizontal jumps: the long jump and the triple jump. The discussions range from the run-up through the takeoff and include what happens in the air as well as the phases and landing. From beginning jumps of lower intensity to more advanced jumps of high intensity and high technical execution, the teaching progressions for each part of the jump are addressed separately and then put together.

Rules of the Horizontal Jumps

In the long jump and triple jump, each competitor has three attempts in the preliminary rounds. A predetermined number of competitors with the best marks move on to the finals, where they receive three more attempts. The jumper's best mark of the competition determines the place, regardless of whether it occurred in the preliminary or final rounds. In the case of a tie, the second-best jump of the tying competitors decides the higher place.

The jumper must take off from behind the scratch line, the edge of the takeoff board nearest the sandpit. Jumps are measured from the scratch line perpendicularly to the nearest impact point in the landing area. The long jumper must jump from one foot, and the triple jumper must use a right-right-left or left-left-right sequence before landing. Check marks are not allowed on the runway or in the pit, but an athlete may place markers along the side of the runway. Jumpers are allowed to pass on attempts for strategic purposes.

Safety in the Horizontal Jumps

Sandpits should meet minimal measurements as indicated in the appropriate rulebook. Pits should be free of debris, regularly spaded so the sand is loose, and watered periodically to keep the sand somewhat moist. The material surrounding the sandpit should be level with the runway and the ground around the pit. The sand must be kept at the level of the boards and runway.

The area around the pit and runway should be free of obstructions, including the area behind the pit so that athletes may run through safely. The takeoff board should be visible, stable, in good condition, and located at a reasonable distance from the sandpit.

Athletes should wear proper footwear and be properly instructed and supervised at all times.

Long Jump

This section addresses the segments of the long jump approach from acceleration to transition, maximal-velocity sprinting, the penultimate step, takeoff, flight, and landing. It also provides teaching progressions and drills to help jumpers acquire the proper technique and approach for success.

Approach

The long jump approach is a smooth, consistent acceleration to near-maximal velocity. Minimal disruption to the sprint cycle should occur late in the approach as the athlete prepares to take off. A common error of jumpers is making significant changes in the final few steps in anticipation of takeoff. Such changes disrupt the elastic cycle, compromise horizontal velocity, and inhibit proper takeoff positions. Jumpers have an inherent steering ability that allows them to adjust steps late in the approach to hit the takeoff board. They should practice the approach for consistency so that late adjustments are not needed. Significant repetition gives athletes both consistency and confidence in the approach run.

As a visual cue, the jumper can look at the board early in the approach, but he should adjust his visual focus to a point just beyond the pit when nearing the takeoff. Check marks used by both coach and jumper aid in ensuring consistency in the approach. Besides the obvious starting mark, the athlete may use a second mark four steps into the approach as an indicator of consistency. Because most step problems at the board are due to inconsistency in the first four steps, this is a very useful mark. A covert check mark four to six steps before the board permits the coach to gauge approach

FIGURE 13.1   Long jump penultimate step and takeoff.

accuracy while eliminating the distraction of adjustments occurring in the last four steps.

The long jumper's penultimate step should prepare the body for takeoff by lowering its center of mass with minimal deceleration (figure 13.1). The body should move well past the grounded penultimate foot, setting up a strong swing of the free leg. Maintaining an elastic cycle through the last four steps is crucial to minimizing deceleration.

The coach should help the athlete find the optimal approach length for her strength and ability level. The approach run should be lengthened only as the athlete's strength allows. The coach can observe the athlete from multiple angles to watch for changes in body lean, arm action, and posture. The approach rhythm must be smooth and progressive without obvious breaks in the phases. The jumper needs to be upright and without forward pelvic tilt at the penultimate step. A neutral pelvic angle must be set at the start of the approach.

Maintaining horizontal velocity is crucial through the last two steps. The jumper must be active on both of the last two foot strikes. Floating through the penultimate step causes

deceleration and negatively affects elastic energy maintenance in the last two steps. The ankle of the penultimate foot must be braced and ready for impact. As the body moves over the penultimate foot, the foot bridges at the ball of the foot. The ankle itself is braced to stay at 90 degrees. The penultimate foot does not fully extend out the back.

Takeoff Mechanics

The takeoff foot should be slightly in front of the body as it contacts the board. Placing it too far in front is a common error as the jumper attempts to gain too large a vertical component, decreasing crucial horizontal velocity. Because horizontal velocity is far more important than vertical velocity at takeoff, the jumper should make every effort to maintain velocity through an active and complete firing of the takeoff leg. Incomplete extension or firing of the takeoff leg when on the board is a common error in the long jump. The extension from the board should project the jumper forward and up.

The rise associated with takeoff should not begin until the body is over the takeoff foot and extension of the takeoff leg occurs. A common mistake is beginning to rise too early, a function of incomplete firing while on the board. The arms perform a powerful, opposing swinging movement at takeoff. The action of the free leg is a function of its action in the penultimate step. If active through the penultimate step, the free leg will recover aggressively forward and up and aid in loading the takeoff leg.

The jumper must drive fully off the takeoff foot and not rush the action on the board. The free foot is recovered high to the hip to speed its recovery. The thigh on the free-leg side continues forward and up until it is parallel to the ground.

Table 13.1 summarizes some common errors and corrections for the long jump.

TABLE 13.1   Common Errors and Corrections for Long Jump

Fault	Reasons	Corrections
Decelerating into takeoff	• Too long of an approach • Accelerating too quickly • Braking to create too much of a vertical component at takeoff	• Shorten the approach or work on approach distribution. • Correct and drill penultimate mechanics to conserve horizontal velocity into the takeoff step.
Forward lean at takeoff	• Too short of an approach • Still accelerating • Looking down at the board at takeoff	• Make sure the approach is long enough so you can be upright before the penultimate step. • Visually focus on a point just above the end of the pit.
Premature flight mechanics	• Being in a hurry to jump and not completing the takeoff step	• Perform short-run jumps. Focus on proper penultimate mechanics and a complete firing of the takeoff leg while on the board.
Overrotating while in the air and dropping the feet into the sand too early	• Inefficient penultimate mechanics • Being on the takeoff board too long • Not using long arm actions in flight to slow forward rotation	• Drill penultimate mechanics. • Make sure the approach length is appropriate for your strength. • Practice long arm rotations and reach while in flight. Begin by using a short box.

Flight

All jumpers exhibit a forward rotation of the body in flight. Once in flight, the jumper has two goals: to slow the forward rotation of the body and to place the body in the best position to land. On takeoff, the thigh of the free leg should be parallel to the ground. As the body leaves the ground and the athlete ascends to the peak of the flight parabola, the free leg straightens as the thigh drops under the center of mass, assisting in controlling rotation.

The torso remains upright throughout flight. This allows the athlete to time the landing and maintain an upright position later in the landing sequence. This has a direct effect on the leg position at the initial point of contact with the sand.

The major goal of flight is to minimize forward rotation. The long arm rotation for the hitch-kick technique and the high reach for the hang technique both slow forward rotation. The jumper must fold at the waist as late as possible to prepare to land. Practicing this off a low box provides increased air time.

The hang technique (figure 13.2) involves extending the arms and, to a lesser degree, the legs in flight to slow forward rotation.

The hitch-kick technique (figure 13.3) involves forward circular movements of the arms and legs in flight to slow forward rotation.

FIGURE 13.2   For the hang technique, the jumper lengthens the body in flight to slow forward rotation.

FIGURE 13.3   For the hitch-kick technique, the jumper uses circular movements of the arms and legs to slow forward rotation.

Landing

An effective landing (figure 13.4) enables the jumper to maximize distance at the end of the jump. The failure to attain a good landing posi- tion is normally the result of excessive forward rotation caused by poor takeoff mechanics. These problems can be addressed by drilling the approach and penultimate mechanics.

FIGURE 13.4   Long jump midflight to landing.

The athlete begins preparing for landing while near the peak of flight. The torso remains upright. The arms sweep down, fully extended from an overhead position. This continues until the hands are near the hips when landing occurs. The legs should be extended in front of the body. On impact, the hips and knees flex to allow forward movement to continue. The buttocks move toward the heels. As the buttocks approach the heels, the legs kick out in front of the jumper, allowing the buttocks to touch down in the hole made by the feet. The jumper needs to think about making a hole in the sand and following it with the hips.

Drill Progressions for the Long Jump

Following are practice goals for the long jumper:

- Developing maximal, controlled horizontal velocity into takeoff
- Creating the necessary vertical component at takeoff to achieve an optimal takeoff angle while minimizing loss of horizontal velocity
- Achieving flight mechanics that manage forward rotation and place the jumper.

Drills help the jumper develop approach, takeoff, flight, and landing skills. General drills can be implemented on a regular basis, even as part of a daily warm-up routine. Approach and takeoff mechanics are crucial to the flight and landing, so significant time should be spent developing and drilling these techniques. Nearly all of these drills encompass various loads of elastic (plyometric) training and must be carefully designed to ensure the necessary recovery.

General cyclic drills such as skipping, hopping, bounding, and running should be part of the long jumper's training plan. These drills are covered in chapter 12.

Approach Runs

The approach run is very much a cause-and-effect process. How the athlete accelerates out of the back has a direct impact on the high-velocity mechanics that follow. The high-velocity mechanics then directly affect the penultimate and takeoff mechanics. Long jumpers should spend ample time on each phase before progressing.

DRIVE PHASE REPEAT

Drive phase repeats are quality repeats of the first six steps of the approach. This drill should be used early in the training process and performed at least once per week. Most issues with inconsistency at takeoff happen in the first six steps. Place a six-step mark and do drive phase repeats to work on consistency in this phase.

Be sure the long arm action matches the long ground contact times at the start. Run with the head in line with the trunk; don't look down or up. Push hard during the run. The trunk angle should be 45 degrees at the first drive step. After becoming upright on the sixth step, step over the other knee. At maximal velocity, apply force into the ground like a piston. Sprinting at high velocity is not a clawing action.

DRIVE PHASE REPEAT WITH RESISTANCE

Set up a rope or bungee system and attach a belt around your waist. Perform drive phase repeats with the coach applying resistance through the rope or cable. Focus on a full extension of the leg during the push. Drive!

INS AND OUTS

Ins and outs are variations of runs with changing tempos, with some segments at high velocity. Ins and outs teach high-velocity relaxation and the ability to change speeds.

Segments can vary based on the goals of the session. Here is a sample session:

1. Acceleration: focus on excellent acceleration dynamics.
2. Maximal velocity.
3. Float: fast and elastic, but relaxed.
4. Maximal velocity: focus on the piston action of the leg into the ground.
5. Deceleration: decelerate slowly to protect the shins.

The distance of each segment can be adapted to your needs; for example:

- 30-20-30-20-30 meters
- 30-30-30-30-30 meters
- 30-20-30-40-30 meters

Penultimate Step Drills

When teaching athletes the penultimate step, coaches should ensure that they land with the knee over the ankle and the ankle braced for the landing. This is an active landing. The leg fully extends at the hip to get the takeoff foot ahead of the center of mass. An active penultimate step sets up a strong knee drive off the nonsupport leg at takeoff. It conserves horizontal velocity.

Long jumpers should drill the penultimate step often, if not daily. The run-run-bound drill can be part of the warm-up routine.

THREE-STEP RUN OVER HURDLES

This drill trains penultimate step lowering and extension at takeoff. Use 6- to 12-inch (around 15 to 30 cm) mini hurdles. Set hurdles to allow a three-step rhythm between them, about 5 meters apart. Use a right-left-right or left-right-left cadence with the second step as the penultimate step and the third step as the takeoff. Exaggerate high knees. As horizontal speed increases, lengthen the distance between the hurdles.

RUN-RUN-BOUND WITH ALTERNATING TAKEOFF LEG ON BOUNDS

Repeat run-run-bound over 40 to 50 meters. Use a right-left-right-penultimate jump sequence into a left-right-left penultimate jump sequence in a forward direction. Be sure the ankles stay dorsiflexed and the thigh of the free leg on the bound drives up to parallel with the ground. Do two or three repeats on the runway (12 contacts).

RUN-RUN-RUN-BOUND WITH SAME-LEG TAKEOFF FOR JUMP

Repeat run-run-run-bound over 40 to 50 meters. In this variation, take off on the bound with the same leg each time. Use a left-right-left-right-penultimate jump sequence or a right-left-right-left-penultimate jump sequence repetitively in a forward direction. Do several repeats on the runway.

LONG JUMP GROUCHOS

Grouchos are runs performed in a slight squat position (the center of mass is dropped 2 to 3 in., or 5 to 8 cm). Grouchos are best done with a broomstick across the shoulders. Perform 20- to 30-meter repeats, keeping the body's center of mass level and 2 to 3 inches (5 to 8 cm) lower than normal. Run fast, but without fully extending the foot at the back.

Takeoff Drills

Takeoff drills develop the skills the athlete needs to create a flight pattern after running up to the board. These drills teach not only proper body position, but also the kinematic sequencing of the leg to prepare for takeoff at high velocity.

STANDING LONG JUMP

The standing long jump teaches full extension of the legs at takeoff. Using both feet, jump from the edge of the pit into the sand. Land on both feet in a squat position. Jump and land again on both feet in a squat position, sweeping the arms from front to back as the heels push out and the buttocks slide into the foot-landing position. Finally, jump off both feet and land with the heels in the sand, sweeping the arms from front to back. As the heels make contact with the sand, bend the knees and bring the buttocks to the hole made by the feet.

LONG JUMP THREE-STEP HURDLE RUN

Use 6- to 12-inch (around 15 to 30 cm) mini hurdles placed about 5 meters apart. Run with high knees and jump over each hurdle. Use a sequence of one step, penultimate step, and takeoff.

LONG JUMP BOX DRILL

Perform takeoffs from a 2- to 4-inch (5 to 10 cm) plyometric box (figure 13.5). Run six to eight steps using a high-knee running style. Take off from the box to help increase vertical lift. Drive off the box, bringing the thigh of the free leg to parallel. The arms block to help transfer momentum. The arm opposite the free leg stops and creates a 90-degree angle between the biceps and forearm. Hold this position to learn patience when delaying the flight sequence and to counter forward rotation. Achieve full extension off the board and big amplitude at the hips off the box. Push all the way until the foot is off the box. A common problem with young jumpers is not fully firing the leg.

FIGURE 13.5   Long jump box drill.

LONG JUMP TAKEOFF WITHOUT BOX

Perform takeoffs without the plyometric box. Run six to eight steps using a high-knee running style. Take off, bringing the thigh of the free leg to parallel. The arms block to help transfer momentum. The arm opposite the free leg stops and creates a 90-degree angle between the biceps and forearm. Hold this position to learn patience when delaying the flight sequence and to counter forward rotation.

Flight Drills

Flight drills teach the athlete the flight sequence using either a hitch-kick or hang technique. Flight is considered the time spent off the ground before touching down into the sand. Teaching arm movement, leg movement, and the timing of each rotating sequence is important for each flight style. A 2- to 4-inch (5 to 10 cm) plyometric box can be used to increase air time.

ARM CYCLE

As you leave the board, your arm actions are crucial to create displacement and minimize forward rotation while in the air. The arm in opposition to the takeoff leg drives down and to the rear, extending at the elbow and then rotating over you while in flight. The arm opposite the free leg drives and blocks at the moment of takeoff, thus transferring momentum to the whole body. The arm actions are best trained when ample flight time is available. This is best accomplished by doing short run jumps off a 4- to 6-inch (10 to 15 cm) box. Again, the arm actions should reflect the leg actions; the two must work in concert to create a harmonious rhythm.

LUNGES INTO SAND

This drill emphasizes the lunge position necessary at the moment just after takeoff. Drive off the takeoff with full extension off the board, driving the lead knee forward and up to a point at which the thigh is parallel to the ground (figure 13.6a). Hold that split position (figure 13.6b) and land in the sand in the lunge position (figure 13.6c). The keys to this drill are a tall and vertical upper body at takeoff and fully firing the takeoff leg off the board. The arms mimic the split of the legs, rotating powerfully at the shoulder joints.

FIGURE 13.6 Lunges into sand: *(a)* takeoff; *(b)* mid-flight; *(c)* landing.

DOUBLE LUNGE

This drill, a progression of the lunge drill, is helpful when learning the hitch-kick technique. First master the lunge into sand drill before progressing to the double lunge drill. Because this drill requires more air time, use a short box for takeoff. Drive off the board into a single lunge position; then cycle through to a lunge position so the lead leg from takeoff ends up being the rear leg on landing. Do not hurry into the initial lunge position off takeoff; doing so will compromise displacement.

Landing Drills

When performing landing drills for the long jump, the athlete should use her normal flight technique, hang or hitch kick. The landing sequence begins with the heels leading into the sand, followed by an accordion-like action of the legs with the buttocks following into the hole made by the heels. Landing drills can occur from a standing long jump position and can progress to short-run jumps, both with a short box and without.

ACCORDION DRILL

Make a hole in the sandpit with your feet. Jump into the sandpit from a static standing position, or use a modified short-approach jump from two to four steps. Drive through the hole. The hips and feet should go through the hole. Move the hands forward to keep the center of mass forward at landing. The landing begins with the heels leading into the sand, followed by an accordion-like action of the legs with the buttocks following into the hole made by the heels.

Microcycles for the Long Jump

The following microcycles (figures 13.7 to 13.9) demonstrate how to load the athlete in a progressive manner at different times of the training year. The total load on a given day is a function of both volume and intensity and thematically reflects the goal of that day, whether it be technical work, speed development, strength, fitness work, or restoration.

Microcycle #	Dates:	Event group: Long jump
Phase: General preparation	Comments:	
Sunday	Monday	Tuesday
Active rest	Warm-up Acceleration drills Basic long jump drive runs Acceleration sprint work Body balance drills Medicine ball work Weight room: General strength, Olympic lifts Cool-down Prehabilitation work	Warm-up Speed development drills Basic long jump takeoff drills Speed development work Hurdle mobility work Functional movement and body awareness drills Weight room: Static lifts Cool-down
Wednesday	Thursday	Friday
Abbreviated warm-up Balance drills Circuit training Core strength work Pool or bike work: Low intensity, medium volume	Warm-up Speed development drills Gymnastics or long jump flight awareness drills Maximum velocity mechanics work Medicine ball work Weight room: Mixed static and Olympic day Cool-down Prehabilitation work	Abbreviated warm-up Plyometric day Medicine ball drills Hurdle drills Cool-down Contrast bath cool/warm
Saturday	Intensity of load by day	Post-workout comments
Controlled runs or striders		

	Su	M	Tu	W	Th	F	Sa
Hard		x			x		
Medium			x			x	
Easy				x			x
Rest	x						

FIGURE 13.7 Sample seven-day microcycle for the long jump: general preparation phase of training.

Microcycle # Phase: Specific preparation	Dates: Comments:	Event group: Long jump
Sunday	**Monday**	**Tuesday**
Active rest	Warm-up Acceleration drills Long jump approach runs Acceleration sprint work: Block starts Body balance drills Medicine ball work Weight room: Olympic lifts Cool-down Prehabilitation work	Warm-up Speed development drills Long jump short approach jumps Speed development work Hurdle mobility work Functional movement and body awareness drills Weight room: Static lifts Cool-down
Wednesday	**Thursday**	**Friday**
Abbreviated warm-up Balance drills and yoga Circuit training Core strength and physioball work Pool or bike work: Low intensity, medium volume	Warm-up Speed development drills Long jump technique Maximum velocity work Medicine ball work Weight room: Mixed static and Olympic day Cool-down Prehabilitation work	Abbreviated warm-up Tendon ligament strength work Medicine ball drills Hurdle drills Cool-down Contrast bath cool/warm
Saturday	**Intensity of load by day**	**Post-workout comments**
Warm-up Extensive temp work	(intensity table below)	

Intensity of load by day:

	Su	M	Tu	W	Th	F	Sa
Hard		x			x		
Medium			x			x	
Easy				x			x
Rest	x						

FIGURE 13.8 Sample seven-day microcycle for the long jump: specific preparation phase of training.

Microcycle # Phase: Competitive phase	Dates: Comments:	Event group: Long jump
Sunday	Monday	Tuesday

Active rest	Warm-up
	Acceleration drills
	Long jump approach runs and modified
	  takeoffs
	Acceleration sprint work: Block starts
	Body balance drills
	Medicine ball work
	Weight room: Olympic lifts
	Cool-down
	Prehabilitation work
		Warm-up
		Speed development drills
		Long jump short approach jumps
		Speed development work
		Hurdle mobility work
		Functional movement and body awareness
		  drills
		Weight room: Static lifts
		Cool-down

Wednesday	Thursday	Friday
Abbreviated warm-up Balance drills and yoga Circuit training Core strength work and physioball work	Warm-up Speed development drills Long jump technique Maximum velocity work and multijumps Medicine ball work Weight room: Mixed static and Olympic day Cool-down Prehabilitation work	Pre-meet warm-up Shake out Rhythm runs Modified takeoffs Accelerations
Saturday	Intensity of load by day	Post-workout comments
Meet day	(table below)	

	Su	M	Tu	W	Th	F	Sa
Hard		x			x		x
Medium			x				
Easy				x		x	
Rest	x						

FIGURE 13.9 Sample seven-day microcycle for the long jump: competitive phase of training.

Triple Jump

The triple jump is composed of an approach followed by a takeoff to a hop, step, and jump. The sequence of the triple jump can be either left, left, right or right, right, left. The goal is to maintain speed through each of the phases. Much like a rock skipping on water, the movement in each phase needs to be low and fast.

Approach

The triple jump approach consists of the same smooth, consistent acceleration to the board used in the other jumping events. It is crucial that the athlete use proper acceleration mechanics and reach correct maximal velocity, because accuracy and correct body position at takeoff depend on these factors.

Triple jump approaches are frequently (but not always) shorter than long jump approaches because of the more complicated, high-demand nature of the event. Less-experienced jumpers should use a shorter approach until they increase in strength and technical competency. As in the long jump, the athlete makes stride length adjustments in the triple jump to hit the board. For this reason, the visual focus techniques and check mark systems used in coaching the long jump are used in this jump as well.

The coach should find the optimal approach length for the athlete's strength and ability level. The approach run should be lengthened only as the athlete's strength allows. The coach can observe from multiple angles to watch for changes in body lean, arm action, and posture. Teaching proper approach dynamics, such as body lean and arm action, is important. The approach rhythm must be smooth and progressive without obvious phases. To work on takeoff mark consistency, the athlete can tape a board on the track. The athlete needs to be upright and without forward pelvic tilt at the penultimate step, and must set a neutral pelvic angle at the start of the approach.

General Considerations for Preparation and Takeoff

As in all jumping events, conserving maximal-velocity mechanics in the final steps of the approach is crucial to ensuring a good body position at takeoff. One noted difference between the triple jump and other jumping events is that the triple jumper does not make radical mechanical changes on the penultimate step. Unlike the long jump and pole vault, the triple jump requires a lower takeoff angle (figure 13.10). Too high a takeoff angle off the

FIGURE 13.10 The takeoff position for the triple jump is at a lower angle.

board is perhaps the most common fault in the event and creates a domino effect of problems to follow.

The vertical push-off associated with maximal-velocity mechanics is especially important in the final steps of the triple jump approach. Young triple jumpers frequently overreach in the final step and take off at too high an angle, or they push more horizontally in the final steps in anticipation of a low takeoff angle. This can cause the feet to fall behind the jumper in these final steps, causing shorter phases, approach inaccuracy, and forward rotation.

In the final steps, a single- or double-arm action is used. Basically, a single-arm action is a continuation of cyclic sprinting mechanics. A double-arm action provides additional impulse off the ground but also disrupts the sprint cycle into takeoff; therefore, it must be practiced to minimize deceleration into takeoff.

Takeoff From the Board

The takeoff step should be grounded under the body's center of mass. No forward or backward trunk lean should occur at this point. The elastic cycle continues throughout the time the foot is on the board. Very little rise should occur. The body should displace so that it is well past the takeoff foot before the jumper leaves the ground, to an even greater extent than in the long jump. The nonsupport leg swings powerfully forward and upward. This helps to conserve pelvic alignment throughout takeoff and controls forward rotation in flight. Controlling forward rotation with each successive foot strike is a primary goal of the triple jumper. The body displacement and free-leg action set up proper techniques for the phases. Most problems in the phases can be traced to errors in preparation for takeoff.

The arms swing powerfully at takeoff. For the jumper to maintain balance and rhythm through each phase of the jump, the arm actions must match, in opposition, the leg actions. A single-arm technique at takeoff can help the jumper run more aggressively through the board, but it does not create the power of a double-arm technique. A double-arm action, on the other hand, can add impulse and provide stability and balance at takeoff, but at a loss of velocity and cyclic rhythm. Regardless of whether the jumper uses a single- or double-arm technique, the goal should be to minimize the loss of horizontal velocity through takeoff.

For takeoff, the athlete drives fully off the takeoff foot. He must not rush the action on the board. The triple jump takeoff has a lower angle than that of the long jump. A good cue is "Run off the board aggressively." The athlete should displace out, not up. The free leg must displace forward and up. A good cue for the athlete is "Lead with the thigh." The athlete must minimize lowering the center of mass through the penultimate step.

Table 13.2 summarizes some common errors and corrections for the triple jump.

General Considerations for the Phases

The hop, step, and jump phases of the triple jump share three key concepts: posture conservation, ground contact patterns, and swinging movements.

1. **Posture conservation.** Proper alignment of the core of the body is a primary factor in triple jump success. The alignments desired are similar to those required in sprinting. The head remains in neutral alignment with respect to the spine. The pelvis, although not rigid, should remain in neutral alignment as well. In addition, the athlete must be strong enough to keep the body in these

TABLE 13.2 Common Errors and Corrections for Triple Jump

Fault	Reasons	Corrections
Decelerating into takeoff	• Too long of an approach • Accelerating too quickly • Braking to create a vertical component at takeoff	• Shorten the approach, or work on approach distribution. • Correct and drill penultimate step mechanics to conserve horizontal velocity into the takeoff step.
Pronounced forward lean at takeoff	• Too short of an approach • Still accelerating, resulting in forward lean • Looking down at the board at takeoff	• Make sure the approach is long enough to permit you to be upright into the penultimate step. • Visually focus on a point just above the end of the pit.
Being too high during the flight of the hop phase, resulting in a short step phase	• Too much vertical component at takeoff • Not running off the takeoff step	• Drill running off the takeoff step. There is no penultimate setup as in the long jump.
Not maintaining horizontal velocity on the landing of each phase	• Being unprepared for the landing or using an active landing	• Drill an active cycle with large ranges of motion and aggressive landings for each phase. • Make sure the arm action is long and aggressive to match the leg action.
Overrotating on the jump and dropping the feet into the sand too early	• Forward rotation is common and typically increases with each phase.	• Make the body as long as possible in flight to slow forward rotation. • Drill with a step-step-jump into the pit. • Drill vertical posture during each phase.

alignments under the stress of impact. Forward lean, backward lean, and butt-out postures are frequent mistakes in all phases of the jump.

2. **Ground contact patterns.** The ground contact patterns throughout the phases of the triple jump are comparable. Ground contact occurs slightly in front of the body's center of mass to preserve horizontal velocity. Reaching forward at takeoff results in braking. The ankle is stable in a dorsiflexed position prior to impact. The jumper must be prepared and braced for the impact of each landing. A heel-to-toe, active rolling action of the foot should occur on ground contact. The active nature of the motion is due to good elastic cyclic mechanics that continue through each phase of the jump. There should be only minimal give (amortization) in the joints on landing to set up appropriate stretch reflex patterns. Because the time to apply force on each foot strike is limited, the jumper must be braced and ready for impact. The leg should extend continually and completely during each contact, something young jumpers who are in a hurry to complete the jump often struggle with. The jumper's body should continue to move forward while the foot is on the ground. Trying to grab or claw excessively at the ground is unwise. The active backward movement of the foot displayed by good triple jumpers just prior to impact is a natural result of reflexes and the continuation of good cyclic mechanics.

3. **Common swinging movements.** The swinging movements throughout the triple jump phases are similar. The free leg swings powerfully through a large range of motion. As the swing begins, the leg is somewhat straight, and so heel recovery is low. Overemphasizing knee lift in the free-leg swing is a common mistake. Proper swinging of the free leg produces force at takeoff and also conserves good pelvic posture and maximizes stretch reflexes. When the leg swings in a somewhat straight position, the pelvis moves forward with it, conserving good alignment through takeoff. Whether a single- or double-arm action is used, the arms swing powerfully and through a large range of motion. Arm swing is dynamic and from the shoulder joint.

Phases of the Triple Jump

The major goals of flight mechanics are to minimize forward rotation and prepare for the next foot contact. Foot contacts are flat-footed with a slight rolling from heel to toe. Long leg rotations minimize forward rotation and allow the foot to be planted appropriately for each landing. The blocking of the arms coordinates with the braking, support, and propulsion of each phase of the hop, step, and jump. Although the goal is to limit vertical forces at takeoff to conserve horizontal forces, each succeeding impact should have a greater vertical component.

Hop Phase

After the athlete leaves the board, the free leg straightens and falls back underneath the body as the athlete effectively takes a stride in the air. This helps control forward rotation. The recovery of the hop leg is relaxed and late. The foot is left behind as the body displaces beyond the board, and then allowed to naturally lift from the board and fall underneath the body as the leg prepares for impact. This is similar to a hurdler's displacement at takeoff and trail-leg action. Attempting to perform a butt-kicking technique, or jerking the foot off the board disrupts posture, causes deceleration at landing, and destroys the step phase. The hop phase (figure 13.11) should be the lowest of the three phases. Excess height can increase instability on landing, disrupt rhythm, and contribute to a short step phase.

FIGURE 13.11   Triple jump hop phase.

Step Phase

A somewhat straight and low recovery of the swing leg as the takeoff into the step phase begins aids posture and balance. The nonsupport leg drives forward and up as the athlete lands to begin the step phase (figure 13.12). Driving the knee in the step phase cannot be overemphasized. Success in the step phase is determined by maintaining pelvic alignment, posture, and cyclic mechanics from the hop phase. The ability to maintain, or ride, the step phase is always determined by pelvic posture. Errors in the step can usually be attributed to issues that occurred in the hop phase.

FIGURE 13.12   Triple jump step phase.

Jump Phase

Forward rotation typically increases with each foot strike in the triple jump. Forward lean during takeoff is a common error that results in the feet dropping too early into the sand. To slow forward rotation, the athlete lengthens the body as much as possible during flight to create a long moment arm. Flight time restraints usually dictate using a hang technique, as described in the long jump discussion, during the jump phase (figure 13.13). In the hang technique, the athlete drives the thigh of the free leg to parallel. With the double-arm technique, the athlete blocks both arms, stop-

FIGURE 13.13   Triple jump jump phase.

ping them in front at eye level, while driving the free leg and pushing off from a single-leg stance. With the single-arm technique, the athlete blocks with the arm opposite the free leg while driving off the ground with the support leg. The athlete extends the hands over the head and uses the hang position at the apex of the jump parabola. During the fall from the parabola and into the pit, both arms sweep in from overhead to behind as the athlete enters the landing. This causes the chest to come forward in a jackknife position. Moments later, the heels touch the sand. The sweeping of the arms is followed by a bending of the knees to create an accordion-like effect of the body. The athlete's buttocks enter the sand in the hole created by the heels.

Landing

The landing is the final sequence in the jump process. The landing cannot add distance to the total jump, but faulty landing technique can decrease total distance.

In the landing, the upper body leans forward. Both feet are in front, similar to a pike position. The heels are the first part of the feet to enter the sand. The legs collapse and the butt follows into the hole the heels have made. The momentum created allows for the body to follow into the hole.

Drill Progressions for the Triple Jump

Following are the goals of the triple jumper:

- Develop maximal, controlled horizontal velocity into takeoff.
- Create the necessary vertical component at takeoff to achieve optimal takeoff angle and minimize the loss of horizontal velocity.
- Achieve flight mechanics that manage forward rotation and result in the best position for maintaining horizontal velocity through each phase.

- Maintain postural integrity and elastic cycling through the phases to limit the loss of horizontal momentum and minimize braking forces.
- Coordinate arm actions using either single- or double-arm blocking to provide balance and help in energy transfer.

The following drills develop approach, takeoff, phases, and landing skills. General drills can be implemented on a regular basis, even as part of a daily warm-up routine. Because approach and takeoff mechanics are crucial to the phases that follow, significant time should be spent developing and drilling both the approach and the takeoff. Almost all of these drills encompass various loads of elastic (plyometric) training and must be carefully designed to ensure the necessary recovery.

General cyclic drills such as skipping, hopping, bounding, and running should be part of the triple jumper's training plan. These drills are covered in chapter 12.

Approach Runs

Approach run drills teach athletes the distinct phases of the approach. Athletes need to be able to distinguish among the mechanics required to create a successful acceleration, the transition from acceleration to maximal-velocity sprint mechanics, and maximal sprint mechanics. This creates better body position and accuracy in the approach. See the drive phase repeat, drive phase repeat with resistance, and ins and outs drills in the long jump section.

Takeoff Drills

Takeoff drills for the triple jump employ a lower takeoff, which is more like a run off the ground or board. The lower trajectory is necessary to maintain horizontal velocity on each support landing sequence of the jump. In the triple jump, too high a takeoff can cause braking and a loss of speed at the finish of the hop phase.

STANDING TRIPLE JUMP

The standing triple jump teaches synchronization of the arms and legs while minimizing the large-impact forces that occur with the approach run. Use a double-leg takeoff, or hop, to a single-leg support step, into a single-leg support jump on the other leg. Finish with a hang landing. Use a sequence of both feet-right-left or both feet-left-right.

TRIPLE JUMP THREE-STEP HURDLE RUN

Use the same pattern as with the long jump three-step hurdle run but with a more horizontal and lower flight pattern. Use 6- to 12-inch (about 15 to 30 cm) mini hurdles placed about 5 meters apart. Run with high knees and jump over each hurdle. Use a sequence of one step, penultimate step, and takeoff.

FIRST PHASE RUNOFF DRILL

The motion in this drill is more horizontal. Run 4 to 18 steps and run off the board, simulating a takeoff but with only the hop phase of the triple jump. Use either a single-arm or double-arm takeoff. Minimize the loss of horizontal velocity and vertical forces for a lower takeoff angle. Focus on postural integrity. The thigh of the free leg should be parallel to the ground. Focus on horizontal hip displacement from toe-down at takeoff to toe-off from the board.

TRIPLE JUMP BOX DRILL

Place 2- to 4-inch (5 to 10 cm) plyometric boxes at your estimated takeoff, hop landing, and step landing distances. Land each single-leg support step on top of the box. Move horizontally; the box creates the vertical component. The key is to get the thigh of the free leg parallel to the ground during each midair sequence. Begin with a static start; then use two steps, and then four steps.

Focus on horizontal movement, full extension off the board, and big amplitude at the hips off the box. Push all the way until the foot is off the box. An incomplete push is a common problem with young jumpers.

TRIPLE JUMP TAKEOFF WITHOUT BOX

Perform triple jumps without boxes. The key is to get the thigh of the free leg parallel to the ground during each midair sequence. Begin with a static start; then use two steps, and then four steps.

Focus on horizontal movement, full extension off the board, and big amplitude at the hips. Push all the way off the feet.

Phase Drills

Phase drills teach each part of the hop, step, and jump sequence of the triple jump. They can be part drills or whole sequence drills. Each should start at a lower intensity and lower speed and increase in intensity and speed as the athlete masters it.

ARM BLOCK DRILL

Whether using a single- or double-arm technique, drive and block the arms in concert with the extension of the support leg during each phase. The drive and block action results in a transference of momentum from body parts (arms) to the whole body. The result is greater displacement and maintenance of horizontal momentum.

STEP-STEP-STEP INTO SAND

This drill involves three bounds with big amplitudes at the hips and active landings. The final bound is done into the sand, with a two-leg landing. This drill teaches big amplitude at the hip joints, and also landing skills.

HOP-JUMP INTO SAND

This drill is very good for teaching an active push off the hop landing. Use a short run of two to six steps, take off into a hop, and then jump off the hop and land in the sand. This is very good for learning an active landing on the hop. As you progress and build strength, lengthen the approach.

HOP-STEP INTO SAND

This drill teaches the rhythmic cycling of the legs. It is done just like the hop-jump into sand drill, but you land on a single leg (step) and run through the sand.

HOP-STEP-STEP INTO SAND

The emphases in this drill are a full push off the board and a big amplitude at the hips in both the hop and steps. Execute a proper hop phase; then move into a step, followed by another step into the sand, followed by a run out of the sand.

SHORT-RUN TRIPLE JUMP

This drill is done with a short run of two to eight steps. Focus on driving off the board, even-length phases, big hip amplitudes, and active landings for each ground contact.

Landing Drills

Landing drills for the triple jump should be done using a hang technique. The shorter distance created because of the three phases and loss of speed on each phase results in less air time. The landing begins with the heels leading into the sand, followed by an accordion-like action of the legs and the buttocks following into the hole made by the heels. See the accordion drill in the long jump section.

SHORT-RUN TRIPLE JUMP WITH JUMP OFF BOX

Take four to six steps into a triple jump with the jump phase off a short box (2 to 4 in., or 5 to 10 cm). This provides more air time for practicing landing preparation and technique.

Microcycles for the Triple Jump

The following microcycles (figures 13.14 to 13.16) demonstrate how to load the athlete in a progressive manner at different times of the training year. The total load on a given day is a function of both volume and intensity and thematically reflects the goal of that day, whether it be technical work, speed development, strength, fitness work, or restoration.

Microcycle # Phase: General preparation	Dates: Comments:	Event group: Triple jump
Sunday	**Monday**	**Tuesday**
Active rest	Warm-up Acceleration drills Basic triple jump drive runs Acceleration sprint work Body balance drills Medicine ball work Weight room: General strength, Olympic lifts Cool-down Prehabilitation work	Warm-up Speed development drills Basic triple jump takeoff drills Speed development work Hurdle mobility work Functional movement and body awareness drills Weight room: Static lifts Cool-down
Wednesday	**Thursday**	**Friday**
Abbreviated warm-up Balance drills Circuit training Core strength work Pool or bike work: Low intensity, medium volume	Warm-up Speed development drills Gymnastics or triple jump phase awareness drills Maximum velocity mechanics work Medicine ball work Weight room: Mixed static and Olympic day Cool-down Prehabilitation work	Abbreviated warm-up Plyometric day Medicine ball drills Hurdle drills Cool-down Contrast bath cool/warm
Saturday	**Intensity of load by day**	**Post-workout comments**
Controlled runs or striders	(table below)	

	Su	M	Tu	W	Th	F	Sa
Hard		x			x		
Medium			x			x	
Easy				x			x
Rest	x						

FIGURE 13.14 Sample seven-day microcycle for the triple jump: general preparation phase of training.

Microcycle # Phase: Specific preparation	Dates: Comments:	Event group: Triple jump
Sunday	Monday	Tuesday
Active rest	Warm-up Acceleration drills Triple jump approach runs Acceleration sprint work: Block starts Body balance drills Medicine ball work Weight room: Olympic lifts Cool-down Prehabilitation work	Warm-up Speed development drills Triple jump short approach jumps Speed development work Hurdle mobility work Functional movement and body awareness drills Weight room: Static lifts Cool-down
Wednesday	Thursday	Friday
Abbreviated warm-up Balance drills and yoga Circuit training Core strength work and physioball work Pool or bike work: Low intensity, medium volume	Warm-up Speed development drills Triple jump technique Maximum velocity work Medicine ball work Weight room: Mixed static and Olympic day Cool-down Prehabilitation work	Abbreviated warm-up Tendon ligament strength work Medicine ball drills Hurdle drills Cool-down Contrast bath cool/warm
Saturday	Intensity of load by day	Post-workout comments
Warm-up Extensive tempo work	(see table below)	

	Su	M	Tu	W	Th	F	Sa
Hard		x			x		
Medium			x			x	
Easy				x			x
Rest	x						

FIGURE 13.15 Sample seven-day microcycle for the triple jump: specific preparation phase of training.

Microcycle # Phase: Competitive	Dates: Comments:	Event group: Triple jump
Sunday	Monday	Tuesday
Active rest	Warm-up Acceleration drills Triple jump approach runs, modified takeoffs Acceleration sprint work: Block starts Body balance drills Medicine ball work Weight room: Olympic lifts Cool-down Prehabilitation work	Warm-up Speed development drills Triple jump short approach jumps Speed development work Hurdle mobility work Functional movement and body awareness drills Weight room: Static lifts Cool-down
Wednesday	Thursday	Friday
Abbreviated warm-up Balance drills and yoga Circuit training Core strength work and physioball work	Warm-up Speed development drills Triple jump technique Maximum velocity work and multijumps Medicine ball work Weight room: Mixed static and Olympic day Cool-down Prehabilitation work	Pre-meet warm-up Shake out Rhythm runs Modified takeoffs Accelerations
Saturday	Intensity of load by day	Post-workout comments
Meet day	(see table below)	

	Su	M	Tu	W	Th	F	Sa
Hard		x			x		x
Medium			x				
Easy				x		x	
Rest	x						

FIGURE 13.16   Sample seven-day microcycle for the triple jump: competitive phase of training.

Conclusion

In the horizontal jumps, speed and body position are very important. The acceleration phase must be performed with consistent technical execution. The jumper transitions from a functional acceleration mechanic to a controlled maximal-velocity sprint mechanic into takeoff. Maintaining good posture and horizontal momentum is crucial. Accuracy and consistency in the approach and takeoff are the goals and must be reflected in training.

14

Vertical Jumps

Jeremy Fischer

This chapter addresses the rules, technical models, and teaching progressions for the two vertical jumps: the high jump and the pole vault. Although similar to the horizontal jumps, the vertical jumps have distinct characteristics. The high jump has curvilinear components and speeds that are much less than those seen in the horizontal jumps. It also has much greater vertical forces and different takeoff techniques. The pole vault has similar approach and takeoff components but the use of a pole at takeoff results in technical demands not seen in the other events.

Basic Rules for the Vertical Jumps

In the high jump and pole vault, officials establish a progression of heights. Competitors may begin at any of these heights and, if needed, receive up to three attempts at each height. When all competitors have either passed the height, cleared the bar, or completed their trials, the bar is raised and the process repeats. Jumpers are allowed to pass on attempts for strategic purposes. Three consecutive failures at one or more heights eliminates a competitor from the competition. The last competitor eliminated is the winner, the second to last eliminated finishes second, and so on. The last height cleared is the first criterion used to decide final placing. If a tie results, tie-breaking procedures exist based on the number of failed attempts at the height at which the tie

occurred and in the entire competition. The coach should be familiar with these procedures and other rules, because strategy often comes into play when determining starting heights and when to pass on attempts. Vertical jumpers must take off from one foot.

Safety in the High Jump

As in all track and field events, safety should always be a priority. For the safety of the athletes, coaches and competition officials should ensure that landing pits meet the size requirements outlined in the appropriate rulebooks and that they are in good condition. The pads and the top cover should be properly and tightly fastened together. The position of the pit should be checked after each jump to make sure it has not moved, and the takeoff area should be swept clean. The standards should be properly spaced and located with respect to the pit. Finally, athletes should be properly instructed and supervised at all times and should wear proper footwear.

Safety in the Pole Vault

Pole vaulters should be properly instructed and supervised at all times. The landing pit and the front extensions that surround the box should meet the minimal size standards outlined in the appropriate rulebook. Larger is always better. The pads and the top cover should be properly and tightly fastened together. Coaches should consult the rules governing their competition level for exact dimensions and specifications on the landing area, which should be close to the box. The area between the box and the landing pit should be equipped with a padded collar that meets current ASTM standards. The pit should be kept in the proper position and should be adjusted if it moves.

Padding should cover the bases of the standards and any projections on the standards, and the bases of the standards should be adequately weighted or fixed to prevent toppling. The area surrounding the landing area should be free of obstacles and hazards; hard and unyielding surfaces and obstacles should be covered.

The angle of the back wall of the plant box is 105 degrees, and the sides are 120 degrees. The box is 8 inches (about 20 cm) deep at its lowest point.

Poles should be stored in a case to ensure that they are not damaged, stepped on, or spiked. Poles with nicks, scratches, and cuts should not be used, and poles should not be altered in any way. Athletes and coaches should not bend the poles in the box to loosen them up prior to use because doing so is dangerous and may damage them. Pole plugs should be in good condition, of proper size, and changed periodically to prevent damage to the pole. The pole may be taped where the athlete holds it to provide an adequate grip surface. The use of head protection should be considered. Finally, vaulting should not be attempted in poor weather conditions.

High Jump

This section outlines the technical demands and teaching progressions for the high jump. Because of the more curvilinear and three-dimensional aspect of this event, the teaching progressions and technical demands are very event specific. The approach, takeoff, and flight mechanics make the high jump different from all three of the other jumps.

Approach

The high jump approach is unique. It begins with a straight drive phase before progressing into a curve. This curved approach assists takeoff efficiency by creating additional forces (centripetal) at takeoff. On takeoff, this tangential force propels the jumper toward the crossbar, eliminating the need to jump at the bar.

Regardless of the length of the approach, the final five steps occur on the curve. Most high jumpers employ a two-check-mark system to ensure a consistent takeoff mark. The first check mark is placed at the start of the run. The second is placed on a line connecting the standards, usually 10 to 16 feet (around 3 to 5 m) out from the near standard. The line connecting the check marks is perpendicular to the crossbar. This second check mark ensures that the first part of the run is straight and perpendicular to the bar. Stronger, faster jumpers use a larger turn radius on the curve.

Coaches should use a triangulation system to guarantee that the approach is laid out properly, and that the angle formed between the line marking the straight part of the jumper's approach and the crossbar extended is constant. To use this system, the coach marks a right triangle, one leg of which is the line of the crossbar extended, another is the line marking the straight part of the jumper's approach, and the hypotenuse is the line from the starting check mark to the near standard (figure 14.1). Measurements can be established for any triangle once a 90-degree angle between the two legs is verified.

The transition from the straight to the curve should occur smoothly, without excessive decelerating, accelerating, cutting, or leaning forward. A unique element of running on the curve is that the body leans inward. This demands a slight change in arm movement. The arms should balance and counter the actions of the legs and should not be overemphasized. Each step should touch down on the curve, and the foot axis at touchdown should follow the curve. A common fault is stepping out while on the curve. The athlete should maintain hip oscillation through the turn.

Table 14.1 summarizes the common faults and corrections for the high jump.

Visual focus should be on the second check mark during the first few steps. Just prior to initiating the curve, the athlete should shift visual focus toward the near standard to gauge the takeoff point. In the middle of the curve, the athlete should shift visual focus to the intersection of the far standard and the

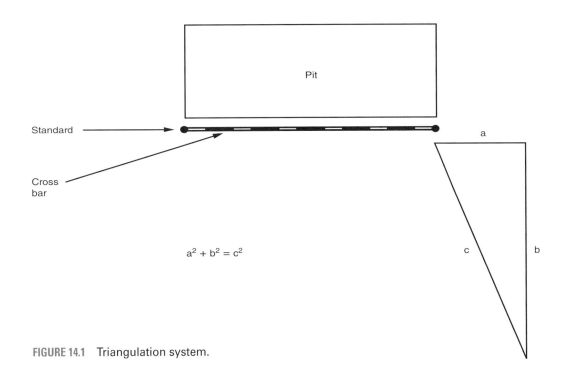

$a^2 + b^2 = c^2$

FIGURE 14.1   Triangulation system.

TABLE 14.1   **Common Errors and Corrections for High Jump**

Fault	Reasons	Corrections
Lack of consistency in the approach takeoff mark	• Inconsistent approach rhythm	• Drill the proper drive phase and approach rhythm. • Check the takeoff marks for consistency.
Jumping into the bar, not up	• Running too fast for one's strength level • Flawed mechanics on the penultimate step • Inability to achieve the appropriate position to apply force to direct the center of mass up	• Shorten the approach and work on proper penultimate mechanics. • Increase strength.
Dragging off the bar with the legs	• Lack of rotation around the bar caused by a lack of inward lean at takeoff, which inhibits rotation around the bar • Not tucking the chin to initiate folding at the waist and raising the legs over the bar	• Develop the approach run and turn radius to create an inward lean. This creates the needed rotation around the bar. • Practice clearance from a standing position. Work on tucking the chin to raise the feet over the bar.
Not rotating longitudinally to face away from the bar during the jump	• Not creating angular velocity around the longitudinal axis of the body at takeoff	• Drive the free knee across the body while on the takeoff foot. This initiates the longitudinal rotation that occurs after takeoff.

crossbar. This provides a target from which to gauge inward lean and provides information about crossbar location.

The coach needs to find the optimal approach length for the athlete's strength and ability level and lengthen the approach run only as the athlete's strength allows. Observing the approach from multiple angles can help the coach note any change in body lean, arm action, and posture. All high jumpers should learn proper approach dynamics including body lean and arm action. The approach rhythm needs to be smooth and progressive without obvious phases. Chalk can be used to draw the approach run on the approach surface so both the coach and the athlete can see whether the feet are following the line through each step into the takeoff.

Preparation for Takeoff

The high jumper's penultimate step prepares the body for takeoff by lowering the center of mass. An active penultimate step is crucial to avoid deceleration onto the takeoff foot and to conserve elastic reflexes in the cycle. The body should move well past the penultimate foot when it is grounded. This action sets up a strong swing of the free leg. Because of the rotational aspects of the curved approach, maintaining postural integrity and good curve-running mechanics is important in relation to the penultimate step. Most errors in body position occur in preparation for takeoff in the penultimate step.

Athletes should drill the penultimate step often, if not daily. These drills can be part of the warm-up routine with the run-run-run-jump drill. The jumper should focus on maintaining horizontal velocity through the last two steps and be active on both of the last two foot impacts. Floating through the penultimate step causes deceleration and negatively affects elastic energy development in the last two steps. The ankle must be braced and ready for impact on the penultimate step. As the body moves over the foot, the foot bridges at the ball. The ankle is braced at 90 degrees. The penultimate foot does not fully extend out the back. The high jumper must maintain the penultimate step in line with the curve-running foot's contact alignment.

Takeoff

The high jump takeoff (figure 14.2) accomplishes two goals: (1) it creates vertical lift and (2) it sets up the rotations that turn the jumper's back to the bar and then rotates the jumper around the bar.

The takeoff foot is directed toward the crossbar so that it points behind the far standard. The takeoff location varies with the jumper's ability level. Better jumpers take off farther from the plane of the crossbar and farther from the center of the crossbar than novice jumpers do.

The jumper exhibits a double lean at takeoff: leaning in, as a result of running the curve, and leaning slightly back because of an aggressive penultimate step that places the takeoff foot well in front of the body's center of mass. The forward placement of the takeoff foot and the corresponding backward lean create the catapult effect at takeoff. Tangential forces created by the double lean direct the jumper vertically. The combination of running on the curve and driving the free leg knee up and across the body during the takeoff step rotates the body longitudinally. The arms and free leg swing powerfully with great range of motion through the takeoff step. The free leg swings so the knee is up at the moment of takeoff. The knee stays up in flight. Dropping the free leg normally indicates a rotation problem, which often can be traced to poor mechanics over the last three steps of the approach.

The high jumper can use either a single- or double-arm action into the takeoff. Both techniques are used at the highest levels of the event. Although in theory, the double-arm action may provide greater transference of momentum at takeoff, it also disrupts the rhythm of the penultimate step. The coach and athlete should work in concert to determine which works better for the athlete. Whether a single- or double-arm action is used, the arms should swing powerfully to transfer momentum at takeoff.

At takeoff, the high jumper drives fully off the takeoff foot. The free foot is recovered high to the hip to speed its recovery. The free thigh drives to a parallel position and slightly across the body to aid rotation. The inside arm blocks

FIGURE 14.2   Good high jump takeoff mechanics.

to aid in the transfer of energy. The vertical positioning of the shoulders and spine creates a vertical takeoff position.

Flight Mechanics

The jumper's primary goal during flight is to accelerate rotation around the bar (figure 14.3). This rotation begins as a result of forces applied while the jumper is still on the ground. Once the jumper is in the air, the path of the center of mass is set, but the jumper can shorten the effective length of the body around the bar. The athlete lies back and extends the hips slightly into a slight arch. The knees should be flexed and apart in flight. Keeping the free leg up in flight is key to this.

In flight, the arms are returned to the sides so that the hands are near the hips. The jumper should take care not to overarch. Overarching tends to cause the feet to drop under the bar, often resulting in hitting the bar with the heels. In the final stages of flight, the head is lifted toward the chest to facilitate lifting the feet over the crossbar.

In flight, the athlete allows the body to lift and maintain vertical direction in the initial air

position. The drive knee should be maintained at a 90-degree angle as long as possible. The body gradually falls or drapes over the bar. The athlete should resist the urge to try to bend over the bar or to throw the head back to create arch.

Landing

At landing, the athlete tucks the chin into the chest and braces the backs of the shoulders for landing on the mat. Landing square on the shoulders and keeping the chin tucked protects the head and spine from the impact of landing on the mat. Athletes do this naturally because instinctually they want to protect the head and spine, like a falling cat. Coaches need to pay extra attention when athletes are landing on short mats or when they create excess rotation.

Drill Progressions for the High Jump

Following are the goals of the high jumper:

- Developing maximal, controlled vertical and horizontal velocity at takeoff

© Human Kinetics

FIGURE 14.3 High jumper in position over the bar.

- Creating the necessary vertical component at takeoff to achieve the optimal takeoff angle while minimizing a loss of horizontal velocity
- Achieving flight mechanics that create a somersault rotation and optimize a flight parabola over the bar

Drills for the high jumper develop the approach, takeoff, flight, and landing. General drills can be implemented on a regular basis, even as part of a daily warm-up routine. Approach and takeoff mechanics are crucial to the flight and landing, so significant time should be spent developing and drilling the approach and takeoff. Almost all of these drills provide various loads of elastic (plyometric)

training and must be carefully designed to ensure the necessary recovery.

Approach Runs

The high jump approach run is probably the most difficult of any of the approach runs used in jumping. The curvilinear aspect of the approach makes accuracy and measurement more difficult for the coach to check and the jumper to manage. A curve that is too deep can cause the athlete to jump down the bar and shallowly into the pit. A curve that is too shallow can cause ankle and foot injuries because of the torque created at takeoff. Finding the adequate depth, speed, and tempo is critical to success in the high jump.

HIGH JUMP DRIVE PHASE REPEATS

Drive phase repeats are quality repeats of the first six steps of the approach. This drill should be used early in the training process and performed at least once per week. Most issues with inconsistency at takeoff happen in the first five steps. Place a five-step mark and do drive phase repeats to work on consistency in this phase.

Be sure the long arm action matches the long ground contact times at the start. Run with the head in line with the trunk; don't look down or up. Push hard during the run. The trunk angle should be 45 degrees at the first drive step. After becoming upright on the sixth step, step over the other knee. At maximal velocity, apply force into the ground like a piston. Sprinting at high velocity is not a clawing action.

HIGH JUMP INS AND OUTS WITH CONES

High-velocity mechanics should be addressed at least once a week. Set cones at the starting mark, at 30 meters, and at 50 meters. Accelerate over the first 30 meters to the first cone. Remain upright and fully cyclic at the first cone. Focus on using a big range of motion at the hip and stepping over the other knee from 30 meters to 50 meters. The foot strike is a pistonlike action, not a clawing action. Slowly decelerate to a stop to minimize stress on the shins. Recover for two to three minutes between runs.

SERPENTINE RUN

Draw a line to designate a serpentine path. Run with the feet in line with the running line. Use good sprint mechanics. The radius of each turn is a reflection of velocity. The faster the run is, the wider the turn radius will be. Maintain shoulder position with an inward lean into the curve and neutral head, spine, and hip alignment.

CIRCLE AND OVAL RUN

Use cones to lay out a circle with a diameter of 30 to 50 feet (about 9 to 15 m) across. Circle runs are performed running with body lean into the curve and good maximal sprint mechanics. Run with the feet in line with the circle. Use good maximal sprint mechanics. Maintain shoulder position with an inward lean into the curve and neutral head, spine, and hip alignment.

Oval runs are a progression of the circle run. The oval runs provide a straight section that leads into the turn, just as an approach run does. The oval can use a 30- to 50-foot (about 9 to 15 m) radius, with a straight section of up to 75 feet (about 23 m).

RHYTHM RUN

Run the approach at 70 to 80 percent of full speed using the same rhythm as a full-speed approach.

Penultimate Step Drills

For the penultimate step, the athlete should land with the knee over the ankle and the ankle braced for the landing. This is called an active landing. The leg fully extends at the hip to get the takeoff foot ahead of the center of mass.

An active penultimate step sets up a strong knee drive off the nonsupport leg at takeoff. It also conserves horizontal velocity.

The long jump grouchos drill in chapter 13 may be used for the high jumper as well.

THREE-STEP RUN OVER TRAINING HURDLES

This drill trains penultimate step lowering and extension at takeoff. Use three to five hurdles that are 30 to 33 inches (about 76 to 84 cm) high. Set hurdles about 7 meters apart, enough to allow a three-step rhythm between hurdles. Concentrate on horizontal velocity while moving over each barrier using a left-right-left or right-left-right sequence between hurdles.

HIGH JUMP RUN-RUN-JUMP, ALTERNATING LEG

Repeat run-run-jump over 40 to 50 meters. Do two or three repeats on the runway. Finish with a last jump into the sand. The drill also can be done with a curvilinear pattern that leads into the high jump mat.

HIGH JUMP RUN-RUN-RUN-JUMP, SAME LEG

Repeat run-run-run-jump over 40 to 50 meters. Do two or three repeats on the runway. Finish with a last jump into the sand. The drill also can be done with a curvilinear pattern that leads into the high jump mat.

DAPENA DRILL

The Dapena drill works on the last two steps of the takeoff. It teaches both the penultimate step and the takeoff.

Using the penultimate foot as the base, align the body with an inward lean and inside shoulder lean into the curve. Drive the knee of the penultimate foot in line with the curve. As the body passes over the grounded penultimate foot, step forward with the takeoff leg. The heel of the free leg stays tight and drives up and across. The drill should mimic the last two steps used in the takeoff of a full high jump.

Takeoff Drills

Takeoff drills develop the takeoff mechanics required for the high jump. Because the high jump is a curvilinear event, some event-specific drills can help create the rotational values needed.

HIGH JUMP THREE-STEP HURDLE RUN

Place hurdles ab out 5 meters apart in a curvilinear (C) pattern. Use 6- to 12-inch (about 15 to 30 cm) mini hurdles. Run with high knees and jump over the hurdles, making sure to step with one step, a penultimate, and then take off.

SCISSOR DRILL

Using four to six steps, take off and scissor over a bar at submaximal height. Practice the vertical free-leg drive and the takeoff position. Land on your feet on top of the mat.

HURDLE DRILL

Jump over hurdles to create a more vertical takeoff. Place hurdles about 5 meters apart, either in a straight or curvilinear pattern. Hurdles should be high enough to force you to exhibit a penultimate step that increases the vertical component.

MINI HURDLE TAKEOFF DRILL

Place 6- to 12-inch (about 15 to 30 cm) hurdles about 5 meters apart. Run, run, and jump over each hurdle.

BACK-OVER DRILL

Perform takeoffs from a 2- to 4-inch (about 5 to 10 cm) plyometric box (figure 14.4). Begin with four steps; then take six, and then eight. Achieve full extension off the board and big amplitude at the hips off the box. Push all the way until the foot is off the box. A common problem with young jumpers is not fully firing or extending the takeoff leg. The drill also can be done without a box.

FIGURE 14.4   Back-over drill with box.

Flight Drills

Flight drills work on body position while in the air during the high jump. During a high jump, the athlete loses visual contact with the bar and experiences a moment of blind flight time. In the upward part of the trajectory, patience is key because the athlete wants to use the somersaulting action created at takeoff from the ground. At the peak of the jump, the body arcs so that the center of mass travels underneath the bar. After bar clearance, the body senses that it's falling. High jumpers need to adapt to the falling feeling, because their natural tendency is to protect themselves when they sense this. These drills work on all of these components. A 6- to 18-inch (about 15 to 46 cm) plyometric box can be used to increase air time.

STANDING BACK-OVER

Stand on both feet with your back to the bar. Jump and rotate over the bar. Arch the back. Just before landing on the mat, tuck the chin into the chest. Land on the back of the shoulders.

BACK-OVER WITH BOX

Do a standing back-over, but use a 6- to 18-inch (about 15 to 46 cm) box. This increases the falling feeling and teaches you to be patient in the layout position.

Bar Clearance Drills

Bar clearance drills focus on arching over the bar and executing a layout position with the small of the back directly on top of the bar. These drills help the athlete develop back arch and the subsequent drop of the center of mass underneath the bar, which can help with bar clearance.

BRIDGE

Lie on a mat. With the feet and shoulders on the mat, press the hips up. The shoulders stay on the mat. The small of the back is curved and off the mat with the feet planted flat.

Once you can perform the bridge on the shoulders, attempt a hand–foot bridge in which the hands and feet remain on the mat as you press the hips up and arch the back. The next progression is to bring the hands and feet together to create a jackknife position.

BACK LAYOUT

Jump backward onto a mat. Arch the back. Right before landing on the mat, tuck the chin into the chest. Land on the backs of the shoulders.

Microcycles for the High Jump

The following microcycles (figure 14.5 to 14.7) demonstrate how to load the athlete in a progressive manner at different times of the training year. The total load on a given day is a function of both volume and intensity and thematically reflects the goal of that day, whether it be technical work, speed development, strength, fitness work, or restoration.

Microcycle #	Dates:	Event group: High jump
Phase: General preparation	Comments:	
Sunday	Monday	Tuesday
Active rest	Warm-up Acceleration drills Basic high jump approach drills Acceleration sprint work Body balance drills Medicine ball work Weight room: General strength and Olympic lifts Cool-down Prehabilitation work	Warm-up Speed development drills Basic high jump takeoff drills Speed development work Hurdle mobility work Functional movement and body awareness drills Weight room: Static lifts Cool-down
Wednesday	Thursday	Friday
Abbreviated warm-up Balance drills Circuit training Core strength work Pool or bike work: Low intensity, medium volume	Warm-up Speed development drills Gymnastics or high jump flight awareness drills Maximum velocity mechanics work Medicine ball work Weight room: Mixed static and Olympic day Cool-down Prehabilitation work	Abbreviated warm-up Plyometric day Medicine ball drills Hurdle drills Cool-down Contrast bath cool/warm
Saturday	Intensity of load by day	Post-workout comments
Controlled runs or striders		

	Su	M	Tu	W	Th	F	Sa
Hard		x			x		
Medium			x			x	
Easy				x			x
Rest	x						

FIGURE 14.5   Sample seven-day microcycle for the high jump: general preparation phase of training.

| Microcycle # | Dates: | Event group: High jump |
| Phase: Specific preparation | Comments: | |

Sunday	Monday	Tuesday
Active rest	Warm-up Acceleration drills High jump approach drills Acceleration sprint work: Block starts Body balance drills Medicine ball work Weight room: Olympic lifts Cool-down Prehabilitation work	Warm-up Speed development drills High jump short approach drills Speed development work Hurdle mobility work Functional movement and body awareness drills Weight room: Static lifts Cool-down

Wednesday	Thursday	Friday
Abbreviated warm-up Balance drills and yoga Circuit training Core strength work and physioball work Pool or bike work: Low intensity, medium volume	Warm-up Speed development drills High jump technique Maximum velocity work Medicine ball work Weight room: Mixed static and Olympic day Cool-down Prehabilitation work	Abbreviated warm-up Tendon ligament strength work Medicine ball drills Hurdle drills Cool-down Contrast bath cool/warm

Saturday	Intensity of load by day	Post-workout comments
Warm-up Extensive tempo work	(see table below)	

	Su	M	Tu	W	Th	F	Sa
Hard		x			x		
Medium			x			x	
Easy				x			x
Rest	x						

FIGURE 14.6   Sample seven-day microcycle for the high jump: specific preparation phase of training.

Microcycle # Phase: Competitive	Dates: Comments:	Event group: High jump
Sunday	**Monday**	**Tuesday**
Active rest	Warm-up Acceleration drills High jump approach runs Acceleration sprint work: Block starts Body balance drills Medicine ball work Weight room: Olympic lifts Cool-down Prehabilitation work	Warm-up Speed development drills High jump short approach jumps Snake runs, curve runs Hurdle mobility work Functional movement and body awareness drills Weight room: Static lifts Cool-down
Wednesday	**Thursday**	**Friday**
Abbreviated warm-up Balance drills and yoga Circuit training Core strength work and physioball work Pool or bike work: Low intensity, medium volume	Warm-up Speed development drills High jump technique and multijumps Maximum velocity work: Circle runs, figure 8s Medicine ball work Weight room: Mixed static and Olympic day Cool-down Prehabilitation work	Abbreviated warm-up Approach runs Low bar jumps Accelerations
Saturday	**Intensity of load by day**	**Post-workout comments**
Meet day	*(see table below)*	

	Su	M	Tu	W	Th	F	Sa
Hard		x			x		x
Medium			x				
Easy				x		x	
Rest	x						

FIGURE 14.7   Sample seven-day microcycle for the high jump: competitive phase of training.

Pole Vault

The ultimate goal of pole vaulting is to clear the bar safely. Preliminary goals at takeoff ensure the best chance to reach the ultimate goal. The goals of vaulting high and safely go hand in hand.

The first goal is to move the pole to vertical. The vaulter must move the pole from its position at takeoff to a vertical position to facilitate clearance. This means that takeoff forces should be directed in a way that moves the pole, not just in a way that bends the pole.

The second goal is to create appropriate pole speed, which refers to the speed of movement as it rotates to a vertical position. Inadequate pole speed makes it difficult to get the pole to a vertical position, causing the vaulter to come up short of the bar. Excessive pole speed denies the vaulter adequate time to prepare for bar clearance and causes the vaulter to encounter the bar too quickly.

The final goal is to conserve horizontal velocity off the ground. This goal is consistent with the first two goals. Although the pole vault is a vertical jump, during the takeoff and the moments immediately following takeoff, the vaulter travels primarily horizontally. The conversion to a more vertical direction occurs later.

Special Considerations for the Pole Vault

Because of the unique nature of the pole vault, coaches need to understand special situations for teaching the vault and using vault equipment correctly.

Teaching Guidelines for the Pole Vault

From the earliest stages of teaching, the coach must help the vaulter understand that sufficient pole speed promotes success and safety. Early emphasis should be on the horizontal movements of the vaulter and pole. From the first day of jumping, athletes should focus on landing in the center of the pit and not on bending the pole. In fact, stiff-pole vaulting is a part of a good teaching progression that moves to bent-pole vaulting.

A safe, functional teaching progression emphasizes vault efficiency over excessively high handgrips, which can mask serious mechanical issues. The focus should be on mastery of the skill before high grips.

Standard Placement

Rules allow for the standards to be moved in a direction parallel to the runway. Normally, the standards are set at some distance behind the back edge of the box, as the vaulter attempts to achieve peak height directly over the bar. Adjustment often is needed as a result of environmental factors and pole characteristics. Coaches should consult the rules governing their competition levels for limitations on the movement of the standards during competition. The coach and athlete should aim to set the standards as far back as the rules allow. Keeping them closer to the rearmost position helps teach the vaulter to develop the horizontal characteristics at takeoff necessary for safety and success in the event.

Often, in competition, vaulters who achieve the peak of their flight in front of the crossbar instinctively react by moving the standards forward. However, this problem is caused by errors in the run, plant, or takeoff, or by using the wrong pole. Any of these factors will result in failure to maintain pole speed through takeoff. Moving the standards up causes the vaulter to disrupt horizontal movement even more, further compounding the problem. Moving the standards should never be used as compensation for a lack of penetration into the pit.

Pole Classification

Poles are classified according to pole length and body weight. Shorter poles enable developing vaulters to grip lower, and longer poles enable more advanced vaulters to grip higher. Moving to longer poles and higher grips should occur only after developing appropriate speed and skill. All poles are designed to be gripped 6 to 18 inches (about 15 to 46 cm) from the end.

Each pole is assigned a body weight rating that represents the maximal body weight for using that pole. A vaulter should not use a pole rated below his body weight. Poles with higher body weight ratings are stiffer. The stiffer the pole is, the higher the vault will be. However, a stiffer pole is harder to load, making penetration and technical efficiency more difficult to achieve. An athlete in competition should use the stiffest pole possible, but not so stiff that pole speed and penetration are sacrificed.

Variables Governing Pole Selection

The two major variables that govern pole choice are penetration into the pit and the amount of pole bend. Penetration is the distance achieved in the vault in the direction of the landing pit. It depends on grip height, pole speed, and pole movement. Pole bend is the amount of bend that occurs in the pole during the vault. The degree of pole bend is often misleading; it may or may not dictate pole choice. If technique is good, excessive pole bend dictates the need for a stiffer pole. However, technical problems such as stopping at takeoff, being under the bar, and having a low takeoff angle produce excessive pole bend. In these instances, penetration is normally poor.

Pole Selection Guidelines

The following five guidelines will help govern decisions about grip height, pole length, and pole stiffness. This information can help coaches maximize the progression of vaulters' technical development and keep them safe through the learning process.

1. If the athlete is getting poor penetration with a large pole bend, lower the grip.

2. If the athlete is getting poor penetration with a small pole bend, choose a softer pole that is still rated at or above the athlete's body weight.

3. If the athlete is getting excessive penetration with a large pole bend, choose a stiffer pole.

4. If the athlete is getting excessive penetration with a small pole bend, raise the grip.

5. If the athlete is landing to the left or right of center, regardless of pole bend, lower the grip.

Approach

The pole vault approach has many unique characteristics. Although the pole carry distinguishes the vault approach from other events, success in the vault approach depends on the fundamentals of acceleration and maximal-velocity mechanics found in other jump events.

The hands grip the pole slightly wider than shoulder-width apart (figure 14.8). The top hand is positioned within the assigned grip range of the pole. The hands are positioned so that when the pole is held overhead, both palms face inward.

In the pole carry, the top hand is slightly behind the hip. The bottom hand is near the center of the chest, with the wrist flexed so that the pole rests on the webbing between the thumb and first finger. Both hands are closed loosely around the pole.

The approach starts with the pole tip relatively high. During the first steps, the vaulter drives aggressively, building momentum quickly. Displacement produced by the vault-

FIGURE 14.8   Pole vault grip.

er's steps is directed along the axis of the pole, so that the pole is effectively being pushed down the runway.

After the first few steps of the approach, the pole tip drops progressively with each step. The vaulter uses the top (rear) hand to control the drop; the bottom (front) hand acts as a fulcrum. The pole tip should be at or below the height of the vaulter's forehead as the penultimate foot strikes the ground. Dropping the tip too early produces poor posture or forward lean, making it difficult to take off properly. Dropping the tip too late forces the vaulter to slow down and disrupts the rhythm of the plant action.

Most coaches use a check mark four to six steps from the takeoff at the start of the transition phase. This helps them gauge approach accuracy while eliminating the distraction of adjustments in the last six steps. The athlete's position with respect to this check mark is often more important than the position at takeoff.

Coaches must continually monitor the takeoff location to ensure consistency. Vaulters who take off too close to the box are said to be under, and those taking off too far away are said to be out. Consistency in takeoff position is best practiced through repetitions on the track. As with all jumping events, consistency over the first four to six steps is crucial to hitting a consistent takeoff mark. Most issues with takeoff marks are due to problems in the first four to six steps.

The coach and athlete need to find the optimal approach length for the athlete's strength and ability. The approach should be lengthened only as the athlete's strength allows. Observing the athlete from multiple angles can help the coach note any changes in body lean, arm action, and posture. All pole vaulters should learn proper approach dynamics such as body lean and arm action. The approach rhythm needs to be smooth and progressive without obvious phases. Taping down a box on the track can help the vaulter work on the approach rhythm.

The vaulter must be upright and without forward pelvic tilt at the penultimate step. A neutral pelvic angle must be set at the start of the approach.

Table 14.2 summarizes some common faults and corrections for pole vault.

Plant and Takeoff

Planting is a curl–press action (figure 14.9). The elbow of the top arm flexes, bringing the hand near the ear. In the press that follows, both arms are fully extended up. During the curl, the vaulter keeps the pole as close to the body as possible to prevent deceleration and postural problems. The hands move in the same upward and slightly forward direction to conserve pole speed. "Active hands" is a good cue.

The goal of the plant is to move the pole to vertical. Therefore, the pole should be as high as possible when it impacts the box. Prior to impact, the vaulter should be in a tall position, with the arms fully extended (figure 14.10). The takeoff foot should be directly under the top hand at takeoff.

TABLE 14.2   Common Errors and Corrections for Pole Vault

Fault	Reasons	Corrections
Decelerating into takeoff	• An approach that is too long • Accelerating too quickly	• Shorten the approach. • Work on approach distribution.
Inconsistent takeoff mark	• Ineffective approach rhythm and lack of harmony • Inconsistency in the first six steps	Drill the drive phase of the approach until the drive phase is consistent.
Late pole drop, causing late plant action	• Incorrect timing of the pole drop	• Train an earlier drop on the track into a taped box or towel.
Swinging too early	• Bent trail leg during the swing • Not bracing with the bottom arm, causing the hips to lead the shoulders during the swing • Not fully firing the takeoff leg to full extension	• Drill the swing so that trail leg is long throughout the swing. Sand vaults are good for this. • Learn to press both arms up and to lead with the chest at takeoff. This will cause the arms to be compressed backward, which is OK.
Lack of pole speed and penetration into the pit	• The grip is too high. • The pole is too stiff.	• Lower the grip. • Switch to a softer pole.

FIGURE 14.9 Curl–press action of the plant.

On the penultimate step, the vaulter lands with the knee over the ankle and the ankle braced for the landing. The foot landing progresses from the heel to a flat foot to the ball of the foot (rolling action). The top hand curls the pole from the hip to the ear. The bottom hand slightly rotates and stabilizes the pole. The penultimate step is an active landing. The leg fully extends at the hip to get the takeoff foot ahead of the center of mass. An active penultimate step sets up a strong knee drive off the nonsupport leg at takeoff. It also conserves horizontal velocity.

Vaulters should drill the penultimate step often, if not daily. These drills can be part of a warm-up routine with the run-run-run-jump drill. The coach should emphasize maintaining horizontal velocity through the last two steps. The vaulter must be active on both of the last two foot impacts. Floating through the penultimate step causes deceleration and negatively affects the elastic energy development in the last two steps. The penultimate ankle must be braced and ready for impact. As the body moves over the penultimate foot, that foot bridges at the ball. The ankle is braced at 90

FIGURE 14.10 Arms are high before the pole impacts the box.

degrees. The penultimate foot does not fully extend out the back. The vaulter should take a longer second-to-last step and a shorter, quicker last step.

At takeoff, the shoulders are parallel with the crossbar, the top arm is extended com-pletely up, and the bottom hand is in front of the opposite shoulder (figure 14.11). The top hand should not be outside of that shoulder. These points ensure travel toward the center of the pit and proper pole loading, and prevent turning about the pole.

FIGURE 14.11   Takeoff.

The takeoff angle in the pole vault resem-bles that of the long jump. As in the long jump, the penultimate step creates an increased vertical component at takeoff. The vaulter aggressively jumps off the ground forward and upward, ensuring effective loading of the pole. At impact and immediately after, the hor-izontal movement continues and rock-back is delayed. The shoulders and hips continue to move forward so that they are significantly past the top hand and takeoff foot at liftoff. Also, the vaulter attempts to remain vertical immediately after takeoff by keeping the body extended.

During takeoff, the vaulter must drive fully off the takeoff foot and not rush the action off the ground. The free foot is recovered high to the hip to speed its recovery. The vaulter moves the hands up throughout the takeoff phase and plants the pole with the top hand directly above the takeoff foot. A good cue is "Active hands" that push up, not forward and up. The vaulter jumps off the ground and maintains postural integrity and a tall upright position.

Immediately after impact, the shoulders and hips keep moving forward past the top hand and takeoff foot, demonstrating a symmetrical C or reverse C alignment, depending on the side from which the action is being viewed (figure 14.12). This sets up a powerful succeeding swing of the trailing leg. The takeoff leg and top arm remain extended during the swing phase. As the swing slows, the vaulter bends at the waist so that the shins come near the pole. Shortening the body lever speeds up rotational velocity. As the swing is completed, the hips are extended forcefully so that the body is extended and nearly in line with the pole.

Pole Recoil

As the pole recoils, the top arm rows across the body from the torso to the opposite hip. This arm movement creates a rotational action around the pole, turning the athlete.

The vaulter pushes the bottom hand against the pole to reduce the compressive forces needed to bend the pole and transfer energy into it. The vaulter must keep the arms as straight as possible to reduce braking forces. A good cue is "Active hands."

On the swing to inversion, the vaulter maintains a long extended body during the first half of the swing. This activates the stretch reflex of the hip flexors, trunk flexors, and shoulder extensors. The vaulter uses a dynamic swinging of the trail leg and an active dynamic rowing of the top hand to the opposite hip to achieve vertical pole and body alignment.

Clearance

Just before clearing the bar, the vaulter bends at the waist to set up a rotation over the bar and move the center of mass to a more favorable location with respect to the bar. In the final stages of clearance, after the pole is released, the vaulter lifts and rotates the elbows out to avoid contact with the bar (figure 14.13).

During the turn to bar clearance, the vaulter continues to swing and pull past the top of the pole. The top arm is close to the body, and the bottom hand is near the head. The vaulter's body rotates around the pole, moving from facing the runway to facing the bar. Completing the unbending of the pole aids in catapulting the vaulter up and away from the top of the pole.

FIGURE 14.12 The C position.

FIGURE 14.13   Pole vault bar clearance.

Landing

While falling from the height of the bar, the athlete should prepare to land on the square of the back. Young vaulters have a tendency to land on their feet; injuries from sprained ankles result from this landing tendency. The athlete should brace himself as he lands on his back (figure 14.14). The arms and legs need to be out away from the body so they are not caught under the athlete in the landing sequence. The neck and head should be slightly forward to prevent a whiplashing effect when the athlete crashes onto the mat.

FIGURE 14.14   Landing on the back.

Drill Progressions for the Pole Vault

Following are the goals of the pole vaulter:

- Developing maximal, controlled horizontal velocity into takeoff.
- Creating the necessary vertical component at takeoff to achieve an optimal takeoff angle while minimizing the loss of horizontal velocity.
- Achieving a high degree of vertical velocity so that energy is transferred into the pole, creating vertical lift and maximizing pole speed.

Drills for the pole vaulter develop the approach, takeoff, and flight. General drills can be implemented on a regular basis, even as part of a daily warm-up routine. Doing drills and runs with a pole or a modified pole (or stubby) can help create the sprint mechanics needed while carrying a pole. The approach and takeoff mechanics are crucial to the flight and bar clearance that follow, so significant time should be spent in developing and drilling both the approach and the takeoff. Almost all of these drills provide various loads of elastic (plyometric) training and must be carefully designed to ensure the necessary recovery.

Approach Runs

Specific forces are created in the pole vault event, such as the impact of the pole hitting the back of the box. Pole vault drills and teaching progressions are required for athlete success, health, and development. Developing accuracy, creating a sound technical model, and improving the strength needed to carry and plant the pole so that it can store the energy needed to move from horizontal to vertical are fundamental in protecting athletes and helping them achieve success.

Pole vaulters can also use the high jump ins and outs with cones drill.

POLE VAULT DRIVE PHASE REPEATS

Drive phase repeats are quality repeats of the first six steps of the approach. This drill should be used early in the training process and performed at least once per week. Most issues with inconsistency at takeoff happen in the first six steps. Place a six-step mark and do drive phase repeats to work on consistency in this phase.

Be sure the long arm action matches the long ground contact times at the start. Run with the head in line with the trunk; don't look down or up. Push hard during the run. The trunk angle should be 45 degrees at the first drive step. After becoming upright on the sixth step, step over the other knee. At maximal velocity, apply force into the ground like a piston. Sprinting at high velocity is not a clawing action.

POLE VAULT DRIVE PHASE REPEATS WITH RESISTANCE

Set up a rope or bungee system and attach a belt around your waist. Using a modified shortened pole or a regular pole, perform drive phase repeats with the coach applying resistance through the rope or cable. Focus on a full extension of the leg during the push. Drive!

APPROACHES ON THE TRACK

This drill involves approach mimicry on the track so you can learn approach dynamics without the concern of having to plant and take off. The purpose is to develop approach rhythm and pole drop timing. Place an approach mark on the track, and use a tape box or towel to designate the box. A four- or six-step visual mark at the back of the approach is highly recommended.

Penultimate Step Drills

These drills teach the progression required to develop vertical forces to create lift and the transfer of horizontal to vertical velocity. The lowering of the center of mass also aids in transferring energy into the pole.

The grouchos drill also can be used to teach the penultimate step to pole vaulters.

THREE-STEP RUN OVER HURDLES

This drill trains penultimate step lowering and extension at takeoff. Set hurdles to allow a three-step rhythm between them. Use a piece of a broken pole (stubby) about the length of a broom handle. Press the hands over the head when jumping over the hurdles.

POLE VAULT RUN-RUN-JUMP, ALTERNATING LEG

Repeat run-run-jump over 40 to 50 meters. Do two or three repeats on the runway. Finish with a last jump into the sand. Use the same pattern as that in the long jump drill. Using a stubby pole, repeat the drill with a modified pole vault takeoff. Press the hands over the head.

POLE VAULT RUN-RUN-RUN-JUMP, SAME LEG

Repeat run-run-run-jump over 40 to 50 meters. Do two or three repeats on the runway. Finish with a last jump into the sand. Use the same pattern as that in the long jump drill. Using a stubby pole, repeat the drill with a modified pole vault takeoff. Press the hands over the head.

POLE CURL DRILL

In a standing position, curl the pole from the hip to the ear to practice the timing of the pole drop and the preparation for takeoff. The goal is to keep the pole close to the body when curling it to the shoulder. Once you are comfortable with the curl action, add a walking approach that ends with a curl–press action.

Plant and Takeoff Drills

Like the other jumps, the pole vault employs a takeoff. Unlike in the other jumps, the athlete experiences impact forces at or slightly after takeoff from the pole hitting the back of the pole vault box. These drills teach the athlete the takeoff and body position needed when taking off with a pole and getting it to go from horizontal to vertical.

RUN-RUN-BOUND WITH A STUBBY POLE

Perform the run-run-bound drill as described in chapter 13. Then carry a stubby pole and perform the drill. While stepping into the penultimate step, the top hand curls from the hip to the ear. The bottom hand aids in dropping the pole and rotates 45 degrees. Going into the jump, press the pole overhead with the arms fully extended.

THREE-STEP HURDLE RUN

Holding a stubby pole, perform the run-run-bound over a small hurdle. Step into the penultimate step. The top hand curls from hip to ear. The bottom hand helps drop the pole and rotates 45 degrees. Press the pole overhead with the arms fully extended, and bound over the hurdle.

FOUR-STEP SAND DRILL

Place the top hand high on the pole. From a standing position, run four steps and plant the pole end into the sand of a long jump pit. Only the top hand stays on the pole. Keep the top arm straight and swing through the pendulum. Land on the takeoff foot in the sand and run out.

FOUR-STEP SINGLE-ARM TAKEOFF

Place the top hand high on the pole. From a standing position, run four steps and plant the pole end into the pole vault plant box. Only the top hand stays on the pole. Keep the top arm straight and swing through the pendulum, landing on the mat.

FULL-APPROACH SLIDE BOX DRILL

From a full approach, run and plant the pole into a modified plant box that slides. Jump into takeoff and press the hands over the head, arms fully extended.

Swing to Inversion Drills

These drills mimic the movement pattern needed to get the athlete inverted during the vault sequence. They help the athlete get comfortable with the feeling of inversion and strength when moving from vertical to horizontal to inverted.

BUBKAS ON A BAR

Grip a pull-up bar using an alternating grip (one hand is palm down, the other is palm up). Bend the legs so the thigh of the free leg is parallel to the ground and the takeoff leg is fully extended. Swing and pull yourself into an upside-down position so the hips are even with the hands. This position mimics the vertical upside-down position of the full vault.

FOUR-STEP HOUVIAN DRILL

Using the pole vault runway and mat, take four steps and plant the pole. Fully extend both arms. The pole does not bend. Use a rowing action to bring the top hand to the opposite hip, and ride the layout position onto the mat.

ROPE SWING

Grip a rope in the same hand positions used for vaulting, and jump onto the rope. As the rope swings, get into takeoff position. Use the swing of the takeoff leg to create momentum and invert the body. Hold this position for a count of three.

Push and Turn and Bar Clearance Drills

These drills mimic the body positioning and movements needed to replicate the push off the pole and the clearance over the bar. These are part drills but can provide a sense of the movements needed during this sequence of the vault.

BUNGEE ROW

Attach a bungee cord to the end of a stubby or modified pole. Place the hands in takeoff position. Row the top hand to the opposite hip. The bungee cord creates resistance.

SEATED ROW

Sit with the takeoff leg straight and the free leg bent. Hold a modified pole. Rock back onto the shoulders. Row the top hand to the opposite hip.

ROUNDOFF

Perform this drill on the grass. Take two steps and catapult onto the hands so that the feet rise straight into the air. Bring the feet together, push off the ground with the hands, and rotate over. As the body begins to right itself, hollow out the chest. End with the feet on the ground and the arms extended overhead about shoulder-width apart.

ROUNDOFF WITH BOX

Use a 4- to 12-inch (about 10 to 30 cm) box. Take two steps and catapult onto your hands. Place the bottom hand on the ground and the top hand on the box. The feet should rise straight in the air. Bring the feet together, push off the ground and the box with your hands, and rotate over. As the body begins to right itself, hollow out the chest. End with the feet on the ground and the arms extended overhead about shoulder-width apart.

Microcycles for the Pole Vault

The following microcycles (figure 14.15 to 14.17) demonstrate how to load the athlete in a progressive manner at different times of the training year. The total load on a given day is a function of both volume and intensity and thematically reflects the goal of that day, whether it be technical work, speed development, strength, fitness work, or restoration.

Microcycle #	Dates:	Event group: Pole vault
Phase: General preparation	Comments:	
Sunday	Monday	Tuesday
Active rest	Warm-up Acceleration drills Basic pole vault approach drills Acceleration sprint work Body balance drills Medicine ball work Weight room: General strength and Olympic lifts Cool-down Prehabilitation work	Warm-up Speed development drills Basic pole vault takeoff drills Speed development work Hurdle mobility work Functional movement and body awareness drills Weight room: Static lifts Cool-down
Wednesday	Thursday	Friday
Abbreviated warm-up Balance drills Circuit training Core strength work Pool or bike work: Low intensity, medium volume	Warm-up Speed development drills Gymnastics or pole vault flight awareness drills Maximum velocity mechanics work Medicine ball work Weight room: Mixed static and Olympic day Cool-down Prehabilitation work	Abbreviated warm-up Plyometric day Medicine ball drills Hurdle drills Cool-down Contrast bath cool/warm
Saturday	Intensity of load by day	Post-workout comments
Controlled runs or striders	(table below)	

	Su	M	Tu	W	Th	F	Sa
Hard		x			x		
Medium			x			x	
Easy							x
Rest	x						

FIGURE 14.15 Sample seven-day microcycle for the pole vault: general preparation phase of training.

Microcycle #	Dates:	Event group: Pole vault
Phase: Specific preparation	Comments:	

Sunday	Monday	Tuesday
Active rest	Warm-up Acceleration drills Pole vault approach runs Acceleration sprint work: Block starts Body balance drills Medicine ball work Weight room: Olympic lifts Cool-down Prehabilitation work	Warm-up Speed development drills Pole vault short approach jumps Speed development work Hurdle mobility work Functional movement and body awareness drills Weight room: Static lifts Cool-down

Wednesday	Thursday	Friday
Abbreviated warm-up Balance drills and yoga Circuit training Core strength work and physioball work Pool or bike work: Low intensity, medium volume	Warm-up Speed development drills Pole vault jump technique Maximum velocity work Medicine ball work Weight room: Mixed static and Olympic day Cool-down Prehabilitation work	Abbreviated warm-up Tendon ligament strength work Medicine ball drills Hurdle drills Cool-down Contrast bath cool/warm

Saturday	Intensity of load by day	Post-workout comments
Warm-up Extensive tempo work	(see table below)	

	Su	M	Tu	W	Th	F	Sa
Hard		x			x		
Medium			x			x	
Easy				x			x
Rest	x						

FIGURE 14.16   Sample seven-day microcycle for the pole vault: specific preparation phase of training.

Microcycle # Phase: Competitive	Dates: Comments:	Event group: Pole vault
Sunday	Monday	Tuesday
Active rest	Warm-up Acceleration drills Pole vault approach runs, modified takeoffs Acceleration sprint work: Block starts Body balance drills Medicine ball work Weight room: Olympic lifts Cool-down Prehabilitation work	Warm-up Speed development drills Pole vault short approach jumps Speed development work Hurdle mobility work Functional movement and body awareness drills Weight room: Static lifts Cool-down
Wednesday	Thursday	Friday
Abbreviated warm-up Balance drills and yoga Circuit training Core strength work and physioball work	Warm-up Speed development drills Pole vault technique Maximum velocity work and multijumps Medicine ball work Weight room: Mixed static and Olympic day Cool-down Prehabilitation work	Pre-meet warm-up Shake out Rhythm runs Modified takeoffs Accelerations
Saturday	Intensity of load by day	Post-workout comments
Meet day		

	Su	M	Tu	W	Th	F	Sa
Hard		x			x		x
Medium			x				
Easy				x		x	
Rest	x						

FIGURE 14.17 Sample seven-day microcycle for the pole vault: competitive phase of training.

Conclusion

The vertical jumps are two of the most complex events in all of track and field. Both have a significant vertical component and specific technical demands. Therefore, they require specific teaching progressions that are critical for safety and success. Coaches should always practice safe teaching in safe environments when working with both high jumpers and pole vaulters.

PART V

Throws

15

Coaching Throwing Events

Lawrence W. Judge, PhD

Track and field events that involve the propelling of an implement—the hammer, shot put, discus, and javelin—are collectively called the throwing events. High muscular forces coupled with high muscular contraction velocity contribute to the high power output that throwers need to develop. Although strength is an asset for athletes competing in throwing events, success in throwing events depends on the interaction of variables such as natural talent or genetics, technical components, and influential coaching. Effective coaches identify the right combination of these variables for each competitor. To identify the performance model that will work best for each thrower, the coach must develop an individual training program that systematically and progressively builds the skills that lead to the achievement of peak performance. This chapter examines the variables that influence the level of success for track and field athletes who compete in throwing events.

Talent Demands for the Throws

Great throwers are athletic. High-level performance in track and field relies heavily on strength. Strength can be defined as the ability to use muscular activity (enhanced by the use of weights) to exert resistance on external forces to overcome those forces. Throwing strength involves holding the positions necessary to master techniques and improve performance. Proper technique is optimized through a set of muscle contractions and relaxations coordinated and synchronized to produce maximal acceleration of the implement. Body size helps, but size is

no substitute for athletic ability. Athletes who have had success in other speed and power sports and events may find that their natural athletic ability lends itself well to throwing events. Football and basketball players often possess the physical tools and size to become great throwers and often compete in the shot put and discus in the off-season. Because speed and power are essential components of throwing, a mediocre sprinter may end up becoming a better thrower than a bigger, but slower athlete. Volleyball players often are well-developed athletes who have speed and power, which they can translate into success in the javelin throw.

The concept of natural athletic talent has been a theme throughout the history of sports. Stories of athletes who dominate from early ages are common across all sports and events. How heavily does genetics weigh on the success of an athlete? Genetics may provide an excellent foundation for athletic ability, but coaches and athletes have risen above genetic destinies with sport expansion and sophisticated training methods and technology. Given proper training and basic athletic ability, many dedicated, committed athletes achieve success in athletic competition. Such drive and dedication can eclipse natural athletic ability in throwing events, especially when nurtured through good coaching techniques.

General Analysis of the Throwing Events

The competitive performance of a thrower in track and field is an aggressive display of strength, power, and technique. The throws are complicated movements performed at high speed in limited spaces. From a training perspective, the hammer, weight throw, shot put, discus, and javelin are classified as the speed and power events. Although each event is unique, they share many qualities needed for success. Although physical condition and athleticism are both imperative, an athlete's technical ability contributes significantly to overall performance. At the elite level of the sport, many believe that technique is the largest discriminating factor among athletes. Some have suggested recently that coaches have placed too much emphasis on strength and power at the expense of technique. In addition, the literature argues that a lack of scientific research into throwing may hinder the development of the sport. Given this lack of scientific knowledge, coaches of throwing athletes must help their athletes build and maintain strength while also developing refined techniques.

Release Parameters

Three parameters—release velocity, release angle, and release height—dictate the quality of performance on any throw, and all technical teaching is geared toward improving these parameters. When the implement is released, its horizontal displacement depends on its velocity, angle, and height. Release velocity is the most important parameter because the horizontal displacement of the implement is proportional to the release velocity squared. Release angle and release height may help to produce better aerodynamics for the discus and javelin, potentially minimizing the effect of wind shear and the degenerative effect on release velocity. The shot put uses high release angles. The shot is released from a greater height above the ground and with a lower release speed, resulting in a shorter throwing distance. Small deviations in release angle are tolerable because, at angles close to the optimal release angle, the flight distance is insensitive to release angle. Throwing with a high release speed is more important to performance than throwing at the optimal release angle.

Often, velocity is referred to as the critical parameter in throwing. The two primary ways to increase release velocity are to improve strength and power and to optimize technique to maximize the use of strength and power. Coaches should keep in mind that technique may be limited by strength and power.

To take advantage of these forces, the thrower must fully understand the static positions and the temporal patterns involved in the throw. Understanding the mechanics involved in generating the necessary power and momentum during the throw allows the coach to adjust when necessary and devise procedures to improve the athlete's performance. Each position and its associated patterns fall into distinct phases, allowing throwers to develop good mechanics throughout the throw.

Phases of the Throw

Researchers sometimes disagree about the number of phases of the throw and have different criteria for determining each phase. They have divided the throw into as few as 4 and as many as 11 phases. Various methods have been used to divide the movement. Hay (1993), for instance, divided the throw into motor tasks such as initial stance, glide, delivery, and reverse. Each division includes the external qualities of the movement rather than the accelerations of the implement or the kinetics of the performance, which makes it difficult to interpret and compare the results of various researchers. This chapter uses standardized terminology to facilitate application, and five terms to define the phases of the throw: starting position, preparation phase, power position, delivery, and follow-through or reverse.

Starting Position

The thrower begins the throw from a stationary position and leaves the circle or runway under control after completing the attempt. The starting position is the body position the thrower achieves prior to initiating the attempt, including the grip. The starting position can vary from athlete to athlete, but some basic technical concepts such as balance and stability remain constant. Minute changes (as little as 2 cm, or less than an inch) to this position influence the subsequent structure of the throw. For example, athletes in the shot put, discus, and hammer throw sometimes maintain superior balance and stability in the starting position by using a wider base.

Preparation Phase

Each of the throwing events contains some type of preliminary movement, such as the glide in the shot put, the turns in the discus, the approach and crossovers in the javelin, and the winds and turns in the hammer. The preparatory phase begins with the initiation of the throwing movement and concludes at the moment of takeoff. The preliminary movements develop momentum and velocity, which contribute to the distance of the throw and also position the body and implement to create the foundation needed for the correct performance of the delivery phase of the throw. Achieving the correct body position is as important as developing velocity, especially when developing technique.

The period of time in which the athlete moves toward the front of the throwing circle and has no contact with the throwing surface is the flight phase. Rear-foot touchdown (RFTD) is the point at which the thrower's rear foot makes contact with the throwing circle following the flight phase. Likewise, front-foot touchdown (FFTD) is the point at which the thrower's front foot makes contact with the throwing circle following the flight phase. Following the completion of the preparation phase and the touchdown of both feet, the power position is established.

Power Position

The preliminary movements put the body in the best position for executing the delivery phase of the throw. This position is called the power position. The power position is unique to each throw, but there are similarities among the events. Some advocate an almost simultaneous landing of the rear and front feet, although most agree that the rear foot should land prior to the front foot. Although a shorter transition time is beneficial, some researchers suggest that a simultaneous RFTD and FFTD may halt the forward momentum of the athlete and the implement. The upcoming chapters address the throwing mechanics for each implement, including similarities in the power positions of all of the throwing events.

Delivery

The time between RFTD and release is the delivery phase. This phase starts when the body arrives in the power position and begins the throw itself. The delivery phase is sub-divided into the transition phase, the time between RFTD and FFTD, and the completion phase, the time between FFTD and release.

The delivery phase consists of the movements of both the lower and upper bodies. Movements of the upper body during the throw are referred to as the strike. The final part of the throw is the delivery phase, which commences at the end of the power position and culminates with the release of the implement. The lower body is fixed to provide a stable base against which the upper extremity, especially the throwing arm in the case of the discus, javelin, and shot put, may exert force. During this time, the thrower accelerates the implement up and over the shoulder. The thrower does this by extending the knees, hips, back, and shoulders, releasing the implement at approximately shoulder height or higher. The explosive lifting and rotating actions of the lower extremity are closely mirrored in the movement of the hips. Along with the legs, the hips both rotate and extend during the delivery phase. These high-intensity and short-duration movements contribute to the leg joint motions of ankle plantar flexion, knee extension, and hip extension (also called the triple extension) during the final phase or release of the throwing implement.

Once a thrower has developed a technique that consistently results in optimal release height and angle, emphasis should then be placed on technique alterations that can improve release speed. In all throwing events, maximal speed is necessary to achieve the highest possible release velocity, just as maximal force is necessary to accelerate the implement. Consecutive acceleration and deceleration of the main body segments maximizes movement coordination during the release.

This is called blocking the nonthrowing side and is beneficial because it accelerates the throwing side and allows for greater transfer of momentum to the implement.

Follow-Through and Reverse

An attempt is considered a failure if the athlete improperly releases the implement or touches any part of the ground outside of the runway or circle between the time she steps inside the ring to begin the throw and the moment the implement lands after the throw. Movement strategies such as the follow-through and reverse prevent a foul by having the athlete land outside of the front of the circle or foul line, thus preserving a legal throw. For example, the objective of the follow-through in the shot put is to achieve proper throwing arm mechanics, including arm extension and wrist action and hand follow-through. The reverse allows the thrower to follow through and chase after the implement. The athlete stops forward momentum by braking in the final moments of the delivery phase and immediately following release.

In general, three movement strategies preserve a legal throw in the shot put and discus. In the first option, the athlete stops forward momentum by applying braking forces in the final moments of the delivery phase and immediately following release. This is referred to as the nonreverse because, unlike the other two methods, the athlete does not switch the position of the feet following the release.

As indicated previously, the two other methods of preserving a throw involve an exchange in the position of the front and rear feet. The first such technique is called the step reverse or delayed reverse. Using this method, the athlete stops forward momentum without a full exchange of foot positioning. However, the athlete does step forward with the rear foot after a considerable delay following the release.

The final method used to preserve a legal throw is the reverse. This is a maneuver that enables the shot put and discus thrower to follow through, recover, and maintain or regain balance after the throw to prevent fouling. In this technique the athlete exchanges the front and rear foot positions so that the rear foot can be used to stop forward momentum of the body and the implement. Several authors have advocated this method as best for stopping momentum.

In the hammer and javelin throws, event-specific follow-throughs follow the throw. These are described in the chapters addressing these events (chapters 18 and 19, respectively).

Implements

A basic knowledge of the implements is important. Implements vary in weight, materials, and feel, and throwers should choose those that support their own styles and match their abilities. The coach may want to purchase some implements for practice and others for use primarily in competition. Modified or light implements may help athletes progress in the early stages of learning. For example, a cone can be substituted for a discus, a ball or club for a javelin, and a weighted baseball bat for a hammer. The event-specific chapters have more information to assist in the selection process.

Skills of the Throwing Events

Success in the throws depends on the consistent performance of skills and techniques. Some of the skills required for throwing may seem unnatural at first. The summation of all forces leading up to the release of the implement directly affects the throw. Although the throwing events are similar in some aspects, the movements that lead up to the release may vary.

The shot put consists of three movements: the glide or rotation, the standing power position, and the release. Movements involved in the hammer and discus include body rotation within the boundaries of a ring and rely on centripetal forces and torque, culminating with a release. Unlike the hammer and discus, the javelin requires the athlete to build speed over a linear distance. A successful throw in any of these four events requires the transfer of explosive strength and maximal muscular force onto the object in the shortest possible time.

The importance of muscular strength drives the requirement for throwers to develop leg strength in the early stages of their careers. Strength is so important for a thrower that it often becomes a limiting factor in technique development. Weaker athletes simply cannot develop and refine technique as quickly or effectively as stronger throwers can.

The schema theory of Schmidt (1975) proposes that skill learning is a process of recall and recognition. Schema learning occurs as the motor program stores information such as body position, skill parameters, accuracy, and sensory input (Judge 2007). Each throwing event requires the development of near-maximal force production in a limited time while maintaining precise execution of the skill.

Consistent Implement Acceleration

Although mechanics are important, rhythm is equally important for quality throws. Proper acceleration is a key component of rhythm. For example, the final action of shot-putting in the direction of the throw starts when the rotation of the hips and shoulders stops. At the end of the rotation of the hips and shoulders, the velocity of the shot is just over 6 m/s. After the throwing arm has taken part in the release action through the extension of the elbow and shoulders, the shot velocity increases to just under 7 m/s. The acceleration of the implement must be consistent and positive. The idea of a consistent, progressive acceleration seems simple, but it is often violated. A common error is accelerating the implement too quickly only to decelerate it later. Progressive acceleration is important in both the preliminary movements and the delivery. On a graph, the acceleration rate should map as a gradual curve, without large spikes and dips.

Summation of Force

Force generation normally begins in the proximal joints. The large muscles of the legs and torso initiate the movement and overcome inertia, so that the smaller muscles of the shoulders and arms can further increase

the velocity of the implement in the delivery phase. The initial force generated by the proximal-to-distal sequencing of hip extension, knee extension, and plantar flexion accelerates the athlete-and-implement system. This force must be transmitted to the ground or to an implement through other (distal) joints. For example, although the shoulder (proximal joint) may be producing the force, the force is being transmitted to the shot put through the elbow and wrist (distal joints). Upper-body activity in the delivery and arm strike results from a summation of forces. Although throws differ slightly, proximal-to-distal firing must be preserved. Overall, an optimal coordination pattern appears to be one in which muscle activation and segment acceleration occur in a proximal-to-distal manner with an optimally timed deceleration of body segments leading up to the moment of release.

One of the benefits of a proximal-to-distal coordination pattern is that it generates a whiplike motion. When the upper leg and trunk musculature are the first to contract, greater separation is developed between the shoulders and hips. This results in a whip effect as the hips decelerate and the shoulders accelerate as they uncoil and the implement is released. This deceleration of the hips is critical in an acceleration–deceleration coordination pattern. If the extremity muscles are strong but the core is weak, an adequate summation of forces cannot be created. The result is often technical breakdown and a less-than-optimal performance.

Lengthening the Path of Implement Acceleration

The longer force is applied to the implement, the greater the momentum and velocity will be. To lengthen the amount of time force is applied, the athlete must achieve maximal length in the path of the implement during the delivery. Two ways to lengthen the acceleration path are weight transfer and turning, or using closed throwing positions.

During the delivery phase, body weight is transferred from the back foot to the front foot to increase the body's range of movement and the path of the implement. This transfer of body weight is a crucial component of the throw. The front leg should extend almost completely at the moment of release. However, the timing of initiation and the magnitude of the action of the lower extremity differ considerably between the glide and rotational techniques. Unlike in the glide technique, in the rotational technique the workload is more evenly distributed between the legs during delivery. That is, instead of an initial push with the rear leg and a weight transfer to the front leg, rotators push more simultaneously with both legs.

After arriving in the power position and during the delivery, the center of mass (proximal joints) of the body turns smoothly and progressively in the direction of the throw. This turning, or rotation, is a crucial component of the throw. The body is turned away from the direction of the throw in the start and power positions, enabling it to turn through a greater angle as the implement is delivered. For more advanced throwers, a slight forward lean of the trunk while in double support helps to maintain balance when the angular velocity of the body is reduced and the absolute velocity of the implement is relatively high. A thrower of shorter stature can take advantage of a longer radius, which allows for a smoother change of kinematic indicators.

Important implications are associated with producing a larger radius in the early parts of the throw. For a given linear speed, a larger radius provides a system that allows the thrower to rotate with a slower angular velocity. A slower rate of rotation permits slower contractions of the muscles involved, which allows these muscles to exert larger forces. This is due to the force–velocity relationship for skeletal muscle. In turn, a larger muscle force results in a larger torque and an increase in the overall angular momentum of the system. Therefore, using a longer radius in the early parts of the throw increases the angular momentum of the system and lengthens the path of the implement.

Separation and Torque

Although the body turns smoothly and progressively in the direction of the throw, in most situations the upper body and lower body do not turn from the same positions at the same time. This is called separation, referring to the separation between the hip and shoulder about the rotational axis. In addition, throwers generally start to turn the lower body before turning the upper body. This twists the core of the body and creates torque. Force is a push or a pull that changes the linear state of motion of an object or body. The angular equivalent of force is torque. Torque is the turning effect created by a force about an axis. Torque can be increased either by applying greater force or by increasing the radius of rotation. When the upper leg and trunk musculature are the first to contract, greater separation occurs between the shoulders and hips. As the hips decelerate and the shoulders accelerate as they uncoil, the implement is released; this separation results in a whip effect. Separation and torque exist in different degrees in the various throwing events. Both serve to establish a summation of rotational forces, beginning with the lower body and finishing with the upper body.

Blocking

The thrower must eventually stop the momentum created in the body to transfer it to the implement. A good way to do this is to harmoniously blend the left-leg block and the left-arm block. The blocking actions of the upper body in the shot put, discus, and javelin differ slightly based on the unique release mechanics of these events. For example, in the discus, the throwing arm is ideally 90 degrees from the body to maximize radius. The left-side block would be initiated and positioned opposite and equal to the throwing side.

Left-Leg Block

In the left-leg block, the left leg plants firmly in the power position with the left heel pushing into the ground and stopping the horizontal and rotational movement of the left side of the thrower's lower body. This action transfers momentum to the upper body and implement. Proper alignment of the feet is essential to proper blocking. A common error in the shot put, discus, and javelin is to put the left leg too far left of center making blocking impossible.

The error of planting the left foot too far to the left is commonly called being in the bucket.

Left-Arm Block

During the delivery phase, the athlete has a long left arm to slow the rotation of the upper body, creating an eccentric stretch of the upper-body musculature and allowing the hips to fire ahead of the upper body. The shoulder girdle movement is a key factor in throwing performance. The left arm begins to shorten at the midline of the body to create a forceful shortening and summation of forces. Desired forceful contractions in athletic endeavors usually are elastic and reflexive, setting up a powerful response of eccentrically stretched muscles, referred to as a volitional concentric response. If the volitional contractions are improperly timed or voluntary involvement by any muscle group is too great, the elastic energy generation of the entire system is diminished, reducing efficiency. The left arm remains long until delivery is initiated, at which time it moves in close to the side of the thrower to help stop the left side of the upper body and transfer momentum to the nonthrowing side. The action of throwing occurs much more efficiently when these stretch reflexes are invoked and elastic energy is developed.

When teaching athletic techniques, coaches should create situations that prestretch the muscles. The hammer is an exception to this rule because it is thrown with both arms. However, on release, the left side of the hammer thrower blocks as the thrower attempts to maximize radius and lift the implement.

Posture

As in many athletic disciplines, posture is an important component of throwing events. Because the core is at the center of nearly all sport movements, the core musculature is a key element of energy generation. The torso's ability to support effective arm and leg actions (core stability) is essential to performance and injury prevention in many sports.

Postural integrity is directly linked to elastic energy generation. Body parts must be stabilized in proper alignment for applied forces to produce displacement without excessive distortion and rotation. Excessive instability or postural misalignment cause postural muscles to overwork to compensate and maintain balance, which restricts their ability to function elastically. However, the postural unit should not be stabilized in a way that restricts movement. Proper posture during athletic endeavors should not be associated with total rigidity, which compromises elastic energy production. Proper alignment of the core of the body is important for movement efficiency and injury prevention.

An important element of posture is head alignment, and it is important in throwing events for several reasons. Improper head alignment affects the technical execution of a skill by impairing limb function. Balance may also be affected, because most of the body's vestibular equipment is disturbed. Finally, the head is quite heavy, so extraneous movements may produce instability. Improper alignment may cause instability, which can elicit stiffening, multilink, or grounding strategies and interrupt the technical flow of the throw, causing inconsistencies in performance. Proper alignment of the head ensures relaxation and balance and helps create a good release or arm strike. Dropping the head and turning the head away during the throw are common errors.

Another component of posture, pelvic alignment, is also crucial for efficient throwing. Pelvic misalignment significantly affects the function of the legs and nearly always produces instability. The instability resulting from pelvic misalignment also elicits harmful stiffening, multilink, or grounding strategies, which disrupt throwing technique. A neutral alignment of the pelvis with respect to the spine promotes relaxation, proper leg function, and good turning. Excessive bending at the waist after arriving in the power position, a common mistake, places the pelvis in an inferior position.

Teaching and Training the Throws

The goal of a training program for the throws is to optimize skill performance and fitness while minimizing fatigue on the day of the competition. Proper sequencing and appropriate intensities of training activities contribute to peak performance. Each technical training session must have a clearly defined objective for both coach and athlete. Once the objective is established, the coach must tailor feedback to that objective. Specific guidelines for setting up throwing workouts are outlined at the end of each event chapter.

When correcting mistakes made by a beginning thrower, the coach should focus more heavily on strengths than on areas in need of improvement. A strategy known as the positive sandwich can be helpful. It involves beginning the conversation with a positive comment regarding one of the athlete's strengths, then discussing how to correct an error, and ending with a positive comment. This approach helps athletes stay energized and confident.

Although correcting errors is important, coaches should be careful to avoid creating mental overload in the athlete. A common coaching error that leads to mental overload is identifying a fault on every throw. A good plan is to establish a technical theme for each session and focus feedback cues on that theme. Also, coaches should limit the number of feedback cues overall. Athletes cannot process several comments at once, and they need to repeat motor skills to develop motor planning. To achieve mastery, athletes must focus their thoughts, energy, and repetitive behavior. Addressing too many areas delays the mastery of any motor skill. For these reasons, the coach must prioritize motor skills and encourage athletes to focus on one skill until they can demonstrate mastery. A mastered skill is remembered for a long time.

The durable memory makes motor skill learning an interesting paradigm for the study of learning and memory mechanisms. Skill learning is a continuous and dynamic process without distinct stages. For convenience, however, the following general stages can be considered:

- **Acquisition (cognitive) stage.** This stage occurs during the initial instruction and practice of a skill and involves what-to-do decisions. The acquisition phase is characterized by fast learning (within sessions) and slow learning

(between sessions). In this stage the learner forms a cognitive picture of the skill and the requirements for performing it. The movements in this initial stage are sometimes jerky, halting, and poorly timed.

- **Associative (practice) stage.** This stage involves carryover as throwers demonstrate their newly acquired skill after initial practice; it involves how-to-do decisions. The associative stage is quite long. In fact, some throwers might never move beyond it. In this stage, the fundamentals and mechanics of the skill have been learned, and performance is less variable and more consistent.

- **Autonomous (automatic) stage.** In this stage, most of the skill is performed without thinking because the thrower requires less attention to basics. As a result, more selective attention can be given to higher-order cognitive activities, such as competition strategies or external cues as in the angle of attack in the discus or the wrap in the javelin. In this stage, improvements come slowly, but there is good consistency of performance as the thrower demonstrates the skill in a new context. This stage involves how-to-succeed decisions that can involve more advanced technical execution.

Most people move from stage to stage as they learn skills. However, some might not arrive at the last stage as a result of the training demands, the complexity of the task, or a lack of motivation.

Risk Management

Risk management must be an active part of a coach's duty. Staff training, facility upkeep and maintenance, and a proper risk management plan for emergency situations work together to prevent risk. Proper risk assessment and management for track and field venues requires a layered understanding of the specific sporting event, the amount of spectator participation, and what constitutes a safe facility.

Event facilities for the throws in track and field are of specific concern. Vulnerability in hammer and discus cage safety has been overlooked. There are definitely inherent dangers associated with the hammer throw event aside from facility neglect. Athletes, coaches, and spectators participating in the event are at risk. Hammers (4 kg, or 8.8 lb, for women and 7.26 kg, or 16 lb, for men) are implements of steel hurled through the air at great speeds and distances, and they are often difficult to spot in flight.

Coaches must never neglect safety considerations, and they should always provide adequate supervision. The infield is generally the only appropriate place for throws training. Proper signage that is visible is crucial. Coaches should instill in their athletes the habit of not crossing the infield to get from one side of the track to the other, even when throwing is not taking place. The hammer and discus cage must be safe; and the cage doors, appropriately set. The discus, shot, and hammer throwing circles should be inspected to make sure they are dry and clear of foreign objects. The landing area must be clear before an athlete enters the ring or runway.

The events in track and field require a variety of footwear. Throwing shoes should be flexible with a wide, flat-bottom sole. Here are some basic guidelines for selecting specialty shoes for the throwing events:

- **Hammer and weight throw.** The ideal shoe has a smooth sole. This allows more natural contact with the side edges of the foot while the athlete is rotating in the circle.
- **Discus and rotational shot put.** Heel roundness is not as important in these events because the throwing action is on the balls of the feet. Instead, the best shoe has a broad, flat, wide base. The sole should have some texture or be made with a tackier rubber so it has a better grip of the throwing ring surface.
- **Glide shot put.** The best type of shoe for this event is slightly curved with a wide, flat heel. This promotes lateral

balance and prevents the athlete from wobbling back and forth. It also makes it easier to place the heel against the back of the circle rim.

- **Javelin.** Javelin shoes or boots come in low-cut, high-cut, and mid-cut versions. They are modeled this way to provide more support and protection around the ankle of the plant foot. The javelin shoe has 11 spikes, usually 7 in the front and 4 at the heel. According to the IAAF, the maximal number of spikes allowed on a shoe is 11, and they cannot exceed 12 millimeters (about half an inch) in length.

Prior to training and competition, coaches should assist athletes in inspecting equipment and footwear to ensure that all are in good condition to prevent injury and poor performance.

Coaches should address and demand good technique in everything the athlete does in training. The training program (running, multijumping, multithrowing, and even lifting workouts) is an opportunity to teach throwing fundamentals whenever possible. Workouts should be stopped when fatigue creates technique problems. Coaches should break down movements into easily practiced and mastered parts, and teach the release of the implement first. The next skill to teach is the throw from the power position, and so on. Working back toward the start of the event, coaches should gradually add more velocity and preliminary movement.

Athletes should not attempt full throws until they have shown consistency in the start and preliminary movements. Simplified techniques, such as shortening the javelin approach or throwing the hammer from only one or two turns, can be useful to the developing thrower.

Premature reversing is a common error in which the thrower reverses before completing force application to the implement, compromising performance. To combat this problem, the coach should de-emphasize the reverse in practice and not allow the athlete to reverse in the developmental stages of learning.

Conclusion

Although success in throwing events depends on the interaction of several variables, we cannot ignore the impact of natural talent and genetics. Great throwers are athletic by nature. Success also depends on an aggressive display of strength, power, and technique as well as consistency in the technical components of the throw. Although each event is unique, they all share many qualities needed for success. Initial velocity, release angle, and release height work together to dictate the success of the throw, although release velocity is the most important.

Understanding the mechanics of the throws allows the coach to modify the athlete's technique when necessary and devise ways to improve performance. The coach plays a vital role in the development of a successful athlete. Training the technical aspects of the throw must include a clearly defined objective for both coach and athlete. Once the objective is established, the coach must tailor feedback to that objective. Providing structure to the training regimen ensures clarity for both the coach and the athlete and empowers the athlete to more effectively apply newly learned skills.

16

Shot Put

Lawrence W. Judge, PhD

The shot put is a traditional throwing event with origins in Scottish Highland games. It is one of the oldest events in track and field; competitions have been held at the modern Summer Olympic Games since their inception in 1896. The arm strike in shot-putting is unique to the event; no other sport requires a push from the front deltoid with the elbow at a 90-degree angle to the body. Shot-putters must develop a set of skills that at first may seem unnatural. They must learn posture and balance and feel comfortable pivoting on the ball of the foot.

Each drill in this chapter teaches a specific skill. For example, an athlete's natural shoulder mobility is rarely even close to the mobility necessary to execute a solid arm strike. The blocking motion of the free arm prior to the arm strike is another skill that must be developed with drills such as the partner high five drill, described later in this chapter.

Current elite male and female athletes use both the glide and the rotational technique with equal success. Therefore, this chapter addresses both. To develop the parts of the throw in their athletes, coaches must introduce a series of drills to teach shot put specifics.

Regardless of the technique they eventually use, all shot-putters need to learn and master fundamental skills such as the block, arm strike, and hip movement.

The current rules governing the shot put event are established by the IAAF and are fully explained in the IAAF rulebook. The rules state that the shot must be spherical and made of a metal no softer than copper or a shell of such metal filled with lead or another material. For indoor throwing, the shot may be made of plastic or enveloped in rubber. The shot must be smooth and without irregularities on its surface. Table 16.1 lists the weights and diameters of shots for junior and senior men and women. Typically, competition shots are made of iron or steel. Cast-iron shots range in cost from $20 to $50, and turned-iron and steel shots range from $50 to $100. Turned shots are more precisely weighted and balanced.

Shot-putters, whether glide or rotational throwers, develop an important set of skills that may, at first, seem a bit peculiar to the aspiring novice. For example, an athlete's natural hip mobility is rarely even close to the mobility necessary to execute solid shot put technique. The rotational motion of the torso at

TABLE 16.1 Weights and Diameters of the Shot

	Weight	Diameter
Senior men	7.26 kg (16 lb)	110 to 130 mm (4.3 to 5.1 in.)
Junior men	6 kg (13.2 lb)	110 to 130 mm (4.3 to 5.1 in.)
Senior women	4 kg (8.8 lb)	95 to 110 mm (3.7 to 4.3 in.)
Junior women	4 kg (8.8 lb)	95 to 110 mm (3.7 to 4.3 in.)

the initiation of the delivery is another unnatural motion that must be developed through repetitive drill and special strength work. A good coach focuses on the fundamentals of shot-putting before introducing glide or rotational mechanics.

Becoming a successful shot put thrower requires a considerable level of discipline, dedication, and commitment. Even young, highly athletic, and naturally talented athletes dedicate years of work to develop the necessary skills. Long-term development may be limited by progressing into the rotational technique before mastering the basics of the arm strike, block, and power position throw.

Regardless of the athlete's competitive level, there are always skills to learn and improve. The complexities of the footwork of the rotational technique keep aspiring young throwers learning new skills for years. American-record holder Jill Camarena-Williams is a perfect example of an athlete who mastered the basics with the glide technique (18.15 m) and went on to become a world-class (20.18 m) shot-putter with the rotational technique. The rudimentary rotational mechanics discussed in the discus chapter (chapter 17) can easily be used by the glide shot-putter who has mastered the basics.

Starting Position

For the sake of clarity and simplicity, the discussion in this chapter assumes a right-handed athlete. The thrower must assume a starting position and ultimately a power position that promotes posture and balance. Balance is a state of equilibrium characterized by the cancellation of all forces by equally opposing forces. Stability refers to the body's resistance to toppling over. Although the definitions are not the same, stability and balance are intertwined and do affect one another, making it very difficult to talk about one and not the other.

In the shot put, forces must be applied from a stable base to produce efficient displacements. The core of the body must be stable when the body applies force to the ground or the implement. Novice throwers have a tendency to round the back and drop the head in the starting position. Dropping the head results in the following series of mistakes made in an effort to correct the first:

1. The head moves forward, shifting the center of gravity.
2. To compensate, the upper body drifts backward.
3. To compensate for the upper-body tilt, the hips shift forward.

A stable stickman (upright) position with the head and vertebrae stacked and minimal bend in the torso places young throwers in a position of strength. This athletic position is similar to the position just prior to the shrug in the hang clean in the weight room. Positioning the head properly with respect to the spine and pelvis are the primary concerns when creating a stickman position.

Grip and Neck Placement

The shot is placed in the hand so that it rests on the base of the fingers (figure 16.1). The fingers are comfortably spread, with the three strongest fingers touching the shot and the thumb and little finger on the sides to balance

FIGURE 16.1   Grip.

the shot. The wrist is flexed, and the shot is cradled against the neck close to the chin, so that the thumb touches the collarbone. With the elbow bent, the shot is placed on the neck by the jawline. Some coaches say that the protrusion on the back of the jawbone was made for the shot-putters of the world. Spinners (those who use the rotational technique) often carry the implement high on the neck near the ear (figure 16.2a). Most gliders carry the shot low on the neck underneath the chin (figure 16.2b). The placement on the neck is largely determined by the flexibility in the wrist, forearm, triceps, and shoulder girdle. The power clean is a good exercise for shot-putters who need to develop and maintain upper-body flexibility.

FIGURE 16.2   Shot position on the neck: (a) American record holder Michelle Carter places the shot higher on the neck; (b) Some shot putters prefer to place the shot lower.

A faulty starting position can cause the athlete to drop the elbow at release, which diminishes the velocity of the arm strike. A common error is to rest the shot on the clavicle with the hand and wrist facing the midline of the body. This error often is due to a lack of upper-body mobility and specific strength. Although elbow positions may vary, in general the elbow is slightly elevated. A good technique to teach proper neck placement is to instruct the athlete to place the shot and the throwing hand at the approximate angle of release, between 32 and 36 degrees, and then lower the shot into the neck with the thumb down and elbow out. The nonthrowing hand helps to position the implement against the neck.

Preliminary Stance

In the preliminary stance, the foot of the drive leg is flat and near the rear edge of the circle; the toes point away from the direction of the throw (figure 16.3). Prior to initiating the glide, the athlete may use one of two basic starting positions in what is termed the preparation phase:

1. Begin with an upright posture. Drop onto the drive leg to perform the dynamic glide.

2. Use the crouch start or T-position start. In the T-position start, assume a low position, loading approximately 70 percent of the body weight onto the drive leg in the back of the ring before initiating movement toward the toe board.

Preliminary Movements

The preliminary movements and the throw should be a rhythmic whole. The coach should keep rhythm in mind when teaching these movements. Shot-putters have many ways to start prior to initiating movement across the ring. They may begin in an upright position, a medium position, or a low position. The static start (figure 16.4), which starts from a low position with no preliminary movement, is best for beginners. More advanced athletes may choose a start such as the Timmerman start, a rolling start from a more upright stance (figure 16.5). The coach and the athlete should work together to determine the style and rhythm of the athlete's preliminary movements.

FIGURE 16.3   Preliminary stance.

FIGURE 16.4   Static start.

FIGURE 16.5   Timmerman start.

Preparation for the Glide

To initiate the glide, the thrower lifts the left leg; then lowers the body weight completely onto the right leg, flexing the knee and hip. Simultaneously, the left leg moves toward the right leg so that the knees are near each other at maximal flexion. The torso and head remain in their original positions, and the shoulders and left arm remain closed. The shot remains behind the right foot.

Glide

The glide results from three distinct movements: the unseating of the hips, the extension of the left leg, and the push and pull of the right leg (figure 16.6). As the preparation phase is completed, the athlete begins unseating the hips. Once the athlete's center of mass passes the right heel, the left leg extends so that the left foot moves toward the toe board. Almost simultaneously, the right leg pushes forcefully so that the body displaces as one unit toward the front of the ring. This push uses the entire surface of the right foot, so that the heel is the last to lose contact with the surface as the right leg is extended. As the right leg pushes, the hips begin to open gradually toward the thrower's left. The torso begins to rise slightly, but the shoulders remain square to the back of the circle. The head remains aligned with the stacked vertebrae, the left arm remains closed, and the shot is kept back with the eyes focused on a fixed location 6 to 8 feet (1.8 to 2.4 m) behind the ring.

Two primary technical glide styles have been used over the last several decades: long glide, short base (long–short); and short glide, long base (short–long). Of the top-level gliders in the world, most use the short–long style of throwing, although many coaches believe in the long–short method. The coach and athlete should determine together the technique best suited for the athlete. Common errors and their corrections can be found in table 16.2.

FIGURE 16.6   Glide.

TABLE 16.2   Common Errors and Corrections for Glide Shot Put

Fault	Reasons	Corrections
Late-hanging left foot to the front of the circle	• Even if the athlete extends the left foot straight back, it initially may lift above hip level. In this case, have the athlete sweep the left foot across the circle, keeping light contact with the surface as the foot reaches back for the board. • Poor use of the left leg; improper extension toward the toe board; kicking the left foot up above the hips with a pronounced bend in the knee. Drilling is required to teach the athlete that the left foot must explode straight back to the toe board.	• Practice the A drill. • Place a medicine ball directly behind the left foot and punch or push the ball with the left foot while driving the left foot to the toe board. • With a rubber cable tied to your left ankle, hold on to a fence, punching the foot back repeatedly and completely extending the left leg. For an added dimension, perform glides with the rubber cable attached to the left ankle. The resistance forces you to use the left leg more aggressively.

Fault	Reasons	Corrections
Driving off the ball of the foot in the back of the circle	• Pushing off the ball of the foot rather than rolling onto the heel during the drive due to inadequate leg strength	• Stand flat on your right foot with the center of gravity over the right heel. When entering the crouch position, keep the center of gravity over the right heel. When you unseat, you will naturally roll off the right heel. • Practice the A drill. • Start high on the toes in the back of the circle while in the low position. This removes the option of pushing vertically rather than horizontally. Drive aggressively from this position toward the toe board.
Raising the trunk during the glide	• Inadequate strength (an indication of this would be throwing the left arm down and back to facilitate gliding across the circle) • Poor habit • Insufficient angle in the right knee	• Keep in mind that the legs do the work and concentrate on maintaining good trunk lean to the rear, focusing the eyes on the back rim of the circle. • To deepen the angle of the right knee and develop right-leg strength, perform the locked left-knee glide drill. Sink as deeply as possible at the back of the circle. The chest must be as low as possible on the right thigh, and the left leg must be stretched out with the knee locked. It is critical that the knee is bent deeply and the chest is literally against the thigh. From this position, glide across the circle as far as possible and put the shot. As you improve and master this skill, begin using overweight shots.
The right foot is too far under the body, and the trunk is extended too far back over the right leg	• Extending the left leg too high and above the hips during the glide, which causes the upper body to tilt forward and the right foot to pull out of the back of the circle too soon, so that it travels too far into the front half of the circle	• Practice the A drill and similar drills to train the left-leg action. • Concentrate on keeping the left leg locked at extension and planting both feet at the same time to land in a balanced power position.

(continued)

243

Table 16.2 *(continued)*

Fault	Reasons	Corrections
Looking over the left shoulder and causing the shoulders to rotate to the left (open) during the glide across the circle	• Not keeping the eyes focused on the back rim of the circle, thus losing control of the head	• Hold one end of a towel in your left hand while the coach holds the other end. Glide across the circle as the coach holds your left shoulder back by pulling on the towel. When you reach the power position and are ready to throw, the coach releases the towel. • Stand with the coach on your left. The coach's right hand is resting gently on your upper left arm. As you glide across the circle, the coach's hand keeps contact until you reach the power position. • Place a broom handle or piece of PVC pipe across the back of your shoulders and practice gliding. The broom handle should keep your shoulders square and prevent them from opening up.

Flight and Transition Phase

As the rear (right) foot loses contact with the ground, a flight phase begins as the right foot is pulled under the athlete's center of gravity. In the flight phase, after the right leg completes its push, it should be pulled back underneath the body. The right foot is turned so that it points 90 to 135 degrees from the direction of the throw to the thrower's left.

The transition phase continues as the right foot is grounded followed by the grounding of the left (front) foot. The implement decelerates during this nonsupport phase; the objective is the harmonious blending of the horizontal action of the glide and the vertical action of the power position. Beginners have a tendency to pause during this phase, but this will diminish with gains in strength and technical proficiency. At the grounding of the front foot, the hips continue to open slightly. The torso remains firm but slightly tilted, and the shoulders and left arm remain closed. The shot is kept back as much as possible.

Power Position

The power position is a position from which the athlete is able to explode; balance is essential.

The athlete must land in a good power position (figure 16.7) to be ready to deliver the shot. The body weight is placed on the ball of the right foot, which is near the center of the circle and

FIGURE 16.7   Power position.

turned somewhat to the thrower's right, so that it is directed 90 to 135 degrees from the direction of the throw. The right leg is bent at the knee. The left leg lands in a slightly flexed but firm position about an inch (2.5 cm) from the toe board and just left of center. The hip axis is 90 degrees from the direction of the throw. The torso is slightly tilted but not so low that the body is bent excessively at the waist. The head is aligned, the shoulders and left arm are closed, and the shot is in back of the right foot. The power position should feel comfortable, although the athlete will feel some tension in the torso. The eyes are focused on a fixed location 6 to 8 feet (1.8 to 2.4 m) behind the ring.

Delivery

The delivery phase accounts for nearly 70 percent of the distance achieved in a full throw. It has two parts: the initiation of the throw and the strike.

Initiation of the Throw

The delivery starts with the stronger and slower proximal joints and finishes with the weaker and faster distal joints. Three actions occur subsequent to the landing in the power position:

1. Rotation of the hips
2. Drifting of the hips
3. Forceful lifting of the legs

The throw is initiated in the lower body as the hips turn and the body weight transfers from the back foot to the front foot. This action is coupled with a forceful lifting of the legs. Sequentially, the left arm and upper body turn and move forward as well; the right arm remains in position so that the elbow stays in line with the path of the shot. Later, the left arm blocks this rotation by pulling down and close to the side. Head alignment is preserved as turning occurs. The objective is to maximize the potential of the small, fast joints by building momentum with the more powerful joints.

A common error is turning the head prior to turning the upper body; this causes the joints to fire out of order. The thrower must keep the eyes focused on the original fixed location 6 to 8 feet (1.8 to 2.4 m) beyond the back of the circle to maintain the torque position with the shot behind the hip of the drive leg for maximal distance.

Strike

The arm strike (figure 16.8) begins when the lower-body and upper-body movements are nearly complete. The strike features a pushing movement, using first the shoulder and elbow and finishing with a strong snap of the wrist. The shot comes off the neck to a position over the deltoid. The elbow is high and in line with the shot's path so that the thumb points down during the strike. The head maintains alignment as the strike occurs. A common error is dropping the head or turning it to the left during the arm strike. The arm strike is primarily horizontal but with a slight vertical component; the release angle is approximately 32 to 36 degrees. Athletes cannot throw at the same speed for all angles of projection; as the angle increases, velocity often decreases.

FIGURE 16.8   Arm strike.

Follow-Through and Reverse

The thrower should vigorously strike through the shot. A vigorous release brings the arm across the chest at the completion of the throw.

The reverse is a function of the explosive extension of the hips and legs, which leads to the delivery of the shot and the long shoulder hit. To reverse properly after the shot is released, the athlete moves the right foot forward toward the toe board, where the left (front) foot has just been planted. The left foot drops back and up, and the chest lowers and turns toward the thrower's right (figure 16.9).

The thrower should not watch the flight of the shot. Watching the shot will almost certainly result in the thrower going over the toe board, resulting in a foul. An effective coaching cue is "Choose a location in the back of the ring to focus on during the reverse." Focusing on a spot behind the ring helps the thrower regain balance and avoid scratching.

Rotational Shot Put

Not since Dick Fosbury turned the high jump into a flop has track and field witnessed as significant a technical advance as the rotational shot put. The put with a discus-style turn actually predates the flop-style high jump, although the first person to achieve international success with this style was Soviet great Alexander Barishnikov in 1976. The first generation of rotational throwers who developed their technical patterns during their formative years is now coaching, and the rotational technique has become a more traveled technique. More research has been conducted, and athletes are breaking new barriers with this technique.

Although the glide technique is well established, the rotational technique has many mechanical advantages over the glide technique. For example, the rotational shot put increases the range over which the shot can be accelerated. The rotational technique results in a longer path, which enables the athlete to generate force over a greater period of time. The pathway created using the rotational path equals 14 feet 0 inches (4.27 m) with 10 to 12 inches (25.4 to 30.4 cm) of lift at release, whereas the pathway created using the glide technique equals only 9 feet 8 inches (2.95 m) with 4 to 6 inches (10.2 to 15.2 cm) of lift at release. As a result of the increased application of force, the athlete can obtain greater release velocities and leg lift at delivery. The tremendous kinetic energy generated from the back to the front of the circle along with the powerful torque in the power position and the two-legged lift at the time of the release makes the rotational technique more explosive than the glide technique.

Inconsistency in technique sometimes plagues the rotational shot-putter (see table 16.3). However, the rotational technique can produce dramatic results when all forces are in sync because it places the thrower in a more favorable putting position and produces harmonious rhythmic qualities that facilitate greater torque. In addition to the technical advantages, the rotational technique provides opportunities for athletes of shorter stature and modest strength. It may place less stress on the body because it mimics many training elements found in the discus throw. Although the rotational technique provides the

FIGURE 16.9   Reverse.

TABLE 16.3 Common Errors and Corrections for Rotational Shot Put

Fault	Reasons	Corrections
Overrotation at the back of the circle resulting in imbalances when coming out of the back of the circle	• Overrotation during the rhythmic swing to the right, which may result in a fall into the circle when beginning to rotate back to the left over the left leg	• Do not rush into the turn. Concentrate on reducing the rhythmic swing to the right. Focus on maintaining control. • Remember that the upper body does not rotate during a shot put throw the way it does during a discus throw. • Practice the 360-degree turn drill.
Falling off balance into the center of the circle	• Allowing the left shoulder and head to lead the body into the turn	• Concentrate on shifting the weight to the left. Do not rush into the turn. Focus on aligning the head and trunk with the eyes focused straight ahead. The shoulders should be level with the left arm and directly over the left leg. As the left foot begins to rotate, keep the right foot on the ground until the chest faces 3 o'clock. Practice quarter and half turns.
The right shoulder and shot fall ahead of the legs resulting in a loss of balance when the center of gravity shifts. Also, falling out of the circle toward the left.	• The left shoulder drops when the hips reach the 3 o'clock position.	• Concentrate on maintaining level shoulders. • Complete 360-degree (full) turns with a PVC pipe on the shoulders. This develops the kinesthetic feel of maintaining level shoulders.
Falling seat-first into the circle instead of shifting over the left leg even though the shoulders are level	• The shoulders face the 5 or 6 o'clock position.	• Keep the left arm and shoulder over the left knee. Ensure that the center of gravity transitions onto the left leg. Maintain balance. • Use a broom or PVC pipe to practice imitations. This helps develop the feel of rotating on top of the left leg and foot.
Falling into the turn	• Rolling to the outer edge of the foot during the start of the first turn, causing the center of gravity to transfer to the outside of the left leg	• Practice many imitation turns in the back of the circle. • Concentrate on staying on the ball of the foot. • Practice the start drill.
Lack of adequate space to accommodate a solid power position base	• Traveling too much coming out of the back of the circle	• Maintain balance and control over the left leg and initiate an aggressive, yet controlled jump turn from the ankle and foot. Slow down and focus on maintaining control. • Practice the jump the stream drill.

(continued)

Table 16.3 *(continued)*

Fault	Reasons	Corrections
Overrotation into the circle when turning the shoulders toward 9 o'clock instead of to the front	• Blocking with the left leg while still overrotating (this may result in a throw down the right sector line, even though the force vector of the body is to the left) • Failure to provide a left-leg block resulting in the forces being to the left, which frequently causes a foul or results in pushing the shot down the left sector line	• Maintain the right foot on the circle until the shoulders and hips face 3 o'clock. When the right foot is thrown into the center of the circle, select a focal point at 12 o'clock and direct the drive toward that point. Drive the left shoulder down the left sector line. If you tend to overrotate while correcting, drive the left shoulder to a focal point in the direction of 12 o'clock. • Practice the quarter turn and South African drills.
Leaning back and throwing across the chest, and falling to the left out of the circle	• Dropping the right heel causing the right foot to stop turning (the most common and most serious error in the rotational technique)	• Complete many drills without the shot. Concentrate on keeping the right heel up and maintaining the right-foot turn. This ensures that the center of gravity remains cleanly on top of the right foot and leg, preventing the heel from touching the circle. • Practice the wheel drill.
Backing into the circle. The left foot remains in the back of the circle, causing a very late placement of the left foot in the front of the circle. This results in the left foot landing to the right of the right foot at the board, blocking the hips.	• Jumping into the air as if completing a pirouette in the back of the circle. The left foot is in front as the athlete faces 6 o'clock and the right foot makes contact with the circle.	• You must be on the ball of the right foot and continue turning until you are facing the direction of the throw. The left foot must come down as quickly as possible. Attempt to have both feet land at the same time. Concentrate on quickly pulling the left foot behind the right knee and moving smoothly into the power position. • Practice the half turn drill and the wheel drill.
Shutting down the rotation of the right leg, rushing the throw	• The hips and shoulders are facing 1 o'clock at the time of release because the left leg straightens prior to the complete rotation of the hips to the front.	• Timing is critical. Keep the legs well bent throughout the entire rotation. Keep the left leg soft until ready to drive up onto the left leg at the release of the shot. • Practice multiple repetitions with heavy implements. • Complete many imitations to develop precise timing.
The right leg consumes too much of the circle, creating a narrow base.	• Poor technique in the turn	• Wait until the hips, left foot, and shoulders face the 3 o'clock position before picking up the right foot. There must be a 90-degree angle in the right knee when the right foot is picked up. • Practice the jump the stream drill.

248

opportunity for powerful performances, athletes must endure hours of practice to perfect it.

Beginning shot put throwers typically are introduced to the glide technique. This enables the coach to teach the fundamental aspects of throwing the shot put. The glide technique permits the novice thrower to develop a solid power position with a turning right leg. The turning inward of the right leg is crucial for the development of the rotational technique.

To achieve success with the rotational technique, the thrower must possess the patience and perseverance to meet its precise requirements. For that reason, this technique is not the best fit for every shot-putter. The successful rotational shot put thrower is methodical and even tempered, consistently focused, and intensely committed to the technique. The explosive urge must be under total control. Additionally, the coach may consider the athlete's throwing distance when determining whether to introduce the rotational technique. One rule of thumb is that a high school sophomore who can perform a 140- to 150-foot (42.7 to 45.7 m) throw in the discus may have the rhythm and balance necessary to become a successful rotational shot-putter.

Starting Position

The starting position for the rotational technique can vary from upright to a slightly inclined (tilted) torso. An inclined posture with a more pronounced knee bend allows for a longer path of acceleration and a steeper path of the shot from the rear of the circle through the delivery. It can present problems for the novice thrower because it requires greater overall strength, especially in the core, makes balance in the start difficult, and can limit turning speed potential because of the required strength. Although the shot may be held in the hand and cradled at the neck exactly as in the glide, most rotational throwers tend to hold it under or even behind the ear to increase control of the shot during the turns. As the athlete increases the speed of the turns during the throw, holding the shot to the neck becomes much harder; the higher neck placement helps counteract the centrifugal force.

The thrower straddles the midline of the circle with a base that is a little wider than the shoulders but is eventually adjusted according to individual preference and comfort. Body posture is rigid, although the athlete is slightly bent at the waist with shoulders square and facing the rear of the circle (figure 16.10). An upright (stickman) position is recommended when teaching beginners. Assuming a right-handed thrower, the right hand holds the shot against the neck with the arm level with the shoulder and at a 90-degree angle to the trunk. The left arm is at shoulder level in front of the body and relaxed, slightly bent at the elbow.

Turn

The success of the throw depends on a series of precise movements at the back of the circle. Following a slight rhythmic swing of the trunk to the right, the athlete begins a slow transfer of the center of gravity to the left leg to prepare to punch off the left leg. The knees are bent 90

FIGURE 16.10 Upright posture in the starting position for the rotational shot put.

to 110 degrees, assuming a position similar to that of a front squat (figure 16.11).

As the athlete pivots on the ball of the left foot, there is a delayed push-off of the right foot until the hips face 3 o'clock, resulting in the tension being felt in the hip area. At the same time, the right arm and shot remain over the right knee and foot.

The eyes remain focused on the horizon with the head facing straight ahead in line with the shoulders as they turn. The coach should instruct the athlete to maintain this position and refrain from looking over the left shoulder. The head must remain in line with the shoulders during the turn.

The left arm and shoulder rotate to the left until they are above the left knee and foot, continuing to rotate with the knee and foot until they point to 3 o'clock. At this time, the right foot is lifting, creating a 90-degree bend in the knee joint; then the dorsiflexed foot sweeps in a heart-shaped path to the center of the circle with a swing outside the rim at 4 or 5 o'clock. The angle must be at least 90 degrees. This

FIGURE 16.11   Transfer of the center of gravity to the left leg.

soccer-style sweep (kicking action) of the foot and lower leg results in a quick movement of the feet (hip flip) toward the center of the circle. This also ensures a short and flat jump turn.

The left foot and ankle produce the push-off. The knee is never locked out or straight because that will cause the athlete to jump too high and use up too much of the circle. Too vigorous of an opening or swinging of the left arm will cause instability, and the upper body will fall into the turn, resulting in a balance problem at the front of the circle.

Maintaining level shoulders during the rotation out of the back of the circle is one of the most important aspects of a successful throw. Any dipping or dropping of the left shoulder will result in a critical balance problem in the front of the circle.

As the body rotates to the front of the left foot, the right foot is thrown to the center of the circle. The athlete must drive the left shoulder and arm in the direction of the left sector line. The right foot and leg turn inward from the right hip so that when the right foot comes down, it is pointing from the 9 to the 6 o'clock position.

Some athletes focus the eyes on the left sector line to prevent an overrotation of the shoulders as the left foot pushes the hips to the center of the circle. After the left foot completes its push, it must be rapidly pulled close to the right leg and tucked under the hip for quick placement down in the front of the circle. The slower the left-foot plant, the less torque in the body and the greater the chance for a premature shift of the center of gravity to the left leg.

The left foot must be pulled out of the back of the circle and enter into a 90-degree relationship with the hips to create a more efficient jump turn to the power position, which prevents a late arrival of the left foot to the stop board. The coach can facilitate the timely placement of the left foot at the front of the circle by instructing the athlete to pull the left thigh as close to the right thigh as possible, or attempt to kick the left heel to the buttocks.

Also important is that the athlete stay low on well-bent legs. A common error of novice rotational throwers is rising too soon, which results in expending too much leg strength and possibly reducing the lift from the power position.

Power Position

The right foot makes contact with the circle through the ball of the foot. Active rotation of the right foot depends on the right heel's never coming into contact with the circle throughout the rest of the throw. The left leg and foot move quickly to the front of the circle. This movement results in a much greater torque (shoulder hip separation) with the center of gravity over a well-bent right leg.

The shot and right shoulder should be over the right foot when the left foot comes into contact with the surface. The left arm should be outside of the left (front) leg producing a prestretching of the chest. The hips face the 3 o'clock position, and the feet are in a good left-toe, right-heel alignment. The base of the rotational technique is narrower than that of the glide; the right foot is between 3 and 6 inches (about 8 and 15 cm) in the front half of the circle.

The right (throwing) arm is still shoulder high, pressing the shot against the neck. The eyes are focused hard on a spot 6 to 8 feet (1.8 to 2.4 m) beyond the back of the circle, and the hips are moving ahead of the shoulders.

The right foot continues to aggressively turn while the athlete remains on the ball of the foot and pushes the right hip to the front against a braced left leg (figure 16.12). At the same time, the legs remain bent until the hips face the direction of the throw. The right leg does not straighten as it does in the glide, because of the narrower base of the rotational technique. The important task of the right leg and foot is to thrust the right hip toward the front.

Nearly all rotational shot-putters share a common error: the left leg straightening or locking out too early when the hips are still facing 2 or 1 o'clock. This results in an ineffective lift and release height and a throw that slants toward the right sector line. The center of gravity must remain solidly on the right leg and foot during the turning of the right hip in the direction of the put.

Arm Strike

Both legs are directly involved in a successful shot put throw. However, the primary source of lift comes from the left leg only after the hips are facing the direction of the throw. This is necessary for creating an effective block on the left side (figure 16.13), keeping the athlete in the circle, and preventing a foul.

FIGURE 16.12 Wheel to the power position.

FIGURE 16.13 Block.

A critical component of the rotational technique is precise timing. The right leg lifting prior to the left leg often results in a weak block and a throwing direction down the left sector line. If the left leg lifts prior to the right leg, the athlete may be forced to sit or lean back with the center of gravity behind the left leg, which results in a weak throw.

The left shoulder and arm work with the left leg to establish a strong block as the right arm punches out with an inside-out movement to deliver the shot.

A rotational shot put thrower must learn to wait for the right hip to rotate to the front. The inability to wait often results in a foul as a result of sliding the hips to the front. Many throwers rush the throw and slide the hips to the front so that the shoulders end up in front of the hips at the time of the leg lift and throw.

The head and chest are up, facing the direction of the throw as the right shoulder is punched up and the elbow is high behind the shot. The fingers and wrist execute a powerful flick with the thumb down and the little finger up as the shot leaves the hand.

Recovery (Reverse)

The rotational technique may require the thrower to continue the rotational movement after the release of the shot as a result of the forceful momentum developed by the action of the rotational technique and leg lift. This results in the athlete landing on a slightly flexed right leg, flat footed, and facing the 9 o'clock position. The left leg is swung out wide toward 6 o'clock.

Drill Progressions for the Glide Shot Put

The fundamentals of the shot put are best taught through a series of drills. The thrower must learn requisite skills such as posture and balance and feel comfortable pivoting on the ball of the foot. Each drill teaches a specific skill. A series of drills to teach shot put specifics help throwers develop the parts of the throw.

Regardless of the type of technique eventually used by the shot-putter, these basic skills must be addressed. Once the drills are mastered, the thrower is ready to learn the back-of-the-ring mechanics of the throw and advance to the throwing progression.

Throwing events use the part-whole-part method of teaching. The coach breaks down the event into parts. For the shot put, the power position is taught first, and then the glide. After the athlete acquires an acceptable skill in the power position and the glide, the two are combined into the whole so the athlete learns the rhythm of the event. Because rhythm and timing are vital, coaches must allocate a majority of technical training to the whole event. However, the athlete must use drills to practice parts of the event to reinforce challenging aspects.

The novice athlete must understand that the legs are the most important part of the body in throwing the shot. To build this understanding, the coach can have the athlete complete throws that demonstrate how each part of the body affects the distance of the throw if the sequential timing is in place. Each step eventually leads into the complete throw.

When trying to establish the proper position, the coach and athlete should keep in mind that a weak position has no life; they should strive for positions that create sparks. The stickman position can be the starting point. The athlete should try different styles and adapt techniques as needed. A slight adjustment can make a big difference. When an athlete hits a good position, he should practice it. The coach's task is to solidify the technical model, mold it, and drill it until the athlete knows it instinctively. When the technical model is stable, it is time to introduce heavy and light implements.

Arm Strike and Block Drills

The arm strike is likely the most undercoached component of the shot put throw. Properly performing the inside-out motion of the arm strike often can be the difference between a good throw and a great throw. The putting motion of the arm strike is another unnatural motion that must be developed through drills that develop specific throwing strength. Most athletes are comfortable with the follow-through used when shooting a basketball, which can make teaching the arm strike in the shot put a challenge. The following drills will help athletes master the parts of the technique. The focus is on the fundamentals of the shot put. These drills, which are applicable for the glide and the rotational technique, help throwers feel the desired positions and actions.

MEDICINE BALL PUT

Hold a 2- or 3-kilogram (around 4 or 6 lb) medicine ball with the elbows up and thumbs down (figure 16.14). Throw the ball to a partner or against a fence with an inside-out motion. The thumbs should be down. The hand should follow through outward.

FIGURE 16.14 Medicine ball put.

PARTNER HIGH FIVE

Stand and face a partner, who serves as your target for the drill. Have your throwing arm bent at the elbow with the throwing hand over the shoulder. Hold the opposite arm long at the midline of the body. Your partner lifts a hand in the air to create a target. Strike your partner's hand with your throwing hand (figure 16.15). Maintain the proper alignment of the arm with the thumb down and the elbow up. Use a release angle similar to the one for the actual throw.

After a few repetitions, add the block. The timing of the drill is: block, then strike. You will feel the summation of forces and the additional power achieved with the block.

FIGURE 16.15 Partner high five.

KNEELING THROW

In this drill, you use the shot put to stress the blocking action. If you are right-handed, put your left knee down and hold the shot put off the neck on the shoulder. The left arm is in front, slightly flexed at the midline of the body as you face the landing area. Put the shot (figure 16.16) with the same inside-out motion described in the partner high five drill. The shot should not travel very far. Emphasize good release mechanics.

FIGURE 16.16   Kneeling throw.

SQUARE DRILL

Face the throwing direction and place the right knee on the ground. Relax the blocking arm and hold it at about 35 degrees at the midline of the body extended toward the middle of the throwing sector. Cradle the throwing hand under the shot as you place it in the throwing position over the deltoid (figure 16.17). Push the shot in the throwing direction using correct arm extension and wrist action. The left arm remains extended at the midline of the body.

FIGURE 16.17   Square drill.

BLOCKING DRILL

Place the right knee down, and hold the shot put off the neck on the shoulder. The left arm is in front, slightly flexed at the midline of the body as you face the landing area. Put the shot (figure 16.18) with the same inside-out motion described in the partner high five drill. During the throwing movement, allow the nonthrowing hand to come toward the nonthrowing shoulder, bringing the back of the arm toward the rib cage. Do not allow the shoulders to rotate.

FIGURE 16.18 Blocking drill.

TWISTING DRILL

Put your left knee down and hold the shot put off the neck on the shoulder. The left arm is in front, slightly flexed at the midline of the body as you face the landing area. Rotate the shoulders 90 degrees to the right so that the shot is behind the right hip (figure 16.19). Push the shot in the throwing direction. The shoulders naturally will come to the front without forcefully rotating.

FIGURE 16.19 Twisting drill.

Delivery Drills

Flexibility, balance, and kinesthetic awareness are vital to be a successful shot put thrower. The action in the center of the circle for both the glide and rotational techniques includes a combination of rotation, lift, and hip drift. The action depends on the technique and the athlete's physical qualities. Most twisting happens along the spine; the trunk causes rotation. Torque is established by maintaining partially open hips and closed shoulders. Entering this position creates a spring-loading effect in the torso. The muscles used to put the shot are stretched so they are ready to contract and accelerate the shot. The key is to fire them in the proper order (proximal to distal joints) to maximize force development.

Power position and delivery drills help the athlete obtain a consistent power position with proper balance and alignment. These drills teach proper timing (range and separation) in the movement pattern during the delivery phase, thereby increasing the range of motion that the shot must travel prior to release.

HIP POP

Assume the power position. Keep the shoulders closed and the weight on the drive leg. A partner holds either your free arm (figure 16.20a) or a bungee cord to help you stay back. Turn the hip on the drive leg in the direction of the throw. This movement is similar to grinding a cigarette. In a variation of the drill, move the hip and the left arm (figure 16.20b). The hip pop drill also can be performed with a stick on the shoulders (figure 16.20c).

FIGURE 16.20 Hip pop: *(a)* turning the hip and driving the leg; *(b)* moving the hip and left arm; *(c)* holding a stick on the shoulders.

FRONT PUNCH

Set up with both feet against the toe board, facing the throwing sector with the throwing hand cradled under the shot, which is over the deltoid (figure 16.21). Step back into a shoulder-width stance with the majority of the body weight over the right leg. From this modified power position, forcefully extend the right leg while the right foot turns in. Feel the legs and hips work independently of the upper body. Once the lower body is fully extended and turned to the front, execute a release while the left foot is firmly planted on the ground. The front punch drill is a great way to warm up prior to the standing throw drill.

FIGURE 16.21   Front punch.

STANDING THROW

Stand with feet shoulder-width apart and in a heel–toe position with the back foot turned in the direction of delivery. Bend the right leg, and keep the torso upright and firm. The left leg is rigid and slightly flexed, about an inch (about 2.5 cm) from the toe board and just left of center. The power position should feel comfortable, although you may feel some tension in the torso. Focus on a fixed location 6 to 8 feet (1.8 to 2.4 m) behind the ring. Initiate the throw from the midsection of the body, as the hips turn and the body weight transfers from the back foot to the front foot. Pop the hip by turning on the balls of the feet. The movement starts with the strong, slow proximal joints and finishes with the weak, fast distal joints. The majority of standing throw work should be performed without the reverse. Performing 10 standing throws is a good way to begin a throwing workout.

Glide Drills

Once a thrower can complete a full standing throw under control, she is ready to begin to learn the technique in the back of the ring. Coaches should introduce the glide technique initially. Beginning shot-putters who can throw much farther using a standing throw than using a full technique can use the standing throw in meets until they are ready to use the full glide technique. Coaches may consider introducing the rotational technique at an early age for athletes who exhibit exceptional rotational awareness. The drills in this section teach athletes the mechanics of the glide technique.

STEP BACK

Assume the same starting position as the glide (figure 16.22*a*). Step to the middle of the ring with the right foot slightly turned at a 45-degree angle (figure 16.22*b*), and extend the left foot to the board (figure 16.22*c*). The movement results in a strong power position. You can stop and throw, or go through the total movement without a pause. The goal is to hit a solid and balanced power position while moving the shot from the back of the ring. This drill is great for multievent athletes. After mastering this basic movement, you can move on to learning the mechanics of the glide technique.

FIGURE 16.22   Step back: *(a)* starting position; *(b)* right foot; *(c)* left foot.

A DRILL

Assume the typical starting position and unseat the hips, keeping the majority of the weight on the right heel. Extend the left leg toward the toe board while keeping the right heel planted. During this movement, the hips should stay low and the shoulders should remain square to the back of the ring. Hold a shot or mimic holding a shot (figure 16.23). This extension should create an elongated body position similar to the letter A. This drill helps eliminate the flight phase in the transition phase of the glide. In the glide, this phase must be fluid. Too long a flight phase often causes the left leg to ground late and the shoulders to open prematurely, which reduces valuable time in which to apply force to the shot.

FIGURE 16.23 A drill.

MEDICINE BALL PUSH AND GLIDE

This drill teaches the extension of the left leg in the glide. If you have trouble extending the left leg in the straight line, place a medicine ball behind your left leg. Set up in the back of the ring as if preparing to glide, and kick the ball with the left leg to feel the extension as if gliding (figure 16.24).

FIGURE 16.24 Medicine ball push and glide.

MINI GLIDE

The rhythm of the glide is very important, and deficiencies in core strength may prevent you from learning the proper rhythm. The mini glide drill is a great way to learn the simultaneous grounding of the feet.

Perform a shortened version of the glide (figure 16.25), emphasizing correct rhythm. Start with a glide of 6 inches (about 15 cm) and increase from there. As you understand the rhythm and grow stronger, lengthen the glide.

FIGURE 16.25   Mini glide: *(a)* starting position; *(b)* finish.

PARTNER GLIDE

Keeping the shoulders closed while moving across the ring toward the toe board often is the biggest challenge in the glide shot put. The partner glide drill emphasizes keeping the shoulders closed (square to the back of the circle) in the glide.

Assume a normal starting position in the back of the circle with a partner holding your free arm (figure 16.26*a*). The partner provides mild tension by walking with you during the glide (figure 16.26*b*), ensuring that your shoulders stay closed and square to the back of the circle. Perform sets of five repetitions.

FIGURE 16.26   Partner glide: *(a)* starting position; *(b)* execution.

Drills for the Entire Throw

Each throwing session should include brief warm-up activities such as agility work and running. The session can begin with a power position drill and a glide drill. Each training session should begin with a briefing in which the coach introduces the objectives of the training session. The throwing session should consist of approximately 30 throws with shots of various weights depending on the stage of the training cycle.

GLIDE AND STOP

This drill splits the full throw into two parts. Begin in the same way as you begin a full throw. However, after gliding across the ring, stop in the standing throw position. At this point, the coach observes to see whether you are in the proper position to perform a good throw. After the observation (usually a couple of seconds), the coach tells you to finish the throw by saying "Go" or clapping.

This drill helps the coach assess how well you hit the positions after gliding across the ring. The one thing this drill does not address is the quick transition from the glide to the throw. Therefore, the coach should ensure that you do not become accustomed to stopping in the middle of the ring. Three to five repetitions of the glide and stop drill will help establish the proper kinesthetic feel for the power position.

FULL THROWS WITH NO REVERSE

Initiate the throw in the midsection of the body (proximal to distal), as the hips turn and the body weight transfers from the back foot to the front foot. The movement starts with the strong, slow proximal joints and finishes with the weak, fast distal joints. The majority of throwing in training (70 percent) should be performed without the reverse. All of the standing throws and 10 to 15 of the full throws should be performed without the reverse.

FULL THROWS WITH REVERSE

The reverse is a function of the explosive extension of the hips and legs, which leads to the delivery of the shot and the long shoulder hit. Perform the final 5 to 10 throws of a workout with the reverse, and stay in the ring.

Drill Progressions for the Rotational Shot Put

With a skill as complex as the rotational shot put, it is appropriate to break it down into parts following an introduction of the basic movement. The parts are taught and then linked to develop the final skill. This is referred to as whole-part-whole instruction. The athlete first watches a demonstration of the whole skill to appreciate the product and understand how the parts develop the skill. The parts are then practiced individually, in order, before being linked together and expanded. This approach is sometimes termed the progressive part method. This process is slow, but it allows weaknesses to be targeted and helps the athlete understand the relationship of the parts to the whole technique. This section breaks down the rotational shot put technique into parts in a series of drills.

Power Position Drill

The first step in teaching the rotational technique is teaching the standing throw. The standing throw should be taught the same way for gliders and spinners (rotational throwers). The only difference is that the spinner may use a narrower base than the glider. See the standing throw drill in the preceding section, Delivery Drills.

CRUNCH DRILL

Assume a shoulder-width base with both feet pointing toward 90 degrees. Lean back over the right leg in a side bend motion (figure 16.27). Initiate the throw by pushing with the right leg to create a spring motion through the hip and into the side and shoulder. The left arm blocks. This drill mirrors the power position in the throw and is great for developing core strength.

FIGURE 16.27   Crunch drill.

Transition Drills

When the power position is mastered, the athlete must practice a series of drills to learn the rotational movement. Many of the drills used for the rotational shot put can be modified and used to develop a discus thrower. The drills in this section teach balance and the basic positions of the full movement. Transition drills allow the athlete to acquire consistency in transitioning from the initial starting position into a proper power position. A comfortable and efficient starting position must be established in the back of the ring. These drills also teach the athlete how to create proper timing in the movement pattern during the transition phase (active lower body and passive upper body).

PIVOT STEP BACK LINE DRILL

Stand behind a line with the left foot forward and the hands on the hips. When the coach issues the "Step forward" command, step onto the line with the right foot (figure 16.28). The next command is "Pivot," at which point you pivot on both feet 180 degrees. Following the pivot, when the coach calls "Step back," step straight back along the line with the left foot. The final command is "Pivot," at which point you pivot 180 degrees on both feet back to the original starting position. Repeat the sequence over and over. Progress to an imitation holding the shot.

FIGURE 16.28 Pivot step back line drill.

WHEEL DRILL

Start with the right leg in the center of the ring and pivot to the power position, working on getting the left leg down (figure 16.29). The wheel helps the right foot tuck and turn. Pick up the left foot and rapidly tuck it and turn on the ball of the right foot, performing a 180-degree turn and maintaining the same position throughout the drill. This drill can be repeated in the same spot.

FIGURE 16.29 Wheel drill.

BALANCE WHEEL DRILL

Beginning throwers often have trouble keeping the upper body and lower body moving as a unit. The balance wheel drill teaches you how to keep the majority of your body weight over the throwing side. From the center of the ring, and while holding the outside of the throwing-side knee with the nonthrowing-side (left) hand, perform a half turn in a counterclockwise direction (figure 16.30a). This drill teaches you how to maintain balance and alignment over the throwing-side leg in the center of the ring (figure 16.30b). It also emphasizes the importance of timing and posture during the transition phase and into the power position.

FIGURE 16.30   Balance wheel drill: *(a)* start; *(b)* finish.

CHALLENGE WHEEL DRILL

The challenge wheel drill increases the difficulty of the standard wheel drill. It helps build balance and control in the execution of the wheel drill. The wheel drill is replicated in a continuous turning manner, and the use of verbal cues or preset combinations is recommended. To perform the challenge wheel drill, set up four cones approximately 90 degrees apart (figure 16.31). At the coach's command, turn to a specified position in the ring. Placement options include quarter turn (90 degrees), half turn (180 degrees), three-quarter turn (270 degrees), and full turn (360 degrees).

FIGURE 16.31   Challenge wheel drill.

From the power position, perform a series of multidirectional turns in a counterclockwise direction. A stick behind the neck along the top of the shoulders can be added to increase the difficulty. This drill may also be performed on the nonthrowing-side leg to improve overall balance and coordination.

WHEEL TUCK DRILL

The wheel tuck helps develop the left foot tuck and turn. Line up 3 feet (about 1 m) from a wall or fence starting with the right leg in the center of the ring (figure 16.32a). Perform a wheel and pivot to the power position. Instead of putting the left leg down, squeeze the knees and drive the left leg into the wall. The objective is to support the majority of the body weight over the throwing-side leg, which necessitates driving the nonthrowing-side foot into the wall for support (figure 16.32b). This drill also helps you understand the need for greater torsion between the lower and upper bodies during the transition phase.

FIGURE 16.32   Wheel tuck drill: *(a)* start; *(b)* finish.

Entry Drills

Entry drills help the athlete acquire consistency in obtaining balance and alignment in the initial starting position. These drills teach proper timing in the movement pattern during the entry phase (active lower body and passive upper body).

JUMP THE STREAM

Stand in the back of the ring with the left foot inside the circle, facing 12 o'clock, and the right foot outside the circle (figure 16.33a). Wind up and drive off the left leg to the center of the circle. Land in the center of the circle with the shoulders level, the head raised, and the hips leading. Concentrate on pulling the left foot as quickly as possible behind the right knee, and hold that position in the middle of the ring (figure 16.33b). This drill teaches you how to drive out of the back of the ring and reinforces proper positions in the middle of the ring.

If you have trouble getting off the ground and learning the jump turn, jump into a high jump pit. Focus on performing the jump out of the back so you can eventually perform the jump turn while driving into the center of the ring. If you are a novice, start facing the pit, and as you become more comfortable, perform the windup and entry phases. Place a small object in the middle of the ring to jump over if you like. Right-foot placement should occur on the top of the pit at the completion of this drill. Perform five or more repetitions.

FIGURE 16.33   Jump the stream: (a) start; (b) finish.

SOUTH AFRICAN DRILL

Stand in the back of the ring with the left foot inside the circle, facing 12 o'clock, and the right foot outside the circle. Wind up and drive off the left leg to the center of the circle. Concentrate on pulling the left foot as quickly as possible behind the right knee and continuing into the power position and putting the shot.

MODIFIED SOUTH AFRICAN DRILL

Stand in the back of the ring in the starting position of the full spin. Then, perform a quarter turn. With the left foot inside the circle, facing 12 o'clock, and the right foot outside the circle, perform the South African drill. Wind up and drive off the left leg to the center of the circle. Concentrate on pulling the left foot as quickly as possible behind the right knee and continuing into the power position and putting the shot.

Back of the Ring Drills

These drills teach the compulsory skills for the back of the ring in the rotational technique. The first drill is fairly simple, and the drills progress in difficulty from there. In each drill, the athlete starts by putting the knee over the toes and the armpit over the knee to load the left leg.

The left arm is kept long, in line with the left knee. The left side is locked for a unit turn. The athlete keeps the knees apart while performing each drill, initiates the turn with the left-side pivot, and powers the turn with the right leg. The head is up with the eyes focused on the horizon. The athlete should imagine balancing a stack of books on top of the head.

STEP-AROUND TURN

This drill teaches how to load the left leg and is performed with the left foot in the center of the ring. Assume the starting position with the majority of the body weight on the left leg. Initiate the turn with a slight pivot of the left foot; then step around the clock (figure 16.34). Keep the majority of the body weight (approximately 70 percent) balanced on the left leg.

FIGURE 16.34   Step-around turn.

QUARTER TURN

The quarter turn drill teaches proper balance at the back of the circle. It is very similar to the step-around turn drill, but is slightly more difficult. You can work on lines or in the back of the circle. Place the feet shoulder-width apart, knees bent at 45 degrees. The nonthrowing arm is relaxed and away from the body about shoulder high (figure 16.35). Pivot forward a quarter turn, employing balance skills (knee over toes, armpit over knee, left arm over left leg) and continue pivoting forward to the starting point. Balance is attained by transferring the weight to the left by moving the left shoulder over the left foot. Do not change the angles of the knees and ankles when

FIGURE 16.35   Quarter turn.

transferring to balance and pivot. Unite the left side all the way around with a controlled pivot. Move left, pivot on the left foot, rotate a quarter turn, and keep the knees and thighs apart.

HALF TURN

The half turn drill also teaches proper balance at the back of the circle. It is very similar to the two previous drills, but it requires a bit more balance. You can start in the back of the circle or work on lines. Place the feet parallel, shoulder-width apart, knees bent at approximately 45 degrees. The nonthrowing arm is relaxed and away from the body about shoulder high. Pivot forward a half turn, employing balance skills, and continue pivoting forward to the starting point (figure 16.36). Balance is attained by transferring the weight to the left by moving the left shoulder over the left foot.

Coaching Points

- Stay balanced
- Control transfer and pivot
- Unite the left side
- Keep knees and thighs apart

FIGURE 16.36   Half turn.

360-DEGREE TURN

The 360-degree turn drill is the final drill in the back-of-the-ring series. Assume the starting position in the back of the ring or on the lines. Place the feet on the line, shoulder-width apart, and bend the knees to approximately 45 degrees. The nonthrowing arm is relaxed and away from the body about shoulder high. Pivot forward 360 degrees, employing balance skills, and continue pivoting forward to the starting point. Balance is attained by transferring the weight to the left by moving the left shoulder over the left foot (figure 16.37a). A bar can be added to develop core strength (figure 16.37b). The shot put can be held in the chest pass position for additional balance (figure 16.37c).

FIGURE 16.37   360-degree turn: *(a)* basic drill.

(b) with a bar.

(c) with a shot put.

Putting It All Together

The balance drills can be grouped to teach the full rotation. The quarter turn drill out of the back of the ring is followed by a half turn to the middle of the ring, followed by a half turn backward, or wheel. Combining these drills is an easy way to teach a beginner to rotate. Using the part method keeps beginners from developing the bad habits that can result from teaching the whole movement, which many have a hard time understanding. After step 1 is mastered, the coach can move on to step 2.

When performing the drills, the athlete should keep the left arm out for balance and simulate holding the shot with the right arm. The half turn backward is the wheel and reach drill. Athletes should always finish in a balanced power position. They need to maintain the angles of the knee and ankle during the center pivot. In the wheel, the left leg is kept long and in the front position. Weight should be maintained over the pivot foot, the left foot at the start, and then the right foot in the center. The left arm should be relaxed and long for a long left side. Eyes should be focused outside the circle to the horizon and remain relaxed.

RIGHT LEG TAP AND TURN

This drill emphasizes right-side rotation. Assume the power position with the shoulders closed and the weight back on the right. As you tap the left leg, the right knee turns and the left arm sweeps high in direction of the throw. The head and shoulders stay back over the right leg, and the shoulders arch backward. The left foot comes off the ground as you deliver the shot put. The drill should result in a high, but short throw.

HEADACHE DRILL

Assume the power position with the free arm resting against the forehead and the palm out (figure 16.38*a*). Deliver the shot put from this position (figure 16.38*b*). The headache drill emphasizes getting the left elbow high and a linear over-the-top delivery for the rotational thrower.

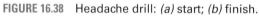

FIGURE 16.38   Headache drill: *(a)* start; *(b)* finish.

Sweep Drills

At the back of the circle, the main action comes from swinging wide and having a very active right leg. Better results can be obtained by stressing the circular action of the right leg sweeping around the left. Athletes should concentrate on sweeping the inside of the right thigh around the left leg. Many athletes lead the action with the top of the right thigh, which is not recommended. The giant step drill and the wall catch drill introduce and refine the very important right-leg sweep.

GIANT STEP DRILL

After you have mastered the combination, the quarter turn and half turn are replaced by the giant step. In the giant step, the sweeping movement is led by the inside of the right thigh at the start, finishing in the middle of the ring (figure 16.39). A circular, heart-shaped, sweeping action is stressed in this drill.

FIGURE 16.39   Giant step drill.

WALL CATCH DRILL

Emphasis in this drill is on turning out of the back of the circle and working the sweep. Standing in front of a wall at arm's length, replicate the windup phase. Following the windup, begin the entry phase movement by lifting the right leg and sweeping it around the body until you can hold yourself up against the wall by reaching out with the left arm and sweeping the right leg (figure 16.40). Perform at least five repetitions.

FIGURE 16.40   Wall catch drill.

Designing Shot Put Workouts

Before developing shot put throwing workouts, coaches should emphasize the importance of acquiring proper technique. They should also carefully consider the relationship between training and teaching. Before teaching a beginner the shot put, a coach must consider the equipment needed, decide on the units of training (including how much time in each unit), and choose key coaching cues.

The thrower should begin each session with 8 to 12 minutes of a general dynamic warm-up that flows smoothly into a specific warm-up that includes shot put drills. Throwing workouts should always start with drills that align with the objectives (technical theme) of the training session. One drill should emphasize the power position, and one should address the mechanics. As the drills conclude, the thrower begins the throwing session, which should consist of approximately 30 throws.

How heavy should the implement be in these workouts? This depends on the training status and training age of the athletes. Many coaches argue that the majority of training should be completed with an implement 2 pounds less or 2 pounds more (about 1 kg) than the competition implement. This is referred to as the 10 percent rule. Keeping weights within 10 percent of the competition implement allows the beginner to adapt to this type of training and does not disrupt the competition rhythm.

As a thrower becomes more advanced, heavier implements may be used. Ultimately, implements that do not exceed the standard weight by 20 percent can be used in the full glide or rotation. This recommendation is especially important for beginner to intermediate athletes. As athletes advance, they can use an implement 4 pounds more or less (about 2 kg) than the standard weight as part of the training regimen, but the majority of the work should still be done with an implement 2 pounds (about 1 kg) over or under standard weight. Technique may be affected if the implement is too light or too heavy.

Most throwers use implements of two or three different weights during each six- to eight-week training period. Too many different weights in a training phase may overwhelm the athlete's nervous system and dampen the development of proper patterns, although varying weights aid the development of the proper reflexes. Techniques are mastered only when muscle contractions and relaxations are coordinated and synchronized to produce maximal total effort relative to throwing. In addition, throwing heavy implements makes the thrower strong in a way that is specific to the technical pattern of the event. It helps develop core strength and enhances the ability to stabilize the midsection during high-velocity throws.

The control and kinesthetic awareness of the legs and the right side of the body in the power position are critical. Heavier implements increase electrical activity in the involved muscles, improving the coordinative potential of the movement, which results in better recruitment of functional motor units.

Microcycles for the Shot Put

The definitive goal of shot put training is the functional reconstruction of the athlete, resulting in an enduring adaptation and the preservation of the training effect. High-quality training plans often include both specific and general exercises. Variables such as training load, training volume, exercise selection, and training frequency should be chosen based on the athlete's training age and strengths and weaknesses, as well as the phase of the training year. An in-season competition program must consider bioenergetics, metabolic parameters, and movement characteristics specific to throwing the shot put, such as force, magnitude, velocity, movement patterns, and time factors.

The objective of microcycles for shot-putters is to coordinate training loads to establish a balance between work and recovery. The plan must ensure sufficient regeneration prior to the start of a new microcycle. The function of a microcycle is to provide a rational approach to the training loads planned for a particular training phase. As a rule, each microcycle concludes with one or two recovery days. Microcycles also include specific goals. The goal of a preparation microcycle (figure 16.41) is to prepare the thrower for the upcoming competition. The goal of the last preparation microcycle (figure 16.42) prior to a competition is to unleash and mobilize the thrower's performance capacities.

The goal of a competition microcycle (figure 16.43) is to organize activities just prior to and immediately after a competition. This involves activities one day before the competition, the day of the competition, and days following the competition. The goal for the competition microcycle depends on the length of the competition, the number of attempts, the frequency of competitions, the performance level of the rivals, and so on. In short, the competition microcycle should be tailored to the needs of the shot-putter.

The most effective organizational structure is one week for each microcycle. However, shot put throwers who train two or three times per day often require slightly shorter microcycles.

Each microcycle must include recovery times between training sessions.

Consistency in scheduling throughout the year is an important component of a microcycle. Additionally, the efficacy of training sessions is maintained when careful consideration is given to any potential interference among the types of training. For example, coaches should ensure that the training activity of day 1 does not interfere with the training activity of day 2.

Microcycle # Phase: General preparation	Dates: Comments:	Event group: Shot put
Sunday	**Monday**	**Tuesday**

Rest	Theme: Neuromuscular development, high demand
	Warm-up jog
	Dynamic flexibility exercises
	Specific warm-up, grind the cigarette drill 3 × 5
	Shot put drills
	    Hip pops with bar 3 × 5
	    Multiple glides with bar 3 × 5
	Standing throw 1 (10), 10% over competition weight
	Glide stop and throw (10), 10% over competition weight
	Multithrow overhead back shot put throws (10), 10% over competition weight
	Weight training
	    Olympic lift
	        Clean pull from floor 6 × 4, 120% of CL 1RM
	    Back squat 4 × 8, 75% 1RM
	    Bench press 4 × 8, 75% 1RM
	Cool-down activity, static stretching
		Theme: General training, energy system and endocrine development
		Warm-up jog
		Dynamic flexibility exercises
		Technical drills for shot put throw
		    Hip pops with partner 3 × 5
		    Partner glide 3 × 5
		Shot put – Standing throw #1 (5 repetitions); glide stop and throw
		    Standing throw 1 (5)
		    Glide stop and throw (10)
		General strength
		    Total body circuit (8 exercises, 20 repetitions each)
		    Abdominal/spinal circuit (1 exercise, 10 repetitions in each plane)
		Bodybuilding lifts (9 exercises, 3 giant sets), 60 sec rest between sets
		Barefoot cool-down and foot strengthening work

Wednesday	**Thursday**	**Friday**

Theme: Neuromuscular development, low demand
Warm-up jog
Dynamic flexibility exercises
Shot put drills
    Partner high five drill 3 × 5
    Hip pops drill with partner 3 × 5
    Partner glide 3 × 5
    Throws on knees 3 × 5, 10% over competition weight,
    focus on block
Ground level plyometrics
    Jump circuit (6 exercises, 10 repetitions), 20 sec rest between exercises
Weight training
    Olympic lift
        Power clean from floor 4 × 3, 85% 1RM
    Step-up 2 × 5
    Lunge walk with twist 2 × 5
    Incline press 4 × 8, 70% 1RM
Build-up 5 × 80 meters
Multithrows 3 × 5, between legs forward, 10% over competitive weight
Cool-down activity, static stretching
	Theme: General training, general strength and strength endurance development
	Warm-up jog
	Dynamic flexibility exercises
	Hurdle mobility
	Technical drills shot put
	    Hip pops with cord 3 × 5
	    Glide to power position 3 × 5
	    Glide and stop drill (10), 10% over competition weight
	Medicine ball circuit (8 exercises, 10 repetitions)
	General strength (8 exercises, 20 repetitions)
	Barefoot cool-down and foot strengthening work
		Theme: Neuromuscular development, high demand
		Warm-up jog
		Dynamic flexibility exercises
		Specific warm-up, grind the cigarette drill 3 × 5
		Shot put drills
		    Hip pops with bar 3 × 5
		    Multiple glides with bar 3 × 5
		    Standing throw 1 (10), 10% over competition weight
		    Glide stop and throw (10), 10% over competition weight
		Weight training
		    Olympic lift
		        Snatch pull from floor 6 × 4, 115% of 1RM
		    Back squat 4 × 8, 70% 1RM
		    Bench press 4 × 8, 70% 1RM
		Cool-down activity, static stretching

Saturday	**Intensity of load by day**	**Post-workout comments**
Theme: General training, energy system and endocrine development Warm-up jog Dynamic flexibility exercises Glide drills down the track 2 × 10 Shot put Standing throw 2 (10), 20% overweight implement Cool-down, static stretching	(see intensity table below)	

	Su	M	Tu	W	Th	F	Sa
Hard		x		x		x	
Medium			x		x		
Easy							x
Rest	x						

FIGURE 16.41   Sample seven-day microcycle for the shot put: general preparation phase of training.

Microcycle #	Dates:	Event group: Shot put
Phase: Specific preparation	Comments:	

Sunday	Monday	Tuesday

Rest	Theme: Neuromuscular development, high demand
	Warm-up jog
	Dynamic flexibility exercises
	Specific warm-up
	  Hip pops with cord 3 × 5
	  Glides with bar (5)
	Standing throw 2, alternating 14 lb and 12 lb
	Glide and stop (2), 14 lb and 12 lb
	Full throws with no reverse, 10 × 2, alternating 14 lb and 20 lb (20 throws)
	Full throws with reverse (5), 12 lb
	Weight training
	  Olympic lift
	      Snatch from floor 6 × 2, 90% 1RM
	  Back squat 6 × 5, 85%
	  Bench press (6, 5, 4, 3, 2), 80%, 90%, 92%, 95%, 98%, increase weight each set
	Multithrows
	  Toe board chest pass explosions (10), 20% over competition weight
	Cool-down activity, static stretching
		Theme: General training, energy system and endocrine development
		Warm-up jog
		Dynamic flexibility exercises
		Specific warm-up
		  Hip pops with bungee cord 3 × 5
		  Partner glides, keep left arm long and head on spot (5)
		  Throws on knees 1 × 5
		Throwing progression (example for male high school thrower)
		  Standing throw 1 × 3 (6k, 6k, 5k)
		  Wheel and throw 1 × 3 (6k, 6k, 5k)
		  Glide stop and throws 1 × 3 (6k, 6k, 5k)
		  Full technique throws 3 × 3 (6k, 6k, 5k)
		  All-out throws (4), 5k, 100%
		  All-out throws with 11 lb weighted vest 4 × 3 (6k, 6k, 5k) 25 full throws
		General strength
		  Abdominal/spinal circuit (5 exercises, 10 repetitions)
		  Bodybuilding lifts (9 exercises, 3 giant sets), 60 sec rest between sets
		  Barefoot cool-down and foot strengthening work

Wednesday	Thursday	Friday

Theme: Neuromuscular development, low demand
Warm-up jog
Dynamic flexibility exercises
Sprint development drills
Specific strength
  Throws on knees (10), 20% over competition weight
Weight training
  Olympic lift
      Clean pull from thigh 6 × 3, 140% 1RM
  Split squat 2 × 6
  Split deadlift 2 × 6
  Pull-over 4 × 6
Acceleration development (3 × 20, 3 × 30, 3 × 40)
Cool-down activity, static stretching
	Theme: General training, general strength and strength endurance development
	Warm-up jog
	Dynamic flexibility exercises
	Specific warm-up
	  Hip pops with cord 3 × 5
	  Glides with bar (5)
	Shot put throwing progression
	  Standing throw 2, alternating 14 lb and 12 lb
	  Glide and stop (2), 14 lb and 12 lb
	  Full throws with no reverse 10 × 2, alternating 14 lb and 12 lb (20 throws)
	  Full throws with reverse (5), 12 lb
	Advanced core exercises (1 exercise, 10 repetitions in each plane of movement)
	Barefoot cool-down and foot strengthening work
		Theme: Neuromuscular development, high demand
		Warm-up jog
		Dynamic flexibility exercises
		Specific warm-up
		  Hip pops with bungee cord 3 × 5
		  Partner glides, keep left arm long and head on spot (5)
		  Throws on knees 1 × 5
		Throwing progression (example for male high school thrower)
		  Standing throw 1 × 3 (6k, 6k, 5k)
		  Wheel and throw 1 × 3 (6k, 6k, 5k)
		  Glide stop and throw 1 × 3 (6k, 6k, 5k)
		  Full technique throws 3 × 3 (6k, 6k, 5k)
		  All-out throws (4), 5k, 100%
		  All-out throws with 11lb weighted vest 4 × 3 (6k, 6k, 5k) 25 full throws
		Depth jump 3 × 5, full recovery
		Olympic lift
		  Hang clean 6 × 4, 85% 1RM
		Half squat 4 × 6, 120% full squat 1RM
		Speed incline press 4 × 6, 50% 1RM
		Cool-down activity, static stretching

Saturday	Intensity of load by day	Post-workout comments

Theme: General training, energy system and endocrine development
Warm-up jog
Dynamic flexibility exercises
Shot put drill; all drills performed with weighted vest
  Glide to power position and hip pop 3 × 5
  Hip pops, stick on shoulders 3 × 5
  Left leg 90-degree drives (5)
  Stand 6k medicine ball (5)
  Wheel 6k medicine ball (5)
  Three-step (L, R, L) throws with 6k medicine ball (10)
Medicine ball circuit (8 exercises, 10 repetitions for power)
Barefoot cool-down and foot strengthening
	<table><tr><td></td><td>Su</td><td>M</td><td>Tu</td><td>W</td><td>Th</td><td>F</td><td>Sa</td></tr><tr><td>Hard</td><td></td><td>x</td><td></td><td>x</td><td></td><td>x</td><td></td></tr><tr><td>Medium</td><td></td><td></td><td>x</td><td></td><td>x</td><td></td><td></td></tr><tr><td>Easy</td><td></td><td></td><td></td><td></td><td></td><td></td><td>x</td></tr><tr><td>Rest</td><td>x</td><td></td><td></td><td></td><td></td><td></td><td></td></tr></table>	

FIGURE 16.42 Sample seven-day microcycle for the shot put: specific preparation phase of training.

Microcycle # Phase: Competitive phase	Dates: Comments:	Event group: Shot put
Sunday	Monday	Tuesday

Rest	Theme: Neuromuscular development, high demand
	Warm-up jog
	Dynamic flexibility exercises
	Specific warm-up
	    Hip pops with partner 3 × 5
	    Glides with bar (5)
	Shot put throwing progression
	    Standing throw 2 (5), 10% above competition
	      weight
	    Glide and stop (2), 10% above competition weight
	    Full throws with no reverse (5), 10 % above
	      competition weight
	    Full throws with reverse (5), competition weight
	    Full throws with reverse (5), 10 % below competition
	      weight 22 throws total
	Weight training
	    Olympic lift
	      Hang snatch 6 × 2, 85 to 95%
	    Bench press 6 × 3, 85 to 90%, 3 to 5 min rest
	      between sets
	    Quarter squat 6 × 3, 130% BS 1RM
	    Russian twist 2 × 8
	Acceleration development 3 × 20, 3 × 30, full recovery
	Cool-down activity, static stretching
	Slow jog 5 min
		Theme: General training and endocrine development
		Warm-up jog
		Dynamic flexibility exercises
		Specific warm-up
		    Hip pops with bungee cord 3 × 5
		    Glides with weighted vest 3 × 5
		Standing throw 2 (5), competition weight
		Glide and stop (2), competition weight
		Full throws with no reverse (5), competition weight
		Full throws with reverse (5), competition weight
		  General strength
		    Abdominal/spinal circuit (5 exercises, 8 repetitions)
		    Medicine ball drills (4 exercises, 5 repetitions for
		      speed)
		Weight training
		    Bodybuilding lifts (9 exercises, 3 giant sets), 60
		      sec rest between sets
		Barefoot cool-down and foot strengthening work

Wednesday	Thursday	Friday

Theme: Neuromuscular development, low demand
Warm-up jog
Dynamic flexibility exercises
Specific warm-up
    Hip pops with partner 3 × 5
    Glides with bar (5)
Shot put throwing progression
    Standing throw 2 (3), competition weight
    Glide and stop (2), competition weight
    Full throws with no reverse (5), competition weight
    Full throws with reverse (5), 10% below
      competition weight 15 throws total
Weight training
    Olympic lift
      Clean pull from knees 6 × 3, 130% 1RM
    Weighted squat jump 4 × 6, 30% 1RM
    Speed incline press 4 × 6, 50% 1RM
    Weighted side bend 2 × 8
Cool-down activity, static stretching
	Theme: Recovery and mental preparation
	Film study, mental preparation
	Dynamic warm-up 8 to 12 min
		Theme: Neuromuscular activation, low demand
		Warm-up jog
		Dynamic flexibility exercises
		Specific warm-up
		    Hip pops with bungee cord 1 × 5
		    Partner glides 1 × 5
		Throwing progression
		    Standing throw (2), competition weight
		    Glide stop and throw (2), competition weight
		    Full technique throws with no reverse (2), competition
		      weight
		    Full technique throws with reverse (2), competition
		      weight 8 throws total
		Acceleration development, 20-meter block starts (4)
		Weight training
		    Olympic lift
		      Hang clean 5 × 2, 75 to 80% 1RM, 3 to 5 min rest
		      between sets
		Multithrows over head back shot put throws (3 to 5)
		  with competition implement
		Cool-down activity, static stretching

Saturday	Intensity of load by day	Post-workout comments
Theme: Competitive readiness Compete in shot put	(see table below)	

	Su	M	Tu	W	Th	F	Sa
Hard		X					X
Medium				X		X	
Easy			X		X		
Rest	X						

FIGURE 16.43 Sample seven-day microcycle for the shot put: competitive phase of training.

Designing an Individual Training Session

In conjunction with individual or event group training sessions, shot put throwers benefit from training sessions uniquely tailored to meet their needs. These may include individual workouts in the weight room or on the field, as well as training units listed on the training inventory. The coach must understand the athlete's physical capabilities before designing a training session. Training sessions that last too long may not be effective; training sessions that are too short may not result in physical adaptations.

Prior to each session, the coach should present the session objective to the athlete. A shot-putter who understands the purpose of the workout is more likely to buy in to the workout activities. Each throwing session should include agility work and running as a brief warm-up. Additionally, throwing drills with or without implements may be used prior to a training session to complete the warm-up.

The session should have one or two specific and measurable goals that have specific benchmarks or activities that ensure progress toward reaching the goal. Throwing activities may be designed to build specific strength or speed. High-volume, high-intensity throwing can improve special strength. However, not all throwing sessions should involve going all out for long throws. The intensity of the throw should be limited to 88 to 92 percent of the athlete's practice personal best; only three to six all-out throws should occur in a practice. The coach should concentrate on correcting or modifying one element in throws performed in the 88 to 92 percent range. Workouts can include heavy and light implements or focus on throwing the standard implement.

A debriefing period at the end of the session helps to reinforce the objective. Coaches and athletes can discuss elements of the session that were highly beneficial as well as areas that need to be tweaked for upcoming sessions. At least once per week, cool-down periods need to include additional running or flexibility work.

Each training session should follow this progression:

1. Warm-up
2. Briefing
3. Skills or technical unit
4. Fitness unit
5. Cool-down
6. Debriefing

Conclusion

A considerable level of discipline, dedication, and commitment are fundamental characteristics of successful shot-putters. Even young, highly athletic, and naturally talented athletes dedicate years of work to develop shot put skills. Regardless of the athlete's competitive level, there is always room to improve and new skills to learn. However, coaches must move cautiously when introducing techniques to novice throwers. The glide technique should be introduced first. Only after the athlete demonstrates consistency and dedication in the glide should the rotational technique be introduced. Shot-putters, whether glide or rotational throwers, develop a set of skills that may, at first, seem unnatural. Both coach and athlete must commit to individualizing the training regimen to maximize performance.

17

Discus

Lawrence W. Judge, PhD

The discus throw requires athletes to exert high forces against the ground through a series of rhythmic movements. Because of the aerodynamic nature of the event, knowledge of the types of implements available is important. The cost of a quality discus ranges from $80 to $300. Rim weight is the most important factor to consider when selecting a discus. Rim weight percentage refers to the ratio of the weight of the rim to the weight of the entire discus. A discus with a high rim weight percentage (greater than 80 percent) is more stable in flight; however, because it is more difficult to control, it is best suited for advanced throwers. A discus with a lower rim weight percentage (70 to 80 percent) is easier to control and is a better choice for beginners. A rubber discus is an inexpensive solution to practice problems or for indoor use, but seldom passes competition inspection and is not viewed as a competition-viable implement.

The discus is lighter in weight and travels faster and farther than the shot, but it is more difficult to control. Fully mastering the mechanics of the release is more difficult in the discus event than it is in the shot put event. Even at elite levels, the discus is thrown from within a cage to protect spectators from errant throws. Novice discus throwers throw from within a cage once they begin using the full, rotational technique. Beginners may use a wooden or rubber discus while developing a controlled technique.

Standard discus implements for women weigh 1 kilogram (about 2.2 lb), and a standard discus for men weighs 2 kilograms (about 4.4 lb). All female throwers use the 1-kilogram (2.2 lb) implement regardless of age, junior boys

use a 1.75-kilogram (3.9 lb) implement, and senior men use the 2-kilogram (4.4 lb) version.

The instruction that follows assumes a right-handed thrower.

Starting Position

The discus is held in the palm so that the first finger joints cup loosely over the rim. The index finger bisects the discus. The index and middle fingers often are closer together than the other fingers are (figure 17.1). The two types of grips common today are the fingers-equal spread and the index and middle fingers together grip. The wrist is very slightly flexed, and the thumb rests comfortably on the flat surface of the discus at approximately a 45-degree angle to the index finger. The wrist

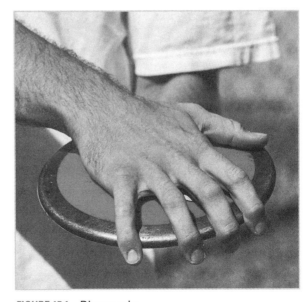

FIGURE 17.1 Discus grip.

is slightly bent so the upper edge of the discus rests against the inner arm and the hollow of the hand never touches the discus. A discus held correctly will fall out of the hand when the hand is not moving. Tangential force generated in the rotational movement holds it in place. Young throwers often hold the discus too tightly.

Table 17.1 summarizes some common errors made by beginning discus throwers and the best ways to correct them.

TABLE 17.1 Common Errors and Corrections for the Discus Throw

Fault	Reasons	Corrections
The discus comes out of the back of the hand.	Improper grip	• Adjust the grip if necessary and relax the arm during the release. Practice the discus bowling drill.
Preliminary swing is too high.	Bending too far forward during the backswing	• Perform multiple windup drills to emphasize keeping a neutral pelvis and a flat windup.
Overrotating out of the back of the circle	Rather than driving to the center of the circle, the athlete is pirouetting in the back of the circle. The athlete is likely leading with the left shoulder into the middle of the ring.	• Pick a focal point in the field and drive the left shoulder and chest toward the front of the circle in a linear path. Load and get off the left leg earlier. • Perform the jump the stream drill.
Pivoting on the left heel out of the back of the circle	Falling back at the start of the turn instead of transferring the body weight directly over the left leg and foot	• Slow down and shift the weight to the ball of the left foot with a slight body lean. • Concentrate on pivoting on the ball of the left foot. • Perform the wind and shift drill.
Left arm and shoulder leading the hips and leg into the center of the circle	Starting the turn with the upper body	• Begin the turn with an aggressive sweep of the left arm, pulling the upper body with it and leading the lower body. • Start slowly and concentrate on keeping the left shoulder and arm above the pivoting left leg and foot. • Perform the wind and shift drill.
The discus is too low or below the shoulder when the left foot lands at the front of the circle.	The athlete is not in a good lay-back position. The athlete is standing too high or straight, which leads to other complications such as the center of gravity being over the left leg.	• Be more aggressive with the hips. The upper body is likely leading the throw. • Perform the standing throw 1 drill to emphasize the pivot, making sure to be in a good lay-back position. If the discus is carried at shoulder level, it will always be at the proper height. • Practice other drills, such as the South African drill, in which you throw and run under the discus to get into a good lay-back position.

Preliminary Position

The preliminary position is standing with the feet approximately shoulder-width apart, the knees and hips slightly flexed, and the chest slightly forward (figure 17.2). The thrower faces away from the direction of the throw, straddling a line marking the direction of the throw. A stable stickman position with the head and vertebrae stacked and minimal bend in the torso places a thrower in a position of strength.

Preliminary Movements

The relative timing, or rhythm, of the discus event is one of the critical components for successful motor sequencing. Rhythm represents the fixed cadence of a motor skill that separates one category of motor skill from another. This fixed rhythmic structure is embedded in all motor skills, regardless of motor skill speed. The preliminary movements (windup) and the throw are a rhythmic whole that has a stable and unique timing structure. When teaching the basic movements, the coach should consider rhythm (i.e., slow to fast) to be as important as mechanics.

Orbit of the Discus

The slanted circular path of the discus is called its orbit. The orbit is positioned so that the lowest point is roughly 180 degrees away from the direction of the throw, and the apex is at a point marking the direction of the throw. Advanced throwers can initiate this orbit in the preliminary swings and maintain it through the remaining phases of the throw. A windup with a flat orbit is advised for a beginning thrower because it makes it easier to stay on balance in the back of the circle.

Preliminary Swings

The athlete may initiate the windup using one of several methods. The most common begins with a stable (nonthrowing) hand in a waiter position. The right-handed thrower holds the discus high in front of the left shoulder. The discus rests on the left palm with the right hand on top of the discus (figure 17.3). The

FIGURE 17.2 F44 world record holder Jeremy Campbell demonstrates the wide preliminary starting position.

FIGURE 17.3 The discus is held high in front of the left shoulder in a waiter position at the start.

athlete swings the discus back and to the right at shoulder level with the back of the right hand turned up. Discus throwers normally perform one preliminary swing with the discus prior to the throw. The discus moves from left to right and back. The body weight shifts slightly, but the majority of body weight remains on the left leg. At the completion of each swing, the discus moves up slightly, and the thrower catches it with the left hand to prevent dropping it. Swings should be slow, rhythmic, and controlled. A common error for novice throwers is fast, nonrhythmical swings. Novice throwers benefit from using less range of motion when executing the windup. The preliminary swings can also help to establish the orbit of the discus. Keeping the discus flat on the windup helps keep the thrower balanced by eliminating undulation in the torso.

Movement Out of the Back of the Circle

The conclusion of the final swing places the body in a position to initiate the throw by creating a separation between the hips and shoulders. The hips face away from the direction of the throw while the shoulders turn more to the thrower's right (figure 17.4). The final swing places the discus in the correct position slightly below shoulder height and at arm's length just behind the right hip (figure

17.5). This swing places the left arm in direct opposition to the right. This positioning of the upper body and discus establishes a single rotating system, whose parts remain in the same relative positions with respect to each other throughout the succeeding turn, jump turn, and flight, and even early in the delivery.

Turn

Three major force-producing movements occur in the back of the ring: unseating (linear important), sweeping the right leg (rotary important), and pushing off with the left leg linear important). The entire left side of the body moves as a unit, pivoting on the ball of the left foot about the axis formed by the left side of the body. The athlete initiates the turn by shifting weight to the left, pivoting on the left foot, lifting the right foot, lowering onto the left leg, and pushing off the left leg. The discus is low as it passes behind the ring. The left leg is loaded throughout the turn.

This pivoting action is accompanied by an unseating action, during which the thrower falls very slightly backward to initiate move-

FIGURE 17.4 The windup is slow and controlled.

FIGURE 17.5 The final swing moves the discus to the correct position.

ment across the ring and moves a low, sweeping right leg. This unseating is carefully directed across the ring to preserve balance and prevent the thrower from going into the bucket (outside the left sector line). The right-leg sweep (figure 17.6) is performed with the leg turned out so the inner thigh and inner knee lead the movement. The right foot is dorsiflexed. The right foot performs a wide soccer-style sweep in the shape of a heart as the athlete drives to the middle of the circle. The athlete should lift the right foot early and move it out in front of the leg before the left foot faces 90 degrees.

Jump Turn

The left-leg push-off results in a subtle jump. In the rotational discus throw, this is thought of as an even more subtle punch off the left leg because of the smaller 7-foot (2.1 m) circle. As the thrower drives, the upper body is relatively erect. As the unseating ends, the thrower drives the right knee up in the direction of the throw and pushes off the left leg, performing a subtle jump that drives the body toward the center of the ring. It is important that the body continues to turn during the push-off. Hip movement during the jump turn, combined with a passiveness in the upper body, serves to maintain or slightly increase the separation as the body leaves the ground. As the jump turn is executed, the discus begins to move higher as the body turns and moves toward the front of the ring.

Flight

During the time the body is in the air, lower-body rotation continues. The body rotates as a unit without changes in the positional relationships of body parts. The left leg recovers and extends out near the front of the ring so that the feet will be properly aligned at landing. The thrower's upper body and the discus become a single rotating system whose parts remain in the same relative positions with respect to each other throughout the flight.

Power Position

The thrower lands in a good power position with the left foot approximately in line with the instep of the right foot. The right foot immediately pivots on landing. If rotation has continued properly, the right foot is between 180 and 240 degrees from the direction of the throw as it touches down. The body weight is over the bent right leg and the ball of the right foot. The right foot and leg continue to turn without hesitating after landing. A common error is shifting weight quickly to the left foot without continuing to turn. The left foot lands quickly after the right in a heel-toe-instep or heel-toe alignment. The body lands with the hip axis directed approximately 90 degrees from the direction of the throw and the shoulders back farther, exhibiting good conservation of the separation established earlier. The discus is located at arm's length over the hip (figure 17.7).

Initiation of the Throw

The throw is initiated in the lower body as the hips turn and the body weight transfers

FIGURE 17.6   Right-leg sweep.

FIGURE 17.7 Power position.

FIGURE 17.8 Delivery of the discus.

from the back foot to the front foot. The right knee moves laterally in the direction of the throw, and the right hip rotates ahead of the right shoulder and arm. The right foot turns as a result of the right hip and knee rotation. This action, along with the blocking action of the left leg, creates lift. Sequentially, the left arm and upper body turn and move forward as well. The left arm blocks this rotation by pulling down and in close to the side. Head alignment is preserved as turning occurs. A common error is turning the head before the upper body.

Release

The arm strike of the discus is a slinging movement. The discus is kept at arm's length from the body throughout. The strike begins slowly, so that the position of the arm and discus with respect to the shoulder does not significantly change until the shoulders are turned in the direction of the throw. The thrower's upper body and the discus remain a single, stable rotating system as the strike begins.

The arm strike begins with the discus high and approximately 270 degrees away from the direction of the throw. The left arm sweeps in coordination with the angle of release. The discus is brought to a low point approximately

180 degrees away from the direction of the throw, and then begins to rise again as the strike is completed (figure 17.8). This orbit of the discus and the leg action produce lift. The discus is delivered off the index finger.

In the final stages of the release, the athlete gently squeezes the discus so that it rolls out of the hand. The side of the index finger gives the final push and imparts a clockwise spin to the implement (figure 17.9).

Follow-Through and Reverse

The thrower vigorously strikes through the discus by imparting clockwise rotation with the index finger. A vigorous release brings the arm across the chest at the completion of the throw. If the athlete has a good block, it is easy to watch the flight of the discus. Some elite athletes hold the block so well that they do not reverse until well after the discus has left the hand. Some top athletes throw the discus very far without reversing. Both styles have advantages.

After the release of the discus, the athlete can reverse the feet to try to stay in the circle. To reverse properly after the discus is released, the thrower moves the right foot forward toward the front of the ring. The left foot drops back and up, and the chest lowers and turns toward the thrower's left side. The right foot is brought forward to the front of the circle. The athlete absorbs the impact by landing on a softly bent knee, while the left leg swings back to the 6 o'clock position and the trunk and shoulders face 9 o'clock (figure 17.10). A common error is to begin to reverse with the feet losing contact with the surface prior to the delivery.

Drill Progressions for the Discus Throw

The discus throw can be broken down into the following parts: grip, power position, wheel, and turn. It can be taught using the three-step whole-part-whole method: demonstrating the general execution first, then the individual parts of the throw, and finally the general execution again. Learners need both auditory and visual models. Coaches should introduce target skills and corresponding drills one at a time, and teach the target skill with a series of drills and short training intervals. Rhythm, or relative timing, is an important pedagogical component that contributes to technical mastery, and must be applied to the teaching progression of the discus throw.

Proper Release Drills

Throwers must learn the proper grip and release before beginning any other discus drills. The thrower's palm rests on top of the discus, which is held in the fingertips. With the nonthrowing hand underneath the discus for support, the top knuckles of the first four fingers (not including the thumb) grip the side of the discus with the fingertips overlapping the edge. The fingers may be spread evenly, or the index and middle fingers may be together. A beginning thrower may wish to try both grips to determine which is more comfortable. A good discus throw includes a proper release. The variables that create the release are discussed in this section.

FIGURE 17.9 American record holder Gia Lewis-Smallwood demonstrates the block as she releases the discus.

FIGURE 17.10 Reverse.

DISCUS SWING

Stand with the feet shoulder-width apart and with the discus in the throwing hand. Place the left hand over the left deltoid in a waiter position. Swing the disc level with the shoulders back and forth, catching it in the left hand. Feel the discus pushing out on the hand.

TOSS-UP

Toss the discus in the air (figure 17.11). Swing the arm so that the discus flies into the air, using the pinching action so that the discus comes off the forefinger. This drill helps establish a feel for the release.

FIGURE 17.11   Toss-up.

DISCUS BOWLING

Use this drill for proper discus release. Place the discus properly in the throwing hand, and then release it using the same arm action as that used in bowling (figure 17.12). When the discus leaves the hand, close the thumb and forefinger in a pinching manner. Bowl the discus to a partner standing 15 feet (about 4.6 m) away. Squeeze out the discus, making sure that it rolls off the index finger and does not wobble. Once you are proficient at 15 feet (4.6 m), move farther from your partner or bowl at a target.

FIGURE 17.12   Discus bowling.

Delivery Drills

Discus throwers must have consistent delivery and flight. The delivery requires a unique set of skills that requires hours of practice to master. Former world-record holder L. Jay Silvester referred to this skill as being able to fly the discus. The following drills introduce and refine the slinging action of the release.

THROW ON KNEES

This drill teaches the basic slinging motion of arm strike mechanics using a cone or bowling pin (figure 17.13). Assume a position on both knees (shoulder-width apart), facing the direction of the throw. Hold a cone or bowling pin in the throwing hand. Place the left hand over the left deltoid in a waiter position. Swing the cone or pin level with the shoulders back and forth, catching it in the left hand. Perform preliminary swings to learn the feel of the drag of the cone or pin. Once comfortable with the preliminary swings, introduce the block and release action. Hold the free arm long at the midline of the body with the knuckles facing the throwing direction. Then bring the free arm into the body by flexing at the elbow to stop the left side of the body. This blocking action initiates the release of the

FIGURE 17.13   Throw on knees.

cone or bowling pin. Perform the block and slinging action on the knees first without an implement until the movement is mastered. A bean bag can then be introduced for additional repetitions. Finally, a cone is added to provide a feel for the drag of the implement, and later a bowling pin is used to increase resistance.

SCALING THE DISCUS

Assume the power position holding a discus. Complete easy standing throws at 30 to 50 percent effort. Keeping the throwing arm at shoulder level, emphasize a perfect flight each time the discus is released. The feet remain grounded; no switching. Walk the field and perform low-intensity standing throws to warm up and feel the implement. A beginning thrower can spend 15 minutes at the start and at the end of the training session walking the field and working on flying the discus. Once the release mechanics are mastered, progress to the standing throw series. Performing 25 repetitions of the scaling drill is helpful when learning the discus throw. The scaling drill is often part of the specific warm-up (four to six repetitions) prior to a competition or practice.

STANDING THROW 1

Practice assuming the power position (shoulder-width base and heel–toe foot position) and pivoting on the right foot, keeping approximately 70 percent of the body weight over the right leg while pivoting the hips to the front. While pivoting, focus on keeping the majority of the body weight on the right foot so that when the hips face the front, you can pick up the left foot. Once you understand the basic motion, perform the movement with the discus. Performing standing throws from the reverse C position is preferable. Finish the specific warm-up with the hip pop drill to loosen up the hips. Begin the throwing workout with this drill, and perform five repetitions.

STANDING THROW 2

Once the lower body is warmed up and the movement pattern of rotating the lower body is acceptable, progress to the standing throw 2. When first learning the mechanics of this drill, use a light nonaerodynamic object such as a shoe.

Assume the power position holding a light object such as a cone (figure 17.14). Complete standing throws combining the lower-body action and C position of the standing throw 1 with an aggressive left-side block and chase with the right side. Swing the arm back to the high point, aggressively pivot on the right foot, and then pull the throwing arm hard in a wide arc and brace the front (left) leg. When the object reaches the low point (6 o'clock), drive the right hip around a braced left side. Emphasize driving the hip toward the direction of the throw (or block leg) as the

FIGURE 17.14   Standing throw 2 with a cone.

right knee rotates counterclockwise and faces down. The front leg is braced and faces 1 o'clock as the heel is driven into the ground. The right hip must be pushed to create an arch in the back. For maximal radius, keep the throwing arm at shoulder level. The feet remain grounded; there is no reverse (switching) on standing throws. Once the mechanics of the movement are mastered, perform the drill with the discus. Five repetitions of standing throw 1 and 10 repetitions of standing throw 2 are typical for a beginning to intermediate thrower.

Turn Drills

When the power position is mastered, the athlete must practice to learn the rotational movement. Drills teach balance and introduce the basic positions in the full movement. Transition drills allow the athlete to acquire consistency in transitioning from the initial starting position to a proper power position. A comfortable and efficient starting position is established in the back of the ring. These drills also teach the athlete to create proper timing in the movement pattern during the transition phase (active lower body, passive upper body).

PIVOT STEP BACK LINE DRILL

Begin the drill standing on a line with the left foot forward, hands on hips. The coach issues the command "Step forward" to begin the drill. Step forward on the line with the right foot (figure 7.15a). The next command is "Pivot," at which point you pivot on both feet to turn 180 degrees (figure 17.15b). Following the pivot, the coach's command is "Step back"; step straight back along the line with the left foot (figure 17.15c). The final command is "Pivot"; pivot 180 degrees on both feet back to the starting position. Repeat the sequence. This drill introduces the concept of pivoting and encourages progress toward an imitation holding the discus.

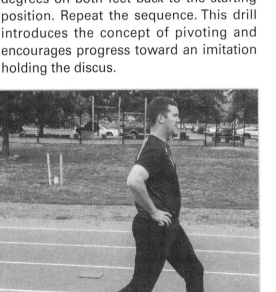

FIGURE 17.15   Pivot step back line drill: (a) step forward; (b) pivot; (c) step back.

Back of the Ring Drills

A series of drills can be used to teach the athlete the compulsory skills for the back of the ring in the rotational technique. The first drill is fairly simple, and they progress in difficulty from there, although they all share some technical cues. In each drill, the athlete starts by loading the left leg by placing the knee over the toes and the armpit over the knee. The left arm is kept long and in position slightly inside the left knee. The left side is locked for a unit turn. The athlete keeps the knees apart while performing each drill, initiating the turn with a left-side pivot and powering the turn with a widely sweeping right leg. The head is up and the eyes are focused on the horizon. To keep the vertebrae aligned (stacked), the athlete imagines balancing a stack of books on top of the head.

STEP-AROUND TURN

This drill emphasizes loading the left leg. Stand with the left foot within the boundaries of the ring. Assume the starting position with the majority of the body weight on the left leg (figure 17.16a). Initiate the turn with a slight pivot of the left foot (figure 17.16b). Step around the clock with a series of small steps. Keep approximately 70 percent of the body weight balanced on the left leg.

FIGURE 17.16   Step-around turn: *(a)* starting position; *(b)* pivoting on the left foot.

QUARTER TURN

The quarter turn drill teaches proper balance at the back of the circle. This drill is similar to the step-around turn drill, but it is slightly more difficult because you cover a slightly longer distance with each step. You can work on lines or in the back of the circle. Place the feet shoulder-width apart and bend the knees to 45 degrees. The nonthrowing arm is relaxed and away from the body at shoulder height and inside the left knee (figure 17.17a). Pivot forward a quarter turn, staying in balance with the knee over the toes, the armpit over the knee, and the left arm over the left leg (figure 17.17b). Continue pivoting forward to the starting point. Transfer weight to the left by moving the left shoulder over the left foot. Do not change the angles of the knees and ankles when transferring to balance and pivot. The left side moves as a controlled unit all the way around. Move left, pivot on the left foot, rotate a quarter turn, and keep the knees and thighs apart while maintaining an upright posture with the eyes focused on the horizon.

FIGURE 17.17   Quarter turn: *(a)* starting position; *(b)* pivoting forward a quarter turn.

HALF TURN

The half turn drill also teaches proper balance at the back of the circle. This drill is similar to the two previous drills, but it requires more balance. Begin in the back of the circle or work on lines. Place the feet parallel and shoulder-width apart, knees bent at approximately 45 degrees. The nonthrowing arm is relaxed away from the body at shoulder height (figure 17.18). Pivot forward a half turn, maintaining balance, and continue pivoting forward to the starting point. Achieve balance by transferring weight to the left by moving the left shoulder over the left foot; maintain an upright posture by keeping the eyes focused on the horizon.

FIGURE 17.18   Half turn.

360-DEGREE TURN

The 360-degree turn drill is the final drill that teaches balance in the back-of-the-ring series. Assume a starting position in the back of the ring or on the lines. Place the feet shoulder-width apart, knees bent at approximately 45 degrees. The nonthrowing arm is relaxed away from the body at shoulder height as the left side is unitized. Pivot forward (counterclockwise) 360 degrees, maintaining balance. Continue pivoting forward to the starting point and maintain an upright posture by keeping the eyes focused on the horizon. Attain balance by transferring weight to the left by moving the left shoulder over the left foot and keep the right leg wide to finish the turn (figure 17.19a). A bar may be added to develop core strength (figure 17.19b). The discus may be held in the chest pass position for additional balance (figure 17.19c).

FIGURE 17.19　360-degree turn: *(a)* pivot: *(b)* add a bar to develop core strength; *(c)* hold the discus in the chest pass position.

WHEEL DRILL

In the wheel drill, begin with the right leg in the center of the ring, the right foot facing 9 o'clock (270 degrees), and the upper body facing 12 o'clock (the middle of the landing area). Assume an upright posture and swing the implement to the rear of the body and pivot to the power position while working to get the left leg down (figure 17.20). This drill trains the right foot to turn and the left foot to squeeze and tuck. As you turn, pick up the left foot and rapidly tuck it. A common cue is "Bring the heel to the glute on the tuck." While positioning the left foot, turn on the ball of the right foot, performing an 180-degree turn while maintaining the position throughout the drill. This drill can be repeated in the same spot.

FIGURE 17.20   Wheel drill: *(a)* start; *(b)* finish.

Combination Drills to Teach the Full Spin

Beginners often have trouble understanding the rotational movement in the discus. Combining the quarter turn, half turn, and wheel drills is an easy way to teach a beginner the full spin. Using the part method in this way avoids the development of the bad habits frequently associated with using the whole movement with a beginner. After the athlete masters step 1 of the teaching progression (quarter turn, half turn, and wheel), the coach may progress to step 2 of the progression (giant step, wheel).

COMBINATION FULL SPIN DRILL

The quarter turn, half turn, and wheel drills may be grouped to teach the full spin. The quarter turn drill out of the back of the ring is followed by a half turn to the middle of the ring, which is followed by a half turn backward or wheel.

Keep the left arm out for balance. Simulate holding the discus with the right arm. Always finish in a balanced power position. Maintain the angles of the knees and ankles during the center pivot. In the wheel, keep the left leg long and to the front. Maintain your weight over the pivot foot—the left foot at the start; then the right foot in the center. Keep the left arm relaxed and long. Focus outside the circle to the horizon and remain relaxed.

Once the teaching progression is mastered, the combination full spin drill can be used as part of the warm-up.

GIANT STEP DRILL

After mastering the combination full spin drill, the quarter turn and half turn are replaced by the giant step. In the giant step, the sweeping movement is led by the inside of the right thigh at the start and it ends in the middle of the ring. This drill stresses the circular, heart-shaped, sweeping action.

Entire Throw Drills

The following drills help the athlete learn consistency in obtaining balance and alignment in the initial starting position. Entry drills teach proper timing in the movement pattern during the entry phase (active lower body, passive upper body).

JUMP THE STREAM

This drill teaches the drive out of the back of the ring and reinforces proper position in the middle of the ring.

Stand in the back of the ring with the left foot inside the circle facing 12 o'clock and the right foot outside the circle (figure 17.21a). Wind up and drive off the left leg to the center of the circle. Land in the center of the circle with the shoulders level, head raised, and hips leading (figure 17.21b). Concentrate on pulling the left foot as quickly as possible behind the right knee and holding that position in the middle of the ring. Perform five or more repetitions.

If getting off the ground and learning the jump turn is difficult, try jumping into a high jump pit (figure 17.21c). Start by facing the pit, and as you become comfortable, perform the windup and entry phases. Right foot placement occurs on the top of the pit at the completion of the drill.

FIGURE 17.21   Jump the stream: *(a)* starting position; *(b)* landing; *(c)* landing in the high jump pit.

SOUTH AFRICAN DRILL

Stand in the back of the ring with the left foot inside the circle facing 12 o'clock and the right foot outside the circle. Wind up and drive off the left leg to the center of the circle. Concentrate on pulling the left foot as quickly as possible behind the right knee and continuing into the power position and throwing the discus.

QUARTER TURN SOUTH AFRICAN DRILL

This is a modified version of the South African drill. Stand in the back of the ring in the starting position for the full spin (figure 17.22a). Perform a quarter turn. With the left foot inside the circle facing 12 o'clock and the right foot outside the circle (figure 17.22b), perform the South African drill. Wind up and drive off the left leg to the center of the circle. Concentrate on pulling the left foot as quickly as possible behind the right knee and continuing into the power position and slinging the discus.

FIGURE 17.22   Quarter turn South African drill: *(a)* starting position; *(b)* left foot inside circle.

FULL THROW

After mastering the quarter turn South African drill, turn to the rear to face 6 o'clock (figure 17.23). From this position, complete the discus throw. (At this phase, in-depth coaching takes place.)

FIGURE 17.23   Full throw.

Designing Discus Throwing Workouts

Before developing discus throwing workouts that use drills, coaches must ensure that the athletes have developed proper technique. They should also carefully consider the relationship between training and teaching. Before teaching a beginner the discus throw, a coach must consider the equipment needed, decide on the units of training (including how much time in each unit), and choose key coaching cues.

The thrower should begin each session with 8 to 12 minutes of a general dynamic warm-up that flows smoothly into a specific warm-up that includes discus throw position drills. Throwing workouts should always start with drills that align with the objectives (technical theme) of the training session. One drill should emphasize the power position, and one drill should address the mechanics of the back of the ring. As the drills conclude, the thrower begins the throwing session, which should consist of approximately 30 throws.

Microcycles for the Discus

The definitive goal of discus training is the functional reconstruction of the athlete, resulting in an enduring adaptation and the preservation of the training effect. High-quality training plans often include both specific and general exercises. Variables such as training load, training volume, exercise selection, and training frequency should be chosen based on factors such as the athlete's training age and strengths and weaknesses, as well as the phase of the training year. An in-season competition program must consider bioenergetics, metabolic parameters, and movement characteristics specific to throwing the discus, such as force, magnitude, velocity, movement patterns, and time factors.

The objective of microcycles for discus throwers is to coordinate training loads to establish a balance between work and recovery. The plan must ensure sufficient regeneration prior to the start of a new microcycle. The function of a microcycle is to provide a rational approach to the training loads planned for a particular training phase. As a rule, each microcycle concludes with one or two recovery days. Microcycles also have specific goals. The goal of a preparation microcycle (figures 17.24 and 17.25) is to prepare the discus thrower for the upcoming competition. The goal of the last preparation microcycle prior to a competition is to unleash and mobilize the discus thrower's performance capacities.

The goal of competition microcycles (figure 17.26) is to organize activities just prior to and immediately after a competition. This involves activities one day before the competition, the day of the competition, and days following the competition. The goal for the competition microcycle depends on the length of the competition, the number of attempts, the frequency of competitions, the performance level of the rivals, and so on. In short, the competition microcycle should be tailored to the needs of the discus thrower.

The most effective organizational structure is one week for each microcycle. However, throwers who train two or three times per day often require slightly shorter microcycles. Each microcycle must include recovery times between training sessions.

Consistency in scheduling throughout the year is an important component of a microcycle. Additionally, the efficacy of training sessions is maintained when careful consideration is given to any potential interference among the types of training. For example, coaches should ensure that the training activity of day 1 does not interfere with the training activity of day 2.

Designing an Individual Training Session

In conjunction with individual or event group training sessions, discus throwers benefit from training sessions uniquely tailored to meet their needs. These may include individual workouts in the weight room or on the field, as well as training units listed on the training inventory. The coach must understand the discus thrower's physical capabilities before designing a training session. Training sessions

Microcycle # Phase: General preparation	Dates: Comments:	Event group: Discus
Sunday	**Monday**	**Tuesday**

Rest	Theme: Neuromuscular development, high demand
	Warm-up jog 5 min
	Dynamic flexibility exercises
	Specific warm-up, grind the cigarette drill 3 × 5
	Discus drills
	    Hip pops with bar 3 × 5
	    Wheel to power position with bar 3 × 5
	Throwing workout
	    Standing throw 1 (10), 10% over competition weight
	    Standing throw (10)
	    Glide stop and throw (10), 10% over competition
	      weight
	    Wheel and throw (10)
	    Multithrow (10) overhead back shot put throws,
	      10% over competition weight
	Weight training
	    Olympic lift
	            Clean pull from floor 6 × 4, 120% CL 1RM
	    Back squat (4 × 8), 75% 1RM
	    Bench press (4 × 8), 75% 1RM
	Cool-down activity, static stretching
		Theme: General training, energy system and endocrine
		  development
		Warm-up jog
		Dynamic flexibility exercises
		Technical drills
		    Discus throw (1/4 turn, 1/2 turn, 360-degree turn),
		      3 × 5 each drill
		Discus
		    Standing throw (10)
		    South African drill and throw drill (10)
		General strength
		    Total body circuit (8 exercises, 20 repetitions each)
		    Abdominal/spinal circuit (1 exercise, 10 repetitions in
		      each plane)
		    Bodybuilding lifts (9 exercises, 3 giant sets, 60 sec
		      rest between sets)
		Barefoot cool-down and foot strengthening work

Wednesday	**Thursday**	**Friday**

Theme: Neuromuscular development, low demand
Warm-up jog
Dynamic flexibility exercises
Discus drills
    Medicine ball slings against the wall 3 × 5
    Partner hip pops drill 3 × 5
    Line drill 3 × 5
    South African drill and throw drill (10), focus on block
Ground level plyometrics
    Jump circuit (6 exercises, 10 repetitions, 20 sec, rest
      between exercises)
Weight training
    Olympic lift
            Power clean from floor 4 × 3, 85% 1RM
    Step-up 2 × 5
    Lunge walk with twist 2 × 5
    Incline press 4 × 8, 70% 1RM
Build-up 5 × 80 meters
Multithrows 3 × 5 (between legs forward), 10% over
  competition weight
Cool-down activity, static stretching
	Theme: General training, general strength and strength
	  endurance development
	Warm-up jog
	Dynamic flexibility exercises
	Hurdle mobility
	Technical discus drills
	    Hip pops with cord 3 × 5
	    Wheel to the power position 3 × 5
	Throwing workout
	    Standing throw (10)
	    Modified South African drill (10)
	Medicine ball circuit (8 exercises, 10 repetitions)
	General strength (8 exercises, 20 repetitions)
	Barefoot cool-down and foot strengthening work
		Theme: Neuromuscular development, high demand
		Warm-up jog
		Dynamic flexibility exercises
		Specific warm-up, grind the cigarette drill 3 × 5
		Discus drills
		    Hip pops with bar 3 × 5
		    Walking South African line drill
		Throwing workout
		    Standing throw (10)
		    Wheel and throw (10)
		Weight training
		    Olympic lift
		            Snatch pull from floor 6 × 4, 115% 1RM
		    Back squat 4 × 8, 70% 1RM
		    Bench press 4 × 8, 70% 1RM
		Cool-down activity, static stretching

Saturday	**Intensity of load by day**	**Post-workout comments**
Theme: General training, energy system and endocrine development Warm-up jog Dynamic flexibility exercises Walking South African drill down the track 2 × 10 Discus, standing throw 2 with cone (10) Cool-down activity, static stretching	<table><tr><td></td><td>Su</td><td>M</td><td>Tu</td><td>W</td><td>Th</td><td>F</td><td>Sa</td></tr><tr><td>Hard</td><td></td><td>x</td><td></td><td></td><td></td><td>x</td><td></td></tr><tr><td>Medium</td><td></td><td></td><td></td><td>x</td><td></td><td></td><td>x</td></tr><tr><td>Easy</td><td></td><td></td><td>x</td><td></td><td>x</td><td></td><td></td></tr><tr><td>Rest</td><td>x</td><td></td><td></td><td></td><td></td><td></td><td></td></tr></table>	

FIGURE 17.24 Sample seven-day microcycle for the discus: general preparation phase of training.

that last too long may not be effective; training sessions that are too short may not result in physical adaptations.

Prior to each session, the coach should present the session objective to the athlete. A discus thrower who understands the purpose of the workout is more likely to buy in to the workout activities. Each throwing session should include agility work and running in a brief warm-up. Additionally, throwing drills with or without implements may be used prior to a training session to complete the warm-up.

The session should have one or two specific and measurable goals that have specific benchmarks or activities that ensure progress toward reaching the goal. Throwing activities may be designed to build specific strength or speed. High-volume, high-intensity throwing can improve special strength. However, not all throwing sessions should involve going all out for long throws. The intensity of the throw should be limited to 88 to 92 percent of the athlete's practice personal best; only three to six all-out throws should occur in a practice.

Microcycle # Phase: Specific preparation	Dates: Comments:	Event group: Discus
Sunday	**Monday**	**Tuesday**

Rest	Theme: Neuromuscular development, high demand
	Warm-up jog
	Dynamic flexibility exercises
	Specific warm-up
	    Hip pops with cord 3 × 5
	    Walking South African drill 3 × 5
	Throwing workout
	    Standing throw (20), 10% over competition weight
	    Wheel and throw (10), 10% over competition weight
	    South African drill and throw drill (20), 10% over
	    competition weight
	Weight training
	    Olympic lift
	        Snatch from floor 6 × 2, 90% 1RM
	    Back squat 6 × 5, 85%
	    Bench press (6, 5, 4, 3, 2,) 80%, 90%, 92%, 95%, 98%
	    (increase weight each set)
	Multithrows
	    Toe board chest pass explosions (10), 20% over
	    competition weight
	Cool-down activity, static stretching
		Theme: General training, energy system and endocrine
		    development
		Warm-up jog
		Dynamic flexibility exercises
		Specific warm-up
		    Hip pops with bungee cord 3 × 5
		    360-degree turns, keep left arm long and leg wide (5)
		    Ball slings into cage 1 × 5
		Throwing progression (example for male high school thrower)
		    Standing throw 1 × 3 (1.75k, 1.6k, 1.6k)
		    Wheel and throw 1 × 3 (1.75k, 1.6k, 1.6k)
		    Drill start shadows (3)
		    Full technique throws 3 × 3 (1.75k, 1.6k, 1.5k)
		    All-out throws (4), 1.6K, 100%
		    All-out throws 5 × 3 (1.75k, 1.6k, 1.6k)
		    25 full throws
		General strength
		    Abdominal/spinal circuit (5 exercises, 10 repetitions)
		    Bodybuilding lifts (9 exercises, 3 giant sets), 60 sec
		    rest between sets
		Barefoot cool-down and foot strengthening work

Wednesday	**Thursday**	**Friday**

Theme: Neuromuscular development, low demand
Warm-up jog
Dynamic flexibility exercises
Sprint development drills
Specific strength
    Throws on knees with an implement, 20% over
    competition weight (10)
Weight training
    Olympic lift
        Clean pull from thigh 6 × 3, 140% 1RM
    Split squat 2 × 6
    Split deadlift 2 × 6
    Pull-over 4 × 6
Acceleration development 3 × 20, 3 × 30, 3 × 40
Cool-down activity, static stretching
	Theme: General training, general strength and strength
	    endurance development
	Warm-up jog
	Dynamic flexibility exercises
	Specific warm-up
	    Hip pops with a cord 3 × 5
	    Walking South African drill 3 × 5
	Throwing progression
	    Standing throw (10), 10% over competition weight
	    Wheel and throw (10), 10% over competition weight
	    South African drill and throw drill (20), 10% over
	    competition weight
	Bodybuilding exercises
	    9 exercises, 3 giant sets, 60 sec rest between sets
	    Advanced core exercises (1 exercise, 10 repetitions in
	    each plane of movement)
	Barefoot cool-down and foot strengthening work
		Theme: Neuromuscular development, high demand
		Warm-up jog
		Dynamic flexibility exercises
		Specific warm-up
		    Hip pops with bungee cord 3 × 5
		    360-degree turns, keep left arm long and leg wide (5)
		    Ball slings into cage 1 × 5
		Throwing progression (example for male high school thrower)
		    Standing throw 1 × 3 (1.75k, 1.6k, 1.5k)
		    Wheel and throw 1 × 3 (1.75k, 1.6k, 1.6k)
		    Drill start shadows (3)
		    Full technique throws 3 × 3 (1.75k, 1.6k, 1.5k)
		    All-out throws (4), 1.6K, 100%
		    All-out throws 4 × 3 (1.75k, 1.6k, 1.6k)
		    25 full throws
		Depth jumps 3 × 5, full recovery
		Olympic lift
		    Hang clean 6 × 4, 85% 1RM
		Half squat 4 × 6, 120% full squat 1RM
		Speed incline press 4 × 6, 50% 1RM
		Cool-down activity, static stretching

Saturday	**Intensity of load by day**	**Post-workout comments**

Theme: General training, energy system and endocrine
    development
Warm-up jog
Dynamic flexibility exercises
Discus drills; all drills performed with weighted vest
    Wheel to power position and hip pops 3 × 5
    360-degree turns, stick on shoulders 3 × 5
    Left leg 90-degree drives (5)
    Stand 2k ball (5)
    Wheel 2k ball (5)
    Full technique throws 2k ball (10)
Medicine ball circuit (8 exercises, 10 repetitions for power)
Barefoot cool-down and foot strengthening
	<table><tr><td></td><td>Su</td><td>M</td><td>Tu</td><td>W</td><td>Th</td><td>F</td><td>Sa</td></tr><tr><td>Hard</td><td></td><td>x</td><td></td><td>x</td><td></td><td>x</td><td></td></tr><tr><td>Medium</td><td></td><td></td><td>x</td><td></td><td>x</td><td></td><td></td></tr><tr><td>Easy</td><td></td><td></td><td></td><td></td><td></td><td></td><td>x</td></tr><tr><td>Rest</td><td>x</td><td></td><td></td><td></td><td></td><td></td><td></td></tr></table>	

FIGURE 17.25   Sample seven-day microcycle for the discus: specific preparation phase of training.

The coach should concentrate on correcting or modifying one element in throws performed in the 88 to 92 percent range. Workouts can include heavy and light implements or focus on throwing the standard implement.

A debriefing period at the end of the session helps to reinforce the objective. Coaches and athletes can discuss elements of the session that were highly beneficial as well as areas that need to be tweaked for upcoming sessions. At least once per week, cool-down periods need to include additional running or flexibility work.

Each training session should follow this progression:

1. Warm-up
2. Briefing
3. Skills or technical unit
4. Fitness unit
5. Cool-down
6. Debriefing

Microcycle # Phase: Competitive	Dates: Comments:	Event group: Discus
Sunday	Monday	Tuesday

Rest	Theme: Neuromuscular development, high demand
	Warm-up jog
	Dynamic flexibility exercises
	Specific warm-up
	   Hip pops with partner 3 × 5
	   Wheel to power position with bar (5)
	Discus throwing progression
	   Standing throw (5), competition weight
	   Wheel and throw (2), competition weight
	   Full throws with no reverse (10), 10% above
	   competition weight (88 to 92%)
	   Full throws with reverse (5), competition weight
	   (100% intensity)
	   Full throws with reverse (5), 10% below competition
	   weight 22 throws total
	Weight training
	   Olympic lift
	      Hang snatch 6 × 2, 95%
	   Weighted squat jump 4 × 6, 30% 1RM
	   Speed incline press 4 × 6, 50% 1RM
	   Russian twist 2 × 8
	Acceleration development (3 × 20, 3 × 30, full recovery)
	Cool-down activity, static stretching
		Theme: General training, energy system and endocrine
		   development
		Warm-up jog
		Dynamic flexibility exercises
		Specific warm-up
		   Hip pops with bungee cord 3 × 5
		   360-degree turns, keep left arm long and leg wide (5)
		   Ball slings into cage 1 × 5
		Throwing progression
		   Standing throw (4)
		   Wheel and throw (4)
		   Drill start shadows
		   Full technique throws (8), 88 to 92%
		   All-out throws (4), 100%
		   12 full throws, 20 throws total
		General strength
		   Abdominal/spinal circuit (5 exercises, 8 repetitions)
		   Medicine ball drills (4 exercises, 5 repetitions for
		   speed)
		Barefoot cool-down and foot strengthening work

Wednesday	Thursday	Friday

Theme: Neuromuscular development, low demand
Warm-up jog
Dynamic flexibility exercises
Specific warm-up
   Hip pops with bungee cord 3 × 5
   360-degree turns, keep left arm long and leg wide (5)
   Ball slings into cage 1 × 5
Throwing progression
   Standing throw (4)
   Wheel and throw (4)
   Drill start shadows
   Full technique throws (8), 88 to 92%
   All-out throws (4), 100%
   12 full throws, 20 throws total
Bodybuilding lifts (9 exercises, 3 giant sets, 60 sec rest
   between sets), 130% 1RM
Cool-down activity, static stretching
	Theme: Recovery and mental preparation
	Film study, mental preparation
		Theme: Neuromuscular development, high demand
		Warm-up jog
		Dynamic flexibility exercises
		Specific warm-up
		   Hip pops with bungee cord 1 × 5
		   360-degree turns, keep left arm long and leg
		   wide (5)
		Throwing progression
		   Standing throw (2)
		   Wheel and throw (2)
		   Drill start shadows
		   Full technique throws (4)
		   8 throws total
		Acceleration development
		   20-meter block starts (4)
		Weight training
		   Olympic lift
		      Hang clean 5 × 2, 95%, 3 to 5 min rest between
		      sets
		Multithrows 5 × over head back throws with competition
		   implement
		Cool-down activity, static stretching

Saturday	Intensity of load by day	Post-workout comments
Theme: General training, energy system and endocrine development Compete in SP and DT	(table below)	

	Su	M	Tu	W	Th	F	Sa
Hard		x		x			x
Medium			x			x	
Easy							
Rest	x				x		

FIGURE 17.26   Sample seven-day microcycle for the discus: competitive phase of training.

Conclusion

The coach should work collaboratively with the discus thrower to develop and implement a unique and individualized training regimen to produce maximal performance. Purposeful and dedicated training increases performance consistency. The strategies and drills outlined in this chapter will prepare coaches to train their discus throwers well.

18

Hammer

Lawrence W. Judge, PhD

Because of its limited popularity and miniscule exposure through literature and research, the hammer throw remains the most ignored and misunderstood event in track and field in the United States. The technical demands of the hammer throw make it very challenging for both the athlete and the coach, possibly second only to the pole vault. The hammer throw has changed considerably since its origin. This includes equipment changes as more precisely manufactured hammers and smooth-soled shoes permit faster spinning, and training methods and throwing distances are now in excess of 280 feet (85 m) for the best men and 250 feet (76 m) for the best women in the world. One aspect of the hammer throwing event that has not changed, however, is the inherent danger associated with it. This chapter dissects the hammer throw by discussing the mechanics and techniques in chronological order.

Equipment

A ball, a length of wire, and a handle make up the hammer (figure 18.1). The overall weight and dimensions of the hammer used in competition differ between men and women. Men use a ball that is 11 to 13 centimeters (4.3 to 5.1 in.) in diameter and weighs 7.26 kilograms (16 lb). Women use a ball that is 9.5 to 11 centimeters (3.7 to 4.3 in.) in diameter and weighs 4 kilograms (8.8 lb). The men's hammer is 117.5 to 121.5 centimeters (46.3 to 47.8 in.) long, and the women's hammer must fall between 116 and 119.5 centimeters (45.7 and 47 in.).

The ball is composed of solid iron or other metals that are no softer than brass. The ball

cannot be filled with any materials that may add to the overall weight. A looped wire is attached to the handle at one end and the ball at the opposite end. The wire measures 3 millimeters (0.1 in.) in diameter. The wire is one piece and is made of a suitable material that does not stretch when placed under the tension of the throw. The wire is securely looped at both ends and is attached directly to the handle and to the ball by a swivel. The handle is a solid piece shaped like an isosceles triangle and does not stretch when placed under the tension of a throw.

FIGURE 18.1   The hammer.

IAAF regulations specify where the center of gravity of the implement can be located. It cannot be more than 0.6 centimeters (0.24 in.) from the center of the ball, and it must be able to balance in the holder of a weighing device with a 1.2-centimeter (0.47 in.) depression.

The cost of a quality hammer ranges from $100 to $450. Turned-steel hammers are more precisely weighed and balanced and typically are built with better-quality swivels. Inexpensive hammers consist of a solid iron head, although steel shells filled with lead or other materials are available. The filling in the solid iron head is immovable. Replacement wires and handles are frequently needed and are kept in stock for quick access. Although wires can be homemade from #11 piano wire, it may be safer to purchase manufactured wires, currently about $8.00 each. Many types of handles are available.

To ensure that the implement meets standards, the coach should check its length and weight prior to competition.

Safety

The hammer throwing circle is protected by a C-shaped cage for the safety of officials, athletes, coaches, and spectators. This is to prevent the hammer from exiting the thrower's hands in unwanted directions. Because the hammer throw presents unique safety issues, the first aspect to consider is the physical space of throwing. The coach needs to ensure the presence of a well-maintained cage that is far enough from other events to ensure safety. Ideally, the cage should meet the recommendations of the IAAF; that is, swinging gates in front that are 10 meters high and 3.2 meters long and can be moved easily. The protective netting or chain-link fence surrounding the hammer ring must be kept in good repair. Proper maintenance of the hammer cage and facility equipment ensures longevity and safety. Coaches should consult the IAAF rulebook for details.

Some schools allow hammer throwing on multiple-use fields. The coach must provide a safe throwing field and be on high alert about anyone being in the line of fire while a throw is taking place. When safety is properly addressed, the hammer throw is a beautiful expression of finesse, rhythm, power, and speed that is unmatched in sport.

In addition to the safety of the facility and space, coaches must consider the throwing field. Some schools use soft-landing training hammers that closely simulate the feel of regulation hammers but do not damage fields. These are available from equipment vendors.

Starting Position

As with the other three throwing disciplines, the aim of the hammer throw is to project the implement as far as possible without committing a foul. Athletes commence a throw by performing preliminary winds, or swings, in which they swing the hammer overhead in a circular arc while facing the rear of the circle. They accelerate the hammer to the point of release by performing turns across the throwing circle.

Grip

Legal gloves are an important piece of equipment for the hammer thrower. Gloves with the fingertips exposed and a smooth front and back may be used.

The hammer is gripped in both hands. A right-handed athlete grips the handle with the left hand (figure 18.2a) in such a manner that the second knuckle of each finger contacts the handle. The right hand covers the left (figure 18.2b).

Preliminary Stance

Grasping the hammer, the thrower stands with the toes abutting the rear edge of the circle. The thrower's feet are shoulder-width apart (approximately 70 to 80 cm, or 28 to 31 in.), bisecting an imaginary line marking the center of the ring. A piece of chalk can be used to draw a line to help beginning throwers obtain a consistent foot position. Advanced throwers often start with the left foot on the centerline of the circle. The hips and shoulders face directly opposite the direction of the throw. Although the rules governing entry into the

 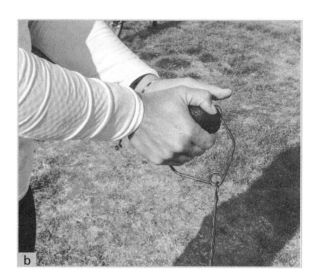

FIGURE 18.2 Hammer grip: *(a)* the left hand grips the handle; *(b)* the right hand covers the left hand.

circle that apply to other throws also apply to the hammer, the implement itself may rest outside the circle prior to initiating the throw. The hammer rests on the ground directly behind the thrower's right foot (figure 18.3). A wide, stable base is important.

FIGURE 18.3 Former American record holder Erin Gilreath demonstrates the wide preliminary stance in the starting position.

Preliminary Movements

A good hammer throw depends heavily on stability and balance during the preliminary movements; this leads to a consistent entry into the initial turn. Athletes commence a throw by performing winds (preliminary swings), in which they swing the hammer overhead in an arc while facing the rear of the circle. The aim of the winds is to give the hammer the proper plane and establish the low point. During the winds, the throwers also maximize the path of the hammer to establish the rhythm of the throw.

Start

To start the throw, the thrower lifts the hammer from the ground and places it on the surface of the circle approximately 1 foot (30 cm) to the right of and 1 foot (30 cm) behind the right foot. While placing the hammer, the thrower turns the shoulders to the right. The left shoulder is lowered, the hips and right foot remain facing away from the direction of the throw, and the majority of the body weight remains on the flexed left leg. From this position, the thrower lifts the hammer from the ground with both hands (figure 18.4) and strokes it along a level path until it is well out to the left.

The slanted circular path of the ball is called the orbit of the hammer. The ideal orbit is one in which the lowest point is approximately 180 degrees from the direction of the throw, and the apex is at a point marking the direction of the throw. The orbit is replicated throughout the winds and later throughout the turns.

Winds

The preliminary swings, or winds, are sometimes referred to as standing turns that the thrower applies to the hammer at the initiation of the throw, without turning the body (figure 18.5). The purpose of the winds is to develop momentum, place the hammer in the optimal position to begin the turns, and establish the thrower and hammer as a single rotating system. The winds also establish the orbit of the implement. Because so many variables are affected by the winds, consistency at the start of the winds is crucial to success in the event. The thrower must learn how to start and execute the winds consistently and correctly prior to learning the throw as a whole movement.

Typically, the hammer thrower executes two winds prior to beginning the turns. Keeping the body weight opposite the ball, the thrower twists the body at the shoulder to catch the ball. The best way to teach winds is to use the cue "Sweep, curl, and twist": sweep the ball, curl the left arm as the ball passes the front of the left leg, and twist the shoulders to catch the hammer properly. The thrower needs to be careful not to allow the right side to be soft and bent at this point. The right leg needs to remain straight and actually block the hip. The thrower must not permit the hands to pass beyond the center of the head.

Throughout the winds, the legs remain slightly but firmly flexed, and the body's mass is positioned to counter the forces created by the swinging ball. The hips and feet are directed away from the direction of the throw. The thrower remains erect and centered in the hammer's orbit. Focusing on keeping the left shoulder lower than the right prevents the common error of dropping the right shoulder.

The arms are flexed as the hammer moves from the thrower's right to the thrower's left. The hands clear the midline of the head by a few inches (around 7 or 8 cm), and the right wrist rolls to a position above the left. The

FIGURE 18.4   Lifting the hammer from the ground.

FIGURE 18.5   Beginning the winds.

upper arms pass very close to the face as the hammer travels behind the thrower's right shoulder (figure 18.6).

When the hammer reaches its apex, the thrower turns the shoulders to the right, drawing the right elbow back as the left upper arm brushes in close to the thrower's face. This movement combination places the body in a position to meet and accelerate the hammer as it descends on the thrower's right. The stationary hips, along with the turning of the shoulders, create separation between the hips and shoulders.

Throwers should practice only three or four winds per set when learning the throw because the low point tends to move increasingly and excessively to the left with each wind. As throwers become comfortable with the movement, sets of 10 or more winds can be used to develop specific strength.

First Wind

Once the start has been completed and the ball is beginning to rise to the thrower's left, the right heel rises slightly as the hammer approaches its apex. The thrower's legs and hips must not sway or drop as the hammer sweeps up and around the left side. The low point of this first wind should be in front of the thrower's right foot. The feet and hips remain facing away from the direction of the throw, with the right foot flat on the ground, creating a block and preventing body sway (figure 18.7). The orbit of the first wind is steeper than that of the second wind.

Second Wind

The thrower smoothly strokes the hammer through the low point of the first wind, sweeping it on a flat path in front of the body with both arms eventually reaching full extension before the hammer reaches the low point (figure 18.8). The path of the hammer must extend well to the left so that the orbit passes outside the left foot. As the hammer begins to rise, clearance characteristics of the hands are identical to those of the first wind. However, the right shoulder and right elbow turn less to the right, allowing the descending hammer to be stroked to a low point directly in front of the

FIGURE 18.6 The hands move behind the body.

FIGURE 18.7 First wind.

FIGURE 18.8 Second wind.

thrower and 180 degrees from the direction of the throw. If additional winds are used, each subsequent one replicates the second wind.

An athlete who has trouble grasping the rhythm of the winds may benefit from observing a demonstration. The coach should pay attention to the rhythm of the skill and the acceleration of the ball as the athlete's hands move deliberately over the midline of the head. In a demonstration, the coach repeats the wind skill rhythm several times and verbally counts "1" for the sweep and curl while keeping the knees rigid, and "2" for the twisting motion of the shoulders while keeping the head fixed.

There is a rhythm in the subtle weight shift from one leg to the other in the wind. As the athlete reaches the curl position, the weight may shift toward that leg. If the athlete turns counterclockwise, the left arm is curling and the weight is on the left leg. As the curl leads into the twist, movement occurs toward the right leg.

Entry Wind

The entry wind immediately precedes the first turn. It is typically the second wind, but may occur later if more winds are used. At the completion of the entry wind, the hammer is stroked earlier from the high point with the shoulders turned less to the right than in pre-

vious winds. This ensures the proper location of the low point of the hammer's orbit directly in front of the thrower. In addition, as the hammer drops, the thrower hooks up with the ball by bending the knees.

Turns

The thrower accelerates the hammer to the instant of release by performing turns across the hammer throw circle, during which the hammer's linear speed fluctuates. The turns are rotations of the hammer and thrower that help the thrower travel across the circle and accelerate the hammer. Each turn consists of a phase of single support, in which one foot is on the ground (left foot for a right-handed thrower), and double support, in which both feet are on the ground. Typically, three or four turns are used, and they resemble each other mechanically.

When entering the first turn from the entry wind, the thrower must stroke the hammer well out away from the center of mass and around the left foot while countering back against the pull of the hammer (figure 18.9).

At the same time, the thrower is ideally rotating on the ball of the left foot (toe turn) or the heel of the left foot (heel turn) and the ball of the right foot until the hammer approaches a position approximately 90 degrees from the direction of the throw (figure 18.10). At this time, the right knee lifts and raises the foot up and over the left ankle with the knees close together. The left foot continues to turn on its front-outside surface as the hammer reaches a position marking the direction of the throw. The left ankle is actively dorsiflexed as the right foot steps over, providing a hard heel as a solid pivot point. After stepping over, the right foot drops quickly to the surface on the ball of the foot. Continuing to turn on the left foot assists this action. Both feet then rotate simultaneously to complete the full turn. Synchronization of the feet in the turns is crucial to maximize efficiency. The thrower must perform these heel–toe rotations with the feet moving simultaneously, never independently.

When the thrower arrives in double support, a subtle amount of separation exists between

FIGURE 18.9   Beginning the entry.

FIGURE 18.10   Entry.

the shoulders and hips (figure 18.11). The thrower then accelerates the hammer during its descent from a position 270 degrees from the direction of the throw to the low point of the hammer's orbit by stroking the ball with the right side of the body and the arms. It is important to hook up with the ball of the hammer by applying force at this time. A common error is failing to apply force and accelerate the hammer at this point. Because of gravitational forces, this descent is the only opportunity to increase the velocity of the ball.

The thrower must learn to turn without using the visual crutch of looking down at the feet or ground to maintain balance. Looking down shortens the effective radius of the hammer and results in shorter throws.

Power, or Catch, Position

The power (or catch) position in the hammer occurs at the completion of each turn, which is the beginning of the double support phase. The thrower's hips and feet are directed away from the direction of the throw with the knees slightly flexed and the body positioned to counter the forces generated by the hammer. The shoulders are turned to the right to meet the hammer so that the hammer may be continuously accelerated into the delivery. The head is in line with the spine as the eyes look slightly above the ball, and the chest remains

FIGURE 18.11   Double support.

concave with the arms extended (figure 18.12). Throwers must counter with the hips in turns 1 and 2 and with the shoulders in turns 3 and 4 because the forces created by the turns at higher speeds become too large for the hip muscles to counter.

Work Phase

During the double support phase of each turn, when both feet are on the ground, large

FIGURE 18.12   Power position just prior to double support.

FIGURE 18.13   Work phase.

torques can be generated. The rotation of the trunk along with the action of the lower body affects the amount of torque exerted. Beginning to intermediate throwers would do well to minimize hip and shoulder torque (only 20 to 40 degrees) to achieve a more stable body position. Landing in the double support phase allows the athlete to firm up the midsection. An effective coaching cue is "Form a wall with the right side of the body."

The work phase consists of three actions: a counterclockwise pivoting action of the right foot toward zero degrees in conjunction with the right arm; a pulling action with the inside of the left thigh to ground the left heel and create a blocking action; and a movement of the chin and shoulders away from the ball as it moves toward the low point to maximize the distance between the back of the head and the hammer. The thrower sits back and moves the shoulders back and the chin away from the hands (figure 18.13). For a description of common errors for the hammer throw and their corrections see table 18.1.

Delivery

The final part of the hammer throw is the delivery phase, which commences at the end of the final turn and culminates with the release of the hammer. During this phase, which is important to throwing success, the thrower accelerates the hammer up as it passes through 0 degrees and over the left shoulder (for a right-handed thrower). This is done by extending the knees, hips, back, and shoulders; the hammer is released at approximately shoulder height. Once a thrower has developed a technique that consistently results in optimal release height and angle, emphasis should then be on technique alterations that can improve release speed. The delivery phase can be broken down into three parts: throw initiation, the release, and the follow-through and reverse, as described in the following sections.

Throw Initiation

The actual throw is initiated in the release turn, the one prior to arriving in the power position and delivering the hammer. Although velocities are greater, the release turn is initiated in the same way previous turns are.

Release

The strike of the hammer in the release turn resembles the acceleration phase of the previous turns with one exception. When the ball

TABLE 18.1   Common Errors and Corrections for the Hammer Throw

Fault	Reasons	Corrections
The hammer hits the ground.	• The hammer is not in proper trajectory.	• Do not lean forward. If you lean forward, you will not be able to control the downward path of the hammer. • The winds may be too steep; flatten them. • Make sure countering is correct.
Arms pulled in, reducing radius	• Tense movements as a result of inexperience or fear of hitting the ground with the ball or of being pulled off balance	• Practice left and right one-arm swings using a lighter hammer. Work for a complete range of motion. • Do regular winds using a lighter ball. Relax the arms and use the correct stance until a wider sweep of the ball is possible. The ball must sweep across the front and wider to the left. • Build on improved technique by using heavier hammers for specific strength drills. • Stress a flatter plane, rather than a steep up-and-down motion.
The body sways too much from side to side.	• Attempting to put more into the wind by exaggerating the slight shift in the body weight	• Keep the body upright throughout the wind. Do not swing the hips from side to side. • Block with the right leg as the hammer begins to pass behind you. Place the heel firmly on the ground, and do not allow any sideways action of the right knee. • Use the cue word "Block."
The right leg lands too far from the left leg resulting in a wide stance.	• Not waiting on the hammer • Dragging the ball and using the upper body too much	• Keep the left leg bent on entry and push hard with the right leg. • Keep the right foot close to the left leg by closing the knees, giving the appearance of stepping over the left ankle. • Place the right foot down with authority.
Too much weight on the right leg at release	• Being off balance, resulting in an error in the final turn, possibly as a result of preparing for the release	• Push the hammer out and around the left foot on all turns, including the final turn. • Work on maintaining good leg bend until the ball hits the low point. • Drive up hard and feel lift as the ball rises. • Get a good drop on the left leg prior to the right foot landing. • Perform the medicine ball release drill against the wall. • Do not lead with the head. Keep the line of vision above the ball.

Fault	Reasons	Corrections
Losing balance in the turns	• Starting the turn with the shoulder and head • Not placing weight on the right leg as the ball moves left. • Not driving the right leg into the beginning of the DS phase in the turn • Lifting the right leg incorrectly • Rushing the upper body around and not using the hips and legs	• Bend at the end of the second wind and sit back to counter the hammer at the low point. • Keep the left leg slightly bent and push the hammer through a wider radius. Do not lean too far forward. • At entry, be sure the center of gravity is near the left foot. • Keep the arms straight. Don't break the triangle after the arms extend at the end of the second wind. • Beginning throwers may need the right foot on the ground at 90 degrees because they are not turning very fast. Better throwers lift off early.
Turning in one spot, commonly termed drilling for oil	• Lack of countering at the low point	• As the ball descends toward zero degrees, prepare to quickly sit against the hammer with the hips while keeping the back upright. • Elite throwers do show some lean-back because of the greater centrifugal force. • The weight will move from the ball of the left foot to the heel during the action. Unless the force is directed opposite the hammer at the low point, you cannot overcome the hammer's force and move down the circle. • Leaning forward will pitch you and the hammer forward, which allows the hammer to take control.
Falling onto the right leg after the turn	• Incorrect left-shoulder movement, head and left-leg action, and balance at entry, which may cause a wide swing of the right leg	• Face the direction of the ball. The arms and shoulders must not pull in. • Keep your eyes on the hammer. When the ball hits the low point, do not bend the neck to look at the ball. • Keep the center of gravity near the left leg and get the hammer wide to the left. To do this, you cannot straighten the left leg or tug with the shoulders. • Keep the right foot closer and be active in placing it on the ground. A delay will affect the whole throw.

reaches its low point, the thrower rises into a higher position by extending the legs, and the head and shoulders move back to counter and continue the acceleration of the ball. The thrower continues to turn until the hammer is released with the hands at shoulder height and the arms at 90 degrees from the direction of the throw. At the moment the hammer is released, the distance from the crown of the thrower's head to the ball is the greatest; the thrower's head is thrust back at this point so that the line of vision is directly vertical.

Follow-Through and Reverse

The thrower's arms remain long and the hands continue to move up and finish high after the release (figure 18.14). The thrower's head is back, and the eyes are focused up toward the sky.

The action of the reverse in the hammer is unique compared to those in the shot put, discus, and javelin. The reverse in the hammer throw is an opposite action to the lifting motion of the release. After releasing the hammer, the thrower drops the center of mass to stay in the ring. This action is challenging if the athlete is off balance when arriving in double support on the final turn.

Drill Progressions for the Hammer Throw Turns

Although physical condition and athleticism are both important in the hammer throw, technical ability contributes significantly to overall performance. At the elite level of the sport, many believe that technique is the largest discriminating factor among athletes. Young

FIGURE 18.14　After the release.

throwers must develop a set of skills that at first may seem unnatural. For this reason, the hammer coach should be familiar with drills for improving these skills.

Beginning Drills

The technical demands of hammer throwing may present a barrier to young throwers. To capture the interest of young throwers, coaches may need to inject some fun into the learning process. One of the first steps is to introduce rotational drills to get young throwers accustomed to turning in a circle.

SPINNING WITH TWO PARTNERS

Athletes' natural ankle flexibility and foot strength are rarely even close to the strength and mobility necessary to execute multiple hammer turns. This drill involves grabbing a partner by the wrists and sitting back to counter the partner's weight. This counter position, as it's called, entails sitting back with your hips while maintaining an upright torso and tight midline, as in front squatting.

Once you have grabbed your partner's wrists, lean back in the counter position and quickly move in a circle around your partner on the balls of your feet to create rotational speed.

Be sure not to bend over or round your shoulders. Perform a total of five turns and then stop. It is crucial not to let go of your partner until you have both returned to a standing position. Once you understand the concept of rotating and countering, the next step is to incorporate a hammer or similar object such as a rope with a weight on the end into your rotational drills. These turns may be completed on the balls of the feet because there is no concern with exact technique at this point. The aim is to develop balance and rotary ability.

SPINNING WITH A MEDICINE BALL ON A SHORT HANDLE (POWER BALL)

The power ball resembles the actual implement, but the weight of the medicine ball is much less. A medicine ball allows for throwers of all ages and sizes to learn to turn. Step the feet around in a counterclockwise direction in small circles, keeping the head, shoulders, hips, and feet all facing the same direction. The medicine ball also needs to stay in front of the body (figure 18.15); do not let it lag behind. Take eight steps around to return to the starting position. Once you can get the body and medicine ball as a unit back to the position you started from, start reducing the number of steps you take to complete the circle. For example, start with eight, and then reduce to six; when you can do that cleanly, reduce to four.

FIGURE 18.15 Spinning with a power ball.

TUG OF WAR WITH A PARTNER

This drill teaches the concept of balancing against the increasing pull of the hammer. You can first perform the drill using a chain-link fence as a partner. When you progress to working with a partner, one partner pretends to be the hammer; and the other, the thrower. One partner tries to gradually increase the pull (figure 18.16). This is an enjoyable way to learn the major hammer concept of the counter.

FIGURE 18.16 Tug of war with a partner.

Teaching the Turns

The first step in learning to become a hammer thrower is learning how to rotate, counter, and maintain balance. This series of position drills introduces the rotary skill, countering, and balance. Athletes should observe the simple step and pivot of the turning rhythm that takes place during the hammer turn. The athlete begins with the feet shoulder-width apart, knees slightly flexed, and head up. The arms are straight and form a triangle in front of the athlete. The athlete places his body weight on the ball of the right foot and the heel of the left foot; then turns until he reaches 90 degrees. He then repeats these 90-degree rotations. Once the athlete can adopt this position, he turns and walks toward 180 degrees. This helps teach the idea of lifting the right foot to complete the turn.

When this skill is mastered, the athlete must learn to complete the turn. The athlete places her body weight on the ball of the right foot and the heel of the left foot; then turns until she reaches approximately 90 degrees. At this point, she picks up the right foot and continues to rotate on the side of the left foot to the ball of the foot. The right leg is kept close to the left as the athlete completes the turn on the left leg and prepares to place the right foot at 270 degrees. Upon completion of the turn, the right leg contacts the ground so the weight is on the ball of the foot and the athlete is prepared to pivot. The athlete must repeatedly practice performing a single turn until performing a single turn feels comfortable.

The coach should explain the moves as a series of heel-toe turns. Throwers learn and practice each turn in segments until they master the positions and can complete one correct heel–toe turn followed by a series of heel–toe turns.

Position Drills

To initiate the position drills, the thrower assumes an athletic position, forming a triangle in front of the body (figure 18.17). The position is characterized by an upright posture and firm midsection with the body weight evenly distributed between both feet.

FIGURE 18.17   Position drills starting position.

POSITION 1 DRILL

Move from the starting position to a position in which the majority of the body weight rests on the right leg. Turn to 90 degrees while keeping the majority of the body weight on the back foot and synchronizing the feet. In the heel turn (figure 18.18a), the left foot is dorsiflexed and the feet are synchronized, facing 90 degrees at the conclusion of the drill. In the toe turn (figure 18.18b), the weight is on the ball of the left foot and the feet are synchronized, facing 90 degrees at the conclusion of the drill.

FIGURE 18.18 Position 1 drill: *(a)* heel turn; *(b)* toe turn.

POSITION 2 DRILL

From position 1, turn and step to 270 degrees (position 2; figure 18.19) by completing a heel turn on the left foot. Step with the right foot to a spot 3 inches (7.6 cm) in front of the turned left foot. Completing this step brings the weight from the left heel down on the ball of the left foot. The key to this movement is to quickly pick up the right foot and put it back down. Ideally, you will have a 20- to 40-degree separation between the hips and shoulders when landing in position 2. Keep the knees close together, step over the left ankle, and stay balanced primarily on the rotating left foot. Keep the shoulders level and the line of vision above the hands.

FIGURE 18.19 Position 2 drill.

POSITION 3 DRILL

From position 2, turn back to the original starting point (0 degrees). This is the work phase of the throw because this is where all the acceleration takes place. In position 3, the right foot is in plantar flexion and all force is pushed through the ball of the right foot. The left foot rocks from the ball of the foot back to the heel as the drill is completed. Sit back and move the shoulders back and the chin away from the hands (figure 18.20).

FIGURE 18.20   Position 3 drill.

Multiple Turn Drills

Before learning turns, the athlete must understand the basic turning pattern and posture. An effective coaching technique is to use a fully extended aluminum crutch with the handle adjusted for the thrower's arm length. The crutch teaches correct hammer throwing posture, the hammer's key orbital positions, and the corresponding technical heel and toe placements to execute technically correct multiple hammer turns. Additional turning drills can be used once the basic pattern is learned.

MULTIPLE TURNS WITH A CRUTCH

Holding a crutch develops a feel for the hammer–thrower system and keeps the feet in front of the body (figure 18.21). Concentrate on the heel and toe action of the left foot and the action on the ball of the right foot. If dizziness occurs, reduce the number of turns until you develop a tolerance and are able to complete multiple balanced turns.

A variation of this drill involves placing a broom handle across the shoulders. This provides a less demanding task because the arms can rest on the broom handle (figure 18.22). Maintain consistent turning by keeping the left leg moving.

FIGURE 18.21   Multiple turns with a crutch.

FIGURE 18.22   Variation with a broom handle across the shoulders.

WALK THE DOG

This is a great drill for learning the basics of the feet in the turns. It can be performed with one wind or the wraparound start. If right-handed, grip the hammer with the left hand (figure 18.23). After dragging the ball on the ground, perform multiple turns with low to medium intensity. Focus on hitting proper positions, not on turning speed. Once the hammer passes the body's centerline, begin moving the feet to follow the hammer, balanced on the ball of the right foot and the heel of the left foot. For beginners, the right foot remains on the ground until the right knee touches the left knee. As the knees close, the right foot is lifted from the ground.

FIGURE 18.23   Walk the dog.

LEFT ARM DRILL

The key to success in the hammer throw is establishing a rhythm and maintaining an intricate throwing system. Dragging the hammer is a common problem and is often difficult to correct. The left arm drill teaches you to wait on the hammer. The feet, knees, hips, torso, arms, and head move together in sync. The body weight is over the right foot, and the left leg is working against the centrifugal force of the hammer. The low back is straight, and the shoulders are relaxed with the left arm extended (figure 18.24). The head is up and the shoulders are level. Eyes are focused on the horizon just above the ball. If right-handed, grip the hammer with the left or gloved hand and rest the right hand on the waist for balance. After starting to move the ball with a single wind, perform multiple turns with low to medium intensity. The focus should be on hitting proper positions and not on turning speed. The idea of the drill is to keep the left arm loose and relaxed and to let the ball turn your body as you gradually accelerate each turn.

FIGURE 18.24   Left arm drill.

Keep your eyes on the horizon and the majority of your body weight opposite the ball. A balanced upright posture is important. The key to efficient execution of this drill is patience at the low point. Sitting back and countering at the low point will help you be more patient and learn to wait on the ball. Make sure the ball passes you at 0 degrees before starting into the next turn. Very effective coaching cues are "Let the ball run left" and "Let the ball turn you." Waiting on the ball often is more of a challenge in this drill in the later turns, which are faster.

RIGHT ARM DRILL

Using the right hand only, perform two slow winds. The right arm will move well to the left (90 degrees) into the entry. The right arm pushes you into the throw, stepping to 180 degrees each time. If winding is difficult, wind with both arms and release the left arm as when going into the entry. Perform sets of five turns to focus on the work phase. Throwing can be performed with the right arm only. The left hand can grab the right hand just below the wrist for additional stability (figure 18.25). Focus on pushing the hammer long to the left and passing the feet on entry. Allow the feet to follow the hammer into the first turn. Work on firming up at the initiation of double sup-

FIGURE 18.25   Right arm drill.

port as the right foot pushes in a counterclockwise direction. Sit back and feel the counter by pressing the left heel into the ground as you move the head and shoulders back before the ball reaches 0 degrees.

Teaching the Winds

Winds are essential in starting the momentum in the hammer throw. Without winds, it would be very difficult to create a rhythm or tempo along with the speed needed to throw the hammer a competitive distance. Athletes should use a medicine ball on a rope when first learning the winding movement, until the correct pattern is established. Practicing multiple winds for 10 practice sets of five repetitions each with one to two minutes of rest between sets is beneficial.

After mastering the winds on one side, the athlete repeats the same regimen working the opposite side. The first focus is on the kines-

thetic feel, keeping the arms long and loose and the body upright. Keeping the knees rigid while initiating hip extension, the athlete practices brushing the hands above the midline of the head. The same regimen of 10 sets of five repetitions is done on the opposite side.

After completing numerous practice repetitions, the athlete can try closing his eyes and repeating the movement to learn the sound of the winding hammer. He should note the difference between the sound of the hammer moving around the body with constant tension in the wire and the sound of the hammer when the hands drop and the hammer moves out of the desired path.

NARROW STANCE WIND

This drill reinforces the feeling of keeping the legs rigid on the winds. Keep the arms long and loose while keeping the legs rigid and body upright (figure 18.26). Key points here are to keep the arms relaxed and use the shoulders to create rotational momentum. In the starting position, stand at the back of the circle facing out. Standing in the back of the ring, feet close together and parallel to each other and legs bent, hold the hammer on the ground behind the right side of the body. Swing the hammer out in front of the body by straightening the legs and pulling with the left arm. Curl the left arm as the hammer passes overhead. Rotate the shoulders to the right and sweep the hammer out in front again. Perform sets of 10 winds right- and left-handed.

FIGURE 18.26 Narrow stance wind.

ONE-ARM WIND

The one-arm wind drill develops shoulder mobility and provides an opportunity to feel the relaxed long arms necessary for good winding mechanics. Complete this drill slowly, using either hand. Mimic the correct pattern of the arm, as if holding the handle with two hands (figure 18.27). If you are an advanced athlete, perform a one-handed wind and then enter into a turn and perform a delivery, although slower than normal.

FIGURE 18.27 One-arm wind.

TWO WINDS AND RELEASE

Stand with the heels approximately 12 inches (about 30 cm) from the front rim of the circle with the feet equally straddling the line that bisects the circle. Execute two winds. After the slower first wind, the hammer significantly speeds up in the second stroke across the front and in the back half of the second wind. Sling the hammer across the front and up; the legs, hips, rotating feet, and arching back drive the hammer into a release.

WIND AND TURN

This drill is a favorite among world-class throwers. It serves as a good warm-up exercise as well as a teaching tool. Complete two relaxed and fairly slow preliminary winds, push the hammer (not too fast) across the front into a wide orbit around the turning left leg, execute one heel–toe turn, and stop all foot movement after the right foot touches down at the completion of the turn. Immediately execute two more winds and another single heel–toe turn, repeating this drill across the throwing surface until three or four winds–turn, winds–turn sequences have been completed. Stay centered and balanced throughout. If you lose balance when stopping the turn after the winds, execute as many additional preliminary winds as needed to achieve balance before proceeding with the remainder of the two-winds, one-turn, stop drill.

Young athletes may have difficulty with the ball speed and may miss the windup on occasion. Coaches should be patient because this drill builds special throwing strength while emphasizing technical execution.

Teaching the Release

The release can be safely taught with everyday equipment such as a medicine ball. The thrower stands with the feet no more than shoulder-width apart, grasping a medicine ball of an appropriate weight, based on age and experience.

MEDICINE BALL WALL THROW

Stand approximately 4 feet (1.2 m) from a wall or fence, facing away from it. While keeping the hips and feet square to the front, swing the ball with straight arms to the right side with the line of vision following over the top of the ball. Sling the ball around and up to the left as the feet and hips rotate around toward the wall (figure 18.28). Release the ball with the head and shoulders back and the eyes up. The line of vision remains above and with the medicine ball throughout the movement. The ball will strike the wall above the head and to the left. Prepare to catch the ball immediately. With straight arms, rotate it back to the starting position. Immediately repeat the release, establishing a flowing rhythm without pause until the set is complete. The goal is to create a rhythm and string the throws together. Try to complete three good sets of 10 to 12 throws.

FIGURE 18.28   Medicine ball wall throw.

Alternate the sets from right-side releases to left-side releases to maintain balanced body development.

HAMMER DELIVERY

This is one of the most important hammer drills because throwers must be able to easily handle the implement. Throwers under the age of 12 use a hammer that weighs 2 kilograms (4.4 lb) or less. Junior athletes (high school age) may use up to 4 kilograms (boys) and 3 kilograms (girls) (8.8 and 6.6 lb, respectively). Top athletes perform many repetitions with a 5- to 10-kilogram (11 to 22 lb) implement.

Having five or more implements available is helpful in this drill. Stand in the front of the hammer ring. Perform two winds to get the ball moving. Using the correct delivery action, throw the ball into the sector higher than the head. Initially, grab another ball, stop, and repeat. For an advanced drill, repeat the drill over the other shoulder. Alternate left-handed and right-handed releases into the throwing field.

Throwing the Hammer From the Circle Drills

Throwing the hammer from the 7-foot (about 2 m) circle should not be attempted until the thrower can execute two preliminary wind sets of 10 to 12 rhythmic turns in a straight line, with the hammer. Technical mistakes acquired from premature throwing from the circle are very difficult to correct. Athletes should devote at least one month to basic hammer-throwing skills before practicing hammer throwing from the circle.

TWO WINDS, ONE TURN, AND RELEASE

Begin by winding twice (easy) and then turn (easy-stop). After one or two repetitions, proceed with four or five continuous repetitions (still easy) without concentrating on increasing ball speed. To add the release, perform two winds, one turn, and release. Stay with this basic drill until you can deliver the ball and maintain balance. Focus on staying on the legs and maintaining good posture.

These drills help maintain balance and the axis of rotation in the center of the hammer's orbit. Never bail out and stop the movement of the hammer once the drill begins. If you lose your balance, steady yourself by continuing to wind and even walk back to the starting point while winding until you are balanced enough to perform the drill. During the drill, the back must remain in a straight position, not rounded and humped over. When you can repeat the two winds, one turn, and release drill, proceed to the following advanced applications:

- Two winds, one turn, stop, two winds, one turn, stop, two winds, one turn, release
- Two winds, one turn, stop, two winds, two turns, release
- Two winds, one turn, stop, two winds, three turns, release

TWO WINDS, TWO TURNS, AND RELEASE

Once you have mastered the two winds, one turn, and release drill, add an extra turn. This simple drill progression provides good preparation for a low-level competition. Adding the second turn helps you learn to accelerate the ball. It also adds rhythm to the throw. If you are inexperienced, you may compete with this simple technique.

TWO WINDS, THREE TURNS, AND RELEASE

Once you have mastered the two winds, two turns, and release drill, it is time to add an extra turn. The current world record was set with three heel turns. The two winds, three turns, and release drill is the final step for some throwers, serving as their competitive technical model. You also have the option of learning the toe turn and performing two winds and four turns. The four-turn throw (one toe and three heel turns) is the most common technique used today.

Designing Hammer Throwing Workouts

Prior to developing a hammer throw, the coach should provide throwing workouts that use various weight implements and emphasize proper technique. An understanding of the relationship between training and teaching is crucial. Before teaching a beginner the hammer throw, the coach needs to consider the equipment needed, decide on the units of training (including how much time in each unit), and choose key coaching cues.

Each session should begin with 8 to 12 minutes of a general dynamic warm-up that flows seamlessly into a specific warm-up that includes hammer throw drills. All drills should align with the objectives of the training session. One drill should emphasize the winds, and one should address the mechanics of the turns. As the drills conclude, the thrower begins the throwing session, which should consist of approximately 30 throws.

Microcycles for the Hammer Throw

The definitive goal of training hammer throwers is the functional reconstruction of the athlete, resulting in an enduring adaptation and the preservation of the training effect. High-quality training plans often include both specific and general exercises. Variables such as training load, training volume, exercise selection, and training frequency should be chosen based on the athlete's training age and strengths and weaknesses, as well as the phase of the training year. A training program must consider bioenergetics, metabolic parameters, and movement characteristics specific to throwing the hammer, such as force, magnitude, velocity, movement patterns, and time factors. Athletes react to training stimuli differently. Accordingly, a training plan should be specifically adapted to the athlete's physiology and strengths to ensure that the athlete obtains the most from the program.

The objective of microcycles for hammer throwers is to coordinate training loads to establish a balance between work and recovery. The plan must ensure sufficient regeneration prior to the start of a new microcycle. The function of a microcycle is to provide a rational approach to the training loads planned for a particular training phase. As a rule, each microcycle concludes with one or two recovery days. Microcycles also have specific goals. The goal of a preparation microcycle (figure 18.29) is to prepare the hammer thrower for the upcoming competition. The goal of the last preparation microcycle (figure 18.30) prior to a competition is to unleash and mobilize the thrower's performance capacities.

The goal of a competition microcycle (figure 18.31) is to organize activities just prior to and immediately after a competition. This involves activities one day before the competition, the day of the competition, and days following the competition. The goal for the competition microcycle depends on the length of the competition, the number of attempts, the frequency of competitions, the performance level of the rivals, and so on. In short, the competition microcycle should be tailored to the needs of the hammer thrower.

The most effective organizational structure is one week for each microcycle. However, hammer throwers who train two or three times per day often require slightly shorter microcycles. Each microcycle must include recovery times between training sessions.

Consistency in scheduling throughout the year is an important component of a microcycle. Additionally, the efficacy of training sessions is maintained when careful consideration is given to any potential interference among the types of training. For example, coaches should ensure that the training activity of day 1 does not interfere with the training activity of day 2.

Designing an Individual Training Session

In conjunction with team or event group training sessions, hammer throwers benefit from training sessions uniquely tailored to meet their needs. These may include individual

Microcycle # Phase: General preparation	Dates: Comments:	Event group: Hammer
Sunday	**Monday**	**Tuesday**

Rest	Theme: Neuromuscular development, high demand
	Warm-up jog
	Dynamic flexibility exercises
	Specific warm-up, position drill 3 × 5
	Hammer drills
	    Turns with bar 3 × 5
	    Multiple winds with hammer 3 × 5 each side
	    One turn and release (10), 10% over competition
	      weight
	    Five turns and release (10), 10% over competition
	      weight
	Multithrow overhead back shot put throws (10), 10%
	  over competition weight
	Weight training
	    Olympic lift
	      Clean pull from floor 6 × 4, 120% of CL 1RM
	    Back squat 4 × 8, 75% 1RM
	    Bench press 4 × 8, 75% 1RM
	Cool-down activity, static stretching
		Theme: General training, energy system and endocrine
		  development
		Warm-up jog
		Dynamic flexibility exercises
		Technical drills
		    Two winds and turn drill 3 × 5
		    Multiple turns 5 × 5
		Hammer
		    Two winds, one turn drill with release (5)
		    Competition technique throws (10)
		General strength
		    Total body circuit (8 exercises, 20 repetitions)
		    Abdominal/spinal circuit (1 exercise, 10 repetitions in
		      each plane)
		    Bodybuilding lifts (9 exercises, 3 giant sets)
		    60 sec rest between sets
		Barefoot cool-down and foot strengthening work

Wednesday	**Thursday**	**Friday**

Theme: Neuromuscular development, low demand
Warm-up jog
Dynamic flexibility exercises
Hammer drills
    Position drills 3 × 5, right- and left-handed
    Walk the dog drill 3 × 5
    Wind and release with pud 3 × 5 each side, focus
      on block
Ground level plyometrics
    Jump circuit (6 exercises, 10 repetitions), 20 sec
      rest between exercises
Weight training
    Olympic lift
      Power clean from floor 4 × 3, 85% 1RM
    Step-ups 2 × 5
    Lunge walks with twist 2 × 5
    Incline press 4 × 8, 70% 1RM
Build-ups 5 × 80 meters
Multithrows 3 × 5, between legs forward, 10% over
  competition weight
Cool-down activity, static stretching
	Theme: General training, general strength and strength
	  endurance development
	Warm-up jog
	Dynamic flexibility exercises
	Hurdle mobility
	Hammer drills
	    Turn with bar 3 × 5
	    Multiple winds with hammer 3 × 5 each side
	    One turn and release (10), 10% over competition
	      weight
	    Five turns and release (10), 10% over competition
	      weight
	Medicine ball circuit (8 exercises, 10 repetitions)
	General strength (8 exercises, 20 repetitions)
	Barefoot cool-down and foot strengthening work
		Theme: Neuromuscular development, high demand
		Warm-up jog
		Dynamic flexibility exercises
		Specific warm-up
		    Position drills 3 × 5
		Technical drills–Two winds and turn drill
		    Two winds and turn drill 3 × 5
		    Multiple turns 5 × 5
		Hammer
		    Two winds, one turn drill with release (5)
		    Competition technique throws (10)
		Weight training
		    Olympic lift
		      Snatch pull from floor 6 × 4, 115% 1RM
		    Back squat 4 × 8, 70% 1RM
		    Bench press 4 × 8, 70% 1RM
		Cool-down activity, static stretching

Saturday	**Intensity of load by day**	**Post-workout comments**

Theme: General training, energy system and endocrine
  development
Warm-up jog
Dynamic flexibility exercises
Walking two winds, one turn drill down the pad 2 × 10
  each side
Hammer
    One turn and release with 10k pud (10)
Cool down, static stretching
	<table><tr><td></td><td>Su</td><td>M</td><td>Tu</td><td>W</td><td>Th</td><td>F</td><td>Sa</td></tr><tr><td>Hard</td><td></td><td>x</td><td></td><td>x</td><td></td><td>x</td><td></td></tr><tr><td>Medium</td><td></td><td></td><td>x</td><td></td><td>x</td><td></td><td></td></tr><tr><td>Easy</td><td></td><td></td><td></td><td></td><td></td><td></td><td>x</td></tr><tr><td>Rest</td><td>x</td><td></td><td></td><td></td><td></td><td></td><td></td></tr></table>	

FIGURE 18.29 Sample seven-day microcycle for the hammer throw: general preparation phase of training.

workouts in the weight room or on the field as well as training units listed on the training inventory. The coach must understand the hammer thrower's physical capabilities before designing a training session. Training sessions that last too long may not be effective; training sessions that are too short may not result in physical adaptations.

Prior to each session, the coach should present the session objective to the hammer thrower. An athlete who understands the purpose of the workout is more likely to buy in to the workout activities. Each throwing session

should include agility work and running in a brief warm-up. Additionally, throwing drills with or without implements may be used prior to a training session to complete the warm-up.

The session should have one or two specific and measurable goals that have specific benchmarks or activities that ensure progress toward reaching the goal. Throwing activities may be designed to build specific strength or speed. High-volume, high-intensity throwing can improve special strength. However, not all hammer-throwing sessions should involve

Microcycle #	Dates:	Event group: Hammer
Phase: Specific preparation	Comments:	

Sunday	Monday	Tuesday

Rest	Theme: Neuromuscular development, high demand
	Warm-up jog
	Dynamic flexibility exercises
	Specific warm-up
	   Position drills with shot put 3 × 5
	   Turns with bar (5)
	Throwing
	   Entry drills 3 × 5
	   Full throws 10 × 2, alternating 14 lb and 12 lb
	   Full throws with competition implement 12 lb (5)
	Weight training
	   Olympic lift
	      Snatch from floor 6 × 2, 90% 1RM
	   Back squat 6 × 5, 85%
	   Push jerk (6, 5, 4, 3, 2) 80%, 90%, 92%, 95%, 98%
	Multithrows
	   Toe board chest pass explosion (10), 20% over
	   competition weight
	Cool-down activity, static stretching
		Theme: General training, energy system and endocrine
		  development
		Warm-up jog
		Dynamic flexibility exercises
		Specific warm-up
		   Position drills 3 × 5
		   Left arm drill, keep left arm long and knees tight (5)
		   Left arm drills with release 3 × 5
		Throwing progression (example for female high school thrower)
		   Full technique throws 5 × 3 (5k, 4.5k, 4.5k), 88 to 92%
		   of maximum
		   All-out throws (4) 4k, 100%
		   Full technique throws 5 × 3 (5k, 4.5k, 4.5k) 88 to 92% maximum
		   34 full throws
		Special strength work
		   Wind and release with 8k pud 3 × 5 each side
		General strength
		   Abdominal/spinal circuit (5 exercises, 10 repetitions)
		   Bodybuilding lifts (9 exercises, 3 giant sets), 60 sec rest
		   between sets
		Barefoot cool-down and foot strengthening work

Wednesday	Thursday	Friday

Theme: Neuromuscular development, low demand
Warm-up jog
Dynamic flexibility exercises
Sprint development drills
Specific strength
   One-turn throws (10), implement 20% over competition
   weight
Weight training
   Olympic lift
      Clean pull from thigh 6 × 3, 140% 1RM
   Split squat 2 × 6
   Split deadlift 2 × 6
   Russian twist with weight 4 × 6
Acceleration development 3 × 20, 3 × 30, 3 × 40
Cool-down activity, static stretching
	Theme: General training, general strength and strength
	  endurance development
	Warm-up jog
	Dynamic flexibility exercises
	Specific warm-up
	   Position drills with shot put 3 × 5
	   Turns with bar (5)
	Throwing
	   Entry drills 3 × 5
	   Full throws 10 × 2, alternating 14 lb and 12 lb
	   Full throws with competition implement 12 lb (5)
	Advanced core exercises (1 exercise, 10 repetitions in each
	  plane of movement)
	Barefoot cool-down and foot strengthening work
		Theme: Neuromuscular development, high demand
		Warm-up jog
		Dynamic flexibility exercises
		Specific warm-up
		   Position drills 3 × 5
		   Left arm drill, keep left arm long and knees tight (5)
		   Left arm drills with release 3 × 5
		Throwing progression (example for female high school thrower)
		   Full technique throws 5 × 3 (5k, 4.5k, 4.5k), 88 to 92%
		   of maximum
		   All-out throws (4) 4k, 100%
		   Full technique throws 5 × 3 (5k, 4.5k, 4.5k), 88 to 92%
		   of maximum
		   34 full throws
		Special strength work
		   Wind and release with 8k pud 3 × 5 each side
		Depth jump 3 × 5, full recovery
		Olympic lift
		   Hang clean 6 × 4, 85% 1RM
		Half squat 4 × 6, 120% full squat 1RM
		Speed incline press 4 × 6, 50% 1RM
		Cool-down activity, static stretching

Saturday	Intensity of load by day	Post-workout comments

Theme: General training, energy system and endocrine
  development
Warm-up jog
Dynamic flexibility exercises
Hammer drills; all drills performed with competition implement
   Position drills 3 × 5
   Turn with stick on shoulders 3 × 5
   Walk the dog drill (5)
   Left arm drill (5)
   Right arm drill (5)
   Turn under control, waiting on hammer each turn 10 × 10
Medicine ball circuit (8 exercises, 10 repetitions for power)
Barefoot cool-down and foot strengthening		

	Su	M	Tu	W	Th	F	Sa
Hard		x			x		
Medium			x			x	
Easy				x			x
Rest	x						

FIGURE 18.30 Sample seven-day microcycle for the hammer throw: specific preparation phase of training.

going all out for long throws. The intensity of the throw should be limited to 88 to 92 percent of the athlete's practice personal best; only three to six all-out throws should occur in a practice. The coach should concentrate on correcting or modifying one element in throws performed in the 88 to 92 percent range. Workouts can include heavy and light implements or focus on throwing the standard implement.

A debriefing period at the end of the session helps to reinforce the objective. Coaches and athletes can discuss elements of the session that were highly beneficial as well as areas that need to be tweaked for upcoming sessions. At least once per week, cool-down periods need to include additional running or flexibility work.

Each training session should follow this progression:

1. Warm-up
2. Briefing
3. Skills or technical unit
4. Fitness unit
5. Cool-down
6. Debriefing

Microcycle # Phase: Competitive preparation	Dates: Comments:	Event group: Hammer
Sunday	**Monday**	**Tuesday**

Rest	Theme: Neuromuscular development, high demand
	Warm-up jog
	Dynamic flexibility exercises
	Specific warm-up
	    Position drill 3 × 5
	    One-arm winds (5)
	Hammer throwing progression
	    Entry (start) drill (5), competition weight
	    Full throws (10), competition weight, 88 to 92%
	    Full throws (5), competition weight, 100% intensity
	    Full throws (7), 10% above competition weight,
	    88 to 92% 22 throws total
	Weight training
	    Olympic lift
	        Hang snatch 6 × 2, 95%
	    Weighted squat jump 4 × 6, 30% 1RM
	    Speed incline press 4 × 6, 50% 1RM
	    Russian twist 2 × 8
	Acceleration development 3 × 20, 3 × 30, full recovery
	Cool-down activity, static stretching
		Theme: General training, energy system and endocrine
		  development
		Warm-up jog
		Dynamic flexibility exercises
		    Position drill 3 × 5
		    One-arm winds (5)
		Hammer throwing progression
		    Entry (start) drill (5), competition weight
		    Full throws (10), competition weight, 88 to 92%
		    Full throws (5), competition weight, 100% intensity
		    Full throws (7), 10% below competition weight, 88
		    to 92% 22 throws total
		General strength
		    Abdominal/spinal circuit (5 exercises, 8 repetitions)
		    Medicine ball drills (4 exercises, 5 repetitions for
		    speed)
		Barefoot cool-down and foot strengthening work

Wednesday	**Thursday**	**Friday**

Theme: Neuromuscular development, low demand
Warm-up jog
Dynamic flexibility exercises
Specific warm-up
    Position drill 3 × 5
    One-arm winds (5)
Hammer throwing progression
    Entry (start) drill (5), competition weight
    Full throws (10), competition weight, 88 to 92%
    Full throws (5), competition weight, 100% intensity
    Full throws (7), 10% below competition weight, 88
    to 92% 22 throws total
Olympic lift
    Clean pull from knees 6 × 3, 130% 1RM
Bodybuilding lifts (9 exercises, 3 giant sets), 60 sec rest
  between sets
Cool-down activity, static stretching
	Theme: General training, general strength and strength
	  endurance development
	Film study, mental preparation
		Theme: Neuromuscular development, high demand
		Warm-up jog
		Dynamic flexibility exercises
		Specific warm-up
		    Position drills 3 × 5
		    Two winds, one turn drill (3)
		Throwing progression
		    Start drill (5)
		    Full technique throws (2 to 4), competition
		    implement
		Acceleration development, 20-meter block starts (4)
		Weight training
		    Olympic lift
		        Hang clean 5 × 2, 60%, fast, 2 to 3 min rest
		        between sets
		Multithrows overhead back shot put throws, competition
		  implement (5)
		Cool-down activity, static stretching

Saturday	**Intensity of load by day**	**Post-workout comments**
Theme: General training, energy system and endocrine development Compete	<table><tr><td></td><td>Su</td><td>M</td><td>Tu</td><td>W</td><td>Th</td><td>F</td><td>Sa</td></tr><tr><td>Hard</td><td></td><td>x</td><td></td><td>x</td><td></td><td></td><td>x</td></tr><tr><td>Medium</td><td></td><td></td><td>x</td><td></td><td>x</td><td></td><td></td></tr><tr><td>Easy</td><td></td><td></td><td></td><td></td><td></td><td></td><td></td></tr><tr><td>Rest</td><td>x</td><td></td><td></td><td></td><td>x</td><td></td><td></td></tr></table>	

FIGURE 18.31 Sample seven-day microcycle for the hammer throw: competitive phase of training.

Conclusion

The hammer-throwing event presents unique safety issues. For these reasons, it requires extreme caution and awareness; the coach must consider the physical space and the equipment that will be used during training and competition. Additionally, the technical demands of the hammer throw make it very challenging for both athlete and coach. To train a thrower well, the coach must create and implement a uniquely individual training regimen. The techniques, strategies, and drills outlined in this chapter will prepare coaches to help hammer throwers reach their maximal performance capabilities.

19

Javelin

Lawrence W. Judge, PhD

The lightest implement of the four throwing events, the javelin weighs 800 grams (1.76 lb) in the men's event and 600 grams (1.32 lb) in the women's event. Unlike other throwing events, the javelin allows the competitor to build speed over a considerable distance. In addition to core and upper-body strength, javelin throwers benefit from the agility and athleticism typically associated with running and jumping events. Successful javelin throwers often share more physical characteristics with sprinters and jumpers than with athletes in the other throwing events. However, javelin throwers still require the power associated with larger and heavier athletes.

Because javelin throwing can be stressful on the shoulder and arm, proper technique is particularly important. As with all sporting events, safety is of utmost concern. The javelin throw requires a consistent and purposeful dedication to safety. Extra care should be taken during training and competition to maintain an awareness of the dangers surrounding the javelin. Both ends of the javelin can cause injury. While observing or waiting for a throw, everyone should stand at throwing side, some distance behind the foul line. For safety reasons, the javelin should be carried vertically at all times.

The cost of a quality javelin ranges from $200 to $1,450. Javelins are assigned a distance rating, which helps consumers choose one that is most closely aligned with the thrower's ability. Another variance in javelins is the stiffness of the metal. Stiffer javelins are more stable in flight; because they are more difficult to throw, however, they are reserved for more advanced throwers.

This chapter examines the mechanics and technique of the javelin throw. The technique descriptions assume a right-handed athlete.

Starting Position

The javelin consists of three parts: the point (metal head) at the end, the shaft, and a cord grip around the javelin's center of gravity. The javelin is a long implement. The men's javelin is 2.6 to 2.7 meters long, and the women's is 2.2 to 2.3 meters long. The javelin is held horizontally in the palm. Three accepted grips are used: the Finnish grip (gripping the cord between the thumb and middle finger); the American grip (gripping the cord between the thumb and index finger); and the fork grip (gripping the cord between the index and middle fingers). Beginners may benefit from trying all three grips to determine the one that feels the most comfortable. Regardless of grip style, the javelin always rests diagonally in an upturned palm. The grip is relaxed, similar to gripping a bar of soap, to lessen the tension in the arm and shoulders.

In the Finnish grip, the javelin rests diagonally across the palm. The hand is closed so that the index finger is partially extended along and curled about the shaft (figure 19.1). The middle finger circles the javelin just behind the grip, but is still touching the grip. The other fingers are loosely closed around the grip.

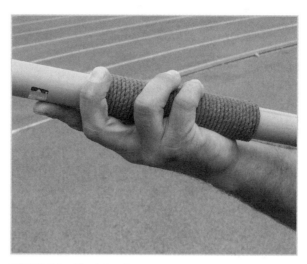

FIGURE 19.1   Finnish grip.

FIGURE 19.2   American grip.

FIGURE 19.3   Fork grip.

In the American grip, the javelin is also diagonal across the palm. The hand is closed so the index finger circles the javelin just behind the grip, but is touching the grip (figure 19.2). The other fingers are loosely closed around the grip.

As in the other grips, in the fork grip, the javelin rests diagonally across the palm. The hand is closed so the javelin lies in the fork formed by the index and middle fingers (figure 19.3), which are flexed so they contact the javelin and the rear of the grip on each side. The other fingers are loosely closed around the grip.

Prior to the approach, the hand holding the javelin is near the forehead and the javelin is level (figure 19.4a). The thrower holds the javelin high, over the right shoulder (for a right-handed thrower). Ideally, the elbow is up and pointed forward. The javelin is aimed in the target direction with the point tipped slightly down (figure 19.4b).

FIGURE 19.4 Position of the javelin: *(a)* hand near forehead; *(b)* tip pointed down.

Preliminary Movements

A good javelin throw is characterized by consistent and accurate preliminary movements that lead up to the release. These include the approach, run, withdrawal, cross steps, flight, and power position.

Approach

The approach begins with a run that accelerates smoothly toward the throwing line. The run-up starts at a check mark with the left foot forward; the thrower runs straight ahead with the hips perpendicular to the target area. The thrower maintains the position of the javelin during the run. Generally, beginners use fewer than 12 strides before throwing. Experienced throwers may use 13 to 17 strides.

The javelin throw begins with a run followed by a withdrawal of the javelin and the completion of a number of cross steps. The term *cross steps* may be misleading and cause athletes to decrease the rate of forward progression. The left foot reaches a mild angle and the right foot reaches a medium angle (figure 19.5). The final cross steps bring the athlete in position to throw.

FIGURE 19.5 Cross step during the carry.

Table 19.1 examines the running portion of the approach, the withdrawal of the javelin, and the angle cross steps. Novice throwers should begin by learning the angle cross steps, usually five to seven steps. Novice throwers should not begin in the withdrawn position.

TABLE 19.1   Common Errors and Corrections for the Javelin Throw

Fault	Reasons	Corrections
The javelin is released with the nose down, creating a short flight. The javelin rotates forward.	• Incorrect approach rhythm • Poor placement of the hand, javelin, and forearm • A lift in the final action that is more dominant than the horizontal thrust	• Improve the rhythm of the approach run. • Correct the relative positioning and action of the shoulder and all upper extremities. • Adjust the timing of the rear-leg strike. • Perform simulation drills of single-handed throwing from a standing position and from other approaches, making the line of pull along the intended line of flight.
A trajectory that is too low	• Incorrect rhythm in the approach run • Lack of mobility or coordination • Late timing of the delivery	• Practice approach runs and cross steps. • Increase the amount of mobility and conditioning work. • Incorporate simulation drills that involve the use of the legs and hips to achieve a bow position at delivery. • Use simulation drills to delay the arm action until the legs and hips have done their work. • Use easy throws to work on aspects of both sets of simulation drills.
Misalignment to the right (javelin lands pointing to the right or goes out to the right of the sector)	• The javelin is misaligned to the right during withdrawal. • The thrower leans too far away to the left at delivery. • The left arm is too active in delivery. • The front foot is in the bucket as the result of a bad cross step. • The chest comes to the front too soon because the thrower cannot tolerate the wound-up position of the cross step. • At delivery, rear-leg activity is weak. • The thrower breaks at the waist.	• Practice keeping the javelin tip close to the ear after withdrawal. • Practice keeping the hips to the front during the cross step. • Drill the approach with the withdrawal and cross step. • Perform simulation drills, placing the rear foot on the line of run in the delivery position. • Practice maintaining straight-line, forward momentum.

Fault	Reasons	Corrections
Ineffective right-leg action	• Weak right leg • Poorly executed simulation drills • Cross step (knee drive) that is too high • Passive landing of the right foot • Lack of anticipatory hip rotation from the pelvis before left-foot placement	• Repeat the practice of withdrawals through to transition. • Perform simulation drills involving the rotation of the pelvis linked with an outward rotation of the left foot. • Perform simulation drills involving turning the right knee in or the right heel out.
The nose of the javelin is up, stalling the javelin and producing a short flight.	• The grip on the javelin is slack. A slack throwing wrist causes hyper-extension. • The thrower lowers the throwing hand and arm. • The final throwing effect does not go through the point. • The last stride is too long. • The front leg is flexed or allowed to collapse.	• Use the correct grip and tension in the wrist. • Perform repeated withdrawals while standing, walking, running, and using cross steps; maintain a high hand. • Check the location of the check mark. • Perform simulations from a standing position, off three strides, and off five strides, using correct front-leg activity in predelivery and delivery. Use various implements. • Practice a short, elastic final stride. • Perform jumping and conditioning drills to develop the legs, including two-handed weight throwing.
A trajectory that is too steep resulting in a short flight with a marked nose dive	• The thrower fails to adequately drive over the front leg at delivery. • The point is too high. • The javelin is misaligned during withdrawal. • Power is applied vertically rather than through the point of the javelin. • The throwing arm gets ahead of the final action of the trunk.	• Perform drills to correct this fault including using the correct placement of the front leg and its braking action. • Practice supporting the javelin in the throwing hand during the withdrawal and cross steps. • Practice the correct withdrawal. • Do simulation drills using sling balls, a shot, and a javelin. Stand and throw two-handed from behind the head off three strides and from a run. • Perform high chopping with a hand ax, easy standing throws, and throws from a short approach.
The javelin is misaligned to the left. It lands pointing to the left or goes out to the left.	• Misalignment of the javelin to the left during withdrawal • Taking the throwing shoulder too far around to the rear • Letting the left side go soft during delivery	• Practice running with the javelin. • Perform simulation drills, preferably in front of a mirror. Practice a smooth withdrawal begun by the left shoulder. • Practice simulation drills to improve the left-side brace. • Perform easy throws off three or five strides and a three-quarters approach.

Run

The runway is 4 meters wide and at least 30 meters long. It ends in a curved arc from which the throw is measured. Athletes use the length of the runway to gain momentum in a run-up to the throw. The run portion of the approach is a controlled acceleration, building momentum so that the angle cross steps can be executed easily. A suitable run-up speed is about two-thirds of maximal sprinting speed. Leading male throwers reach speeds of 7 to 8 meters per second (15.7 to 17.9 mph); female throwers, 6 to 7 meter per second (13.4 to 15.7 mph). Ideal running is performed on the balls of the feet, avoiding bouncing or stamping. Common errors are accelerating too fast and decreasing momentum during the angle steps. The final speed must allow the thrower to move into an efficient predelivery position to be ready for the beginning of the delivery. The run is initiated when the athlete reaches a predetermined location along the runway. The javelin is carried above the shoulder with the palm up and horizontally, although this can vary slightly.

Withdrawal

The final stage of the run-up begins when the left foot hits the second check mark. The javelin-withdrawal strides begin with the rotation of the shoulder girdle to the right. This movement occurs smoothly without interrupting the forward travel of the body. The most common, simplest, and most effective is the three-stride variation—two strides for the withdrawal of the javelin and one impulse stride. The withdrawal is initiated when the left foot reaches a second predetermined location on the runway. The athlete pushes off the left foot, and the right leg moves forward. The athlete withdraws the javelin by turning the shoulders to a position 90 degrees from the direction of the throw and extending the throwing arm back so that the tip of the javelin is near the forehead (figure 19.6). The javelin remains horizontal. The palm is up, and the wrist is straight in the withdrawn position. The head faces the direction of the throw. Hip axis orientations vary, but the hips face approximately 45 degrees from the direction of the throw.

Angle Cross Steps

The angle cross steps are not sideways running. Instead, they are rhythmic steps with no decrease in forward progression. It is more an issue of rhythm than of bounding. The shoulder axis is aligned at approximately 90 degrees from the direction of the throw. The hips should not rotate far beyond 45 degrees. Throughout the angle cross steps, the head faces the direction of the throw, upright posture is maintained, and the javelin remains in the withdrawn position (figure 19.7). Common errors that take place during the angle steps include permitting the javelin to creep forward, turning the body toward the direction of the throw, and leaning back.

The final angle cross step begins with a strong push off the left leg, which drives the body forward. This brings the body to the power position. A sweeping movement of the right leg accompanies this push. The sweep is performed with the leg turned out, so that the inner thigh and inner knee lead the movement (figure 19.8). Hip movement during this strong push and the passiveness of the upper body increase separation as the body leaves the ground.

FIGURE 19.6   Withdrawn position.

FIGURE 19.7   Cross step.

FIGURE 19.8   American record holder Kara Patterson demonstrates the final cross step prior to initiating the power position.

Flight

The delivery stride, unlike the other strides that focus on forward movement, breaks the forward movement of the legs and hips. The primary difference between the final cross step and the previous steps is the speed at which the left leg is recovered. During the flight after the final cross step, the left leg recovers quickly. It is pulled forward and extended in front of the body (figure 19.9) so that it touches down as quickly as possible after the right foot does. Throughout this process, the javelin is maintained in the withdrawn position.

Power Position

The thrower lands in a good power position, ready to deliver the javelin. The right foot points 45 degrees from the direction of the throw. The right foot does not land too far in front of the hips, because excessive stopping would result. The center of gravity passes quickly in front of the right foot, enabling a very active push from the right to get the hips forward so they almost face the direction of the throw. The shoulders remain in position with

FIGURE 19.9   Left leg recovers forward during flight.

the javelin (figure 19.10). The left foot lands quickly after the right, heel first and slightly flexed. Body weight is over the right leg, and the long axis of the body is tilted slightly back. The shoulders are approximately 90 degrees from the direction of the throw, and the hips are ahead of the shoulders. The javelin is maintained in the withdrawn position.

Delivery

After the preliminary movements, the delivery phase of the javelin throw ultimately leads to the release of the implement. An efficient predelivery position following the impulse stride has these characteristics:

- The body leans back 30 to 35 degrees, and the left shoulder points in the throwing direction.
- The eyes look slightly up in the throwing direction, 30 to 35 degrees upward and forward.
- The throwing arm, shoulder, and elbow are extended back, opposite the throwing direction, with the hand at about ear level.

FIGURE 19.10   Power position.

- The left arm, bent in the elbow, is at about shoulder height.
- The front end of the javelin is held close to the head, approximately level with the eyes.
- The three axes (javelin, shoulder, hip) are virtually parallel to the direction of the throw.

The following sections discuss the delivery phase of the javelin throw.

Throw Initiation

Once the right foot lands, the throw is initiated in the lower body. The moment the right foot lands at the end of the impulse stride can be regarded as the kinematic dividing line between the run-up and the delivery phases. This is the predelivery position. The hips turn and the body weight transfers from the back foot to the front foot. On landing, the right leg is flexed slightly to allow the center of mass to move forward. The active right leg comes into play and precedes the firm planting of the left foot. Sequentially, the left arm and upper body turn and move forward, and the left arm blocks this rotation by pulling down and close to the side. Head alignment is preserved as turning occurs. A common error is turning the head prior to turning the upper body.

Arm Strike

The arm strike begins after the lower- and upper-body movements are nearly complete. The arm strike features a sequential, overhand throwing movement using the shoulder, elbow, and wrist. The strike is initiated by a forward and upward movement of the shoulder, accompanied by a slight inward rotation of the forearm and slight flexion of the elbow, which places it in a high position to set up the overhand throw (figure 19.11a).

The arm strike continues as the hand applies force along the shaft of the javelin, finishing well in front of the body with a pronation of the hand and the thumb pointed downward (figure 19.11b). The strike, combined with the blocking action of the left side, supplies lift to the javelin. Delivering the javelin with the

FIGURE 19.11   Arm strike: *(a)* elbow in high position; *(b)* follow-through.

elbow lower than the shoulder is a common error and places the arm at great risk for injury.

At release, a javelin can reach speeds approaching 113 kilometers per hour (70 mph).

Follow-Through and Reverse

The thrower vigorously strikes through the point of the javelin. A vigorous release brings the arm across the chest to a position near the left hip at the completion of the throw.

The reverse is completed following the release of the javelin. To properly reverse, the thrower takes a long step with the right foot to completely stop forward movement. The thrower releases the javelin approximately 5 feet (1.5 m) behind the scratch line. This provides the space needed to move forward aggressively during the final cross step and the throw, as well as the distance needed to execute the reverse and, ultimately, avoid scratching.

Teaching Progression

The javelin event possesses many variables: implement, footwear, and runway. The coach's knowledge of proper technique and safety is crucial. For this reason, a beginning javelin coach needs a mentor.

The coach must select a javelin that closely aligns with the ability of the athlete. Reading catalogs and seeking input from experienced coaches can be very helpful. The coach must also avoid buying an expensive implement for a beginner.

Quality footwear is important for javelin throwers. Those just learning to throw must have a javelin boot, a J-heel, or spiked shoes for both feet. Because the javelin is dangerous, appropriate footwear is vital even for novice throwers.

Many schools have only grass runways. These must be trimmed and as smooth as possible. Athletes running on grass need longer spikes than those using rubberized runways.

Throwers should practice the components of the javelin throw in progression to establish a link between the basic movements and the desired result. Because each portion of the throw is set up by the action of the previous one, throwers must be consistent and practice the movements to perfection so that the components flow smoothly into each other.

GRIP

Beginners may benefit from trying all three accepted grips and use the one that feels the most comfortable. Most beginners benefit from trying the Finnish grip first.

FLICKS

Pull back the javelin with the tip pointing down and the tail pointing up at 45 degrees (figure 19.12). Flick the javelin into the ground approximately 10 feet (3 m) in front of you. Feel the rotation of the javelin off the index finger followed by the final inward rotation of the hand to a thumbs-down position. Repeat this action many times until you can control the rotation.

FIGURE 19.12   Flicks.

TWO-HANDED THROW

Select a grip. Hold the javelin as in the flick drill: javelin pulled back, tip pointing down, tail pointing 45 degrees up. Place the left hand over the right. Stand with feet parallel and lean back into the C position. Step into the throw (figure 19.13), or throw from a staggered position. Choose a target approximately 3 meters away and try to hit it. Work your way down the field, slightly increasing the distance of the target.

FIGURE 19.13   Two-handed throw.

SHORT THROW (STAB)

Begin with the javelin above the right shoulder and the elbow level with the ear and ideally pointing in the direction of the throw. Aim at a target approximately 10 meters away; start with 10 meters and increase as you are able. With the left foot in front and pointing in the direction of the throw (figure 19.14), push off the rear foot and step forward past the left leg to push the javelin at the target. Emphasize the use of the right side of the body to pull the javelin through.

FIGURE 19.14   Short throw.

STANDING THROW

Point both feet forward in the direction of the throw with the left leg in front. The body weight is placed onto the flexed rear right leg (figure 19.15). The javelin is withdrawn with the arm fully extended behind the body and the hand above the shoulder. Shoulders are turned so they are parallel to the javelin and in the direction of the throw, and the left arm is folded around the chest under the point of the javelin. The left elbow is pointing in the direction of the throw. The throwing action begins by extending the right leg, which moves the right hip up and forward to pull the javelin through. The right elbow leads the javelin. As you pass over the flexed but firm left leg, release the javelin over the right shoulder with a fast arm strike, pushing against the binding with the whole hand. The palm is turned up to impart maximal release speed at an optimal angle of 35 degrees.

FIGURE 19.15   Standing throw.

THREE-STEP THROW

The javelin is withdrawn and the right foot is in front of the left (figure 19.16). Keep the left arm up and slightly bent with the palm facing down (thumb down). The chin is near the left shoulder. The step pattern for the three-step throw is left-right-left. In the power position, keep the right side moving (pushing and turning) while the left side enters into position.

FIGURE 19.16   Three-step throw, starting position.

FIVE-STEP THROW

The javelin is withdrawn and the right foot is in front of the left. Keep the left arm up and slightly bent with the palm facing out (thumb down). The chin is near the left shoulder. The step pattern for the five-step throw is left-right-left-right-left. In the power position, keep the right side moving (pushing and turning) while the left side enters into position.

WALK-IN THROW

Begin with the javelin in the overhead carry position, over the shoulder and horizontal or with the nose slightly down. Step with the left foot; then step with the right foot and begin the withdrawal. Step with the left foot with the javelin withdrawn (figure 19.17). (At this point, the coach should observe the position of the javelin and the left arm for accurate positioning.) Repeat. Once you have practiced this drill walking, jogging, and running, use it with a five-step approach.

FIGURE 19.17   Walk-in throw.

FULL-APPROACH THROW

Begin an 11-stride approach with a left step. Walk the approach, counting the number of steps. Decide on which step to begin the withdrawal. Practice without a javelin from a walk, jog, and run.

After practicing without the javelin, add it and proceed in the same fashion, walking, jogging, and running. There is no need to actually throw the javelin.

Next, mark where the left foot (the block leg) lands when running through the approach. Once you have marked four to six approaches, note the distance and add a javelin length to it. Measure the entire approach using javelin lengths or a measuring tape. Complete this drill on the same surface or a similar one to the one on which you will throw.

Javelin-Specific Medicine Ball Throw Drills

Movements required by the javelin throw, such as jumping, involve extension at the ankle, knee, and hip and require the use of the entire body. Throwing medicine balls teaches athletes to summate forces and incorporate the entire body when delivering an implement. Drills that use a medicine ball move from overhead throws to throws that involve a blocking of one side. For these drills, use medicine balls that bounce and weigh 4 to 7 pounds (1.8 to 3.2 kg). Complete one to three sets of 6 to 10 repetitions.

MEDICINE BALL STANDING THROW

Assume the power position with the body weight on the back leg and both hands on the medicine ball. To initiate the throw, rotate on the ball of the right foot, step forward into the throw, and deliver the medicine ball against a wall (figure 19.18). Keep the arms relaxed and rotate the lower body prior to using the upper body. Focus on finesse, not distance.

FIGURE 19.18   Medicine ball standing throw.

MEDICINE BALL THREE-STEP THROW

Hold the medicine ball overhead with both hands and stand with the right foot in front of the left (figure 19.19). The chin is near the left shoulder. The step pattern for the three-step throw is left-right-left. In the power position, keep the right side moving (pushing and turning) while the left side enters into position.

FIGURE 19.19   Medicine ball three-step throw.

MEDICINE BALL FIVE-STEP THROW

Hold the medicine ball overhead with both hands, and stand with the right foot in front of the left. The chin is near the left shoulder. The step pattern for the five-step throw is left-right-left-right-left. In the power position, keep the right side moving (pushing and turning) while the left side enters into position.

TWIST WITH THE MEDICINE BALL

Begin with the medicine ball at the waistline, arms slightly bent. Move the ball to one side (figure 19.20). There are two crucial points in this exercise: turning at the waist while keeping the toes pointed straight ahead and shifting the body weight completely from one side to the other on each twist. Move continuously from right to left.

FIGURE 19.20   Twist with the medicine ball.

Javelin-Specific Weighted Ball Throws

Using other implements such as medicine balls, knocken, or javelin balls helps the athlete learn delivery mechanics. Standing throws, three-step throws, and five-step throws can be performed with weighted balls. Athletes should begin with the basics and proceed to advanced delivery mechanics.

SEATED WEIGHTED BALL THROW

The seated weighted ball throw can be done with a weighted ball or a medicine ball. Sit with both feet firmly on the ground and the back straight. With the ball in the throwing hand, draw the throwing arm straight back. The nonthrowing arm is extended toward the direction of the throw. The shoulders are turned back approximately 90 degrees, creating a comfortable position. The throwing hand is slightly above the throwing shoulder. From this position, throw the weighted ball. Focus on pulling over the top as the throwing elbow comes through at a level higher than the throwing shoulder. Release the ball at a point above the head. The nonthrowing hand may come toward the nonthrowing shoulder, but be careful not to pull too aggressively with the nonthrowing arm. Overrotation of the shoulders may cause the throwing arm to drop and the implement to be thrown with a sidearm delivery.

Drills With the Javelin

Because the javelin throw is very different from the other throws, special consideration is required when developing a training program to produce event-specific strength. Coaches must remember that athletes' adaptations to training occur based on the stress placed on them. A good javelin coach creates and implements exercises and drills that meet the needs of individual athletes.

Current research suggests that preactivity dynamic stretching increases sport-specific flexibility, strength, power, agility, and sprint performance. On the other hand, recent evidence demonstrates that preactivity static stretching may actually decrease athletic performance; it is alternately recommended as a component of a postactivity cool-down routine. Following the hip pop drill are a few drills with the javelin that address flexibility.

HIP POP

In this drill, it is important to keep the right side moving (pushing and turning) while the left side enters the power position (figure 19.21). Set the feet as if in the power position, loading nearly all the body weight onto the power leg. This action involves twisting the foot into the ground and creating a twist that rises up the leg to the hip.

FIGURE 19.21 Hip pop.

DISLOCATES

This drill involves a dynamic stretch that increases flexibility and mobility in the shoulders. It develops and strengthens the full range of throwing motion in the javelin. Grip the javelin with both hands spread shoulder-width apart. Take the implement behind the body with the hands as wide as possible (figure 19.22).

FIGURE 19.22 Dislocates.

ROTATOR CUFF DRILL

Rotator cuff exercises involve external rotation movements. Hold the elbow along the side of the trunk and bend it to 90 degrees. Pull the javelin across the body to full external rotation (figure 19.23). The rotation centers around the humerus (upper arm), so do not lift the elbow to complete the rotation.

This drill may be done with a dumbbell while lying on the floor on your side. Lift the dumbbell straight off the ground.

Complete this exercise from the delivery position as well. Hold the elbow (bent at 90 degrees) straight out from the shoulder (at 90 degrees of abduction), and pull a stretch tube attached to a fixed object at ankle height up and back as the arm rotates around the axis of the humerus. Point the elbow at something for reference, and do not let it move forward or back.

FIGURE 19.23   Rotator cuff drill.

Because the muscles worked by this drill are small and frequently used, increase endurance by incorporating two sets of 20 repetitions. Concentrate on very slow eccentric movement. Ease the weight down very slowly; this action develops and strengthens the targeted muscle groups. The eccentric movements of the posterior shoulder muscles stabilize the shoulder at the joint and decelerate the arm after the throw. The weight should be light enough to allow perfect form. Start with no weight and train the movements first.

TWIST WITH THE JAVELIN

Stand with the javelin on the shoulders and hold it securely with both hands as far from the center as possible (figure 19.24). Twist the upper body in one direction; then, before the torso is fully rotated, twist in the opposite direction. Repeat. This drill strengthens the trunk muscles.

FIGURE 19.24   Twist with the javelin.

Running Drills

Running is the most event-specific exercise and is the backbone of the training program for the javelin thrower during all phases of the training year. Weight training and plyometrics are secondary components. Because exercises such as sprinting are holistic activities, it is difficult to separate them into components. However, javelin throwers need to develop specific running skills involving the implement (i.e., carries, withdrawals, and crossovers).

JAVELIN CARRY

The most accomplished javelin throwers use very fast approaches and run with the eyes and head pointing forward. Sprinting various short distances while carrying the javelin above the head (figure 19.25) helps build speed on the approach. Relaxed sprinters sprint better. Being able to turn muscle contractions on and off very quickly is the essence of good running technique with the javelin. This results in the next contraction occurring without the tension that can hinder the speed and force of the contraction. Like any learning process, to become second nature, relaxation must be practiced and focused on during training. Concentrate on both individual muscle groups and total body relaxation when running. This can be a part of everyday training. Jog 10 steps while carrying the javelin above the head. Increase step count as you build strength.

FIGURE 19.25 Javelin carry.

WITHDRAWAL DRILL

Jog 10 steps carrying the javelin above your head; then perform 10 continuous cross steps with the javelin withdrawn at arm's length and the hand above the shoulder (figure 19.26). Turn the shoulders parallel to the javelin, and face the hips in the direction of the run. The left shoulder is high with the elbow pointing in the direction of the run. Complete six sets out and six sets back, equaling 24 steps total.

FIGURE 19.26 Withdrawal drill.

CROSSOVER DRILL

Set the hips parallel to the javelin, and point the feet away from the body at right angles to the hips. Move sideways to the right, lift the left foot to cross the right foot in front, and then pull the right foot to the side to uncross the legs. There is some variability in the position of the hips in crossovers because some athletes use a more linear approach to maximize running speed. Next, cross the right foot over the left foot and pull the left foot to the left to uncross the legs. Repeat, walking, jogging, or running. You can perform this drill without the javelin and with the arms held straight, parallel to the hips, or out in front at right angles to the hips. Later, you can attempt cross step front bounding (figure 19.27). Complete these drills on grass or on a slight incline.

FIGURE 19.27   Crossover drill.

Designing Javelin Throwing Workouts

The thrower should begin each workout session with 8 to 12 minutes of a general dynamic warm-up that flows smoothly into a specific warm-up that includes javelin drills. The drills should align with the objectives of the training session. One drill should emphasize the power position, and one drill should address the mechanics of the approach. As the drills conclude, the athlete begins the throwing session, which should consist of approximately 30 throws.

The coach should break down the run-up and throw drills into smaller sections to emphasize specific concepts. The athlete should practice running while carrying the javelin in a horizontal position to practice staying relaxed and balanced with the implement. While running, she should practice the approach technique by timing the steps and imagining the transition into the release. The athlete should accelerate into the moment of release rather than come to a stop. The javelin should be thrown only two or three days per week, and nonthrowing days should focus on conditioning and technique, as well as flexibility training, running drills, and medicine ball throwing.

Microcycles for the Javelin

The definitive goal of javelin training is the functional reconstruction of the athlete, resulting in an enduring adaptation and the preservation of the training effect. High-quality training plans often include both specific and general exercises. Variables such as training load, training volume, exercise selection, and training frequency should be chosen based on factors such as the athlete's training age and strengths and weaknesses, as well as the phase of the training year. An in-season competition program must consider bioenergetics, metabolic parameters, and movement characteristics specific to throwing the javelin, such as force, magnitude, velocity, movement patterns, and time factors.

The objective of microcycles for a javelin thrower is to coordinate training loads to establish a balance between work and recovery. The plan must ensure sufficient regeneration prior to the start of a new microcycle. The function of a microcycle (figure 19.28)

Microcycle #	Dates:	Event group: Javelin
Phase: General preparation	Comments:	
Sunday	**Monday**	**Tuesday**

Rest	Theme: Neuromuscular development, high demand
	Warm-up jog
	Dynamic flexibility exercises
	Specific warm-up, grind the cigarette drill 3 × 5
	Arm injury prevention: Wilk thrower's 10
	Medicine balls
	    Two hands OH to wall
	    Two hands OH with twist
	    LL forward, jump into power position, ball OH, throw
	    Seated parallel to wall, twist, throw into wall, repeat
	Multithrow overhead back shot put throws (10), 10%
	    over competition weight
	Weight training
	    Olympic lift
	        Clean pull from floor 6 × 4, 120% of CL 1RM
	    Back squat 4 × 8, 75% 1RM
	    Bench press 4 × 8, 75% 1RM
	Cool-down activity, static stretching
		Theme: General training, energy system and endocrine
		    development
		Warm-up jog
		Dynamic flexibility exercises
		Technical drills
		    Walk javelin down field, flick, thumb down at release
		    Two step: LL forward, thrust off left; RF touch as
		        COG passes, active right drive hip around;
		        LF plant; throw
		    Three step: RL forward, spring off RL; then do the
		        two step
		    Short approach, work on full steps; for five steps
		        rhythm is L...R...L......R..L
		Bodybuilding lifts (9 exercises, 3 giant sets), 60 sec rest
		    between sets
		Barefoot cool-down and foot strengthening work

Wednesday	**Thursday**	**Friday**

Theme: Neuromuscular development, low demand
Warm-up jog
Dynamic flexibility exercises
Shot put drills
    Partner high five drill 3 × 5
    Partner hip pops drill 3 × 5
    Partner glide 3 × 5
Throws on knees 3 × 5, 10% over competition weight,
    focus on block
Ground level plyometrics
    Jump circuit (6 exercises, 10 repetitions), 20 sec
        rest between exercises
Weight training
    Olympic lift
        Power clean pull from floor 4 × 3, 85% 1RM
    Step-up 2 × 5
    Lunge walk with twist 2 × 5
    Incline press 4 × 8, 70% 1RM
Build-up 5 × 80 meters
Multithrows 3 × 5, between legs forward, 10% over
    competition weight
Cool-down activity, static stretching
	Theme: General training, general strength endurance
	    development
	Warm-up jog
	Dynamic flexibility exercises
	Technical drills
	    Walk javelin down field, flick thumb down at release
	    Two step: LL forward, thrust off left; RF touch
	        as COG passes, active right drive hip
	        around; LF plant; throw
	    Three step: RL forward, spring off RL; then do the
	        two step
	    Short approach, work on full steps; for five steps
	        rhythm is L...R...L......R..L
	Medicine ball work as on Monday
	Aerobic run
		Theme: Neuromuscular development, high demand
		Warm-up jog
		Dynamic flexibility exercises with rubber cables
		Wilk thrower's 10
		Sprint 4 × 60 good speed
		Bounding exercises
		Olympic lift
		    Snatch pull from floor 6 × 4, 115% 1RM
		Back squat 4 × 8, 70% 1RM
		Bench press 4 × 8, 70% 1RM
		Cool-down activity, static stretching

Saturday	**Intensity of load by day**	**Post-workout comments**
Theme: General training, energy system and endocrine development Warm-up jog Dynamic flexibility exercises Walking South African drill down the track 2 × 10 Standing throw 2 with traffic cone (10) Cool-down, static stretching	(see intensity table below)	

	Su	M	Tu	W	Th	F	Sa
Hard		x		x		x	
Medium			x		x		
Easy							x
Rest	x						

FIGURE 19.28 Sample seven-day microcycle for the javelin: general preparation phase of training.

is to provide a rational approach to the training loads planned for a particular training phase. As a rule, each microcycle concludes with one or two recovery days. Microcycles also have specific goals. The goal of a preparation microcycle is to prepare the thrower for the upcoming competition. The goal of the last preparation microcycle (figure 19.29) prior to a competition is to unleash and mobilize the thrower's performance capacities.

The goal of a competition microcycle (figure 19.30) is to organize activities just prior to and immediately after a competition. This involves activities one day before the competition, the day of the competition, and days following the competition. The goal for the competition microcycle depends on the

Microcycle #	Dates:	Event group: Javelin
Phase: Specific preparation	Comments:	
Sunday	Monday	Tuesday

Rest	Theme: Neuromuscular development, high demand
	Warm-up jog
	Dynamic flexibility exercises
	Specific warm-up
	    Wilk thrower's 10
	    Medicine balls OH two hand, OH two hands twist, OH one hand
	Throwing
	    30 min run through hitting all marks
	    15 min two-step throw, work on technique
	    30 min hard throws from shorter run
	    15 min work on technical elements
	Weight training
	    Olympic lift
	        Snatch from floor 6×2, 90% 1RM
	    Back squat 6×5, 85%
	    Pull-over (6, 5, 4, 3, 2), 80%, 90%, 95%, 98%
	Multithrows
	    Toe board chest pass explosion (10), 20% over competition weight
	Cool-down activity, static stretching
		Theme: General training, energy system and endocrine development
		Warm-up jog
		Dynamic flexibility exercises
		Specific warm-up
		    Bounding
		    Box jump
		    Runway without javelin
		Medicine ball throwing progression
		    OH two hands to wall 3×10
		    OH two hands to wall with twist 3×10
		    Jump into PP, OH throw to wall 3×10
		    One-handed, two step into wall 2×10
		    Gambetta shoulder crawl 4×10
		    Seated twist into wall, both sides 4×10
		General strength
		    Abdominal/spinal circuit (5 exercises, 10 repetitions)
		    Bodybuilding lifts (9 exercises, 3 giant sets), 60 sec rest between sets
		Barefoot cool-down and foot strengthening work

Wednesday	Thursday	Friday

Theme: Neuromuscular development, low demand
Warm-up jog
Dynamic flexibility exercises
Sprint development drills
Throwing
    Two-step throws, work on elements
    Javelin throws with 600 gram javelin (20)
Weight training
    Olympic lift
        Clean pull from thigh 6×3, 140% 1RM
    Split squat 2×6
    Split deadlift 2×6
    Pull-over 4×6
Acceleration development 3×20, 3×30, 3×40
Cool-down activity, static stretching
	Theme: General training, general strength and strength endurance development
	Warm-up jog
	Dynamic flexibility exercises
	Specific warm-up
	    Wilk thrower's 10
	    Medicine ball series
	Throwing progression
	    30 min run through hitting all marks
	    15 min two-step throw, work on technique
	    30 min hard throws from shorter run
	    15 min work on technical elements
	Advanced core exercises (1 exercise, 10 repetitions in each plane of movement)
	Barefoot cool-down and foot strengthening work
		Theme: Neuromuscular development, high demand
		Warm-up jog
		Dynamic flexibility exercises
		Specific warm-up
		    Gambetta shoulder crawl
		    Work with rubber cables
		Throwing progression
		    20 min run through hitting all marks
		    10 min two-step throw
		    30 min hard throws from shorter run
		    15 min work on technical elements
		Depth jump 3×5, full recovery
		Olympic lift
		    Hang clean 6×4, 85% 1RM
		Half squat 4×6, 120% full squat 1RM
		Speed incline press 4×6, 50% 1RM
		Cool-down activity, static stretching

Saturday	Intensity of load by day	Post-workout comments

Theme: General training, energy system and endocrine development
Warm-up jog
Dynamic flexibility exercises
Javelin throwing sequence
    Easy standing throws
    Two-step light throws
    Short approach, no throwing
    Work on angle steps
    Check technical elements of release
Medicine ball circuit (8 exercises, 10 repetitions for power)
Barefoot cool-down and foot strengthening
	(see intensity table below)	

	Su	M	Tu	W	Th	F	Sa
Hard		x		x		x	
Medium			x		x		
Easy							x
Rest	x						

FIGURE 19.29 Sample seven-day microcycle for the javelin: specific preparation phase of training.

length of the competition, the number of attempts, the frequency of competitions, the performance level of the rivals, and so on. In short, the competition microcycle should be tailored to the needs of the javelin thrower.

The most effective organizational structure is one week for each microcycle. However, javelin throwers who train two or three times per day often require slightly shorter microcycles. Each microcycle must include recovery times between training sessions.

Consistency in scheduling throughout the year is an important component of a microcycle. Additionally, the efficacy of training sessions is maintained when careful consideration is given to any potential interference among the types of training. For example, coaches should ensure that the training activity of day one does not interfere with the training activity of day two.

Microcycle # Phase: Competitive phase	Dates: Comments:	Event group: Javelin
Sunday	**Monday**	**Tuesday**

Rest	Theme: Neuromuscular development, high demand
	Warm-up jog
	Dynamic flexibility exercises
	Specific warm-up
	    Wilk thrower's 10
	    Gambetta shoulder crawls
	Throwing progression
	    Light medicine ball
	    Two step, hard, 10 throws
	    Full approach, hard, 6 throws; analyze
	    Full approach, work on corrections
	    Full approach, light throws
	Weight training
	    Olympic lift
	        Hang snatch 6 × 2, 95% 1RM
	    Weighted squat jump 4 × 6, 30% 1RM
	    Pull-over 3 × 8
	    Russian twist 2 × 8
	Acceleration development 3 × 20, 3 × 30, full recovery
	Cool-down activity, static stretching
		Theme: General training, energy system and endocrine
		   development
		Warm-up jog
		Dynamic flexibility exercises
		Specific warm-up
		    Medicine balls (3 exercises) 2 × 10
		    Bounding
		    Javelin flexibility
		    Easy sprints 3 × 20 meters
		Throwing progression
		    Two step, easy, 10 throws
		    Short approach, medium, 10 throws; analyze
		    Short approach, work on corrections
		    Short approach, work on hitting marks, no throws
		Easy sprints
		General strength
		    Abdominal/spinal circuit (5 exercises, 8 repetitions)
		Medicine ball drills (4 exercises, 5 repetitions for speed)
		Barefoot cool-down and foot strengthening work

Wednesday	**Thursday**	**Friday**

Theme: Neuromuscular development, low demand
Warm-up jog
Dynamic flexibility exercises
Specific warm-up
    Hip drills with rubber cable
    Javelin flexibility
Throwing progression
    Three step throw, work on arm delay
    Full approach, hard, 6 throws; analyze
    Full approach, work on corrections
    Full approach, work on steps, no throws
Weight training
    Olympic lift
        Clean pull from knees 6 × 3, 130% 1RM
    Bodybuilding lifts (9 exercises, 3 giant sets), 60 sec
    rest
    between sets
Cool-down activity, static stretching
	Theme: Film study and mental preparation
	Film study, mental preparation
	Dynamic warm-up
	    Wilk thrower's 10
	    Gambetta shoulder crawls
		Theme: Neuromuscular development, high demand
		Warm-up jog
		Dynamic warm-up
		    Wilk thrower's 10
		    Gambetta shoulder crawls
		Throwing progression
		    Two step throws; analyze
		    Work on good L... then R..L
		    Short approach, get good left drive
		    Full approach, work on steps, no throws
		Cool-down activity, static stretching

Saturday	**Intensity of load by day**	**Post-workout comments**
Theme: General training, energy system and endocrine development Compete in javelin	(see table below)	

	Su	M	Tu	W	Th	F	Sa
Hard		x		x			x
Medium			x			x	
Easy					x		
Rest	x						

FIGURE 19.30 Sample seven-day microcycle for the javelin: competitive phase of training.

Designing an Individual Training Session

In conjunction with team or event group training sessions, javelin throwers benefit from training sessions uniquely tailored to meet their needs. These may include individual workouts in the weight room or on the field as well as training units listed on the training inventory. The coach must understand the athlete's physical capabilities when designing a training session. Training sessions that last too long may not be effective; training sessions that are too short may not result in physical adaptations.

Prior to each session, the coach should present the session objective to the javelin thrower. An athlete who understands the purpose of the workout is more likely to buy in to the workout activities. Each throwing session should include agility work and running in a brief warm-up. Additionally, throwing drills with or without implements may be used prior to a training session to complete the warm-up.

The session should have one or two specific and measurable goals that have benchmarks or activities to ensure progress toward reaching the goal. Throwing activities may be designed to build specific strength or speed. High-volume, high-intensity throwing can improve special strength. However, not all throwing sessions should involve going all-out for long throws. The intensity of the throw should be limited to 88 to 92 percent of the athlete's practice personal best; only three to six all-out throws should occur in a practice. The coach should concentrate on correcting or modifying one element in throws performed in the 88 to 92 percent range. Workouts can include heavy and light implements or focus on throwing the standard javelin.

A debriefing period at the end of the session helps to reinforce the objective. Coaches and athletes can discuss elements of the session that were highly beneficial as well as areas that need to be tweaked for upcoming sessions. At least once per week, cool-down periods need to include additional running or flexibility work.

Each training session should follow this progression:

1. Warm-up
2. Briefing
3. Skills or technical unit
4. Fitness unit
5. Cool-down
6. Debriefing

Conclusion

Because the javelin is the lightest of the throwing implements, the throw is unique in that it allows the athlete to build momentum over an extended distance. Elite javelin throwers have reached throwing velocities in excess of 30 meters per second (67 mph), whereas a shot put release is less than 14 meters per second (31 mph).

Because of the greater emphasis on speed than in other throws, javelin-specific training should never be done at slow speeds. The technical components of the javelin throw require the coach to develop and implement a unique training regimen for each javelin thrower. The careful planning and selection of training methods and exercises is important to develop the neural adaptation and muscular strength required to maximize an athlete's performance in this event. The strategies, drills, and activities in this chapter will prepare the javelin coach to train throwers well.

Final Thoughts

Will Freeman

Back in 1990, I was a young college coach with 10 years of experience (actually, just 1 year of experience, repeated 10 times). I thought I had a lot of answers back then. My experience at the USATF Level 2 Coaching School in Colorado Springs proved me wrong. It was a humbling eye-opener for a young coach. That experience inspired me to read and contact those who knew more, and ultimately led me to write about what I have learned in my years of coaching. To be the editor of this project has been very special to me. The contributors to this book are talented coaches and good people making a difference in our sport. I thank them all for their significant input. Our goal with this project was to help our track and field coaches grow. When coaches grow, athletes grow. When athletes grow, the sport grows. Coaches truly make a difference.

Knowledge goes a long way, and it's free! Just read, research, ask others, and apply what you learn. Knowledge is about what we learn from others who have gone before us. In a way, it's about the past. Wisdom is different. It's about combining knowledge, experience, and intuition to be better at what we do. It comes with experience. After 45 years as an athlete, coach, and classroom professor, I would like to share some truths I've learned along the way.

We Accept Mediocrity Because It's Safe

Most of us live in the middle of the bell-shaped curve because it's comfortable. Leaving a comfort zone creates discomfort. To be successful, the athlete must understand that discomfort is something to be practiced and overcome. Pain, fear, and failure are regularly faced in sport. The coach's job is to help the athlete learn from these challenges, and overcome them. We grow stronger as we are tested. The sport

experience, and life itself, is about adaptation. Along the way, courage is learned. The courage to risk also is learned. Our job as coaches is to train athletes so they are tested, so they look forward to challenge and risk. We cannot ask them to risk in competition unless they first face risk in training.

Life Can Be Difficult

Yes, it is. Get over it, learn from it, and move on. I love the metaphor of life being like ocean waves. There are highs and lows, and they keep on coming. We all experience life's highs and lows. It's simply part of the ride we are on. We must remember that it's the lows, not the highs, that offer the greatest potential for growth. Friedrich Nietzsche was right when he said, "That which does not kill us makes us stronger."

Athletes Should Not Fear Competition

We see this kind of fear too often. It comes from a fear of social comparison and from flawed expectations. Competition can be a wonderful motivator, but it also can be a debilitating phenomenon. Athletes should focus only on what they can control. The coach should help athletes understand that they have a choice in the process. They can choose to define themselves, or they can let others define them. The attempt to win in sport is a great motivator, but winning is only one goal of the sport experience.

It's Not the Event That Creates Tension and Stress

The athlete's *perception* of the event creates tension and stress, not the event itself. Two athletes can view a competitive moment in totally different ways. The coach should make every effort to read tension and stress cues from the athlete. How the athlete perceives the situation is everything. When performance is linked to self-worth, the event can be magnified into something far bigger than it really is. When this happens, a poor result can be a significant blow to an athlete's self-esteem. A single performance does not define a person. Improvement, not the result, should be the primary motivation.

Thoughts Drive Behavior

Athletes' thoughts determine their behavior. We can think about only one thing at a time, and we have a choice in what we think. Although input from the coach and significant others is important to athletes, the messages athletes send themselves matter most. The brain is like a computer hard drive. It simply files the inputted information. Whatever is inputted shapes the person's self-concept. What we say to ourselves matters, and we have a choice in what we say.

The Greatest Gift Athletes Can Offer a Program Is Themselves

There are billions of people on this earth, every one unique. As coaches, we allow for individualized training, yet often do not allow for individuals to be who they are. Great coaches know that creating great teams is a balance between building a unified team and allowing athletes to be who they are. Finding that balance is a key to tapping potential.

People Feed Off the Energy of Others

You bet they do. It's the mirror principle. We get what we give. It's not more complicated than that. Positive energy catches on, and misery loves company. What energy do we want to

send out each day and with every person we meet? Remember, we get back what we give.

Those Who Succeed Expect To

Champion athletes choose to be positive, have functional training programs that result in improvement, and visualize success. Quite simply, they are positive, do the work, and see themselves succeeding in advance. An athlete who is improving will not be a problem athlete. The goal of the coach is to teach competence and inspire confidence. These are two crucial things necessary to succeed. An athlete who is competent and improving will increase in confidence.

Balance Is Crucial

Balance, both in and outside of training, is necessary for optimal development. The variables that both coach and athlete must balance include training, recovery, academics, nutrition, social life, the coach–athlete relationship, the team environment, work, family, and the training environment. The coach must understand how these variables interact and how each influences the training process. The disruption of one variable can have a domino effect on the others. Coaches must know their athletes.

Integrity in the Process Is Essential

Integrity is about doing the right things for the right reasons. Training with integrity is crucial to success, and only the athlete knows for sure whether there is integrity to the process. Doing the little things well, even when the coach is not there, is what builds confidence and self-belief. All athletes at the top of the sport are fit. So what separates them? I believe it is integrity in training. The athlete, not the coach, makes the final judgment on integrity. At the moment of the big performance on target day, the last thing the athlete needs to be asking is, "Have I done everything well enough?" Only the athlete knows the answer.

Athletes Remember Relationships the Most

What coaches do is about people. People make the sport, and people make the team. Coaches should do everything they can to help each team member find a role on the team. It's amazing what people will step up and do for those they care about. As coaches, we must invest in the person, not just the athlete. Community matters.

Dependence Must Give Way to Independence

Coaching is like raising kids. As they get older, we give them an increased role in the deci-sion-making process. In effect, we are weaning them from dependence. Athletes benefit greatly from a dependence-to-independence model. It takes courage for the coach to give up control, but nothing is more empowering to the athlete. If our goal is to create stronger people, and not just better athletes, we need to give them increasing input and ownership in the process.

Coaches Must Continue to Learn and Grow

I learned years ago that no coach has all the answers. We must all challenge ourselves to grow and learn as teachers and coaches. Our roles as coaches are far more important than just teaching our athletes to run faster, jump farther and higher, and throw farther. We teach and mentor young people to face far greater challenges than sport. We must challenge our-selves to do it well and to make a difference.

Bibliography

Anderson, L. 1990. Program design: General preparation phase: Female discus thrower. *Strength & Conditioning Journal* 12 (2): 55-73.

Babbitt, D. 2000. Discus. In J.L. Rogers, ed., *USA Track & Field Coaching Manual*. Champaign, IL: Human Kinetics, pp. 235-248.

Bandura, A. 1977. Self-efficacy: Toward a unifying theory of behavior change. *Psychological Review* 84: 191-215.

Bandura, A. 1986. *Social Foundations of Thought and Action: A Social Cognitive Theory*. Englewood Cliffs, NJ: Prentice Hall.

Bartonietz, K. 1996. Biomechanical aspects of the performance structure in throwing events. *Modern Athlete and Coach* 34 (2): 7-11.

Bell, S. 1979. The shot put, as I see it. *Track & Field Quarterly Review* 79 (4): 8-10.

Bompa, Tudor, Haff, G. Gregory. *Periodization*, fifth edition. Human Kinetics Publishing, Company. 2009.

Bosch, Frans, and Klomp, Ronald. *Running – Biomechanics and exercise Physiology Applied in Practice*. London. Elsevier Churchill Livingstone. 2005

Buckingham, M., and C. Coffman. 1999. *First Break All the Rules: What the World's Greatest Managers Do Differently*. New York: Simon and Schuster.

Daniels, Jack. *Jack Daniels Running Formula*, 3rd edition. Human Kinetics Publishing. 2013.

Davids, Keith. Button, Chris. Bennett, Simon. *Dynamics of Skill Acquisition – A Constraints-Led Approach*. Champaign, IL: Human Kinetics Publishing Company. 2008.

Deci, E., and R.M. Ryan. 2006. Facilitate optimal motivation and psychological well-being across life's domain. *Canadian Psychology* 49 (1): 14-23.

Dick, Frank. *Sports Training Principles*. Fifth edition. A&C Black, London. 2007.

Doherty, Ken. *Track & Field Omnibook*. TAFNews Publishing. 1985.

Drabik, J. 1996. *Children and Sports Training*. Island Pond, VT: Stadion Publishing.

Dunn, G.J. 1989. The shot put. In V. Gambetta, ed., *The Athletic Congress's Track and Field Coaching Manual*. Champaign, IL: Leisure Press, pp. 153-165.

Dunn, G., K. McGill, and L.W. Judge. 2014. *The Throws Manual*. Monterey, CA: Coaches Choice.

Dweck, C.S. 2006. *Mindset: The New Psychology of Success*. New York: Random House.

Dyson, Geoffrey. *The Mechanics of Athletics*. Hodder Arnold H&S, 8th edition. 1986.

Freeman, Will. *The Quest: On the Path to Knowledge and Wisdom*. Amazon. 2014.

Furlong, H.J. 1973. Forces acting throughout the put. *Track Technique* 52: 1655.

Gambetta, V.A. 2007. *Athletic Development: The Art and Science of Functional Sports Conditioning*. Champaign, IL: Human Kinetics.

Gastin, P.B. 2001. Energy system interaction and relative contribution during maximal exercise. *Sports Medicine* 31 (10): 725-741.

Godina, B., and R. Backes. 2000. Shot put. In J.L. Rogers, ed., *USA Track & Field Coaching Manual*. Champaign, IL: Human Kinetics, pp. 219-234.

Harre, Dietrich. *Principles of Sports Training – Introduction to the Theory and methods of Training*. Berlin, GDR: Sportverlag. 1982.

Hay, J.G. 1993. *The biomechanics of sport techniques*. San Francisco, CA: Benjamin Cummings.

Issurin, V. 2008. *Principles and Basics of Advanced Athletic Training*. Grand Rapids, MI: Ultimate Athlete Concepts.

Jackson, S., and M. Csikszentmihalyi. 1999. *Flow in Sport: The Keys to Optimal Experiences and Performances*. Champaign, IL: Human Kinetics.

Jacoby, Ed (editor). *Winning Jumps and Pole Vault*. Human Kinetics {Publishing Company. 2009.

Judge, L.W. 1991. Using the dynamic start in the glide. *Track Technique* 116: 3700-3703.

Judge, L.W. 2000a. Technique analysis of the hammer throw for men and women. *Coach and Athletic Director* 69 (7): 37.

Judge, L.W. 2000b. Technique analysis of the hammer throw for men and women. *Coach and Athletic Director* 69 (8): 46.

Judge, L.W. 2007. Developing speed strength: In-season training program for the collegiate thrower. *Strength and Conditioning* 29 (5): 42-54.

Judge, L.W. 2008. *The Complete Track and Field Coaches' Guide to Conditioning for the Throwing Events*. Monterey, CA: Coaches Choice.

Judge, L.W., D. Bellar, J. Petersen, and E. Wanless. 2010. Perception of risk in track and field venue management: Are hammer facilities overlooked? *Kybernetes* 39 (5): 786-799.

Judge, L.W., and K. McGill. 2013. *The hammer throw handbook*. Monterey, CA: Coaches Choice.

Judge, L.W., and J.A. Potteiger. 2000. A battery of tests to identify overtraining in throwers. *Modern Athlete and Coach* 38 (1).

Judge, L.W., and M. Young. 2011. *The shot put handbook*. Monterey, CA: Coaches Choice.

Kurz, T. 2001. *Science of Sports Training*, 2nd ed. Island Pond, VT: Stadion Publishing.

BIBLIOGRAPHY

Leonard, G. 1991. *Mastery: The Keys to Success and Long Term Fulfillment.* Penguin: New York.

Maslow, A.H. 1968. *Toward a Psychology of Being,* 2nd ed. New York: Van Nostrand Reinhold.

McArdle, W.D., F.I. Katch, and V.L. Katch. 2001. *Exercise Physiology: Energy, Nutrition, and Human Performance,* 5th ed. Baltimore, MD: Williams & Wilkins.

McArdle, William D. Katch, Frank I. And Katch, Victor L. Sixth Edition. *Exercise Physiology – Energy, Nutrition and Human Performance.* Baltimore, MD. Williams & Wilkins. 2007.

McCoy, R.W. 1992b. Biomechanical analysis of Ramona Pagel at the 1992 United States Olympic trials (unpublished technical report). Williamsburg, VA: The College of William and Mary.

McGuire, R.T. 2005. Winning kids with sport: A construction model for positive coaching. In R.A. Vernacchia and T. Statler, eds., *The Psychology of High Performance Track and Field.* Mountain View, CA: Track and Field News Publications.

McGuire, R.T. 2008. Thinking right in sport: The critical importance of mental training. *Techniques* 1 (3).

McGuire, R.T. 2012a. *Winning Kids With Sport! Teach, Model, Practice, Inspire.* Ames, IA: Championship Productions.

McGuire, R.T. 2012b. *From the Whistle to the Snap: Building Your Best FOCUS for Winning Football.* Ames, IA: Championship Productions.

McGuire, R.T., and M.E. Schloder. 1998. *Understanding Athletes: A Foundation for Success.* Marina del Rey, CA: Health for Life.

McGuire, R.T., and S. Portenga. 2009. Building success: Critical conditions for fulfilling team experiences. *Techniques* 2 (4).

Mujika, I., and S. Padilla. 2003. Scientific bases for precompetition tapering strategies. *Medicine & Science in Sports & Exercise* 35 (7): 1182-1187.

Olbrecht, J. 2000. *The Science of Winning: Planning, Periodizing, and Optimizing Swim Training.* Luton, England: Swim Shop.

Radcliffe, J.C., and R.C. Farentinos. 1999. *High-Powered Plyometrics.* Champaign, IL: Human Kinetics.

Sawyer, T.H., and L.W. Judge. 2012. *The Management of Fitness, Physical Activity, Recreation, and Sport.* Champaign, IL: Sagamore.

Schmidt, R.A. 1975. Schema theory of discrete motor skill learning. *Psychological Review,* 82 (4): 225-260.

Schmolinsky, Gerhardt (editor). *Track and Field – Textbook for Coaches and Sports Teachers.* 1974.

Scholich, Manfred. *Circuit Training.* Berlin: Sportverlag. 1986.

Seligman, M.E.P. 2002. *Authentic Happiness.* New York: Free Press.

Seligman, M.E.P. 2011. *Flourish: A Visionary New Understanding of Happiness and Well-Being.* New York: Free Press.

Seligman, M.E., and M. Csikszentmihalyi. 2000. Positive psychology: An introduction. *The American Psychologist* 55 (1): 5-14.

Seligman, M.E.P., R.A. Steen, N. Park, and C. Peterson. 2005. Positive psychology progress: Empirical validation of interventions. *American Psychologist* 60: 410-421.

Shields, D.L. 2009. *True Competition: A Guide to Pursuing Excellence in Sport and Society.* Champaign, IL: Human Kinetics.

Simonyi, G. 1973. Form breakdown of Wladyslaw Komar, Poland, Olympic Champion, 69-6. *Scholastic Coach* 42 (7): 7-9, 94-102.

Starzynski, Tadeusz. And Sozanski, Henryk. *Explosive Power and Jumping Ability for all Sports.* Island Pond, VT: Stadion Publishing Company. 1999.

Stone, M.H., M.E. Stone, W.A. Sands, K.P. Pierce, R.U. Newton, G.G. Haff, and J. Carlock. 2006. Maximum strength and strength training: A relationship to endurance. *Strength and Conditioning* 28 (3): 44-53.

Turk, M. 1997. Building a technical model for the shot put. *Track Coach* 141: 4489-4499.

Vernacchia, R. 2003. *Inner Strength: The Mental Dynamics of Athletic Performance.* Palo Alto, CA: Warde.

Vernacchia, R., R.T. McGuire, and D.L. Cook. 1996. *Coaching Mental Excellence: It Does Matter Whether You Win or Lose.* Portola Valley, CA: Warde.

Vigil, Joe. *Road to the Top: A Systematic Approach to Training Distance Runners.* Amazon. 1995.

Wulf, Gabriele. *Attention and Motor Skill Learning.* Champaign, IL: Human Kinetics Publishing Company. 2007.

Zatsiorsky, V.M. 1995. *Science and Practice of Strength Training.* Champaign, IL: Human Kinetics.

Index

Note: Page numbers followed by italicized *f* and *t* indicate information contained in figures and tables, respectively.

About USA Track & Field

USA Track & Field (USATF) is the national governing body for track and field, long-distance running, and racewalking in the United States. Based in Indianapolis, USATF encompasses the world's oldest organized sports, the most-watched events of Olympic broadcasts, the most popular sport in high school and middle school, and more than 30 million adult runners in the United States. Nearly 100,000 people are members of USATF. USATF member organizations include the U.S. Olympic Committee, NCAA, NAIA, Road Runners Club of America, Running USA, and the National Federation of State High School Associations. 57 USATF associations oversee the sport and its 2,500 clubs at the local level. USATF conducts coaching education courses that elevate and standardize the level of coaching across the country. More than 14,000 coaches have been educated under USATF programs.

About the Editor

Will Freeman is the highly-successful track & field and cross country coach at Grinnell College (IA) and a Level 3 certified coach through USA Track & Field (USATF). A former All-American pole vaulter and Olympic Trials finalist for the University of Florida, where he is a member of the UF Athletic Hall of Fame, Coach Freeman is also a former chairman of the USATF Coaching Education Program and former chair of the NCAA Division III track & field and cross country committee.

Coach Freeman has coached beginners to national champions in his 35 years at Grinnell. His teams have won 28 Midwest Conference titles in track & field and cross country. The author of four books; 19 coaching videos; and many articles on track & field, cross country, and the art of coaching, Coach Freeman is a popular clinician and speaker both nationally and internationally.

About the Contributors

Andrew Allden is a 25-year veteran of distance coaching currently serving on the staff at the University of South Carolina. Previously, he served at Coastal Carolina, Tulane, and North Carolina. For nine years he ran AA Elite Coaching in North Carolina, training professional and amateur runners in the Raleigh-Durham area. Allden earned his bachelor's degree in English from Emory University in 1986 and his master's degree in sports administration from Georgia in 1991. He holds USATF level 1 and 2 certifications as a coach and endurance instructor.

Photo courtesy of Indiana University.

Dr. Robert Chapman is an assistant professor in the department of kinesiology at Indiana University and also serves as the associate director of sport science and medicine for USA Track & Field (USATF). Dr. Chapman is well-published in international scientific journals and texts, with research centering on limitations to performance in elite athletes, altitude training for endurance athletes, and ventilatory limitations to exercise performance. He is the former head coach for men's cross country and assistant track & field coach at Indiana University, where he coached three national champions and 19 All-Americans.

Jeremy Fischer is the jumps coach at the Olympic Training Center in Chula Vista, California. He is a USA Track & Field (USATF) Level 2 instructor and IAAF instructor for the jumps. Coach Fischer has an MS in Kinesiology/Nutrition as well as CSCS and USAW certifications. He has coached champions and medalists at the world and Olympic levels.

Vern Gambetta is currently the director of Gambetta Sports Training Systems. He is considered the father of functional sports training. His coaching experience spans 44 years at all levels of competition. His background is track & field, having coached at all levels of the sport. He served as the first director of the TAC Coaching Education Program. Coach Gambetta has authored more than 100 articles and seven books on various aspects of training. He received his BA from Fresno State University and his teaching credentials with a coaching minor from the University of California, Santa Barbara. He attended Stanford University and obtained his MA in education with an emphasis on physical education.

Lawrence W. Judge is an associate professor and coordinator of the graduate coaching program at Ball State University. Throughout his 18-year collegiate coaching career, he has coached more than 100 NCAA All-Americans, 11 NCAA champions, 16 USATF champions, 8 Olympians, and 2 American and world record holders. He coached Jeremy Campbell to a gold medal in the F44 discus throw in the 2012 Paralympics in London and an International Paralympic Committee world championship in the same event in Lyon, France, in 2013. He recently served as the president for the National Association for the Accreditation of Coaches Education and is currently the USATF national chairman for coaching education.

Dr. Rick McGuire is the director of sport psychology for intercollegiate athletics and graduate professor of sport psychology at the University of Missouri. From 1983 to 2010, he was Missouri's head track & field coach. At Missouri, McGuire coached 143 All-Americans, 110 conference champions, 29 USA national team members, 7 NCAA champions, and 5 Olympians, including two Olympic silver medal winners. McGuire was founder and chair of USA Track & Field's sport psychology program for 27 years and served on the staff for 11 USATF national teams, including for the 1992 and 1996 Olympic Games in Barcelona and Atlanta. Dr. McGuire is now the founder and director of the Missouri Institute for Positive Coaching. Dr. McGuire wishes to acknowledge the contributions of Dr. Scotta Morton and Dr. Brian Zuleger in developing the chapter.

Joe Rogers has 48 years of track & field coaching experience. He has coached at the U.S. Military Academy, Ball State University, Hillsdale College, and Olivet College. He has been an instructor for USA Track & Field's Coaching Education Program since 1984 for both Level 1 and Level 2 and has taught at various coaching clinics throughout the United States.

Dr. Joe Vigil serves as a clinician for the International Olympic Committee (IOC), USA Track & Field (USATF), and IAAF domestically and internationally. His athletes have medaled at the Olympic Games, the World Track & Field Championships, and in the World Cross Country Championships. His college teams have won an unprecedented 19 National Championships and 425 All-American recognitions. Coach Vigil has been inducted into 11 halls of fame and has twice been recognized as the Jim Councilman Coach of the Year.